Guides to Information Sources

Information Sources in
Information Technology

Guides to Information Sources

A series under the General Editorship of
D. J. Foskett, MA, FLA
and
M. W. Hill, MA, BSc, MRIC

This series was known previously as 'Butterworths Guide to Information Sources'.

Other titles available are:

Information Sources in Grey Literature
  edited by C. P. Auger

Information Sources in Metallic Materials
  edited by M. N. Patten

Information Sources in the Earth Sciences (Second edition)
  edited by David N. Wood, Joan E. Hardy and Anthony P. Harvey

Information Sources in Polymers and Plastics
  edited by R. T. Adkins

Information Sources in Energy Technology
  edited by L. J. Anthony

Information Sources in Life Sciences
  edited by H. V. Wyatt

Information Sources in Physics (Second edition)
  edited by Dennis F. Shaw

Information Sources in Law
  edited by R. G. Logan

Information Sources in Management and Business (Second edition)
  edited by K. D. C. Vernon

Information Sources in Politics and Political Science: a survey worldwide
  edited by Dermot Englefield and Gavin Drewry

Information Sources in Engineering (Second edition)
  edited by L. J. Anthony

Information Sources in Economics (Second edition)
  edited by John Fletcher

Information Sources in the Medical Sciences (Third edition)
  edited by L. T. Morton and S. Godbolt

Guides to Information Sources

Information Sources in
Information Technology

Editor
David Haynes

London • Melbourne • Munich • New York

© Bowker-Saur Ltd 1990

All rights reserved. No part of this publication may be reproduced or transmitted in any form or by any means (including photocopying and recording) without the written permission of the copyright holder except in accordance with the provisions of the Copyright Act 1956 (as amended) or under the terms of a licence issued by the Copyright Licensing Agency, 7 Ridgmount Street, London WC1E 7AE, England. The written permission of the copyright holder must also be obtained before any part of this publication is stored in a retrieval system of any nature. Applications for the copyright holder's written permission to reproduce, transmit or store in a retrieval system any part of this publication should be addressed to the publisher.

Warning: The doing of an unauthorised act in relation to a copyright work may result in both a civil claim for damages and criminal prosecution.

British Library Cataloguing in Publication Data

Information sources in information technology – (Guides to information sources).
  1. Computer systems. Information sources
  I. Haynes, David II. Series
  004.07
ISBN 0–408–03285–5

Library of Congress Cataloging-in-Publication Data

Information sources in information technology / editor, David Haynes
    pp.   cm.—(Guides to information sources)
    Includes bibliographical references and index.
    ISBN 0–408–03285–5 (acid-free paper)
    1. Library science—Technological innovations—Information services.
    2. Library science—Technological innovations—Bibliography.
    3. Information technology—Information services.
    4. Libraries—Automation—Information services.
    5. Information technology—Bibliography.
    6. Libraries—Automation—Bibliography. I. Haynes, David. II. Series: Guides to information sources (London, England)
Z678.9.I629   1990
020′.285—dc20   90-40725
                                                                                        CIP

Bowker-Saur is part of the Professional Publishing Division of Reed International Books, Borough Green, Sevenoaks, Kent TN15 8PH

Cover design by Calverts Press
Printed on acid-free paper
Printed and bound in Great Britain by
Biddles Ltd, Guildford and King's Lynn

Series Editors' Foreword

Daniel Bell has made it clear in his book *The Post-Industrial Society* that we now live in an age in which information has succeeded raw materials and energy as the primary commodity. We have also seen in recent years the growth of a new discipline, information science. This is in spite of the fact that skill in acquiring and using information has always been one of the distinguishing features of the educated person. As Dr Johnson observed, 'Knowledge is of two kinds. We know a subject ourselves, or we know where we can find information upon it'.

But a new problem faces the modern educated person. We now have an excess of information, and even an excess of sources of information. This is often called the 'information explosion', though it might be more accurately called the 'publication explosion'. Yet it is of a deeper nature than either. The totality of knowledge itself, let alone of theories and opinions about knowledge, seems to have increased to an unbelievable extent, so that the pieces one seeks in order to solve any problem appear to be but a relatively few small straws in a very large haystack. That analogy, however, implies that we are indeed seeking but a few straws. In fact, when information arrives on our desks, we often find those few straws are actually far too big and far too numerous for one person to grasp and use easily. In the jargon used in the information world, efficient retrieval of relevant information often results in information overkill.

Ever since writing was invented, it has been a common practice for men to record and store information; not only fact and figures, but also theories and opinions. The rate of recording accelerated after the invention of printing and moveable type, not because that in itself could increase the amount of recording but because, by making it easy to publish multiple copies of a document and sell them at a profit, recording and distributing information became very lucrative and hence attractive to more people. On the other hand, men and women in whose lives the discovery of the handling of information plays a large part usually devise ways of getting what they want from other people rather than from books in their efforts to avoid information overkill. Conferences, briefings, committee meetings are one means of this; personal contacts through the 'invisible college;' and members of one's club are another. While such people do read, some of them voraciously, the reading of published literature, including in this category newspapers as well as books and journals and even watching television, may provide little more than 10% of the total information that they use.

Computers have increased the opportunities, not merely by acting as more efficient stores and providers of certain kinds of information than libraries, but also by manipulating the data they contain in order to synthesize new information. To give a simple illustration, a computer which holds data on commodity prices in the various trading capitals of the world, and also data on currency exchange rates, can be programmed to indicate comparative costs in different places in one single currency. Computerized data bases, i.e. stores of bibliographic information, are now well established and quite widely available for anyone to use. Also increasing are the number of data banks, i.e. stores of factual information, which are now generally accessible. Anyone who buys a suitable terminal may be able to arrange to draw information directly from these computer systems for their own purposes; the systems are normally linked to the subscriber by means of the telephone network. Equally, an alternative is now being provided by information supply services such as libraries, more and more of which are introducing terminals as part of their regular service.

The number of sources of information on any topic can therefore be very extensive indeed; publications (in the widest sense), people (experts), specialist organizations from research associations to chambers of commerce, and computer stores. The number of channels by which one can have access to these vast collections of information are also very numerous, ranging from professional literature searchers, via computer intermediaries, to Citizens' Advice Bureaux, information marketing services and information brokers.

The aim of the Guides to Information Sources (formerly Butterworths Guides to Information Sources) is to bring all these sources and channels together in a single convenient form and to present a picture of the international scene as it exists in each of the disciplines we plan to cover. Consideration is also being given to volumes that will cover major interdisciplinary areas of what are now sometimes called 'mission-oriented' fields of knowledge. The first stage of the whole project will give greater emphasis to publications and their exploitation, partly because they are so numerous, and partly because more detail is needed to guide them adequately. But it may be that in due course the balance will change, and certainly the balance in each volume will be that which is appropriate to its subject at the time.

The editor of each volume is a person of high standing, with substantial experience of the discipline and of the sources of information in it. With a team of authors of whom each one is a specialist in one aspect of the field, the total volume provides an integrated and highly expert account of the current sources, of all types, in its subject.

D. J. Foskett
Michael Hill

About the contributors

Marshall J. Crawford

Marshall is a qualified librarian with over 20 years experience in the organization and provision of technical and business information. In 1981 he established Chancery Lane Information Brokers, the first information brokerage in Britain. In 1989 he moved to Newcastle upon Tyne where he is currently the Information Manager for National Building Specification. He manages the NBS Library and is developing internal and external information services in support of the technical team at NBS. He is also Chairman of the Construction Industry Information Group.

Jacky Deunette

Jacky was Manager of the Online Information Centre at Aslib from 1979 to 1985. Following a post as Information Consultant with the Marketing Shop, a firm of marketing consultants, she became a freelance information broker in 1987. She has written several articles and guides on topics concerning online databases and is particularly interested in the balance between printed and electronic sources of information.

Chris Donegani

Since graduating from Leicester University, Chris has held a number of posts in UK electronics companies. For the last five years he has worked as Chief Engineer for an East Midlands software development and electronics manufacturing company. In addition, as a director of Smallsoft he provides hardware and software consultancy to the electronics industry and library world.

Diana Edmonds

After working in a number of libraries, including the University of London Library, the British Library of Political and Economic Science and Aberdeen City Libraries, Diana set up an information consultancy in 1983. Her clients include private sector companies, local authorities and professional institutions. She is also a director of Instant Library, a library and information company offering a wide range of services to clients throughout the UK and Europe.

Tamara Eisenschitz

Tamara has a PhD in theoretical physics and an MSc in Information Science. Before being appointed by The City University, London, she worked briefly as a patent searcher. In her research and teaching she has been concerned with constraints put on the availability of information by legal requirements and the form such constrained information takes. She is interested in information policy and the laws and practices this gives rise to. She also teaches about legal information sources and legal searching techniques.

Mary Feeney

Formerly Production Manager at Chadwyck-Healey Ltd, Mary spent three years as Research Affiliate at the Primary Communications Research Centre, University of Leicester, followed by a further year of research at the Department of Library and Information Studies, Loughborough University. She now runs her own company, the Data Workshop, offering services in documentation and technical writing, editing and desktop publishing. Current projects include *Library and Information Briefings*, published jointly by the British Library Research and Development Department and the Library and Information Technology Centre.

David Haynes

David is a partner with The Information Partnership, which was set up in 1986 to provide consultancy services in information management. During this time as a consultant he has advised on information technology applications as well as devising information management strategies. He previously worked for Aslib (the Association for Information Management) as a British Library-funded researcher and later as a consultant. Prior to that he was an information officer at Pira, where he established a new database, Electronic Publishing Abstracts. He is an active member of the Institute of Information Scientists and has served as its Honorary Treasurer.

Lydia Jackson

Lydia has had a varied career in research, publishing and company administration. She has worked in different types of library implementing online cataloguing systems. She gained experience in applying the latest technology to publishing procedures. Projects for the general public included the PROFILE database and Croner's Teleroute. Lydia also started the BBC Data Enquiry Service. Her current interests are quality assurance and telecommunications.

Pamela Mayorcas

Pamela has been involved with translation and information for over twenty years. Trained as a technical translator, she started work at the Iron and Steel Institute in London and then joined the EC Commission in Brussels as a translator in 1973. Her interest and involvement in documentation and information as support services for translation led to an MSc Information Science at The City University in London in 1980–81. Returning to the EC, Pamela ran the Help Desk for the Commission's Internal Database Service and later collaborated on the design phase of an ambitious project in Luxembourg for creating an integrated management and information system for the Commission's Language Service. She currently works as a freelance translator and information consultant in London. Pamela is a founder member of the Institute of Translation and Interpreting, and an elected member of Council. She chairs ITI's Publications Committee and sits on the Education and Training Committee. She is also Membership Secretary of the Aslib Technical Translation Group.

Ronnie Poyser

Ronnie was Subject Librarian for the Department of Computing, Mathematics, Statistics, Office Technology and Office Administration at City Of London Polytechnic from 1985–90. He is now based at Brighton Polytechnic as Course Resources Officer for the Department of Service Sector Management.

Peter Raggett

Peter is Bibliographies Manager at HMSO Books. He is the Head of the section which produces HMSO's lists and catalogues and the bibliographic enquiries section. He qualified with an MA in Librarianship from the University of Sheffield in 1980 and previous to his post at HMSO Books he worked in the Treasury and Cabinet Office Library and the Library of the Department of Education and Science.

Hilary Ramsden

Hilary is a Senior Medical Information Scientist at ICI Pharmaceuticals with a particular interest in the applications of information technology in information work. In 1983, whilst working for the Leatherhead Food Research Association, she was involved in the early development of the online database FOREGE. Shortly afterwards, deciding to develop her interest in the applications of IT, she left to take an MSc in Information Technology at the University of London. For three years Hilary was the Information Specialist in library automation and software at Aslib, where she provided a general IT enquiry service and some consultancy work. She was a co-author of the Aslib Technology Information Surveys 1987 and 1990, and latterly edited the IT newsletter *Automation Notes* (now published under the title *IT Link incorporating Automation Notes*).

Joyce Stroud

Joyce is a Communications Specialist in the computer Services of West Sussex County Council. She is currently responsible for setting up a communications network as part of the County Council's response to Local Management in Schools. Other responsibilities include advising the Library Service and other County Council Departments on voice and data communications issues, such as the implication of Open Systems Interconnection (OSI). Joyce was previously a Communications Analyst and Microcomputer Support Specialist with Westminster City Council where amongst other things she assisted the Westminster Central Reference Library in setting up an online information service. Before that she was a Principal Research Officer at Aslib, looking at the applications of Local Area Networks. (LANs) for information management, funded by BLRDD.

Geraldine Turpie

Before joining Bowker-Saur Ltd as Publisher (Library and Information Science), Geraldine was the online specialist at Aslib, the Association for Information Management, where she gave advice on accessing online databases, lectured and edited a monthly newsletter *Online Notes*. She has also worked for the Metals Society and CAB International.

Contents

Introduction   xv

PART I: Information Sources by Subject
1. Input technologies   3
   D. Haynes
2. Output technologies: printers, plotters, monitors, speech synthesis robotics and process control   14
   D. Edmonds and C. Donegani
3. Software, computer languages and operating systems   51
   D. Haynes
4. Computer hardware and electronic components   62
   D. Haynes
5. Information and data storage   74
   M. Feeney
6. Transmission of information   96
   J. Stroud
7. Information technology applications   122
   H. Ramsden
8. Information policy and statutory control   138
   D. Haynes

PART II: Sources of Information
9. Machine-readable sources   149
   G. Turpie
10. Secondary sources and reference works   166
    D. Haynes
11. Organizations libraries and referral services   177
    R. Poyser

12	Trade statistics and market information *J. Deunette*	213
13	Research *D. Haynes*	229
14	Patent information *T. Eisenschitz*	240
15	Government publications *P. Raggett*	257
16	Periodicals and conferences *D. Haynes*	269
17	Foreign language material. The foreign-language barrier to information on information technology *P. Mayorcas*	285
18	Experts *M. J. Crawford*	315
19	Standards *L. Jackson*	326

Introduction

D. HAYNES

Information technology is a relatively recent concept. It was apparently coined in the late 1970s and has come into its own in the 1980s. It is interesting to note that as late as 1984 the *McGraw-Hill Dictionary of Scientific and Technical Terms* (New York, McGraw-Hill, 1984) did not have an entry for Information Technology. Even today there are sources which do not mention the term even though they cover the technology. Part of the reason may be the diverse and ill-defined nature of the subject and therefore the limited significance of the term 'information technology' in an index.

With such a rapidly changing area it has been difficult to define the topic, let alone pin it down for long enough to write a guide to information sources on information technology. Many people use information technology synonymously with computer science. Others broaden the definition to encompass telecommunications. It is sometimes even taken to include technologies connected with publishing.

In the *Dictionary of Computing* (Oxford, Oxford University Press, 1986) by Valerie Illingworth, information technology is defined as '*Any form of technology i.e. any equipment or technique, used by people to handle information*'. It goes on to say '[information technology] *incorporates the whole of computing and telecommunications technology together with major parts of consumer electronics and broadcasting*'.

The *Macmillan Dictionary of Personal Computing and Communications* (London, Macmillan, 1986) by Dennis Longley and Michael Shain devotes four pages to information technology. They define information technology as '*The acquisition, processing, storage and dissemination of vocal, pictorial, textual and numerical information by microelectronics-based combination of computing, telecommunications and video.* . . . [Information technology] *has arisen as a separate technology by the convergence of computing, telecommunications and video techniques'.*

The *Chambers' Science and Technology Dictionary* (Cambridge, Chambers, 1988) defines information technology as *'The application to information processing of current technologies from computing, telecommunications and microelectronics'.* It goes on to define information processing as *'the organization, manipulation and distribution of information. Central to almost every use of the computer and almost synonymous with computing'.*

It appears there is a general consensus but no specific agreement on what information technology is. A more fruitful line of investigation might be to try and define what it is not, by testing it against specific examples. This would be an interesting exercise, but is not the province of this guide. For the purposes of this book we have been guided by the definition in Jenny M. Rosenberg's *Dictionary of Computers, Information Processing and Telecommunications* (New York, John Wiley, 1986) with its succinct definition: *'the acquisition, processing, storage and dissemination of various types of information via computers and telecommunications'.* Even then there is no guarantee that our interpretation of her definition corresponds to her understanding of the subject. The contents page of this book is perhaps the best clue to our definition of information technology. No doubt there are those who would disagree.

Another source of definitions can be found in the classification schemes of services such as INSPEC or its printed equivalent, *Computer and Control Abstracts* (IEE) and *Electronic Publishing Abstracts* (Pira) and its online equivalent, the EPUBS database and some of the general library classification schemes such as Universal Decimal Classification and Dewey Decimal Classification. In these cases, the technologies, which we take to comprise Information Technology are scattered throughout the schemes, rather than under one heading or group of headings.

Books on information technology provide a guide to accepted definitions of the subject. Useful introductions and wide-ranging reviews of the technology can be found in A.C. Cawkell's *Handbook of Information Technology and Office Systems* (Amsterdam, North-Holland, 1986) and *New Methods and Techniques* edited by Mary Feeney.

This book is intended as a selective guide to information sources. It does not attempt to cover sources comprehensively, and it is not a directory. Sufficient information has been given to

Introduction xvii

identify the sources discussed in this book, and I hope this will act as a starting point for anyone interested in information technology. The contributors have attempted to give a critical review of the most important sources and have freely indicated their opinions of the relative merits of the different sources covered.

Part I deals with the different subject areas which make up information technology. These are based on the classification which I used as editor of *Electronic Publishing Abstracts*. The technologies are defined by function rather than by attribute. So input technologies are grouped together even though they cover diverse attributes such as speech recognition and the technology of computer keyboards. The chapters in Part I are as follows:

- Input technologies
- Output technologies
- Software, computer languages, and operating systems
- Computer hardware and electronic components
- Information and data storage
- Transmission of information
- Information technology applications
- Information policy and statutory control

Part II looks at the different types of information source available. Many of the sources mentioned in Part I are described in detail in Part II. At the beginning of each chapter is a discussion of the attributes of the information sources mentioned. The authors make suggestions on how to go about identifying relevant sources and locating them. Guides to the sources themselves are also discussed. For instance, the chapter on periodicals and conferences covers guides to periodicals and conferences as well as specific publications. Many of these guides are not specific to information technology and some of the principles used here will apply to other subject areas. Again the authors have been selective in their choice of sources.

Part II begins with a chapter by Geraldine Turpie on machine-readable sources. It seems appropriate that the technologies used to deliver much of the available information are themselves the subjects of this book. The technology of online systems is discussed as a subject in Hilary Ramsden's chapter on information technology applications and CD-ROMs in Mary Feeney's chapter on storage technologies. Many of the machine-readable sources are also available in hard-copy as printed directories and abstracts journals. The chapters in Part II are:

- Machine-readable sources
- Secondary sources and reference works

- Organizations, libraries and referral services
- Trade statistics and marketing information
- Research
- Patent information
- Government publications
- Periodicals and conferences
- Foreign-language material
- Experts
- Standards

Acknowledgement

Permission to reproduce UK Patent Application 2 200 225 A has been granted by the Controller of HM Stationery Office.

PART I

Information Sources by Subject

CHAPTER ONE

Input technologies

D. HAYNES

Introduction

The theme of this chapter is the use of technology as a means of converting data into machine-readable form. Input technologies range from the familiar computer keyboard to more exotic technologies such as speech recognition. An increasingly important area is scanning and pattern recognition and recently a number of new products have been released. Although OCR (optical character recognition) characters are theoretically machine-readable, in this chapter we will define machine-readable as binary digits on a magnetic, electronic or optical medium. 'Input technologies' is the term which describes the various technologies which are used to get information into machine-readable form.

General sources

We will deal first with some general sources which do not deal specifically with input technologies, but which regularly feature information on input technologies. A general text on alternatives to keyboards for data entry is M. D. Sorin's *Data Entry Without Keypunching* (Lexington Books).

Libraries and secondary sources

Catalogues and classification schemes can be a useful point of entry into a subject area. Many specialist libraries have developed their own classification schemes to reflect their coverage of the subject. There are several general classification schemes which are widely used in academic and public libraries, notably Dewey

4 Input technologies

Decimal Classification and Universal Decimal Classification (UDC). In UDC classification, which is used in the IEE and the Aslib library, the following codes are relevant:

519	Pattern Recognition
519.766	Speech Recognition
681	Pattern Recognition (including OCR)
681.3	Computer Peripheral Equipment
681.3:327	Codes
681.327	Keyboards

The INSPEC database is a key source of information on all aspects of information technology. Several of the subject headings are relevant to this chapter. The subject headings can be used in online searches of the INSPEC database and can also be used for searching the relevant sections of *Computer & Control Abstracts* (IEE), the hard-copy equivalent. The headings are as follows:

5500	COMPUTER PERIPHERAL EQUIPMENT
5520	Data acquisition equipment and techniques
5530	Pattern recognition equipment
5540B	Interactive-input devices
5560	Data preparation equipment
5585	Speech recognition and synthesis

Another useful source is *Electronic Publishing Abstracts* (Pira), which is available on the Orbit host as the EPUBS database.

Journals

Personal Computer World (VNU) and other popular computing magazines often have product reviews of data input devices. These devices tend to be aimed at the consumer and small business market. Advertisements for products in these magazines provide another useful source of information, not only telling readers about the suppliers and price, but often containing specifications for the products advertised and a short description of the technology where it is new. If you know the names of manufacturers or suppliers, there is usually an advertisers' index in the journal which will enable you to locate the relevant item quickly. Otherwise it is a matter of scanning the journal for advertisements which catch your eye.

Byte and *Datamation* both offer a slightly more technical approach to the subject and they tend to be aimed towards computing professionals. In both cases there are regular reviews of the technology including input technologies and of new products. Other journals with occasional articles on input technologies are:

Electronics and Wireless World; *Systems International*, which is a controlled circulation journal; and *Mini-Micro Systems* which has features, product reviews and news items.

COMPANY TECHNICAL JOURNALS

A number of the large manufacturers produce their own technical journals. These tend to be product specific or to concentrate on technologies of direct interest to the company in question. For instance the *British Telecom Technology Journal* has done a number of reviews on speech input technology. Other high-quality journals reporting research done by the companies include: *AT&T Technical Journal*, *HP World*, *IBM Systems Journal*, *Electrical Communication* (Alcatel N.V.), *Electrical Communication* (ITT), and *Mitsubishi Electric Advance* (Japan).

Organizations

Below is a partial list of the companies which are active in the area of input technologies, either as providers of services and products or as research establishments and sometimes both. They have been identified by looking at the organizational affiliation of authors who have published extensively in the area of input technology. A number of the large manufacturers are represented including:

AT&T Bell Laboratories
Dictaphone Engineering and Technology
GTE Labs Inc.
Hewlett-Packard
Hohe Electronics
Lockheed Engineering and Management Services Company
McDonnell Douglas Astronautics Co.
Mitsubishi
Northrop Research & Technology Centre
Oki Electric Ind. Co. Ltd
RCA Advanced Technology Lab
Standard Elektrik Lorenz AG
Toyota Central Research & Development Labs

Research-oriented organizations include the academic institutions, and nationally funded research centres and industrial research associations. Key organizations include:

BBN Laboratories Inc., USA
Cambridge University, UK
Carnegie Mellon University, USA

6   Input technologies

Centro Studi e Laboratori Telecomunicazioni (CSELT), Italy
Delft University of Technology, Netherlands
Institution of Electrical Engineers (IEE), UK
Institute of Electrical and Electronics Engineers (IEEE), USA
Instituto per la Richerca Scintifica e Tecnologica, Italy
Maryland University, USA
National Aeronautics and Space Administration (NASA), USA
National University of Singapore
National Research Council of Canada
North Carolina State University, USA
Washington University, USA

Some of these organizations are also publishers. For instance CSELT publishes a bimonthly technical journal in English, *CSELT Technical Reports* which contains articles on all aspects of telecommunications research including speech recognition.

Research programmes such as the Alvey Programme have conferences and publish reports and newsletters giving details of progress with specific projects and advances in technology which result from the funded research. For instance there is the *Alvey Programme Annual Report and Poster Supplement*, which has a section devoted to speech systems. The Alvey Programme has officially come to an end and has been subsumed into the Information Engineering Directorate of the UK Government's Department of Trade and Industry.

The *Journal of the Institute of Electronics Information and Communication Engineering in Japan* and *Transactions of the Institute of Electronics Information and Communication Engineering in Japan* are both useful sources of information on input technologies and provide an English-language notification of current research in Japan.

Keyboards

The most commonly used input device for computers is the keyboard. This is especially the case for text-processing systems. This technology is well developed and there is not very much current research in this area, and consequently not much research literature. However because this technology is universal, standards are important. Standards fall into two categories: product-led standards; and official standards. The product-led standards are standards which have come into effect because of the predominance of a single product or group of products. Other manufacturers will often choose to adhere to a commonly used standard rather than an official standard or one of their own devising. Most of the product-led standards are imposed by manufacturers such as IBM, DEC, etc. Official standards are those produced by standards bodies such as the British Standards Institution or, at an international level, the International Standards Organization.

Roman alphabets have become the standard form of communication with machines. Most keyboards, regardless of where they are manufactured or used have a roman alphabet. The keys are arranged in the format devised for typewriters at the turn of the century. This arrangement is called QWERTY (AZERTY in France) after the first six characters on the keyboard, and was devised to prevent typists typing too fast and jamming the keys on the cumbersome, early manual typewriters. A number of alternatives have been explored for keyboards with a more ergonomic arrangement of keys. Well-established alternatives are the Malatron keyboard and the Dvořák keyboard.

Some years ago there was another innovation, the Microwriter which was a hand-held device with seven keys and a modest memory and liquid crystal display. More recently, Microwriter launched a new product, Agenda, which is a personal organizer. It has a calculator-type keyboard with characters arranged alphabetically plus a Microwriter keyboard of five keys as an alternative input device. The advantage of this system is that very little movement of the fingers is needed, enabling users to type in situations where a conventional keyboard would be awkward, such as on a moving train. Experienced users can type faster than they can write, although generally not as fast as they can type on a conventional QWERTY keyboard.

There are a number of other small input devices intended for use on the move. Some of the portable 'lap-top' computers come into this category and have very limited processing power. The Z88 produced by Cambridge Computers is an example. It uses a conventional QWERTY keyboard and works like a conventional desktop computer. For more rugged conditions there are data entry devices such as the Husky Hawk. These devices are sealed so that they are waterproof and dust resistant.

Keyboards are a relatively well-developed technology and this is reflected in the smaller body of research literature in this area compared with speech recognition or OCR. Most of the useful literature is in the form of standards. Product literature is another important source of information. Manufacturers and suppliers (who produce the product literature) can be identified either through advertisements in the general computing press or through trade directories such as *Kompass* and *Thomas*.

Non-roman Alphabets

Keyboards have now been developed for non-roman alphabets including Russian Cyrillic, Greek Cyrillic, Arabic and Japanese Kanji. It is now possible to buy a chip for microcomputers which enables them to display non-roman characters on screen and to accept input from non-roman keyboards. Languages with non-alphabetic characters such as Chinese, and Japanese ideographic characters cause particular problems for data input. Speech recognition is seen as one possible avenue for overcoming this problem. Keyboards are not really practical for these languages, because several thousand keys may be needed to adequately represent a useful vocabulary. Japanese keyboards are used despite these problems. *Computer Processing of Chinese Oriental Languages* (USA), is of particular importance as it deals with non-roman scripts. It covers all aspects of processing oriental languages including input technologies.

Touch-tablets and key pads

There are a number of devices designed to enhance the operation of keyboards or to supplement them. Touch tablets can be added to conventional keyboards so that more function keys are available. Keypads consisting of digits, control keys and cursor control keys are widely used for numeric data input. The arrangement of the keys is more convenient than a conventional QWERTY keyboard with all the numbers along the top of the keyboard. Most conventional keyboards now have a keypad incorporated into them. Touch tablets have soft keys which can be allocated for different functions or types of data. This can depend on specific applications or can be user allocated. Advertisements in the popular computing press such as *Personal Computer World* and in the technical press aimed at IT professionals both yield important information on the types of products available.

Infra-red keyboard links

Keyboards and keypads are normally linked to the computer or terminal by means of a cable. An alternative is via an infra-red link or an ultra-sound link, such as those used for remote controllers for televisions and video recorders. One manufacturer of microcomputers recently introduced a model with a battery-powered keyboard which was linked to the central processing unit by microwave. Such systems can be subject to interference especially if the line of sight between the keyboard and the CPU is blocked.

Mice, joysticks and pointers

With the development of the microcomputer market and the popularization of computing, other methods of interacting with computers have been examined. One example is the mouse input device which is used as a pointer to select items on a menu or screen. It is not a very efficient method of getting text into machine-readable form, but it is good for graphics and for specific applications where there is a lot of interaction between the computer and the user. Joysticks, primarily developed for computer games are a similar type of technology and again standards are governed by a few manufacturers, who pioneered the technology. Products are advertized and occasionally reviewed in the popular computer magazines such as *Personal Computer World*, *Personal Computer Magazine* and *Which Computer?*. Technical research journals and relevant special interest groups of the large societies are other sources of information.

Touch screens

Touch screens are a way of interacting with computers and inputting instructions, usually in the form of a request for information from the system. Some public information devices operate with a touch screen. A good example of this can be seen at the main railway station in Florence where a touch screen interacts with users in four different languages and gives details of train times and fares. There have been reports in the computing press of a keyboardless portable microcomputer based on a touch screen for input of instructions.

Optical character recognition (OCR)

OCR scanners are widely used for converting large volumes of good-quality hard copy into machine-readable form. Recently, the cost of OCR scanners has come down and there are many different models on the market. The principle is generally the same for all the models. OCR machines are made up of a scanner which scans the text line by line. The text is then broken down into individual letters which are matched against parameters associated with each character. Once these attributes are recognized, the character is recognized and stored on the computer. If a character is not successfully matched, an asterisk or other recognized default character is put in its place. This will tell a human operator that the character needs to be reinterpreted. Modern OCR readers often perform to an accuracy of 99.98% (i.e. two characters out of every ten thousand are incorrect).

Special typefaces have been developed specifically for OCR readers. Banks use an OCR typeface on their cheques for instance, and have been doing so for years. More modern OCR scanners are more versatile and will recognize some of the commonly used typefaces such as Courier and Prestige Elite. Some models will recognize many different typefaces and will learn how to decipher new ones by trial and error.

More recently, there has been a lot of research into scanning and recognizing handwriting. There are several products currently on the market which allow users to write on a special pad linked to a computer. The computer then interprets the handwritten characters and displays the results on a screen for correction. Organizations like the Post Office are interested in character recognition and this is a possible avenue for further automation of letter sorting. There is a large body of information on pattern recognition.

The International Society for Optical Engineering based in the USA is a major organizer of conferences and it publishes the proceedings in *SPIE Proceedings*. Each issue is devoted to a single conference and contains the full text of the refereed papers presented. Many of the conferences are organized in conjunction with other groups around the world. Recent topics covered include: pattern recognition; image processing; optical storage; and scanning technology. The International Society for Optical Engineering also publishes a refereed journal, *Optical Engineering*, which covers diverse subjects and also has special issues.

Pattern Recognition published in the UK is the official journal of the Pattern Recognition Society. It is a learned journal with original articles as well as reviews and pedagogical papers. Most of the articles are refereed and include topics such as: visual text recognition; OCR; and contextual word recognition. *Computer Vision, Graphics and Image Processing* contains research papers on processing of pictorial information.

Bar codes

Bar code readers are increasingly popular in retail outlets for rapid identification of items. The advantages are central pricing and the ability to link into an automatic stock controller. There is a group of standards for bar codes governing the quality of print and spacing of bars, as well as governing the contrast of the bars and the background, to ensure that bar codes can be read by readers produced by different manufacturers. The Article Numbering

Association has been particularly active in this area and has published the *Tradacoms Manual of Standards for Electronic Data Exchange*.

Laser scanners are commonly used for scanning and reading bar codes. Light-pens are also widely used, frequently in libraries. Again bar codes are used in the same way for rapid issuing of books and for logging loans so that the stock is effectively managed.

Digitization

Digitization of images for transmission, manipulation or storage is a well-established technology. Facsimile transmission (Fax) machines are an example of this technology. Rather than encoding text and transmitting the character codes, it is scanned as an image. This allows for transmission of both text and graphics. Depending on the class of the Fax machine, the image scanned and transmitted will have different levels of resolution. Scanners can be used for digitizing images such as photographs which can then be manipulated by a computer. The printing industry has used this technology for a number of years now to yield high-quality colour prints. The PIRA Database, available on the Orbit Search Service, is the most important database in this area. *What to Buy for Business* regularly does comprehensive surveys of fax machines.

Flat-bed scanners are used to capture artwork and photographs directly into applications programmes such as desk-top publishing and word processing. Some scanners include OCR software to convert scanned text into ASCII format rather than digitizing the character image. Scanners generally have two modes of operation – black-and-white, for line drawings and text, and half-tone for photographs and graphics with different grey-scales. Hand-held scanners tend to be simpler and cheaper and work to a lower resolution than flatbed scanners. Specific products are covered by the popular press. Exhibitions such as the <u>Print and Publishing Show</u> often feature scanners and OCR devices.

Speech recognition

Perhaps the area of greatest research activity is speech recognition. It is widely believed that the development of this would greatly improve the accessibility of computing techniques. This is reflected in the quantity of information available and the amount of work going on in this area. As one would expect with an undeveloped area, most of this information is research oriented. As the technology develops, standards will become a priority and product information will be a major source of technical information.

Speech recognition allows for more natural interaction with computers. Although we take speech recognition in other people (and ourselves) for granted, the tasks which our brains perform in this seemingly trivial operation are very complex. Much of the research that has been done focuses on the process of speech production and the make up of words. Different branches of study have contributed to developments in this area including: phonetics; phonology; prosodics; syntax; and semantics. In normal speech there are no clear breaks between words. For instance, pauses within words may be longer than pauses between words. This causes enormous problems for automatic speech recognition systems. Once the sounds have been deciphered, they may have to be constructed into some kind of meaning so that the appropriate response is given. There is evidence to suggest that a lot of the redundancy built into human speech improves the rate of error correction and hence the quality of interpretation of speech.

At present there are a number of machines capable of recognizing individual words and work with a strictly limited vocabulary. One microcomputer manufacturer even brought out a portable computer capable of recognizing spoken commands.

For a general introduction to the area of speech recognition and synthesis there are a number of titles including *Speech Synthesis and Recognition Systems* by Yannakoudakis *et al.* and *Speech and Language-based Interaction with Machines. Towards the Conversational Computer* (Ellis Horwood) by Waterworth and Talbot is part of the *Ellis Horwood Books in Information Technology* series. *Speech Recognition by Machine* (Peter Peregrinus/IEE) gives a general review of speech recognition with some technical background and 359 bibliographic references.

IEEE Transactions on Acoustics, Speech and Signal Processing includes articles on speech recognition and synthesis. Being a learned journal the emphasis is on originality and quality and all articles are refereed. *IEE Proceedings–F. Communications, Radar and Signal Processing* is produced by the UK-based Institution of Electrical Engineers (IEE) and is a learned journal with papers on: communications; speech synthesis; and speech recognition. One of the most important journals in this area is *Speech Technology*, which is published in the USA. Another significant publication is *Computer Speech and Language and Speech Communications* (Netherlands).

Organizations developing techniques and standards for assessing speech recognition include: the IEEE Working Group on Speech I/O Performance Assessment in the US; STAG—Speech Technology Assessment Group (Institute of Acoustics, UK); GRECO in France; and the Speech Research Unit at the Department of Communication and Neuroscience at the University of Keele.

Organizations engaged in research range from academic institutions such as the Department of English at Cambridge University to national research bodies such as the National Research Council of Canada, to manufacturers and providers of telecommunications services such as AT&T Bell Lab in Naperville, Illinois, and Dictaphone Engineering and Technology. Particularly active organizations can usually be identified by the affiliations of authors of papers appearing in the literature and from the patent literature for commercial organizations.

Many of the major companies with large research establishments publish their own research journals. Many of them have special issues devoted to a single topic. An example is the *British Telecom Technology Journal* which had a special issue in April 1988 on speech and language processing.

ICASSP (International Conference on Acoustics, Speech and Signal Processing) is one of the major conferences in this area as is SPEECH TECH (Voice Input/Output Applications Show and Conference).

Large research projects such as the Alvey Programme in the UK, the ESPRIT Programme in Europe, and the Fifth Generation Computer project in Japan have funded projects into speech recognition using a variety of approaches including artificial intelligence. Speech recognition is seen as one of the main targets for future systems, and will provide a more flexible interface between computers and people than keyboards.

CHAPTER TWO

Output technologies

Printers, plotters, monitors, speech synthesis, robotics and process control

D. EDMONDS AND C. DONEGANI

Introduction

The literature relating to output technologies falls into two broad categories: product information; and applications information.

Product information is concerned with peripherals—printers, monitors and plotters (graphics hardware). Developments in these fields are product-led: research and publications originate from manufacturers rather than from academic or professional groups. As research is often commercially sensitive, it is usually impossible to obtain information on new developments until it is published in manufacturers' catalogues and brochures. Trade literature is therefore the most important source of information on products; there are few theoretical publications—as research is pragmatic and aims to result in the development of new products rather than the publication of research papers. There are, however, occasional reviews of the state of industry and general developments.

In the area of output technology, applications of current interest include: robotics; process control; and speech synthesis. These applications are of interest both to manufacturers and to the academic world—and ongoing research and development is taking place both in industrial organizations and in academic institutions.

In the applications area, the traditional published sources—journals and research reports—are more important, although each of the three applications has particular characteristics. In the area of robotics, there are vast quantities of information available. Process control is a difficult concept to define—as it forms part of the process of production engineering and overlaps with many aspects of manufacturing. It is difficult to isolate information specifically concerned with process control—and literature on process control can appear in the literature on production engineering and manufacturing technology, as well as engineering and computer applications in their widest sense.

In contrast with the wealth of literature on robotics, there is relatively little current published information on speech synthesis. Much of the initial research in the area of speech synthesis was undertaken in the 1960s—and the principles of producing speech by electronic means have long been established; the initial, theoretical research has been completed and synthesis techniques are now used in a number of applications. Further R&D is likely to be undertaken in-house by manufacturing companies and published information will become increasingly difficult to trace, as it becomes product information. A great deal of information is, however, being published on speech recognition—the recognition of speech by computers—as this is the current research and development area.

Printers, plotters and monitors

Research and development on output technology products—printers, plotters and monitors—is normally undertaken by manufacturers. The results of this R&D process are commercially-sensitive and are not usually released until the product is available on the open market: even then the researcher often can find only the information that the manufacturer is willing to reveal. Sources of information on all products are similar, and so will be considered together.

PRINTERS

Low-quality and low-cost nine-pin matrix printers have traditionally been used for drafting while the more expensive daisy-wheel printers have been used to produce letter-quality output. Some of the more expensive daisy-wheel printers have a relatively large RAM (random access memory), which is used as a print buffer. In recent years, laser printers have become popular: they provide a higher quality output and operate at a higher speed than daisy-wheel printers but are more expensive to purchase and to operate. They are, however, able to produce high-quality graphics images as well as text.

Ink jet and thermal transfer printers are now challenging laser printers in the marketplace: they produce high-quality output at lower initial cost than laser printers. At the lower end of the market, 24-pin matrix printers are also gaining in popularity; these produce 'near letter quality' (NLQ), a typeface which is more like that produced by a daisy-wheel than by pin matrix. A range of colour printers is now available—and it is likely that these will become increasingly popular in the future.

PLOTTERS

Unlike printers, plotters have a line-drawing function, using pens which move across paper in response to data output from the computer; they can be used with various control languages. Plotters have an internal memory (RAM) which reduces the loading on the host computer. They are able to handle larger paper sizes than printers, including A0 and A1. They are also capable of operating with a number of different pens—and a range of multi-colour plotters is available. Manufacturers are now working to produce plotters with increased pen speeds.

The popularity of microcomputer-based CAD packages is resulting in an increased use of plotters. However, these plotters are themselves being challenged by printers which are increasingly capable of handling graphics, especially laser printers.

MONITORS

The market for PC-compatible monitors is very large: most PC producers market their own screens and, in addition, there are specialist monitor manufacturers. The 80-character × 25-line format has now become standard, although taller screens are now being introduced for desk-top publishing. New developments in this area include moves towards higher resolution, flatter screens and non-glare screens. The highest resolution and largest screen size are required for CAD/CAM processes. There is a wide range of dedicated graphics cards on the market which allow the production of high-quality graphics images using PCs; also available are a number of dedicated, full CAD systems which use the highest resolution monitors. Multisync monitors which will work at several resolutions are now coming onto the market; these provide downward compatibility and enable the user to switch between resolutions to suit the requirements of existing equipment.

Journals

In recent years, there has been an increase in the number of commercially-produced journals covering the field of computers and computer technology. Many titles are now available, some aimed at the consumer, others at the trade. Most of the journals concentrate on hardware and many provide monthly product reviews. It is, however, difficult to predict when and where relevant articles will appear.

Some journals covering other industries or professions also provide occasional articles on new developments in computer peripherals. *Accountancy*, for instance, has published several useful articles on computer hardware and software aimed specifically at those working in the financial sector.

Journals produced by professional institutions in the area of computing and electronics are normally primarily concerned with new developments in research, processes and methodology and tend to provide little coverage of peripherals. The journals produced by the British Computer Society, the IEE and the IEEE, are, however, worth scanning as they include occasional articles of relevance. There are also a number of specialist institutional publications in the field of graphics: although these normally concentrate on software, they produce occasional high-quality refereed articles on plotters. Useful titles include the *Association for Computing Machinery Transactions on Graphics* (USA) and *IEEE Computer Graphics and Applications* (USA).

Commercially-published journals are the most important source of current product information. The information available on an individual product may not be particularly detailed—it may for instance only be an advertisement—but it is valuable if it is the only source.

All these journals tend to publish a mix of editorial, trade news (on people, companies and new product releases, for instance), feature articles on selected new products, some 'objective' articles written by editorial staff comparing different branded products, advertisements, and so on.

The large number of titles available makes selection difficult. The serious researcher can eliminate some titles in some circumstances and can for instance, exclude the following:

- those based purely on sales promotion, e.g. *Computer Shopper* (except when selecting items for purchase or comparing product ranges)

18 Output technologies

- those written for specific machines, e.g. *Acorn User*, *Apple Business* (unless the researcher is interested in the specific system)

Some journals concentrate on one type of article. *Computer Weekly*, *Mini/Micro News* and *Computing*, for instance, all concentrate on trade news and may include announcements of new products or provide clues to the R&D programmes being undertaken by individual companies.

A number of general computing titles also provide coverage of the peripherals market; these include *Practical Computing*, *Personal Computer Magazine*, *What Micro?* and *Which Computer?*. Several journals are targeted to meet the computing needs of the business community. These include *Business Equipment Digest* and *Business Systems and Equipment*. *Computing Equipment*, *What's New in Computing* and *Micro Decision* are also aimed at businesspeople using computer equipment in the workplace. Two specialist journals, *PC Magazine* and *Which PC?* cover the large IBM PC-compatible market, and provide details of peripherals which can be used with IBM-compatible equipment.

A number of journals such as *Computer Graphics Forum*, *Computer Graphics World* and *Computers and Graphics* are concerned exclusively with graphics; although the coverage is normally concentrated on software, they contain occasional articles on plotters. Other relevant journals in this area include *Computer Vision, Graphics and Image Processing* and *Computer Images International*.

SECONDARY SOURCES

A number of indexes and abstracts contain information on peripherals. The *ACM Guide to Computing Machinery*, which is published by the (US) Association for Computing Machinery, is a hard-copy publication. The guide includes abstracts of books, journal articles, conference proceedings, theses and so on, and includes author, keyword, classified, subject and source indexes. Its coverage is international.

Computer and Control Abstracts (Inspec) provides particularly good coverage of the peripherals market; it includes abstracts of articles, conference proceedings, books, and so on. *Computer & Control Abstracts* is published monthly in hard copy and is also available online as part of the INSPEC database which is hosted by ESA and by Dialog.

Key Abstracts: Business Automation (Inspec), another Inspec product, also provides useful coverage of peripherals. A new title, first published in 1989, *Key Abstracts: Business Automation*, provides information on all peripherals which are applicable to an office setting; source material includes 'office equipment' and 'business computing' journals, published mainly in the UK and the USA. Again, this publication forms part of the INSPEC database, which is a particularly important source of information on computers and computer systems. The database abstracts articles from over 3000 journals, and also covers monograph publications and conference proceedings.

Computing, Communications and Media Trend Monitor (Aslib/ TMI) is a new title which analyzes and summarizes press and journal coverage of this industry. It includes useful overviews of developments in output technologies and in particular, information on peripherals.

The COMPUTER database available on Dialog also includes abstracts from journals, conference proceedings and books on every aspect of computers. The database contains useful data on peripherals and includes product evaluations and comparisons, and information on computer industry companies.

A number of journals of relevance are now available online in full-text. Section H in TEXTLINE, for instance, includes the full text of a number of useful journals such as: *Business Computing Systems*; *Computer Decisions*; *Computer Graphics World*; and the *Hewlett-Packard Journal*.

NEWSNET also offers relevant journals online, including: *The Business Computer*; *Computer Book Reviews*; and *Computing Today Journal*.

Some products are now available on CD-ROM. *Computer Peripherals Review* and *Computer Terminals Review* are published by Silver Platter on CD-ROM. Both journals place a particularly strong emphasis on North American equipment and research.

COMPANY JOURNALS AND NEWSLETTERS

Most large computer manufacturers, including some active in the peripherals field, publish house journals which may be distributed to customers and potential customers as well as employees. These are usually glossy and professionally produced, often by a commercial publisher on behalf of the company—and they can provide useful information on the company's current development projects. They should, however, be used with care—as they may present a biased view of the quality of company products! And—as house journals cover all company products—information on peripherals may not get front-page attention. *IBM UK News* is published by the IBM company in the UK, primarily for its own employees, while *Digital Review*, which covers the DEC company activities, is published by a commercial publisher. Both are distributed free of charge to selected readers. They provide detailed information on new products and can be useful for tracking product development. Other house journals are more research-based; examples of this style of house journal include the *IBM Journal of Research and Development*, a bimonthly publication, and the *IBM Technical Disclosures Bulletin*, which is issued monthly.

Books

Current product information is normally produced by commercial organizations, and is published in journals, rather than in monographs. There are, however, many titles which are concerned with the hazards of working with monitors. Many trade unions have been particularly concerned with this topic, and have produced a number of advisory pamphlets; the Health and Safety Executive has also produced several titles on the safety issues associated with the use of monitors.

Marketing and trade information

MARKET INFORMATION

Specialist directories can provide an excellent source of information on specific market sectors. Infotech publishes a range of directories covering specialist industry sectors, and has recently produced a directory covering printers and peripherals: it is intended that the directory will be published annually. *Financial Comparison and Market Directory: Industry Sector: Computer Printers and Peripherals* brings together, in alphabetical order, the major UK companies involved in the production of printers and peripherals, and enables a comparison of performance. The top 50 companies are ranked by turnover. A range of detailed financial information is provided for each company and allows the user to make comparisons between companies. But—as it has no subject index—it cannot act as a product index. There are, however, a number of directories which provide information on manufacturers and suppliers of computer peripherals. These include the following:

British Office Technology is published by the British Office Technology Manufacturers Alliance and distributed free of charge. This publication is a buyers' guide which lists the Alliance's member companies, providing contact information and product indexes.

CAD International Directory (Butterworths), is a buyers' guide which includes plotters and monitors because of their importance to CAD systems.

The *Computer Users' Yearbook* (VNU), is in four volumes. Volume 1 includes a guide to peripherals which is arranged in order of manufacturer's name and subdivided by model name. A brief technical summary of each product is provided. The yearbook provides coverage of printers (page and line), serial printers, plotters, visual display equipment and monitors.

Computing Decisions published by the Kemps Group for the NCC includes information on over 6000 suppliers of computer hardware, software, services.

DIAL Computing (Reed Information Services Ltd) provides a classified guide to products (including printers, visual display terminals and plotters) and an alphabetical guide to companies within the sector. *DIAL Industry: Electrical, Electronics, Computing, Instrumentation* (Reed Information Services Ltd) lists manufacturers, suppliers and distributors; information is arranged by product, and there is an alphabetical listing of companies. Both DIAL directories are also available online within the KOMPASS UK database on Dialog.

Directory of Electronics, Instruments and Computers (Morgan-Grampian) provides an alphabetical list of manufacturers, and gives limited contact information (the address, telephone and telex numbers, branches and sales contacts). It also provides a list of trade names in use within the industry, and gives UK distributors of foreign products.

Microcomputer Software and Hardware Guide is produced by R. R. Bowker and Company, and is available online on Dialog. The guide contains information on microcomputer peripherals in SubFile 3. Each record includes ordering information, technical specifications and a brief description of each product. The sources of information from which the guide is derived include manufacturers' catalogues and press releases. The guide is updated monthly, and so provides a useful source of current information.

PC Year Book 1989 (VNU Business Publications) covers IBM PC compatible equipment only. The peripherals section of the yearbook gives key technical information on individual models; it also provides prices. Information is listed in alphabetical order of company name.

22 Output technologies

TRADE INFORMATION

Trade catalogues are of course a valuable source of information on products. These are freely available from individual manufacturers; and as many of the companies involved in this sector are large—and include multinationals such as Canon, Hewlett-Packard and IBM—some manufacturers' literature is substantial (Epson, for instance, produces the extensive *Which Epson?* catalogue). Distributors' catalogues can also be useful, as they often bring together brief technical data on products from a number of manufacturers. Trade exhibitions are one of the best sources of trade literature as it is possible to gather catalogues from a number of manufacturers in a single location.

If you do not have the opportunity to visit a trade exhibition, the task of identifying appropriate products and obtaining the trade catalogues which describe them can be a lengthy process. A number of companies now gather together trade catalogues and make them available in a single location. Particularly relevant in this area is the *British Product Data Service Information Technology, Computer and Communications Hardware Index* (Technical Indexes) which is published twice per year. The publication contains files of manufacturers' catalogues with associated indexes, all of which are regularly up-dated. The index is available both in microfilm and microfiche, for an annual rental. Hard-copy *Product Data Books* (Technical Indexes) are also available with the index; these provide alphabetic listings of all manufacturers with indexes of products and trade names. They also include details of UK distributors for overseas companies.

Standards

The predominance of IBM PC-compatible products in the marketplace has resulted in IBM standards being accepted by other manufacturers who wish to penetrate the IBM market. Apart from the standard interfaces, such as RS232 and Centronics, there is little other standardization between manufacturers.

Monitors provide the exception to the rule. The interaction between monitors and computers is standardized and well established. There are, for instance, video standards; the main standards-issuing body in this area is the Video Electronics Standards Association (VESA) which is concerned with all types of screen. The VESA often acts passively, recognizing standards which have been developed by manufacturers and then submitted to VESA for approval—for instance, NEC have recently developed the 'SuperVGA' monitor which VESA has retrospectively recognized as setting a new standard. This has led to some standardization but such standards are not enforceable as, for example, one manufacturer's product will be a better quality than another's, even for the same specification.

Conferences, exhibitions and trade shows

Although there are many conferences on computing, relatively few are concerned specifically with peripherals. Workshops on peripherals are, however, sometimes held as part of the larger computing conferences, such as the annual Information Technology Conference organized by the National Computing Centre.

Again, there are many conferences on graphics which also hold sessions on hardware. Two annual conferences are particularly important in this area: the Computer Animation Conference, usually held in a European location, and the Association for Computing Machinery's Siggraph Conference, an annual conference on computer graphics and interactive techniques.

Because this is a product-led area, the catalogues of trade exhibitions and shows can provide useful information. Relevant shows and exhibitions including the following:

- Computer Trade Show
- Business to Business Exhibitions
- Scottish Computer Show
- Computer North—the Northern Computer Show
- Which Computer? and Office Update Show
- Personal Computer Show
- European Computer Trade Show
- PC User Show

Details of forthcoming conferences and shows are included in a number of journals, including computing publications such as *What's On in Computing* and generalist sources such as the *Exhibitions Bulletin*.

Organizations

As the majority of the research undertaken in this area is commercial, most of the relevant organizations represent industrial interests. The major American trade organization in this area is the Association for Computing Machinery which is primarily interested in equipment, computing techniques and languages. The Association has a very active publishing programme, producing journals, conference proceedings and the regular abstracting publication, the *ACM Guide to Computing Machinery*.

In the United Kingdom, there are two major organizations which are involved in this sector. The British Office Technology

Manufacturers Alliance is a trade organization which aims to strengthen the competitiveness of the UK office technology sector by encouraging inter-company collaboration. The Alliance produces *British Office Technology*, a useful buyers' guide to hardware and software which is distributed free of charge to interested organizations.

The Computer and Peripherals Equipment Training Association also represents the interests of companies in the UK involved in the manufacture, distribution and use of computer peripherals. As its name suggests, the Association is primarily interested in training—and it organizes a variety of meetings of relevance to those in the industry.

Robotics

Robots are machines which can solve problems. There are two major categories of robots—industrial robots, which are used in industrial applications such as production and assembly, welding and spraying; and 'robots' which may be used in a variety of applications, in a variety of situations including the home. Problem-solving robots are becoming especially important in new robotics applications. The use of robotics now ranges from large-scale applications in heavy engineering, through machine tool robots, to the small-scale robots used in electronics manufacturing industries.

Extensive use of robots is made in manufacturing countries with a high level of capital for investment—where there is also a high level of research and development. These countries include Sweden, the USSR, Japan, West Germany, France, Italy, Australia and USA as well as in the UK.

There is considerable overlap between information sources which cover production engineering, process control and automation in general, and those which relate specifically to robotics. In order to cover the topic of robotics fully, it would be necessary to scan a wide range of general engineering journals. Large quantities of published material are available: journals and monographs proliferate in this field. There is both academic and industrial interest in robotics—and many conferences and exhibitions cover the topic.

Journals

Many journals cover the field of robotics. A number of these are learned journals which publish refereed articles. The *IEEE Jour-*

nal of Robotics and Automation is an authoritative publication which includes international research papers in the area of robotics. The *International Journal of Robotics Research* is a predominantly academic publication, while *Robotica—International Journal of Information, Education and Research in Robotics and AI* includes theoretical articles by both academic and commercial contributors.

A number of journals are reputable but rather more suitable for the general reader. *Industrial Robot* is a glossy publication which has been produced since 1973. It provides both technical and managerial coverage of industrial robots. It includes trade information such as company data, new products information and exhibition reports. It also contains brief technical articles, book reviews and abstracts of articles published in other journals. *Robotics World* also includes new product information and product reviews along with a useful survey of robots in use.

Other relevant journals in this field include titles such as *Automation*, which has a regular robot survey, *Assembly Automation* and *Robotics*.

Although there are many titles specifically on robotics, wider ranging engineering and computing titles are often a source of useful articles, especially for the non-specialist. Particularly important are those dealing with manufacturing, such as *Automation News*, *Manufacturing Technology Horizons* and the *International Journal of Production Research*.

The quickest way to find out about new products in this area is to consult one of the free advertisement-based titles, such as *Industrial Engineering News*. Information on products may not be extensive—but it is current—and therefore valuable.

Most countries which are involved in robotics produce several journals on the topics; these are often published with English translations or English abstracts. The best-known include European titles such as the French publications *Axes Robotiques: Revue Française de Robotique* and the German publication, *Robotersysteme*. A number of publications are produced in the Far East—and include the Japanese titles, *Robot News* and the *Journal of the Robotics Society of Japan*—and *Jiqiren (Robot)*, produced by the Chinese Society of Automation. However, many of these are available only in their original language of publication and so may have a limited relevance to many researchers. The Science Reference and Information Service of the British Library holds a large number of these titles.

Secondary sources

SUBJECT GUIDES

In an area in which there is so much interest, it is perhaps inevitable that a number of specialist guides to information sources have been published. The most recently produced is the *Robotics Sourcebook* (Elsevier, 1988) by V. D. Hunt. An earlier publication by Ken Susnjara is entitled *Robotics, CADCAM Marketplace 1985* (Bowker, 1985). The Susnjara volume is an information guide with a particularly wide coverage; in the research section, for instance, over 700 institutions are listed.

The *Robotics Sourcebook and Dictionary* (New York, Industrial Press, 1983) by D. F. Tver and R. W. Bolz also provides a useful introduction to the field, listing applications and manufacturers, together with a glossary of terms, and specifications of named robots.

A number of bibliographies also cover this area; particularly useful is: *Robotics: an International Bibliography with Abstracts* (Bedford, IFS, 1984), compiled by P. Farmer and A. Gomersall. The bibliography is international in scope and provides qualitative abstracts, with a number of black-and-white photographs, illustrating particular applications. Another IFS publication, the *Robotics Bibliography 1970—1981*, which is also compiled by Farmer and Gomersall, similarly provides a good introduction to this field, although its content is now a little dated.

Dictionaries

There are several dictionaries which cover the area of robotics; a relatively recent publication is the *Dictionary of Robot Technology* (Elsevier, 1986) in four languages: English, German, French, Russian, compiled by E. Burger. The dictionary includes many terms, although it is unfortunately produced in rather small print. Rather more easy on the eye, is the *Dictionary of Artificial Intelligence and Robotics* (1986) by S. M. Rosenberg, which contains over 4000 terms. And—for the real enthusiast—H. D. Jumge's *Pocket Dictionary of Robotics* (Berlin, Ernst, 1986), in English/German, German/English provides a portable introduction to the topic.

Abstracts and indexes

Two of the abstracting services published by Inspec provide a useful introduction to the literature on robotics. *Key Abstracts: Robotics and Control* and *Key Abstracts: Machine Vision* are both produced by IEE/IEEE. They are published monthly in hard copy, and form part of the INSPEC database which is available on ESA and Dialog. COMPENDEX, which covers engineering in general and has significant coverage of industrial robots is available via several online hosts, including Dialog, STN, and ESA-IRS.

The *ACM Guide to Computing Machinery*, a US publication, provides good, international coverage of robotics research, as does *Robomatics Reporter*, a specialist publication which is also available online as ROBOMATIX on ESA-IRS. Other abstracting services to consider in this field are *PERA Abstracts*, a UK publication, and the *ASME Technical Digest*, which provides useful coverage of American research. RBOT ROBOTICS INFORMATION, an online database available on BRS, also provides specialist coverage of this field.

A number of robotics journals are included in full-text on online systems; *Robotics Today* is available as full-text on TEXTLINE, and *Robot News* is available as full-text on NEWSNET.

Monographs

Many monographs have been published on robotics—and it is not easy to select a representative sample. A useful introduction to the topic is the *International Encyclopedia of Robotics: Applications and Automation* (John Wiley, 1988), edited by R. F. Dorf which is produced in three volumes. It includes lengthy articles, illustrated by black-and-white photographs and line drawings. Many of the articles include bibliographies.

Introduction to Robotics (Macmillan, 1985) by A. J. Critchlow provides—just as the title indicates—a useful beginner's guide to the field, while J. F. Engelberger's *Robotics in Practice* guides the reader into the applications. The Health and Safety Executive has recently produced a clear, practical guide to the safety aspects of this field, under the title of *Industrial Robot Safety* (HMSO, 1988).

Trade and marketing information

Robots are a marketable commodity and form the basis of a number of market reports. Keynote, a publisher which regularly produces market surveys, has issued a number of reports on *Industrial Robots* (Keynote, 3rd edn, 1986). The American market for industrial robots is reviewed in *Industrial Robots: a Summary and Forecast* (Tech Tran Consultants, 3rd edn, 1986). The publication provides data on current suppliers, models and specifications in use in the US robot industry, and also speculates on future trends.

Output technologies

The UK robot industry is analyzed in an excellent publication produced by the British Robotics Association. *Robot Facts* describes the geographical and sectoral distribution of robotic applications in the UK, and details their country of origin. It also compares the robot population growth in the UK with that in the USA and West Germany. The Policy Studies Institute has also produced a study of the extent of use of robotics applications in the United Kingdom, based on a postal survey. *Robots in British Industry: Expectations and Experience* (1986) by J. Northcote analyses the extent of use of robots in the UK, and discusses the characteristics of robot users.

COMPANY AND PRODUCT DIRECTORIES

A number of company and product directories cover robotics. The *Robotics World Directory* is published annually as part of the *Robotics World Journal*. The directory covers robots, and robotic and vision systems; it includes lists of robot component and conveyance device suppliers, and of consultants to the robotics industry. There is both a company and a subject index; there is also a glossary.

A list of companies active in the field of robotics is also included in *Who's Who in Automation* (Templar Publications Ltd).

Two European directories cover the robotics industry in France and in Germany. *Le Guide Robots Ingénierie* (G2H Publications), covers French products and also includes distributors for foreign manufacturers. The directory lists French consultants, experts, associations and so on. It also lists robots by application. *Industrie Roboter Katalog* (Vereinigte Fachverlage) edited by H-J. Warnecke and R. D. Schraft, includes technical datasheets on robots, arranged in order of the name of manufacturer and subdivided by model name or number. It is written in German, although the introduction and major headings are translated into English.

SPECIFICATIONS

The *Datafiles of Advanced Manufacturing Technology Equipment and Organizations* (British Robot Association, 1987) lists robot specifications by company name—and also provides a range of additional information on robotics research and the robotics industry.

The Japanese Industrial Robot Association produces a similar publication covering the Japanese industry. *Specifications and Applications of Industrial Robots in Japan* indexes robots by company and by application, and provides one page of information on each robot, including a line drawing and specification.

The applications section shows each robot in its setting within the manufacturing process.

The *International Robot Industry Report* (IFS Publications/Springer-Verlag, 1987) by J. Mortimer and B. Rooks includes descriptive company profiles, in alphabetical order of name, of more than a hundred American, European, and Japanese companies in this field. It includes international robot specifications. However its usefulness is limited by the lack of a product index.

Many trade journals, for example, *Industrial Engineering News* provide reviews of new products. These are often based on information supplied by the manufacturer, and are objective, but are often the only source of information on new products.

Conferences

A number of regular conferences on robotics are held in the United Kingdom. The British Robotics Association organizes an annual conference on the topic and publishes the Proceedings. A number of international conferences are also often held in the UK, including Robotics International which is organized annually by the American Society of Mechanical Engineers (ASME). Again, the proceedings are published and are readily available from a number of libraries. The ASME also holds regular conferences on flexible manufacturing systems and automated manufacturing which cover robotics in a wider setting.

The IEEE is also interested in the area of robotics, and usually organizes an annual international conference on the topic. The venues vary from country to country; the 1989 Robotics and Automation Conference was held in Arizona. The Proceedings are published, and provide a useful source of information on advancements in the field.

A number of conferences cover special applications in the field of robotics; these often concentrate on the use of robotics within a specific industry sector. The Autofact Conference organized by the ASME, for instance, concentrates on automotive technology and automation.

In addition to the conferences organized by trade and professional organizations, there are many commercially organized conferences in this field. These include Advanced Manufacturing Systems Europe, held in Genoa in 1989, and Advanced Manufacturing Systems USA, both of which are organized annually by Cahners. IFS (Conferences) Ltd organizes both the International Conference on Assembly Automation and the International Conference on Advanced Robotics; the proceedings of both conferences are published by IFS (Publications) Ltd.

Two commercially organized exhibitions are particularly useful for monitoring new products. Automan Exhibition (the Advanced Manufacturing Equipment and Services Exhibition) is organized annually by Cahners, and is normally held at the National Exhibition Centre in Birmingham, while the Computers in Manufacturing Show, arranged annually by Independent Exhibitions Ltd travels to different venues around the UK.

Details of forthcoming conferences and exhibitions are included in *What's On in Computing* and in many of the robotics journals.

Organizations

There are a number of national robotics associations. In the UK, the British Robot Association aims to encourage responsible use of robot and other advanced manufacturing technology. The Association holds an annual conference and publishes the proceedings; it also produces a newsletter and a directory, and provides an information service. The membership of the association includes a mixture of corporate and individual members.

Many other countries have similar associations, including the Australian Robot Association, the Association Française de Robotique Industrielle (AFRI), the Japan Industrial Robot Association (JIRA), the Società Italiana Robotica Industriale (SIRI) and the Swedish Industrial Robot Association (SWIRA).

Because of the importance of robotics, many professional associations have specialist subgroups concerned with robotics and automation. These include the robotics subgroup of the British Computer Society; it is an active publisher and organizes many meetings and conferences. The Institution of Electrical Engineers and Institution of Mechanical Engineers (both in UK) and the Institute of Electrical and Electronic Engineers (in the USA), are all interested in the field of robotics, and organize meetings on applications.

Because robots are now installed in manufacturing plant, information on robotics is of interest to engineers and production staff in particular industries, such as the automotive industry where they are used heavily in assembly and other processes. Conferences, publications and research can therefore be found on the application of robotics to particular industrial sectors.

Research

Information on research in robotics—and on the organizations involved in research—is provided in a number of sources. The *World Yearbook of Robotics Research and Development* (Kogan Page, 2nd edn, 1986) edited by P. B. Scott contains a series of articles by different authors on aspects of robotics, current developments and overviews of national funding programmes, arranged by country. The publication also includes a directory of robotics research and development activities, by country, a world index of R&D centres, a world index of researchers, and a subject index to research.

Ken Susnjara's introduction to information sources in robotics (*Robotics, CADCAM Marketplace 1985* (Bowker, 1985)), lists over 700 institutions undertaking research in this area.

Process control

Process control relates to the control of operations in the manufacturing process, and relies on the transfer of control and data between machinery, management computers, control points and consoles. Process control originated in the processing industries and is still extensively used in chemical and food manufacturing; it is now also used increasingly in industries which involve assembly techniques. Process control is not exclusively an output technology—its operation depends on input and feedback, for instance from sensors.

Process control is only one of the techniques used by production engineers to convert the raw material to the finished product. There is considerable overlap between process control and control engineering which is concerned with the use of equipment in the manufacturing process, rather than with the automated control of sections or indeed the whole of the manufacturing process. Consequently it is difficult to define the boundaries of the literature on process control. The word 'control' appears in the titles of many journals, books and conferences which are not concerned with process control. In terms of selecting material, the word 'automation' is often more relevant than the word 'control'.

There is both commercial and academic interest in process control; manufacturers tend to be concerned with specific products, while academic researchers view process control within the wider topic of automated production.

Journals

The most useful journals in this field are commercially-produced titles; these include both *Assembly Automation* and *Automation—the Journal of Automated Production*. *Process Engineering*, *Control Systems* and *Sensor Review* all contain material of relevance to process control.

32 Output technologies

Information on new products in control and automation is available in a number of trade journals which are funded from advertisement revenue, such as *Industrial Engineering News*, *What's New in Industry* and *What's New in Electronics*.

Journals produced by professional associations tend to cover a wider range of interest than process control—but they are the best source for articles and news on theoretical research. The most relevant are *IEEE Transactions on Automatic Control* and the *IEEE Control Systems Magazine* which is produced by the IEEE Control Systems Society. *Measurement and Control* (Institute of Measurement and Control) is a useful source as is *Production Engineer* (Institution of Production Engineers). Also relevant to this area is *Automation and Remote Control* (Instrument Society of America).

Secondary sources

INDEXES AND ABSTRACTS

The major abstracting journal in the area of process control is *Computer & Control Abstracts* (Inspec). The journal is issued monthly and includes short summaries of papers from journals, conference proceedings, monographs and reports, and so on. Its subject coverage includes control engineering, robotics and automated systems. Each issue has a subject guide and indexes, and cumulated indexes are published twice per year.

Other relevant abstracting and indexing services include *Key Abstracts: Robotics and Control* (Inspec) which covers robotic and control applications in the areas of materials handling, industrial production systems and manufacturing processes. *Key Abstracts: Electronic Instrumentation* (Inspec) is also useful as its coverage includes the components of process control such as instrumentation and measuring, sensors and transducers.

A number of the Production Engineering Research Association (PERA) publications are relevant to the area of process control; these include *PERA Abstracts*, *Pera News*, research reports and state-of-the-art reports.

ONLINE DATABASES

The best coverage of process control is contained within general engineering databases such as COMPENDEX (available on ESA, Dialog, STN, Orbit), INSPEC (on ESA, STN and Dialog) and ISMEC (on ESA and Dialog). CAD/CAM on ESA also provides useful coverage.

The TEXTLINE database on electronics and engineering covers a number of relevant titles, including: *Process Equipment News*; *Production and Industrial Equipment Digest*; *Production Engineer*; *Production Engineering*; and *CAD/CAM International*.

DICTIONARIES

It is often difficult for a newcomer to a technical area to understand the jargon—and the *IFIP Glossary of Terms used in Production Control* (Amsterdam, North-Holland, 1987), compiled by J. L. Burbidge is a particularly helpful source in the field of process control.

Books

A key text in the area of process control is the *Systems and Control Encyclopedia: Theory, Technology and Applications* (Pergamon Press, 1987). The eight-volume encyclopedia edited by Madan G. Singh provides lengthy articles on major concepts such as process control. It also provides an extensive bibliography of additional relevant material.

A good introduction to the topic of process control is the *Handbook of Advanced Process Control Systems and Instrumentation* (Houston, TX, Gulf, 1987) which is edited by L. Kane. There is also a useful section on automatic process control within the *Process Instruments and Controls Handbook* (New York, McGraw-Hill, 3rd edn, 1985). A recent book on *Process Control* (1988) by J. G. Balchen and G. Jens provides good coverage of the subject, too.

Also important in the area of process control is the *IFAC Proceedings* (Pergamon) series which is published on behalf of IFAC, and the *NATO ASI (Advanced Science Institute) Series F* (Springer-Verlag) which covers computer and systems science.

Trade and marketing information

An excellent source of market data in the field of process control is the *Annual Review of Engineering Industries and Automation* (HMSO) produced by the United Nations and usually published annually. The review describes national developments and includes data on production, trade and employment in general. It also includes import and export figures. A review of the European advanced manufacturing technology industry is included in *Manufacturing Technology International—Europe* (Sterling Publications), an irregular publication.

Output technologies

TRADE AND PRODUCT DIRECTORIES

A number of directories provide data on products and companies involved in the area of process control. The *Process Control Handbook* (C. H. W. Roles & Associates) is a buyers' guide to valves, valve selection and associated equipment. The directory also includes lists of UK manufacturers and suppliers of process control valves and the actuators and instrumentation used to control them. The *Automated Manufacturing Directory* (Morgan-Grampian) provides contact details for companies involved in process control, CAD, flexible manufacturing systems and production control. The *Process Engineering Directory 1988* (Morgan-Grampian) also includes UK manufacturers and suppliers' addresses, and gives details of UK agents of overseas manufacturers. This directory also includes a buyers' guide covering control and instrumentation products.

A guide to key organizations and associations is included within *Who's Who in Automation 1987* (Templar Publications). The publication also includes a section on process control and on programmable controllers.

Manufacturers are of course a good source of information on specific products; in the area of process control, suppliers rarely issue databooks covering a range of products; it is usually necessary to request individual datasheets on specific products.

Standards

There are a number of key standards in the area of process control. These include several British Standards, such as *BS1646* on graphic symbols, *BS6739* on instrumentation, installation design and practice and *BS1523 Pt 1* which includes a glossary of relevant terms.

Other important standards include two handbooks produced by the Engineering Equipment Users Association: *Handbook No. 34: Installation of Instrumentation and Process Control Systems* and *Handbook No. 38: Guide to the Engineering of Microprocessor-based Systems for Instrumentation and Control*. The Instrument Society of America Standard *S50.1* is also pertinent as it covers compatibility of analog signals for electronic industry process instrumentation.

Conferences

A number of regular conferences cover process control within a wider programme; the amount of time allocated to the topic varies of course, from year to year, and it is advisable to consult the programme to ensure that relevant papers will be included. The International Federation for Automatic Control (IFAC) <u>Conference on Digital Computer Applications to Process Control</u> is of particular interest to those concerned with process control; the proceedings are published. Similarly the annual <u>Control Conference</u> is organized by the Computing and Control Division of the IEE in association with various other engineering bodies; again, the conference proceedings are published, and are widely available. IFS Conferences Ltd organizes the <u>International Conference on Flexible Manufacturing Systems</u>—and this, too, is relevant to those interested in process control.

Other *ad hoc* conferences relevant to process control are held by professional associations such as the Institute of Mechanical Engineers and the IEE. Details of conferences and exhibitions are included in the majority of journals; *What's On in Computing* and the *Exhibitions Bulletin* are both particularly useful sources of information.

Organizations

A number of professional institutions are involved in the broad issues of process control. In the UK, these include the Institution of Electrical Engineers, which has a Computing and Control Division and the Institution of Mechanical Engineers (IME) which covers the broad spectrum of manufacturing industry and also has a special-interest group concerned specifically with process industries. Both the Institute of Measurement and Control and the Institution of Production Engineers are interested in this area, too; they organize meetings and conferences, and are active publishers.

The British Computer Society has a process control subgroup, and relevant material may be found in a number of the society's journals and newsletters, as well as in the specialist conference proceedings which are produced from time to time.

In the USA, a number of professional institutions are concerned with the topic of process control; these include the Institute of Electrical and Electronic Engineers (IEEE), the American Society of Mechanical Engineers (ASME) and the Instrument Society of America—all of which produce relevant publications.

On an international level, the International Federation of Automated Control (IFAC) is an important source of information on process control and on the wider issues of automated control. The *IFAC Proceedings*, for instance, include many papers on process control technology.

Because of the commercial interest in the area of process control, a number of trade associations cover this specialty.

BEAMA Ltd is a national federation of trade associations serving the electrical, electronic and allied manufacturing industries. BEAMA has several federated associations, all contactable at same address; these include the Association of Control Manufacturers.

GAMBICA Association Ltd is the Association for the Instrumentation, Control and Automation Industry in the UK. The Association has a number of subgroups, covering areas such as industrial instrumentation for measuring and control, and computerized industrial process control. The association organizes meetings and conferences, and provides an information service for members. It also publishes a useful product guide.

A number of organizations are concerned with research in process control. The Production Engineering Research Association (PERA) covers manufacturing processes in the widest sense but has particular interests in the area of computerized information operations. PERA produces a number of publications, although most are available only to members of the Association. Other organizations involved in research into process control include the National Engineering Research Laboratory and the National Materials Handling Centre at Cranfield Institute of Technology.

Information on R&D work in electronics and computer science being undertaken throughout the world is included in *Electronics Research Centres—a World Directory of Organizations and Programmes* (Longman, 1986).

Speech synthesis

Within the field of speech synthesis, there are two major areas of research, namely synthesis by analysis and text-to-speech.

SYNTHESIS BY ANALYSIS

Synthesis by analysis involves the synthesis of pre-recorded digital electronics data, normally recorded from original phrases. The principles of developing basic algorithms have been understood since the 1960s—and research in this area is now product-led. The major electronics manufacturers are drawing on the discipline of linguistics to improve speech quality, and to make synthesized speech sound more like human speech. They are also considering how people relate and react to computer speech, in an attempt to make it more 'hearer-friendly'. In order to improve the quality of machine speech, it is also necessary to bring about improvements in data storage facilities; developments are at present hampered by the large amount of storage needed for the production of even a short phrase.

TEXT-TO-SPEECH

Text-to-speech involves the synthesis of letter sounds, both vowel and consonants, to build up a complete vocabulary. This is still very much an academic research area, which draws on linguistics theory. Although a number of advanced text-to-speech algorithms have been developed, they have not yet been seen in the market place due to the computing power required and the concomitant costs.

At present, there are few ready-made 'speech synthesizers' on the market: such equipment tends to be assembled for each specific application. General electronics trade information, contained in directories and journals, can therefore be useful in this field.

Much of the literature tends to concentrate on specific applications of speech synthesis techniques: published information is for instance available on flight synthesizers, on the use of synthesized speech in cars and on aids for disabled people.

Journals

The journals produced by a number of professional institutions are of interest in the area of speech synthesis. *IEEE Transactions: Acoustics, Speech and Signal Processing*, the *Journal of the Acoustic Society of America* and the *Transactions of the Institute of Electronic Information and Communication Engineering (Japan)* all contain articles of relevance in this field.

The commercially-produced journals cover a variety of disciplines which are related to speech synthesis, including electronics, linguistics and ergonomics. *Computer Speech and Language* is a particularly useful source of information on the electronics aspects of speech synthesis. The *British Telecom Technology Journal* again contains relevant articles in this topic area. *Sensor Review* also covers speech synthesis, and has recently published a state-of-the-art review.

Other journals cover linguistics: the most important in this area are *Language Technology*, *Speech Technology* and *Literary and Linguistic Computing*. Articles on the human–computer interface are included in *Human Factors*, *Applied Ergonomics* and *Behaviour and Information Technology*. *Current Psychological Research and Reviews* also publishes articles in this area of output technology.

Secondary sources

The *ACM Guide to Computing Machinery* provides useful coverage of the topic of speech technologies; the guide indexes books, journals, proceedings, reports, theses and so on. Other relevant sources include *Electrical and Electronics Abstracts*, which contains a very good section on speech technology, and *Computer and Control Abstracts*.

Useful online sources include COMPENDEX (on ESA, Dialog, STN and Orbit), INSPEC (on ESA, STN and Dialog) and INSPEC INFORMATION SCIENCE (on ESA). The TEXTLINE Electronics and Engineering section is also a useful source of information on this area.

Books

The majority of published monographs in this area concentrate on speech recognition. Those which cover both speech synthesis and speech recognition include *Speech and Language-based Interaction with Machines: Towards the Conversational Computer*, edited by J. A. Waterworth (Ellis Horwood, 1987). *Microcomputer Speech Synthesis and Recognition* by A. S. Poulton (Sigma Technical Press, 1983) is a very readable survey of the area and is a useful starting point, although it is now somewhat dated.

Other relevant books covering the topic of speech synthesis include the following:

Bristow, G. (Editor). *Electronic Speech Synthesis Techniques, Technology and Applications*, London, Granada, 1984.
Holmes, J. N. *Speech Synthesis and Recognition*, Wokingham, Van Nostrand Reinhold, 1988.
Jack, M. and Lever, J. *Aspects of Speech Technology*, Edinburgh University Press, 1988.
Linggard, R. *Electronic Synthesis of Speech*, CUP, 1985.
Parsons, T. W. *Voice and Speech Processing* (McGraw Hill series in Electrical Engineering Communications and Signal Processing), London, McGraw Hill, 1987.
Sclater, N. *Introduction to Electronic Speech Synthesis*, Indianapolis, IN, H. W. Sams, 1983.
Witten, I. H. *Making Computers Talk: an Introduction to Speech Synthesis*, Englewood-Cliffs, Prentice-Hall, 1986.
Witten, I. H. *Principles of Computer Speech*, London, Academic Press, 1982.

Conferences

Many general conferences and exhibitions include sessions on the theme of speech synthesis within a general programme. The

Output technologies

annual meetings of the Association for Computational Linguistics often cover synthesis; the Association for Computing Machinery (USA) held a <u>Conference on Human Factors in Computing Systems</u> in 1985 which included papers on synthetic speech.

A number of specialist conferences have been held on the topic of speech synthesis; the most recent include the following:

- <u>International Speech Tech '87</u>. 1987 Proceedings published by Media Dimensions Inc., New York.
- <u>Speech Input/Output: Techniques and Applications–International Conference on Speech Input/Output 1986</u>. IEE Science, Education and Technology Division with the British Society of Audiology. Proceedings published in London by IEE in 1986 (IEE Conference publication no. 258).
- <u>Voice Processing: the New Revolution</u>. Proceedings of the International Conference held in London, July 1986. London, Online, 1986 [0–86353–056–7].
- <u>International Conference on Speech Technology, Brighton 1984</u>. IFS (Conferences) Ltd with *Speech Technology* magazine, the Institute of Acoustics and *Sensor Review*.

Organizations

The Institution of Electrical Engineers is a key organization in this subject field; the IEE has organized a number of conferences in the area of speech synthesis and has published a range of relevant material. The British Society of Audiology, the Institute of Acoustics and the Association for Computational Linguistics are all involved in this area because of their interest in patterns of synthesized speech and the impact of machine speech on our understanding of acoustics in general. The telecommunications implications also concern organizations such as CCITT.

Address and contact list

Journals

ACM Transactions on Graphics
Association for Computing Machinery
11 West 42nd Street
New York
NY 10036
USA
Quarterly. Price on application

Accountancy
Institute of Chartered Accountants in England and Wales
40 Bernard Street
London WC1N 1LD
UK
Monthly. £2.25 per issue or annual rates for members

Output technologies

Acorn User
Redwood Publishing Ltd
20–26 Brunswick Place
London N1 6DJ
UK
Monthly. £1.30 per issue

Apple Business
International Magazines plc
Kiln House
210 New Kings Road
London SW6 4NZ
UK
Monthly. Free to selected readers.

Applied Ergonomics
Butterworth Heinemann
PO Box 63
Westbury House
Bury Street
Guildford
Surrey GU2 5BH
UK
Quarterly. £96.00 p.a.

Assembly Automation
IFS Publications
35–39 High Street
Kempston
Bedford MK42 7BT
UK
Quarterly. £69.00 p.a.

Automation—the Journal of Automated Production
United Trade Press Ltd
UTP House
33–35 Bowling Green Lane
London EC1R 0DA
UK
Free to selected readers; £34.00 p.a.

Automation and Remote Control—Journal of the Instrument Society of America
Consultants Bureau
233 Spring Street
New York
NY 10013
USA
Fortnightly. $960.00 p.a.

Automation News
Grant Publications Inc
c/o Friedberg
450 Park Avenue
New York
NY 10022
USA
Fortnightly. $52.00 p.a.

Axes Robotiques: Revue Française de Robotique
Axes Communications
29 Rue Violet
75015 Paris
France
Bimonthly. Price on application.

Behaviour and Information Technology
Taylor & Francis Ltd
4 John Street
London WC1N 2ET
UK
Quarterly. £69.00 p.a.

British Telecom Technology Journal
British Telecommunications plc
81 Newgate Street
London EC1A 7AJ
UK
Quarterly. £18.00 for two years.

Business Equipment Digest
Techpress Publishing
Company Ltd
Northside House
69 Tweedy Road
Bromley
Kent BR1 3WA
UK
Monthly. Free to selected readers; £24.00 p.a.

Business Systems and Equipment
Maclean Hunter Ltd
Maclean Hunter House
Chalk Lane
Cockfosters Road
Barnet
Herts EN4 0BU
UK
Bimonthly. Free to selected readers.

Computer Graphics Forum
Elsevier Science Publishers B.V.
PO Box 211
1000 AE Amsterdam
Netherlands
Quarterly. DFl 255 p.a.

Computer Graphics World
Penn Well Publishing Co.
One Technology Park Drive
PO Box 987
Westford
MA 01886
USA
Monthly. $4.00 per issue

Computer Images International
EMAP–Maclaren
PO Box 109
Maclaren House
Scarbrook Road
Croydon CR9 1QH
UK
Monthly. £20.00 p.a.

Computer Shopper
Dennis Publications Ltd
14 Rathbone Place
London W1P 1DE
UK
Monthly. £0.88 per issue

Computer Speech and Language
Academic Press Ltd
24–28 Oval Road
London NW1 7DX
UK
Quarterly. £60.00 p.a.

Computer Vision, Graphics and Image Processing
Academic Press Inc
Journal Division
1250 Sixth Avenue
San Diego
CA 92101
USA
Monthly. $441.00 p.a.

Computer Weekly
Reed Business Publishing
Quadrant House
The Quadrant
Sutton
Surrey SM2 5AS
UK
Weekly. £65.00 p.a.

Computers and Graphics
Pergamon Press plc (Sciences)
Headington Hill Hall
Oxford OX3 0BW
UK
Quarterly. £180.00 p.a.

Computing
VNU Business Publications
VNU House
32–34 Broadwick Street
London W1A 2HG
UK
Weekly. Free to UK registrants or £70.00 p.a.

42 Output technologies

Computing Equipment
Industrial Media Ltd
Blair House
184–186 High Street
Tonbridge
Kent TN9 1BQ
UK
Monthly. Free to selected readers; £40.00 p.a.

Control Systems
Industrial Media Ltd
Blair House
184–186 High Street
Tonbridge
Kent TN9 1BQ
UK
Monthly. Free to selected readers; £40.00 p.a.

Current Psychological Research and Reviews
Transaction Periodicals Consortium
Rutgers University
Dept 2000
New Brunswick
NJ 08903
USA
Quarterly. $36.00 p.a. individuals; $48.00 p.a. institutions

Digital Review—DEC Computing and Connectivity in the UK
Reed Business Publishing
Quadrant House
The Quadrant
Sutton
Surrey SM2 5AS
UK
10 issues a year. Free to selected readers; £38.00 p.a.

Human Factors
Human Factors Society
Box 1369
Santa Monica
CA 90406
USA
Bimonthly. $60.00 p.a.

IBM Journal of Research and Development
IBM Technical Disclosures Bulletin
IBM Corp
Armonk
NY 10504
USA
Bimonthly. £30.00 p.a.

IBM UK News
IBM UK Ltd
PO Box 41
North Harbour
Portsmouth
Hants PO6 3AU
UK
Every 3 weeks. Free to employees of IBM UK

IEEE Computer Graphics and Applications
Bimonthly

IEEE Transactions. Acoustics, Speech and Signal Processing
Bimonthly

IEEE Transactions. Automatic Control
Bimonthly

IEEE Control Systems
7 issues p.a.

IEEE Journal of Robotics and Automation
Bimonthly

IEEE Inc
345 East 47 Street
New York
NY 10017
USA
For all IEE titles: $20.00 per single copy to non-members. Subscription price on application.

Industrial Engineering News
Pan European Publishing Company
c/o TW Mail Service BV
PO Box 86
NL-1440 AB Purmerend
Netherlands
9 issues a year. Free to selected readers.

Industrial Robot
IFS (Publications) Ltd
35–39 High Street
Kempston
Bedford MK42 7BT
UK
Monthly. £69.00 p.a.

Institute of Electronics and Information Communications Engineers (Japan) Transactions
c/o Kikai Shinko Kaikan
3–5–8 Shiba Koen
Minato-ku
Tokyo 105
Japan
Monthly. 1800 Yen

International Journal of Production Research
Taylor & Francis Ltd
4 John Street
London WC1N 2ET
UK
Monthly. £255.00 p.a.

International Journal of Robotics Research
MIT Press
55 Hayward Street
Cambridge
MA 02142
USA
Bimonthly. $65 p.a. individuals; $130 p.a. institutions

Journal of the Acoustics Society of America
American Institute of Physics
335 East 45 Street
NY 10017
USA
Monthly. $425.00 p.a.

Language Technology
PO Box 70486
1007 KL Amsterdam
Netherlands
Bimonthly. US$50 p.a.

Literary and Linguistic Computing
OUP
Pinkhill House
Southfield Road
Eynsham
Oxford OX8 1JT
UK
Quarterly. £30.00 p.a.

Manufacturing Technology Horizons
Manufacturing Technology Press Inc
Box 206
Geneva WI 53147
USA
Bimonthly. $60.00 p.a.

Measurement and Control—the Journal of the Institute of Measurement and Control
Institute of Measurement and Control
87 Gower Street
London WC1E 6AA
UK
10 issues a year. £60.00 p.a.

Micro Decision
VNU Business Publications
VNU House
32–34 Broadwick Street
London W1A 2HG
UK
Monthly. £1.50 per issue

Mini Micro News
Bofoers Publishing Ltd
Bofoers House
Bentinck Road
West Drayton
Middlesex UB7 7RQ
UK
Monthly. Free to selected readers; £18.00 p.a.

PC Magazine (UK edition)
Reed Business Publishing Ltd
Quadrant House
The Quadrant
Sutton
Surrey SM2 5AS
UK
Monthly. Free to selected readers; £1.95 per issue.

Personal Computer Magazine
VNU Business Publications
VNU House
32–34 Broadwick Street
London W1A 2HG
UK
Monthly.

Practical Computing
Reed Business Publishing Ltd
Quadrant House
The Quadrant
Sutton
Surrey SM2 5AS
UK
Monthly. £22.50 p.a.

Process Engineering
Morgan-Grampian plc
40 Beresford Street
London SE18 6BQ
UK
Monthly. Free to selected readers; £48.00 p.a.

Production Engineer—Journal of the Institution of Production Engineers
Institute of Production Engineers
Rochester House
66 Little Ealing Lane
London W5 4XX
UK
Monthly. £55.00 p.a.

Robotersysteme
Springer-Verlag
175 5th Avenue
New York
NY 10010
USA
Quarterly. DM 178 p.a.

Robotica—International Journal of Information, Education and Research in Robotics and AI
Cambridge University Press
The Edinburgh Building
Shaftesbury Road
Cambridge CB2 2RU
UK
Quarterly. £71.00 p.a.

Robotics
Elsevier Science Publishing B.V.
PO Box 211
1000 AE Amsterdam
Netherlands
Quarterly. $100.75 p.a.

Robotics World
Communication Channels Inc
6255 Barfield Road
Atlanta
GA 30328
USA
Bimonthly. $52 p.a. (outside USA).

Sensor Review—the International Journal of Sensing for Industry
IFS Publications
35–39 High Street
Kempston
Bedford MK42 7BT
UK
Quarterly. £69.00 p.a.

Speech Technology
Media Dimensions Inc
42 East 23rd St
New York
NY 10010
USA
Quarterly. $58 p.a.

What Micro
VNU Business Publications
VNU House
32–34 Broadwick Street
London W1A 2HG
UK
Monthly. £1.25 per issue

What's New in Computing
(£40.00 p.a.)
What's New in Electronics
(£50.00 p.a.)
What's New in Industry
(£45.00 p.a.)
All three titles published by:
Morgan-Grampian plc
Morgan-Grampian House
Calderwood Street
London SE18 6QH
UK
Monthly. All free to selected readers.

Which Computer?
EMAP Business and
Computer Publications Ltd
67 Clerkenwell Road
London EC1R 5BH
UK
Monthly. £1.75 per issue

Conference and exhibition organizers (see also Organizations section)

Cahners Exhibitions
Oriel House
28 The Quadrant
Richmond
Surrey TW9 1BR
UK

IFS (Conferences) Ltd
35–39 High Street
Kempston
Bedford MK42 7BT
UK

46 *Output technologies*

Independent Exhibitions Ltd
Waltrix House
Oak Road
Leatherhead
Surrey KT22 7PG
UK

National Materials Handling Centre
Cranfield Institute of Technology
Cranfield
Bedford MK43 0AL
UK

Further sources

Exhibitions Bulletin
The London Bureau
266–272 Kirkdale
Sydenham
London SE26 4RZ
UK
Monthly. £38.00 p.a.

Forthcoming International Scientific & Technical Conferences
Aslib
Information House
20–24 Old Street
London EC1
UK
Quarterly. £50 p.a.

What's On in Computing
British Informatics Society Ltd
13 Mansfield Street
London W1M 0BP
UK
Quarterly. £12 p.a. (25% discount to BCS members)

Secondary sources

ACM Guide to Computing Machinery
Association for Computing Machinery
11 West 42nd Street
New York
NY 10036
USA

Computer and Control Abstracts
Monthly. £530 p.a.

Electrical and Electronic Abstracts
Monthly. £815 p.a.

Key Abstracts: Business Automation
Key Abstracts: Electronic Instrumentation
Key Abstracts: Robotics and Control
Monthly. £35 p.a. (members); £56 p.a. (non-members) within UK.

All above titles available from:
Inspec Marketing Department
Station House
Nightingale Road
Hitchin
Herts SG5 1RJ
UK

Computing, Communications and Media Trend Monitor
Aslib/TMI
Aspen House
14 Station Road
Kettering
Northants NN15 7HE
UK
Quarterly. £95.00 p.a.

PERA Abstracts
Production Engineering
Research Association
Melton Mowbray LE13 0PB
UK
Available to members only.
Contact PERA for details.

SME Technical Digest
One SME Drive
PO Box 930
Dearborn
Michigan 48128
USA

Online database hosts

BRS
1200 Route 7
Latham
NY 1200
USA

Dialog
3460 Hillview Avenue
Palo Alto
CA 94304
USA

ESA
IRS-Dialtech
Via Galileo Galilei
00044 Frascati
Italy

NEWSNET
NewsNet Inc.
945 Haverford Road
Bryn Mawr
PA 19010
USA

Pergamon ORBIT INFOLINE Inc.
8000 Westpark Drive, Suite 400
McLean
VA 22102
USA

Pergamon Financial Data Services
Achilles House
Western Avenue
London W3 0UA
UK

STN International
Royal Society of Chemistry
Nottingham NG7 2RD
UK

TEXTLINE
Reuters Ltd
85 Fleet Street
London EC4P 4AJ
UK

CD-ROM publishers

Silver Platter Information Services Ltd
10 Barley Mow Passage
Chiswick
London W4 4PH
UK

Organizations

American Society of Mechanical Engineers
(incl. Machine Vision Association of the SME and the Robotics International of the SME)
One SME Drive
PO Box 930
Dearborn
Michigan 48128
USA

48 *Output technologies*

Association for Computational Linguistics
Michael Rosner
54 Route des Accacias
CH-1227 Geneva
Switzerland

Association for Computing Machinery
11 West 42nd Street
New York
NY 10036
USA

Association Française de Robotique Industrielle (AFRI)
89 Rue Falqueire
75015 Paris
France

Australian Robot Association
GPO Box 1527
Sydney
NSW 2001
Australia

BEAMA Ltd
(Federation of British Electrotechnical and Allied Manufacturers Associations)
8 Leicester Street
London WC2H 7BN
UK

British Computer Society
13 Mansfield Street
London W1M 0BP
UK

British Office Technology Manufacturers Alliance
NEDC
Millbank Tower
Millbank
London SW1P 4QX
UK

British Robot Association Ltd
Aston Science Park
Love Lane
Aston Triangle
Birmingham B7 4BJ
UK

British Society of Audiology
80 Brighton Road
Reading RG6 1PS
UK

Computer and Peripherals Equipment Training Association (COMPETA)
1 High Street
Maidenhead
Berks SL6 1JN
UK

GAMBICA Association Ltd
(Association for the Instrumentation, Control and Automation Industry in the UK)
8 Leicester Street
London WC2H 7BN
UK

Institute of Acoustics
25 Chambers Street
Edinburgh EH1 1HU
UK

Institute of Electrical and Electronics Engineers (IEEE)
345 East 47 Street
New York
NY 10017
USA

Institute of Measurement and Control
87 Gower Street
London WC1E 6AA
UK

Output technologies

Institution of Electrical
Engineers (IEE)
Savoy Place
London WC2R 0BL
UK

Institution of Mechanical
Engineers (IME)
1 Birdcage Walk
London SW1H 9JJ
UK

Institution of Production
Engineers (IPE)
66 Little Ealing Lane
London W5 4XX
UK

International Federation for
Automated Control (IFAC)
Schlossplatz 12
A-2361 Laxenburg
Austria

Japan Industrial Robot
Association (JIRA)
Kikai Shinko Kaikan Building
3–5–8 Shiba-Koen
Minato-ku
Tokyo 105
Japan

National Computing Centre
Oxford Road
Manchester M1 7ED
UK

National Engineering
Research Laboratory
East Kilbride
Glasgow G75 0QM
UK

National Materials Handling
Centre
Cranfield Institute of
Technology
Cranfield
Bedford MK43 0AL
UK

Production Engineering
Research Association (PERA)
Melton Mowbray LE13 0PB
UK

Società Italiana Robotica
Industriale (SIRI)
Instituto di Elettrotechnica et
Elettronica
Politecnico di Milano
Piazza Leonardo da Vinci 32
20133 Milano
Italy

Swedish Industrial Robot
Association (SWIRA)
Box 5506
Storgatan 19
S-114 85 Stockholm
Sweden

Publishers of directories (non-mainstream publishers only)

Datapro Services SA
9 Rue St-Martin
CH-1003 Lausanne
Switzerland

DIAL directories series are
published by
Reed Information Services Ltd
Windsor Court
East Grinstead
West Sussex RH19 1XA
UK

Output technologies

G2H Publications
127 Rue Amelot
75011 Paris
France

IFS (Publications) Ltd
35–39 High Street
Kempston
Bedford MK42 7AJ
UK

InfoTech
86 Haywood Road
Mapperley
Nottingham NG3 6AE
UK

Kemps Group (Printers and Publishers) Ltd
Westbury House
701–705 Warwick Road
Solihull
West Midlands B91 3DA
UK

Morgan-Grampian Books Publishing Co Ltd
40 Beresford Street
London SE18 6BQ
UK

C. H. W. Roles & Associates Ltd
PO Box 25
Sunbury-on-Thames
Middlesex TW16 5QB
UK

Sterling Publications Ltd
86–88 Edgware Road
London W2 2YW
UK

Symecora
20 Rue Hamelin
75116 Paris
France

Tech Tran Consultants Inc
PO Box 206
Lake Geneva
Wisconsin 53147
USA

Technical Indexes
Willoughby Road
Bracknell
Berks RG12 4DW
UK

Templar Publications Ltd
Kingfisher House
Letcombe Regis
Oxon OX12 9JJ
UK

Vereinigte Fachverlage
Postfach 2760
6500 Mainz
West Germany

VNU Business Publications
VNU House
32–34 Broadwick Street
London W1A 2HG
UK

CHAPTER THREE

Software, computer languages, and operating systems

D. HAYNES

Introduction

This chapter covers sources of information on: software engineering, programming languages, operating systems and environments, and applications software. The relationship between these elements of data processing is important. Data processing (DP) is strictly speaking independent of technology, although it is widely interpreted as meaning electronic data processing. Manual and mechanical data processing are valid areas of study, but are not included in this chapter. Data processing in this chapter is taken to mean *'the process of collecting and manipulation of data to produce meaningful information'*.

Data processing is covered by a large number of learned journals. These range from specialist journals dealing with a specific language or application to more general journals on the techniques and theory of programming. The fact that a number of commercial publishers have moved into this area of publishing indicates that this is a thriving market.

General sources

Databases such as INSPEC provide comprehensive coverage of data processing. The IEE produces a number of publications based on the INSPEC database. *Key Abstracts: Software Engineering* (Inspec) is a monthly abstracts journal covering a range of topics including:

- Programming support
- High-level languages

- Compilers and interpreters
- Operating systems
- DBMS
  distributed
  relational
- Software engineering management
- Software techniques and other aspects

Other secondary sources covering the research literature on software include: *Software Systems and Techniques Abstracts* (TechGnosis/NCC); *Micro Abstracts* (TechGnosis/NCC); and *Microcomputer Index* (Learned Information), which comes out quarterly. These sources cover other areas, but provide significant coverage of software. Between them they cover the major international software journals.

Software Engineering

Software engineering is the process of developing software to run a computer. What then is software? The implication of the name 'software' is something malleable, which can be manipulated. The *Shorter Oxford English Dictionary* defines it as '*The collection of programs that can be used with a particular kind of computer*'. It goes on to define a program as '*A fully explicit series of instructions which when fed into a computer will automatically direct its operation in carrying out a specific task*'. Software engineering has gained recognition as a distinct discipline which includes systems analysis and design methodologies, computer programming and software testing. Software reliability is becoming increasingly important and there is a growing literature on this subject.

Monographs

Software Development and Management for Microprocessor-based Systems (New Jersey, Prentice-Hall, 1987) by T. G. Rauscher and L. M. Ott describes a set of techniques for developing software for large microprocessor-based systems. This is a text aimed at graduate students and industrialists. *A Practical Handbook for Software Development* (Cambridge, Cambridge University Press, 1985) gives a summary of the range of techniques available for software development and is aimed at software engineers. It is intended as a means of signposting relevant techniques. The methodology for software development is important especially for large projects. *Software Engineering with Systems Analysis and Design* (Monterey, CA, Brooks/Cole Publishing Co., 1987) is aimed at students and practitioners and provides a general introduction to the field of software engineering. It excludes operating systems and programming languages. *Software Engineering Methodology* (Reston, UA, Reston Publishing Co., 1984) is aimed at small software houses. It covers software development methodology to enable more efficient operation and delivery of goods.

Periodicals

Some of the general periodicals, such as the *IBM Systems Journal* contain items of interest. The journal generally publishes single topic issues, which focus on research done in IBM research laboratories. Topics range from operating systems to computer architecture and data storage.
  Software Engineering (IEEE Computer Society) is an example of the learned journals. It contains original papers, which have been subjected to peer review. It publishes original results and empirical studies which have an impact on the construction, analysis or management of software. Springer-Verlag recently brought out a new journal, *Algorithmica* which contains original papers on algorithms and practical applications such as VLSI, distributed computing, parallel processing, automated design, robotics, graphics, database design and software tools. The *Journal of Programming Logic* (North-Holland) is an international journal publishing original research papers, surveys and review articles, and tutorials. The emphasis is academic and the papers are reviewed prior to publication. North-Holland also publishes *Science of Computer Programming*. It is the complementary journal to *Theoretical Computer Science* (North-Holland) which covers automata, languages, algorithms and programs.
  Software engineering covers all aspects of computer programming, from the design of languages to the development of software applications. The *Software Engineering Journal* (IEE/British Computer Society) is a key academic journal in this area. *Programming and Computer Software* (Consultants Bureau) is a translation journal which contains translations of significant articles from the Soviet journal *Programmirovanie*. There is an approximate time lag of nine months between the publication of the original and the translated article.
  Structured Programming (Springer-Verlag) is a highly respected journal with both original, reviewed papers and short technical communications. It is aimed at the professional computing and engineering community and covers programming, programming methodology, programming languages, programming environments, compilers, interpreters, and applications.

Software Practice and Experience (Wiley) is a monthly journal with articles on software design and implementation, case studies and critical appraisals of software systems. It is aimed at designers, implementers and maintenance people. Articles range from short notes to long articles. The emphasis is academic.

Information Processing Letters (North-Holland) is devoted to the rapid publication of short contributions on information processing. It centres around systems architecture and applications programs, including the theoretical aspects of computer and system programming. It also covers the problems of hardware design connected with software production.

Less formal publications include *Software Engineering Notes*, published by the ACM Special Interest Group on Software Engineering (SIGSOFT). It allows for rapid communication and contains a mixture of new items and short papers, mainly from academics. *IEEE Software* (IEEE Computer Society) is a glossy magazine with articles and regular columns. It contains a lot of advertisements, which are themselves useful sources of information. Individual issues tend to focus on specific topics such as parallel programming, maintenance, reverse engineering, and design recovery.

Another glossy, *Software Magazine*, is aimed at managers of corporate software resources. It contains a lot of advertisements as well as feature articles (although not as many as *IEEE Software*). It provides good coverage of industry news. *Software World. An International Journal of Programs and Packages* (ISSN 0038–0652) is a quarterly from A. P. Publications which also publishes *Database and Network Journal* and *PC Business Software*. *Software World* is UK-based and includes informative articles as well as news items and notices of new publications and events. The *Journal of Object Oriented Programming* is another glossy which comes out six times a year. It contains feature articles as well as regular columns and is aimed at professional programmers.

Datalink is a UK-based tabloid which is notable for the number of job advertisements in it (they generally make up half the issue). It is directed at systems analysts and programmers. *Program Now* (UK) is a glossy magazine with feature articles, advertisements and news items which is aimed at professional programmers.

Software maintenance is a new and growing field. It is that part of software engineering which deals with activities undertaken on software after it is first delivered. This is based on the IEEE definition of software maintenance. There have been an increasing number of articles in the popular computing press about this topic lately. The *Journal of Software Maintenance* (John Wiley) was launched in 1989. It contains refereed papers on all aspects of software maintenance. It is a quarterly and includes contributions from academics and practitioners.

Programming Languages

There are different levels of programming languages. The low-level languages start with machine code or machine language. These are the codes which instruct the machine to perform specific actions. The symbolic languages represent individual machine operations with mnemonics and were developed to make programming easier. As programming techniques developed, so higher level languages were invented. In the higher level languages a single command may represent several machine operations. These languages are easier to manipulate and understand, thereby making it easier to check for errors. The high-level languages are also known as object-oriented languages and can be divided into several categories: commercial languages; scientific languages; command languages for operating systems; multipurpose languages; and logic languages. The current generation of languages are known as Fourth Generation Languages or applications generators.

Monographs

The Definition of Programming Languages (Cambridge, Cambridge University Press, 1980) is a part of the *Cambridge Computer Science Texts* series. It tries to arrive at a definition of programming languages and looks at theoretical aspects before going on to discuss specific computer languages. *Computers and Languages. Theory and Practice* (North-Holland, 1988), a part of the series *Studies in Computer Science and Artificial Intelligence*, looks at the history of artificial languages and also looks at developments in artificial intelligence. *Fundamentals of Programming Languages* (Heidelberg, Springer-Verlag, 2nd edn, 1984) focuses on a few concepts and uses this as a framework to define languages. The approach is academic and the text includes exercizes.

Periodicals

Computer Language is a North American glossy magazine with news, informative articles and correspondence. It also contains a fair number of advertisements. The articles tend to be about specific languages and issues related to them or about particular features of the language.

Another general publication is *SIGPLAN Notices*, a monthly published by the ACM Press on behalf of the ACM Special Interest Group on Programming Languages. It is an informal journal with unrefereed articles. It is a useful source of advance notice of conferences because it contains many calls for papers and advertisements for forthcoming events. It also contains reports on meetings and workshops and occasional issues are devoted to the proceedings of SIGPLAN conferences such as the ACM SIGPLAN Workshop on Object-based Concurrent Programming held in September 1988 and published in the April 1989 issue of the journal.

For a more academic approach, *Computer Languages* (Pergamon), which comes out quarterly, contains original articles and review articles on programming systems, structures and theories.

Language-specific journals include: *Ada User*, the journal of Pascal Ada and Modula; *Ada User (UK)* which aims to promote the effective development and use of the Ada language. It contains a range of contributions from full-length papers to short communications, reviews and news items. It also publishes special papers and conference proceedings, such as the proceedings of the Ada UK 8th International Conference 1989. The *Journal of Pascal, Ada and Modula–2* comes out six times a year and includes refereed papers as well as editorial copy. It is published as a glossy magazine with a lot of advertisements. It also contains a lot of code (sample programs). There is even a special-interest group for the Ada language, SIGAda, which publishes *Ada Letters*.

ACM SIGPLAN publishes *Fortran Forum* as a quarterly newsletter with short items and conferences announcements.

Microprogramming is another area of interest. The ACM Special Interest Group on Microprogramming produces *SIGMicro Newsletter*. *Microprocessing and Microprogramming* (North-Holland) published on behalf of the Euromicro Association, is a more academic journal with refereed original articles. It also includes review articles, book reviews, a calendar of events and conference reports.

Conferences

The learned societies such as the ACM, the IEEE, and the IEE organize a number of events, ranging from formal academic conferences with refereed papers, to less formal meetings of the special interest groups. Examples of the former include Logic Programming and European Conference on Object-Oriented Programming.

The Special Interest Groups of the Association of Computing

Machinery are important conference and seminar organizers. The ACM SIGSOFT organizes the Software Process Workshop periodically (about every 18 months). This event is also sponsored by the IEEE Computer Society.

Operating Systems and Environments

An operating system is a suite of programs which takes over the operation of a computer so that applications programs can be run. Examples range from OS/2 and MS-DOS for microcomputers to VMS for the DEC VAX range of minicomputers and UNIX for a wide range of minicomputers and mainframes.

Periodicals

Some journals are devoted to specific operating systems. UNIX is widely used and is becoming increasingly popular with the development of more powerful processors and more memory being incorporated into smaller machines. *Unix Review* is devoted entirely to the Unix operating system and is aimed at systems and solutions developers. It is a glossy magazine with lots of advertisements, with regular columns and features. It also contains reviews of new products.

The *ACM Operating Systems Review* is a quarterly newsletter from the ACM SIG on Operating Systems, SIGOPS.

Market information is provided by *Software Markets* (Blackwell), which comes out twice a month. Like many other rapid publication newsletters, it is expensive, there being a premium on timeliness of information.

Databases

OPERATING SYSTEMS & NETWORKS is a database which contains the full text of the Elsevier newsletter of the same name. It is a part of the PTS NEWSLETTER DATABASE which is available on Dialog and Datastar.

Applications Software

A vast range of software applications has developed with the proliferation of microcomputers. There is a bewildering choice for each type of application and there is a growing demand for reliable sources of information on what products are available. A number of publishers now regularly produce software directories, which can provide a useful starting point for selecting products.

Directories

The *ICP Software Directory*, which is also available on CD-ROM comes in two series—one for mainframe and minicomputer products and one for microcomputers. The directory is published twice a year and has a strong North American emphasis. The mainframe and minicomputer series is in six volumes corresponding to broad areas of applications:

- Systems and Utilities
- General Accounting
- Management and Administration
- Banking, Insurance and Finance
- Manufacturing and Engineering
- Industry Specific Applications

The Microcomputer series is in four volumes:

- Systems and Utilities
- General Accounting
- Office Automation and Business Management
- Industry Specific Applications

Both of the series are general guides with a large number of entries. For specific applications, specialist directories may give more detailed information. The entries in the *ICP Software Directory* give a brief description of the product, price, availability and number of installations (where this is known). Each volume has an alphabetical product index, a classification scheme for products (categories) and an index to the classification. There is also a hardware index.

The *Software Users Year Book 1990* (VNU, 1989) is a UK directory which comes in four volumes and includes details of 9800 software packages. The volumes are:

- Software Suppliers
- Systems Software
- Industry Specific Software
- General Applications

The *PC Yearbook 1990* (VNU, 1989) contains a section on software with details of 5200 products for microcomputers. They are arranged in classified order.

There are a number of databases available which provide information on software. The MICRO SOFTWARE DIRECTORY is available on Dialog and contains detailed descriptions of software for microcomputers. Like all databases it allows users to select software by several criteria at once, such as operating system, hardware, and keyword.

Choosing the appropriate system is difficult and can be hazardous. A. F. Robb's *Management Guide to Choosing and Implementing Computer Systems. A Professional Approach to System Selection (PASS)* (Manchester, National Computer Centre, 1988) provides a useful series of checklists. It details the PASS methodology for specifying and selecting systems.

Databases

With such a rapidly changing field, printed directories of software quickly become out of date. A number of publishers have started to publish software directories as online databases, often in parallel with the printed directories. For instance R. R. Bowker produces the MICROCOMPUTER SOFTWARE GUIDE, which is available on Dialog. The equivalent printed directory is the *Software Encyclopedia*. The database contains details of more than 40 000 software packages including business and professional software, education, and utility programs. Each entry contains details of the environment under which it operates, the type of software it is and a short description of what it does. Ordering information is also available, including the price (in US dollars).

MENU—THE INTERNATIONAL SOFTWARE DATABASE contains more than 30 000 entries about software packages for microcomputers, minicomputers and some mainframes. It corresponds to the series of *Software Catalog* publications and is published by the International Software Database Corp.

The BUSINESS SOFTWARE DATABASE, also available on Dialog (as well as Data-Star, BRS, ESA-IRS and Knowledge Index) provides details about software for mainframe, mini- and microcomputers. The database contains about 12 000 directory records and 5000 review records. The review records contain abstracts of journals articles describing and evaluating the product.

The MICROCOMPUTER INDEX is produced by Learned Information and corresponds to the printed publication *Microcomputer Index*. This is a more general database covering the literature on microcomputers including software and programming. It contains about 90 000 records. Online Inc. produces the ONLINE MICROCOMPUTER SOFTWARE GUIDE AND DIRECTORY which is mounted on the BRS service. It contains details of more than 5700 microcomputer software packages. The entries contain descriptions of the software, references of reviews of the products and operating requirements as well as contact details.

MICROSEARCH is a comprehensive bibliographic database with details of reviews of more than 12 000 microcomputer products including software. The database contains over 40 000 records. It is available on CompuServe Information Service, Orbit and The Source. A rather smaller database, MICROREVIEWS FOR BUSINESS, contains abstracts of 6000 articles on microcomputer software and hardware. Its coverage is mainly US. DIRECT-NET contains details of more than 5000 products for IBM PC-compatible microcomputers. It corresponds to *PC World's Annual Software Review* and *Annual Hardware Review*.

3RD BASE SOFTWARE REGISTRY lists 15 000 software products with details of hardware and operating requirements, price and availability. Information is provided by software vendors who pay an annual fee for each product they want listed.

SOFTWARE is a new database available on Dialog with details of software packages and with summaries of major reviews in the literature.

Specialist databases include EPIE ON-LINE with details of educational software products; and the ENGINEERING & INDUSTRIAL SOFTWARE DIRECTORY with details of engineering software products.

SOFTWARE LOCATOR is an Australian database with details of 1000 software products available in Australia. LOGIBASE plays a similar role in Quebec with 1500 records on microcomputer software packages available in Quebec, Canada. ISIS SOFTWARE DATENBANK contains profiles of software packages available in Austria, Germany and Switzerland. It is available on Data-Star and FIZ Technik and is divided into four files: ISIS software Report; ISIS Personal Computer Report; ISIS Personal Computer Report Schweiz; and ISIS Engineering Report.

NASA produces COSMIC (Computer Software Management and Information Center) with details of 1300 software packages developed by NASA or other Federal agencies and is available on ESA-IRS and NewsNet.

Some suppliers are beginning to make their catalogues available online. An example is Michigan Office Supply which sells a range of products for microcomputers and provides descriptions of its products on MICRO CITY, available on The Source. ELEPHANT WALK COMPUTERS is another example, also available on The Source. COMPUTER EXPRESS has details of 500 hardware and software products and peripherals for a variety of microcomputers.

On the marketing side, the SOFTWARE COMPETITIVE INTEL-

LIGENCE database available on Strategic Intelligence Systems contains abstracts of journal articles about the software industry. It covers general trends in the industry, company news and legal and regulatory developments. The coverage is mainly North American and it is updated daily. Another interesting database is the SOFTWARE SPECIAL INTERVIEW PROGRAM produced by Computer Intelligence. It contains details of the software purchasing plans of corporations with IBM mainframe computers or plug-compatible computers.

CHAPTER FOUR

Computer hardware and electronic components

D. HAYNES

Introduction

Adrian Stokes in his *Concise Encyclopedia of Information Technology* defines hardware as '*The physical equipment comprising a computer system*'. In his definition he includes peripheral devices such as keyboards and monitors as well as the central processing unit. In this chapter we will concentrate on the major categories of computer and the central processing unit and its components. Peripheral devices such as keyboards and VDUs are covered in the chapters on input technologies (Chapter 1) and output technologies (Chapter 2).

General information sources

Research journals

There are two main types of research and development journals covering computer hardware. The learned societies, notably the IEE, IEEE and ACM all produce learned journals which feature hardware technology. Most of the papers are refereed by experts in the field and they provide a forum for notifying the research community of new discoveries. Titles include: *IEE Proceedings: Computers and Digital Techniques (Part E)*, which covers hardware and software and design of integrated circuits; and *IEEE Transactions on Electronic Devices. Transactions of the Institute of Electronic Communication Engineers of Japan. Section E (Japan)* and *IEEE Transactions on Computers* also contain refereed papers on hardware.

Computer hardware and electronic components 63

The *Japan Annual Review in Electronics, Computers & Telecommunications* is a multi-subject series with parallel volumes on different subjects. The papers cover advances in specific technologies. Volumes in the series include: *Optical Devices & Fibres; Semiconductor Technologies, Computer Science and Technologies*; and *Amorphous Semiconductor Technology and Devices*.

Computer (IEEE), is much less academic and is aimed at professionals. It tends to have a lot of product information and information about practice. Also worth consideration are *EDN* (USA), *Electronics* (USA), and *Elektronik* (Germany), which are more popular journals directed at electronic engineers.

The popular science journals such as *Scientific American* and *New Scientist* provide a selective and sometimes useful introduction to various aspects of computer hardware. They can be a good starting point if your interests are general.

Some manufacturers produce their own magazines with a lot of product information and short features about new products or installations using their products. Examples are the *Toshiba Review* (International Edition), and *Siemens Review*.

Market information

Infotech Services Ltd (formerly Infotech Industrial Market Research Consultants) publishes a number of market research reports on different industrial sectors including those related to information technology. An example is *Financial Comparison and Market Directory: Industry Sector: Computer Hardware*. The Department of Trade and Industry's *Business Monitor PQ 3302. Electronic Data Processing Equipment* is also a useful source of information on market sizes and is based on statistics collected by the DTI.

Databases

The major IT related databases such as INSPEC, the COMPUTER DATABASE and COMPENDEX include information on the literature of computer hardware. CHEMICAL ABSTRACTS is a good source of information on the chemical and physical properties of semiconductors such as silicon and gallium arsenide. Patents of semiconductor devices are covered by the DERWENT database and INPADOC (see Chapter 14 on patents).

INSPEC

One of the key sources of information available on all aspects of information technology is INSPEC the online database and the associated abstracts journal *Computer and Control Abstracts*. A useful way of narrowing one's interests is via the classification scheme. Below are listed the main headings in the classification which relate to computer hardware:

5000	COMPUTER HARDWARE	
5100	CIRCUITS AND DEVICES	
	5110	Logic Elements
	5110C	Semiconductor logic elements
	5110D	Optical logic elements
	5110E	Other logic elements
	5120	Logic and switching circuits
	5130	Microprocessor chips
	5140	Firmware
	5150	Other circuits for digital computers
	5160	Analogue circuits
	5180	A/D and D/A convertors
5200	LOGIC DESIGN AND DIGITAL TECHNIQUES	
	5210	Logic design methods
	5210B	Computer-aided logic design
	5220	Computer architecture
	5230	Digital arithmetic methods
	5240	Digital filters
	5250	Microcomputer techniques
	5260	Digital signal processing
	5260B	Computer vision and picture processing
	5270	Optical computing techniques
	5280	Other digital techniques
5400	ANALOGUE AND DIGITAL COMPUTERS AND SYSTEMS	
	5420	Mainframes and minicomputers
	5430	Microcomputers
	5440	Multi-processor systems and techniques
	5450	Analogue and hybrid computers and systems
	5460	Analogue and hybrid computing techniques
	5490	Other aspects

Research programmes

There have been a number of research initiatives launched recently to develop some of the technology, which it is anticipated will be needed for the next generation of computer systems. The

Japanese Fifth Generation Computer project started in the early 1980s and was the first attempt at a centrally funded coordinated research programme involving many manufacturers and research centres. The British response to this was the Alvey Programme, a five-year programme of research which drew to a close in 1988. One of the research areas in this programme was the development of gallium arsenide microprocessors and the design and manufacture of VLSI (very large-scale integrated) devices. The ESPRIT Programme funded by the EEC and now in its second phase, ESPRIT II, is a European-Community wide programme of research looking at a range of information technologies and their applications.

Conference proceedings

The learned societies are major conference organizers in this area. The papers produced for conferences provide a significant proportion of the total literature reported in secondary services such as INSPEC. Conferences covering different aspects of hardware include: <u>ACM Computer Science Conference</u>; and <u>IEEE International Conference on Computer Design</u>.

Books

Various publishers have jumped on the information technology bandwagon by publishing series of titles on computers and information technology. Examples include: *The Information Technology Revolution* (Basil Blackwell, 1985), edited by T. Forester; *The Information Age: Living with Information Technology* (Forbes Publications, 1985) by R. McKee; and *Information Technology and Information Use: Towards a Unified View of Information and Information Technology* (Taylor Graham, 1986). Although a bit dated now, Peter Gillman's chapter on hardware and software in *New Methods and Techniques for Information Management* (Taylor Graham), edited by Mary Feeney gives an excellent introduction to the area.

Mainframe, mini- and microcomputers

Computer hardware can be divided into the following categories:
- Supercomputers
- Mainframe computers
- Minicomputers
- Microcomputers
- Terminals and workstations

The distinction between micro-, mini-, and mainframe computers is becoming less clear. For instance there is now a wide range of supermicros which have the processing power of small minicomputers and which are capable of supporting several terminals at once. Intelligent terminals often have the processing power of microcomputers, although they lack mass data storage devices and normally depend on a minicomputer or mainframe for access to data.

Supercomputers

At the top end of the range there are supercomputers, capable of prodigious data-processing feats. The U.S. Office of Technology Assessment in its 1985 report, *Information Technology Research and Development: Critical Trends and Issues* defined supercomputers as '*the most powerful machines on the market at any* [given] *time*'. Generally supercomputers are distinguished by their large processing capabilities and are used for intensive calculations such as those needed for meteorology and mathematical modelling.

For an introduction to supercomputers there is *Supercomputing. State of the Art* (North-Holland), which includes chapters on: advanced parallel architectures; program restructuring; performance evaluation; numerical algorithms; and industrial applications. It is part of a series published by North-Holland, *Special Topics in Supercomputing*. A brief review of supercomputing can also be found in the Computing in Science supplement to the *New Scientist* (9 September 1989) entitled *Supercomputing in the 1990s*. *Supercomputer Architecture* (Kluwer) looks at specific machines in operation in the late 1980s. *Supercomputers Class VI Systems, Hardware and Software* (North-Holland) looks to the future by introducing the concepts behind supercomputing (vector processors) and then giving detailed descriptions of supercomputers. It is a multi-author work focusing on supercomputers and the sixth generation of computers.

The *Journal of Supercomputer Applications*, and the *Journal of Supercomputing* are two of the many specialist journals being published on this topic. There are also a number of conferences such as the International Conference on Supercomputing.

Mainframe computers

Mainframe computers are usually regarded as devices capable of doing several tasks at once (multi-processing) and handling many users. In practice most mainframe computers operate a time-sharing system where the computer switches its attention to each user in turn. This happens so rapidly that the user is given the impression that only he or she is using the machine.

The market for mainframes is dominated by a few large manufacturers such as IBM, ICL, Honeywell, Unisys, Fujitsu and Prime. Amdahl manufactures machines which are compatible with IBM mainframes. All the manufacturers themselves are a major source of information on hardware and many other sources are directed at users of specific models or manufacturers.

A number of manufacturers have their own technical journals. Some are specialist, others more general. For instance the *Hitachi Review* covers the full range of technical interests of the company, including computer hardware. The technical journals tend to come out in special issues devoted to one particular topic. If you know that a manufacturer has an interest in a particular area it is worth looking through its technical titles.

Manufacturers such as IBM and ICL also have their own research and development journals which cover various topics including design and manufacture of chips. Examples include the *ICL Technical Journal*, *IBM Technical Disclosure Bulletin*, and the *IBM Journal of Research and Development*. The *ICL Technical Journal* comes out twice a year and includes papers on the design and manufacture of chips.

Minicomputers

Minicomputers are also multi-user systems, but with more limited data-processing capabilities and therefore limited scope for multi-processing. Generally minicomputers also have less massive data storage devices attached to them. They are usually used for a single application, such as telecommunications, or database work, rather than multiprocessing. Like mainframes there are a few major manufacturers which dominate this field. DEC is the largest of the minicomputer manufacturers, providing the complete range of minicomputers in its VAX series. Shows and exhibitions dedicated to specific manufacturers are an important source of information and manufacturers will often time product launches to coincide with shows. The DEC User Show is an example of this type of exhibition.

A lot of product related information is to be found in glossy magazines, many of which overlap with the PC market. Notable examples are: *Informatics*; *Systems International*; *PC World*; *Byte*; and *Datamation*.

Microcomputers

Microcomputers are usually marketed as personal computers, capable of operating independently. A microcomputer usually has a mass storage device (such as a magnetic hard disc) as well as a central processing unit (CPU) and peripherals for data entry and output. With larger organizations the benefits of sharing data are recognized and this is reflected in the growing use of local area networks to link together microcomputers. Some of the more powerful microcomputers are capable of supporting several terminals and several simultaneous users, although there is usually a marked degradation in performance with each additional user logged onto the system.

For an introduction to microcomputers Volume 1 of the *Encyclopedia of Microcomputers* (Dekker) provides a description of the concepts involved. The complete encyclopedia will eventually consist of 10 volumes with about 500 articles arranged alphabetically. It is intended as a companion to the *Encyclopedia of Computer Science and Technology* (Dekker), which is in 16 volumes and was published between 1975 and 1981.

The Single Chip Microcomputer (Prentice-Hall, 1987) by S. J. Cahill is a general text on microprocessors. It outlines the history from the first products in 1969 to the Motorola 68020 chip of the mid-1980s.

Product literature provided by manufacturers is a valuable source of information on the specifications of currently available products. Another useful source of information on specific product ranges is the specialist magazines. This is particularly useful for microcomputers such as the IBM PC, the Apple Mac and the Amstrad PC computers. Magazines such as *Macintosh Buyers' Guide* and *Amstrad PC User* are examples. Most of these journals have wide circulations and can be found in the magazine racks of larger newsagents.

The popular computing journals such as *Personal Computer World*, *Practical Computing*, *PC User*, *Byte*, *Datamation* and *Which Computer?* are of more general interest and tend to do comparative reviews and bench-tests of new microcomputers. *Personal Computer World* is particularly good in this respect. *Datamation* and *Byte* cover similar ground. Advertisements in these journals should not be overlooked as a significant source of information on hardware.

The learned societies publish a variety of journals covering microcomputers. *IEEE Micro* and *ACM SIGSMALL Newsletter* are two examples.

Workstations and terminals

Finally there are workstations, which are peripheral devices for multi-user systems. There is a marked trend towards intelligent workstations with a great deal of local processing power. What they lack is data storage devices, as they have direct access to the mainframe or minicomputer's data storage. By processing that data locally they reduce the volume of data which needs to be transferred and the associated cabling costs. Again many of the popular PC magazines review workstations and titles such as: *Personal Computer World*, *Datamation*, and *Byte* are useful sources of information on specific products.

Components of computers

As well as the major categories of computer we can also look at the components which go to make up computers. All computers are based on microprocessors and memory devices. Most of these are based on electronic devices made from semiconductors such as silicon and increasingly gallium arsenide (GaAs) although alternative technologies such as optical devices are being developed.

Semiconductors

There is a lot of research going on in this area and this is reflected in the volume of information which is being generated. Most of the new information is likely to be reported in the learned journals as well as patents for new products. Improving the performance of semiconductors is in the province of solid-state physics.

The EMIS (Electronic Materials Information Service) database, produced by Inspec and available on ESA-IRS and on BRS is a key source of detailed technical information. Inspec also provides a magnetic tape service for customers who wish to mount the database on their own computers. EMIS is a full-text database with data on the physical properties of over 250 semiconductors. There are four different record types:

Original data records: these contain the full text of data contributed by research workers.
Datareviews: prepared by leading scientists and containing reviews of the most up-to-date material available.
Literature-derived data: these records are compiled from journal articles and published conference papers containing data

	and associated text describing material preparations and measurement techniques used.
Handbook-type data:	concise data on basic properties extracted from published compilations.

The electronic services are complemented by the hard-copy *EMIS Datareviews* (Inspec) series which looks at the properties of individual materials such as gallium arsenide, lithium niobate, and mercury cadmium telluride. These publications are collections of datareviews (articles specially written for the EMIS database) containing data, discussion and references to key sources. They are intended to provide an improved understanding of the material reviewed and hence lead to better exploitation of its properties in devices.

For a technical overview of computer architecture *Computer Architecture Concepts and Systems* (Elsevier, 1988), edited by V. M. Milutinovic contains contributions from 21 experts in computer architecture. *Information Technology Manufacturing Europe* is an annual review which provides a useful introduction to IT, and helps to bring readers up to speed quickly on recent advances in the area. It focuses specifically on design and manufacturing technology in the European IT industry. Articles are very short, usually 2–3 pages, and include topics such as system and processor architectures, CAD, and semiconductor components.

The IEEE publishes a number of journals which are likely to be of interest. These range from magazines such as *IEEE Circuits and Devices Magazine* (formerly *IEEE Circuits and Systems Magazine*) to more formal publications with refereed papers: *IEEE Transactions on Semiconductor Manufacture*; *IEEE Transactions on Electron Devices*, which includes papers on techniques for making chips and components; *IEEE Journal of Solid-State Circuits*; and *IEEE Electron Device Letters*, which is devoted to the rapid publication of original contributions relating to theory, design and performance of devices. *Electronics Letters* published as a fortnightly journal by the IEE in the UK has a similar role of rapid publications of research result, with the emphasis on novelty and on applications rather than a theoretical approach.

The *IEEE Design and Test of Computers* is published by the IEEE Computer Society and provides a technical approach to design and design automation of chips. It also contains papers on testing methods.

Other titles worth investigating for details of chip technology are: the *Philips Technical Review*; *Philips Journal of Research*;

Acta Electronica (annual); and *Electronic Components and Applications*. *Electronics Weekly* and *Electronics Times* both contain industry news, news of products, advertisements and short articles.

Meetings and conferences organized by the IEEE and published as conference proceedings include: IEEE Bipolar Circuits and Technology Meeting; IEEE/Cornell Conference on Advanced Concepts in High Speed Semiconductor Devices and Circuits; IEEE International Conference on Computer Design; and the IEEE International Symposium on Circuits and Systems.

Other specialist conferences include: Semiconductor International, held in London; Eurobus; and International Solid State Circuits Conference held in New York.

GALLIUM ARSENIDE

Gallium arsenide has been the focus of a lot of research effort recently. It is widely believed that devices based on gallium arsenide could pack components more compactly than those based on silicon and also generate less waste heat when in use. Both of these are limiting factors in current chip technology and gallium arsenide holds out the prospect of more powerful devices. An introduction to the subject can be found in *Gallium Arsenide for Devices and Integrated Circuits* (IEE, 1986). It contains a series of papers on different aspects of gallium arsenide technology and advances in research. The IEE EMIS database also has a lot of information on gallium arsenide as a substrate for microprocessors. Also of note is the Gallium Arsenide Integrated Circuit Symposium.

Optical computers

Semiconductor microcircuits are electronic devices which depend on the flow of electrons around very small circuits. Alternative technologies are of increasing interest to researchers and in particular optical devices. Instead of electrons, experimental devices based on optical circuits and the transmission of light are being explored. As well as being much faster, less heat is generated (this is a serious problem for densely-packed electronic circuits). Another potential benefit is the development of a new generation of analogue computers capable of dealing with scalar data, the signals not being limited to two states. Another great advantage is the ability of light rays to cross each other's paths without interference. In 1986 the first entirely optical computer was demonstrated at the Hanover Fair.

Optical Computing: Digital and Symbolic (Dekker, 1989), edited by R. Arrathoon gives a detailed review of the technology of optical computers. It is part of the *Optical Engineering* series published by Marcel Dekker and edited by G. J. Thompson. Another general review of the technology (although this is more of a textbook) is: *Optical Computing: A Survey for Computer Scientists* (MIT Press, 1988) by D. G. Feitelson. It provides a good detailed introduction to the topic and is well illustrated. There is a lot of useful reference material in the appendices and the book includes a bibliography of 752 references.

A major source is the Society of Photo-optical Instrumentation Engineers (SPIE) which publishes its proceedings of the many conferences which it organizes or co-organizes. The *Transactions of the Society of Photo-optical Instrumentation Engineers* is a learned journal with refereed papers. The *IEE Proceedings: Optoelectronics (Part J)* is another notable academic journal in this area.

There are also several major events including the International Semiconductor Laser Conference.

Superconductors

Current computer technology is largely based on the manipulation and processing of digital information. Another possible avenue for development of computer hardware is superconductors. With the recent advances made in fabricating high-temperature superconductors there has been some speculation about how this might be applied to computers. This is still a peripheral area for information technology, but could quickly become more important.

Parallel processing and transputers

PARALLEL PROCESSING

Parallel processors (and transputers, see below) are gaining importance in a number of applications, such as speech recognition. These devices can speed up certain tasks by doing a number of operations in parallel, rather than one at a time as is the case with more conventional devices. Again this is an area where there is a lot of research, and developments are regularly reported in the learned journals.

Traditional (von Neumann) computer architecture limits computers to serial processing. Programs are written so that a sequence of operations is performed to manipulate a piece of data. Parallel processors have been developed so that several operations can be performed in parallel, speeding up the computing operation considerably. However this technique is only suitable for certain applications. Several different approaches have been taken to this, namely:

- Strathclyde GAM (Generic Associative Memory)
- ULA (Uncommitted Logic Array)
- ICL CAFS (Content Addressable File Store)
- Hypercube

There are two main categories of parallel processor: coarse-grained and fine-grained. The coarse-grained systems contain a small number of powerful processors and fine-grained systems contain a larger number of less powerful processors. There are a number of specialist journals in this area such as *Parallel Computing* (North-Holland) which includes a calendar and containing refereed articles.

The International Conference on Parallel Processing is an important event in this area.

A notable series of titles produced by MIT Press is the *Series in Scientific Computing* which includes titles such as: *The Massively Parallel Processor*; *Parallel MIMD Computation: HEP Supercomputer and Its Applications*; *Synchronization of Parallel Programs: Algorithms for Mutual Exclusion*; *Cellular Automata Machines: a New Environment for Modelling*; and *Multicomputer Networks: Message-based Parallel Processing*.

Parallel Processing in Control—the Transputer and other Architectures (IEE, 1988), edited by P. J. Fleming contains a series of papers on parallel processing and transputers.

TRANSPUTERS

The transputer is a parallel processor developed by Inmos and there has been a lot of literature generated about this and the operating system designed for it, Occam. Texts on this include *Transputer Technical Notes* (Prentice-Hall) produced by Inmos, which contains a collection of papers by Inmos engineers about transputer technology. It is highly technical and designed to assist in the implementation of transputer systems. Other titles in the series include *Transputer Development System*; *Occam Technical Notes*; *Transputer Technical Notes*; *Transputer Instruction Set: a Computer Writers' Guide*; and *Digital Signal Processing*. The *Transputer Development and IQ Systems Databook* (Inmos, 1989) contains an overview, engineering data and applications information for the Inmos software development tools and products.

CHAPTER FIVE

Information and data storage

M. FEENEY

Introduction to the technology: general sources

Recent years have seen an ever increasing growth in the amounts of data storage available to computer users—and this storage capacity is provided by a variety of new media. New products are being developed in quick succession: hardly has one new technology established itself, it seems, than another emerges to challenge its position, making this one of the most volatile areas in information technology.
   At the forefront of this explosion in storage capacity is optical disk technology. Optical media offer very great storage capacity and the new products appearing on the market have had an impact on the information industry as a whole.
   The demand for mass storage has brought about refinements in existing technologies, particularly in magnetic media. In much the same way that optical disk technology was seen as superseding magnetic media, DAT (Digital Audio Tape) has appeared as a new challenger.
   Optical disk technology has brought in its wake a vast literature. Other forms of data storage are not covered quite so handsomely, and information is often scattered through a number of resources.

State-of-the-art reviews and newsletters

A prime source of up-to-date news is the *Data Storage Report* (Elsevier), a monthly newsletter. It covers all types of data and information storage—magnetic disks and tape (with some items on disk drives), DAT, and optical storage media. The emphasis is very much on news items—new products, company news and events in the marketplace.

Advanced Information Report (Elsevier) (formerly *CTI—Communication Technology Impact*), provides news, features and commentary on all aspects of information technology. Although not its sole interest, information storage is a frequent topic. Again, the emphasis is on up-to-date coverage of the latest events and products. Each issue usually carries an in-depth article on a subject of current concern.

Research news is provided by the *Computer Bulletin* of the British Computer Society. Data storage features in its coverage of research projects and future systems.

Journals

Information Media and Technology (Cimtech), is one of the most useful journals in this field. Its main interests are micrographics, micropublishing and optical media, with other kinds of data storage featured where appropriate. The journal is very topical and includes news and editorial sections with commentary on major developments. Most issues contain a major survey or articles on a particular aspect of information technology and there are frequent reviews of equipment.

Electronic information transfer is the main concern of the *International Journal of Micrographics and Video Technology* (Pergamon). This is a new journal, created from the old *Microdoc* and *Micropublishing of Current Periodicals*, and the change in its interests reflects some of the changes that have taken place within the storage field. The journal concentrates on micrographics, video and optical technologies and their applications in relation to the process of information flow. An unusual feature is the New Patents section (relevant selections from the PERGAMON PATSEARCH online database).

The U.S. Association for Computing Machinery publishes a monthly journal, *Communications of the ACM*, which contains articles on computing practices and research, with regular items on storage. The concerns of the ACM are the development and application of computing techniques for the recognition, storage, retrieval and processing of data of all kinds.

Standards are of great importance in this field, and standards activities are the specific interest of *Computer Standards and Interfaces* (Elsevier). It is concerned with the specification and application of standards in all aspects of computing, including storage and interchange media; optical storage, CD-ROM, interactive video and semiconductor memories are all covered.

76 Information and data storage

The *IEEE Transactions on Consumer Electronics* has very wide coverage, including articles on VCR, videotape recording, semiconductor memories, CMOS and MOS, optical disk recording, magnetic tape, audio compact disk and CD-ROM, as well as many aspects of television and broadcasting. The emphasis is on the technology rather than new products, and all evidence of commercialism, including company names and trademarks, is meticulously avoided. Many of the papers are selected from presentations given at the international conference of the same name.

Secondary sources

Inspec, the information service of the Institution of Electrical Engineers, offers a monthly abstracts service, *Key Abstracts: Computer Communications and Storage*, which provides references and abstracts of relevant articles on all aspects of data storage. The articles are arranged under three headings: magnetic disk and tape storage; semiconductor storage; optical storage.

Electronic Publishing Abstracts, developed by PIRA and published by Pergamon, covers the input, transmission, storage and retrieval of text as an alternative to printed material. The service relates mainly to publishing, but is a useful source of summaries of the scientific and technical literature on information technology. It is also available online as the E-PUBS database on the Orbit Search Service.

Directories and textbooks

New Methods and Techniques for Information Management, published by Taylor Graham for PCRC, contains a section on information storage with articles on magnetic media, micrographics and optical media.

Information on developments in equipment is provided by the *Micrographics and Optical Equipment Review*, an annual publication from Meckler.

Many of the books published in this field concentrate on the archival potential of the various media and emphasize their competitive relationship. Archival quality is a very real concern: recent reports in the popular press that compact disks would 'self-destruct' within ten years have been discounted, but there remain some doubts about new products which lack independent authoritative testing. Two comparative studies which encompass archival quality are *The Archival Storage Potential of Microfilm, Magnetic Media and Optical Data Discs*, by A. M. Hendley, and the more recent *Optical Disks vs Micrographics as Document Storage and Retrieval Technologies*, by W. Saffady.

Conferences

The Annual AIIM Conference and Exposition, organized by the US Association for Information and Image Management, covers many aspects of data storage from micrographics to optical disk, and is a major industry event. The IEEE Symposium on Mass Storage Systems is also a major conference in this field. 1988 was the ninth conference in this series. The IEEE International Conference on Consumer Electronics covers many relevant topics (as described in the journal section), with sessions on emerging technologies.

Organizations

Cimtech, formerly NRCd and still part of Hatfield Polytechnic, is a major contributor to the field. Its interests include information storage, with particular emphasis on micrographics and optical media. Its function is to provide impartial information and this is particularly important when dealing with product and equipment reviews. Of particular note is the enquiry service for users.

Other organizations active in this field include the IEEE Computer Society and the British Computer Society. Both have a professional interest in computers and their applications and aim to promote the exchange of technical information among interested users. Both have publications and conference programmes.

Optical media

There is now a whole range of digital optical products, the best known of which is CD-ROM (Compact Disk—Read Only Memory), which was developed from the Compact Audio Disk. Other forms of read-only disks are OROMs (Optical Read Only Memory), CD-I (Compact Disk Interactive) and DVI (Digital Video Interactive). The latter are being developed for interactive use. A recent development is digital paper, a low-cost permanent storage medium; rather than a rigid disk, digital paper uses a thin flexible polyester, which can be cut to any required shape.

In addition there are disks which allow the user to record information, but not to erase it—these are known variously as WORMs (Write Once Read Many) and WOOD (Write Once Optical Disks). Fully erasable disks are also being developed.

State-of-the-art reviews and newsletters

Meckler publishes an annual state-of-the-art review (*Optical Storage Technology: a State of the Art Review*, by W. Saffady). The

78 Information and data storage

1988 edition was the fourth in the series. As well as covering the technology, product developments and applications, it also looks at new products under development during the year.

The series of *Library & Information Briefings* published by the British Library Research and Development Department and the Library and Information Technology Centre offers two relevant reports, *CD-ROM* (3) and *WORM Discs* (15), both by Ann Clarke. Updates are issued when appropriate.

Newsletters are a particularly volatile source: new publications appear—and disappear—quite regularly. Of the specialist newsletters, *Optical Information Systems Update* (Meckler) is the most frequent, with issues appearing twice a month. Monthly newsletters include: *CD-Data Report* (Langley Publications); *Optical Memory News* (Rothchild Consultants); and *Optical Data Systems* (Microinfo). The latter, as well as covering all types of optical media, also reports on developments in DAT. The French publisher, A. Jour offers two newsletters, *CD-ROM International* and *CD-ROM*, the latter in French. All these specialist newsletters cover similar ground—product announcements, standards activities, industry news, equipment reviews.

CD-I News (Emerging Technologies Publications), specializes in the developing CD-I industry.

Some newsletters representing other aspects of information technology have diversified to cover this new field. *Information World Review* (Learned Information) and its U.S. counterpart, *Information Today* (Learned Information), both provide news on the information industry and include regular items on developments in optical technology and publishing. Both have a newspaper format and the European publication has columns in French, German and Dutch as well as English. *Monitor*, yet another Learned Information publication, offers selective reports on the information market. This is a rather different newsletter, in that it offers informed, critical comment from the Editor, rather than simply reporting news items.

Many newsletters dealing with the online industry also feature optical media. *Online Notes* (Aslib) includes regular items. *Database Searcher* (Meckler) concentrates on databases from the user's viewpoint and features CD-ROM products. *Online Libraries and Microcomputers* (Information Intelligence) and *Library Hi-Tech News* (Pierian Press) cover the field for libraries. In the UK *Electronic Publishing News* (Publishers Association) covers information technology from the publishing point of view.

Journals

As with newsletters, the optical storage field is covered by both specialist and more general journals. *Optical Information Systems* (Meckler) is issued in parallel with the newsletter *Optical Information Systems Update* (Meckler). It contains articles, news and publishing announcements on the development and use of optical media. All types of optical media are covered, from digital optical disk to laser card. *CD-ROM Librarian* (Meckler), concentrates on CD-ROM products with the emphasis on library applications. This journal used to have the rather long-winded title *Optical Information Systems Update/Library and Information Centre Applications*. Along with the title, the contents have been revamped. Both these journals have a strong U.S. bias—all the prices are quoted only in dollars, for instance, and the otherwise useful *Optical Product Review* section tends to overlook European products.

Two specialist journals come from French publishers. *Infotecture* (A. Jour) is the only French-language journal to cover the optical memory field. A parallel English-language publication, *Infotecture Europe* (A. Jour), is also offered. *Mémoires Optiques* (ARCA Ed Sarl), distributed by Learned Information, describes itself as an 'international journal' and is in English. It focuses exclusively on developments in optical disk technology and applications.

Journals in the online field have also seized on optical technology as a way of finding and sustaining new markets. *Online* (Online Inc.), *Database* (Online Inc.), and *Online Review* (Learned Information) are specialist journals for the online information industry but are also good sources of information on optical products.

Electronic Library (Learned Information) and *Library Hi-Tech Journal* (Pierian Press) provide coverage of information technology applications in libraries. Both have regular features and news of CD-ROM and other optical media.

Although not its only interest, extensive coverage of optical storage media is provided by *Electronic and Optical Publishing Review* (Learned Information). The title was changed from *Electronic Publishing Review* in 1986 to reflect this new interest. The journal covers new products, companies news, developments in hardware and software, product and book reviews, along with longer articles on specific topics. The December and June issues include a bibliography of articles and books on optical publishing.

80 *Information and data storage*

Secondary sources

SPECIALIST GUIDES

The state of the CD-ROM industry is the subject of a subscription service from the U.S. Information Workstation Group. *State of the CD-ROM Industry: Applications, Players and Products*, covers industry trends and the marketplace.

The issue of standards is most important to the future development of CD-ROM. A detailed study of this aspect of the technology is provided by *CD-ROM Standards: the Book* (Learned Information) by Julie B. Schwerin. This brings together a great deal of information about CD-ROM standards, their impact on the information market and their implementation in the computer and information industries.

Whilst there are many publications offering advice on online searching, there are few, if any, which deal with searching CD-ROM databases. This aspect of the technology is tackled in the *LISA Online User Manual* (Learned Information), which offers guidance on searching the LISA database and includes a section on the LISA CD-ROM. Search language, search techniques and worked examples are explained and illustrated.

BIBLIOGRAPHIES

A huge amount has been and continues to be written about optical media, to the extent that there are already a number of published bibliographies to guide the reader to the most useful sources. *The CD-ROM Directory* (described below) includes lists of journals, books and newsletters relevant to CD-ROM and optical media generally. The journal, *Electronic and Optical Publishing Review* offers a twice-yearly bibliography of relevant literature, especially of recent articles. *Optical Storage Technology: a Bibliography* (Meckler, 1988) compiled by William Saffady provides an extensive compilation of citations to the published literature.

Directories and textbooks

The growth in CD-ROM and optical media products has seen a corresponding growth in the number of directories giving details of available titles. All the leading publishers in this field have brought out such guides, many of which are in their second or even third editions. The offering from Meckler, with the rather incongruous title *CD-ROMs in Print 1988–89* lists over 235 products and contains eight supporting indexes. A useful feature is the ROM Drive Index which lists CD-ROM drives with the names of the titles that can be read by them. *The CD-ROM Directory* (TFPL Publishing) provides details of available CD-ROM titles and also includes extensive coverage of relevant books, journals, newsletters and conferences. Learned Information's *Optical Publishing Directory* contains details of published CD-ROM titles and includes other optical products. The *CD-ROM Sourcebook* (Diversified Data Resources), consists of a directory of all products and services for CD-ROM. Issued in parallel are monthly industry analyses with sections on mastering, players, search software, data preparation, titles available, and publications.

The online directories are also beginning to incorporate CD-ROM products. One such is the *Eusidic Database Guide* (Learned Information). The 1989 edition has a special emphasis on CD-ROM with details of almost 200 databases.

Optical Disks for Data and Document Storage (Meckler) by W. Saffady is a survey of the hardware and software currently available. It is divided into three parts: read-only optical disks, read/write optical media and turnkey systems.

Books which explain how the technology works and discuss its implications for the information industry also abound. *CD-ROM: the New Papyrus* by Stephen Lambert and Suzanne Ropiequet was the first of a series published by Microsoft and has become something of a classic. The other volumes in the series are *CD-ROM Optical Publishing* by Suzanne Ropiequet, which examines the technology from the publishing angle, and *CD-I* by David Chell, which deals with Compact Disk Interactive.

CD-ROM: Fundamentals to Applications (Butterworths) edited by Charles Oppenheim covers the area suggested by the title, with chapters on optical technology, the logistics and cost of product creation, product case histories, software issues and market considerations.

Videodiscs, Compact Discs and Digital Optical Disk Systems (Cimtech/Learned Information) by Tony Hendley guides the reader through the wide range of technologies and examines their potential for storage, retrieval and dissemination. Another volume from the same stable, *CD-ROM and Optical Publishing Systems*, assesses the impact of optical read-only systems on the information industry and compares them with paper, microfilm and online publishing systems.

A very useful introduction to the technology is provided by *CD-ROM and the Migration from Print: the 500 Megabyte Solution*, the 1987 CLSI Annual Lecture on Library Automation, by David Whitaker. This brief guide describes the technology in non-technical terms and also explains what CD-ROM cannot do.

The archival quality of optical technology is a particular concern. Several studies involving accelerated ageing tests have been carried out and the results of these are now beginning to be made public. *Life Expectancy of Write Once Digital Optical Discs* (British Library), BL Research Paper No. 66, by D. R. Winterbottom and R. G. Fiddes, summarizes the main archival tests in use to date.

Real-life experience often reveals more of a technology's particular strengths and weaknesses than more general discussions. Two accounts of such experience are *The British Library's Compact Disk Experiment* (British Library) by Ann Clarke, which also offers two demonstration disks, and *Data Storage on Optical Disk—an Experiment* (HMSO), which describes an experiment to assess the advantages of optical digital disk technology as an alternative to magnetic tape for the archival storage of computer-generated data for government departments.

A number of text books and guides are targetted at specific groups in the information community. Librarians are served by *The Librarian's CD-ROM Handbook* (Meckler) by Norman Desmarais, which includes advice on how to evaluate and select CD-ROM products and equipment and a section on management issues. A more specialized library-oriented book is *Library Applications of Optical Disk and CD-ROM Technology* by Nancy Melin Nelson, Volume 8 of Meckler's series *The Essential Guide to the Library IBM PC*. This is dedicated to CD-ROM products for the IBM-PC and covers databases, public access catalogues and catalogue production systems. Publishers are catered for by *CD-ROM: Publisher's Guide* (Blueprint Publishing), which is part of a series geared to the publishing perspective, and *Publishing with CD-ROM* (Meckler) by Patti Myers. This examines the current usage of CD-ROM as a publishing medium and describes the actual publishing process.

The market for CD-ROM products forms another group of publications. Two reports from Link Resources in the UK deal with this topic. *Database Delivery Options in Europe* dissects the structure of the database industry with special emphasis on database use within Europe. It discusses database delivery options, including decentralized databases on optical media, and analyses the pressures of the marketplace with particular reference to the European Commission and 1992. *Market Opportunities for CD-ROM in Europe* examines the optical publishing industry in Europe by country and by activity. Factors affecting the market are discussed, including standards, language barriers, the installed base of hardware and pricing.

CD-ROM Applications and Markets (Meckler) looks at applications of CD-ROM in different contexts—the library, science and medicine, government and the law—and also examines the marketing of CD-ROM. An evaluation of the library optical publishing market is provided by the *CD-ROM Library Market Study* (Meckler) by Nancy Melin Nelson. This study is intended to help publishers effectively assess their market position.

Trade literature

CD-ROM equipment producers have rightly gauged the need for more information on available databases if they are to increase the installed equipment base and so ensure their share of the market. A number of free newsletters have appeared with this aim in mind. *CD-ROM Directions* (Hitachi New Media) is a quarterly newsletter reporting on the latest developments, standards, software and available databases for CD-ROM drives. *CD-ROM Newsletter* (Microinfo) started as a free publication giving news of their own CD-ROM database services, but in January 1989 changed to a subscription-based service with greater frequency and wider scope.

Whitaker's CD-ROM newsletter *News from Whitaker* is a free, very informal news sheet with information presented as the answers to questions that they themselves have received about *British Books in Print* on CD-ROM and about CD-ROM in general.

Conferences

There is now a large number of annual conferences devoted to CD-ROM and other optical storage media. In addition, a number of the established information technology conferences have brought optical technology into their aegis. A full list of relevant conferences is included in *The CD-ROM Directory* (described above).

The U.S. company Microsoft sponsors a yearly <u>CD-ROM Conference</u>. The first, in 1986, was something of a trailblazer for the emerging industry: it was the first major conference dedicated to CD-ROM and the first opportunity for showing product prototypes. It has been described as the 'Woodstock of CD-ROM', and is now a showcase for the industry. The conference has also become a forum for announcing new products: in 1986 Philips announced CD-I and caused a certain amount of confusion and dismay to those who felt that CD-ROM itself was still in a fledgling condition; Digital Video Interactive (DVI) was announced by RCA at the 1987 conference.

Meckler and Cimtech co-sponsor <u>Optical Information Systems (OIS) International</u>, Europe's largest optical media conference and exhibition. A parallel conference is also held in the USA. Proceedings of both conferences are published and are available from Meckler.

Optica 87 was the first of a series of conferences organized in Amsterdam by Learned Information. The second, in 1988 was called OpticalInfo. All the technologies of optical publishing are covered and the proceedings are published. The 1989 Conference includes a parallel event—OnlineInfo—which covers the emerging links between the online and optical industries. Learned Information also sponsors an annual conference in the USA, Optical Publishing and Storage.

Rothchild Consultants in the USA organize a whole series of optical technology conferences under the general title of Technology Opportunity Conference and Study Missions. Most are held in the USA, with one in London and one in Tokyo. The themes of these conferences include: the future of optical memory technology; optical drive and media manufacturing; optical memory applications; optical storage of documents and images; optical storage for large systems; optical storage for small systems.

An annual conference is held in France by the Groupement Français des Fournisseurs d'Information en Ligne (GFFIL), the French trade association for electronic publishing. CD '88 was the third in the series and covered the techniques and applications of CD-ROM, CD-I and CD-V.

Optical technology also figures prominently in conferences whose interests are not so specialized. The International Online Meeting (IOLIM), organized by Learned Information, is mainly concerned with online, but also features CD-ROM. IOLIM is a well established forum for users and producers of information services. There is a parallel exhibition and numerous satellite events. The 1987 conference incorporated a CD-ROM Lab, and in 1988 there was a CD-ROM Gallery where visitors could try out many CD-ROM products. Learned Information also co-sponsors many seminars both before and after the main conference. The National Online Meeting is the U.S. version of IOLIM and is also organized by Learned Information. Proceedings of both conferences are published.

The Electronic Publishing and Print Show, held annually in London by Online International Ltd, covers current topics and issues affecting electronic publishing. Optical technology features regularly in the discussion. The Proceedings are published and make very informative and useful publications.

Organizations

Learned Information, Meckler and Microsoft are all involved in optical media conferences and are all prolific publishers to the extent that they have built up considerable expertise and reputations in this field.

Rothchild Consultants in the USA offers marketing and technical consultancy services in the optical memory industry. The company publishes books and newsletters and organizes the Technology Opportunity Conferences (TOC). They also offer an Optical Systems Information Service (OSIS), aimed at both users and vendors, which provides an enquiry service, regular information bulletins and optional consultancy services.

Microinfo is an independent company which specializes in the production of technical newsletters in the field of information storage. It is also involved in conferences and is the official distributor for several important U.S. and international bodies.

Standards are a key issue in the development of optical information products. There are two kinds of standards involved: physical, relating to the physical characteristics of the disks, the drives and the way data is recorded on the disks, and logical, relating to the way information files are organized. The former are developed as specifications by the principal manufacturers—in the case of CD-ROM by Philips and Sony—and are referred to by the colour of their cover (Yellow Book for CD-ROM and Green Book for CD-I, for example). Activity is now focused on the second type of standard. The High Sierra Group, a voluntary industry group named after the hotel in which it first met, has been active in this field. In Europe the Optical Disk Forum has been established by Learned Information, with financial assistance from the European Commission, to represent the European information industry and keep it up to date on standards activities.

Standards proposals are forwarded to the national and international standards bodies for development and acceptance. The U.S. National Information Standards Organization (NISO) and American National Standards Institute (ANSI) are both involved in standards for the optical storage industry.

At the international level is ISO, the International Organization for Standardization. The *ISO Catalogue of Standards* is published annually; the standards themselves are also published and available from ISO. Information is also provided by ISONET, a worldwide network of national standards information centres established through ISO. There are many databases providing information on standards, including PERINORM on CD-ROM. The British Standards Institute offers news of British and international standards in *BSI News* and BITS—BSI Information Technology Service.

Videodisc, videotape and interactive video

Strictly, videodisc belongs to optical technology in terms of how it works, whereas videotape is a magnetic medium. However, they have applications in common and are often covered together in the literature. Most information sources also deal with interactive media, such as CD-I and DVI, and hybrid technologies, such as CD-Video.

State-of-the-art reviews and newsletters

The University of London Audio-Visual Centre and the British Universities Film and Video Council (BUFVC) jointly publish a quarterly *Videodisc Newsletter*, which covers interactive media generally, videodisc and, to a lesser extent, videotape. This is a useful publication covering new projects, especially educational and training applications, new equipment and products, and news from companies. There is also a hints, tips and problems section.

The French publisher, A. Jour, publishes a French language newsletter, *Vidéodisque*, which covers videodisc and other interactive media, including CD-I.

Journals

The *Videodisc Monitor* (Future Systems) from the USA, is one of the oldest and best-established journals in the field, having started in 1983. It covers technology and applications for both interactive video and the new interactive CD products.

Secondary sources

SPECIALIST GUIDE

The rapid development of the interactive video industry has stimulated interest in the task of authoring—the process of assembling all the various aspects that go to make up a program, from graphics and design to script and video. A handbook, *Authoring Systems: a Guide for Interactive Videodisc Authors* (Meckler) by Peter Crowell, looks at the complete process of authoring and examines the various software packages designed to facilitate interactive programming.

Directories and textbooks

Detailed technical information on all aspects of videodisc technology is offered by *Videodisc and Optical Memory Systems* (Prentice-Hall) by Jordan Isailovic. The book discusses recording processes, mastering and replication, playback, standards and applications. There is also a comparison of videodisc with videotape and with other optical media. A very technical volume, and not for the faint-hearted.

There is increasing interest in interactive video. Two books on this topic are the *Introduction to Interactive Video* (NIVC) and the *Essential Guide to Interactive Videodisc Hardware and Applications* (Meckler) by Charles R. Miller. The latter, as well as covering the basic principles of interactive videodisc systems, provides an overview of the hardware currently available.

Conferences

The British Interactive Video Association (BIVA) organizes an annual Interactive Technology Briefing and Exhibition, held in Brighton. This is the most important exhibition for the UK industry; the 1988 exhibition was the eighth in the series.

The BUFVC holds an annual conference which gives extensive coverage of interactive video and videodisc, with particular emphasis on their role in education and training.

In the USA, Video Computing holds a series of regional and international conferences and trade shows with the collective title Laseractive. The focus is on the applications of interactive video and other optical storage media.

Organizations

The National Interactive Video Centre (NIVC) in London offers advice on interactive video to industry, commerce and the educational sector. It also offers equipment and product demonstrations to interested parties and surveys the use of interactive video. A number of development groups have been set up under its aegis, including the UK Interactive Video User Group. The NIVC hosts IVIS, the Interactive Video in Schools project, sponsored by the Department of Trade and Industry, which is investigating the potential of interactive video in the classroom.

BIVA, the British Interactive Video Association, presents the public face of commercial and industrial videodisc activity in the UK. It organizes an annual conference and exhibition and works in close association with the NIVC.

The British Universities Film and Video Council also organizes an annual conference and is co-publisher of the *Videodisc Newsletter*.

Micrographics

With the emergence of new technologies, such as optical media, micrographics often appear as the Cinderella of information storage technology. Many of the organizations and publications which grew out of the microfilm boom of the 1960s have now diversified to cover the new technologies, and there has been something of a decline in the intellectual interest in micrographics. Nevertheless, it remains a viable medium and new developments have done much to reinforce its position in the field of information storage.

State-of-the-art reviews and newsletters

Microinfo's *Microfilm News* is a monthly management review of worldwide micrographics technology and markets. It covers all aspects of microfilm and microfiche and associated developments in the fields of COM and CAR. The U.S. publication *Micrographics Newsletter* (Microform Publishing Co.), also provides industry and product news, with an annual review of the year's developments as an additional feature.

Microfilm and Imaging Systems (Spectrum), published six times a year, offers short articles, news and reviews on many aspects of information storage. The emphasis is on microform, but this is not the only interest: there are also items on electronic and micro publishing, and each issue includes a special section on optical storage.

Journals

Microform Review is one of the oldest and best known journals in the field of micrographics. Published by the Microfilm Association of Great Britain, it offers detailed reviews of microform products.

Directories and textbooks

Micrographics: a User's Manual (John Wiley), by Joseph L. Kish, offers a very thorough and detailed grounding in all aspects of micrographics. It is written in non-technical language and is accessible to the non-specialist. Topics covered include: the various kinds of microform in current use (fiche, film, COM, aperture cards, jacket fiche, ultrafiche); hardware (cameras, readers, processors and duplicators); types of film used (silver halide, diazo); storage and retrieval techniques; applications and management considerations.

The annual *Guide to Microforms in Print* (Meckler) gives bibliographic details of all micropublications currently available from publishers worldwide. Over 125 000 titles are listed—an indication of the continuing popularity of the medium. A Supplement is issued six months after the main publication which gives details of new titles just appeared.

Another Meckler publication, *Microform Market Place*, is also updated annually and provides a comprehensive international directory to micropublishers.

Conferences

Cimtech offers an occasional two-day seminar on micrographics, Micrographics—the Situation to Date, which deals with both the fundamental principles of the technology and recent developments and applications.

Organizations

The Microfilm Association of Great Britain (MAGB) covers all aspects of microfilm and offers a full list of publications.

Magnetic media

There is still a growing market for magnetic disks and tape, with demand increasing because of continued strong computer sales, especially of workstations and personal computers. The capacity of magnetic media is increased by developments such as perpendicular magnetic recording techniques. New encoding methods, such as ADRT (Advanced Data Recording Technique) use data compaction and encryption techniques to provide increased capacities.

Despite great interest, DAT products are taking time to materialize: suppliers are counting on the consumer market to drive down the cost of DAT drives, but resistance on the part of recording companies may make this a slow process.

State-of-the-art reviews and newsletters

Two useful sources which include regular items on magnetic storage are *Systems International*, a monthly magazine aimed at systems designers, scientists and computer managers, and *Elec-*

tronics and Computing, also monthly but aimed more at the enthusiast. The latter concentrates on small computers and offers items on tape, disk, ROM and RAM. *Systems International* has a new products section, which includes memory and storage, and it also has an interest in DAT.

Information on magnetic storage media can be found throughout a whole range of newsletters which deal with all aspects of computing, rather than with storage alone. One such is *IEEE Micro* (IEEE Computer Society), which offers articles, news and reviews on all aspects of microcomputers, including storage, in a readable but informative style.

Many computer glossy magazines also carry regular items on storage—*Personal Computer World*, *Personal Computer Magazine* and *Byte* are examples. *Micro Decision*, aimed at business users, is another. *What Micro*, published monthly, offers advice on choosing equipment; each issue includes a Buyers' Guide, which gives specifications of a whole range of computing equipment, including details of storage capacity and compatible drives.

Journals

A similar pattern is evident in the journals: many of the computing journals have an interest in data storage. For example, there is a whole clutch of journals from the Institute of Electrical and Electronic Engineers (IEEE), which all contain relevant information, including: *Computer*; *IEEE Transactions on Computers*; and *IEEE Design and Test of Computers*. The first contains up-to-date discussions of the latest developments in hardware and software systems and new products. The *IEEE Transactions on Computers* is an authoritative journal with technical articles intended for the professional systems designer, while *IEEE Design and Test of Computers* covers all aspects of the design and test of chips, assemblies and systems. *IEEE Spectrum* is more accessible and wide-ranging than the more specialized IEEE publications.

New Electronics offers news and features on all aspects of electronics and computer technology, including microprocessors and digital design. Various kinds of data storage are dealt with and memory is a regular feature.

Another useful source, *Computing Techniques*, offers an annual review of various computing topics; the data storage review appears in the July/August issue.

Secondary sources

Computer Abstracts (Technical Information) provides bibliographic details and abstracts of very technical literature on all aspects of computers and computing technology. A section on data storage is included.

The quarterly *Computer Books Review* supplies brief comments on new books; six categories are included—hardware, software, data, applications, people, and sources of information.

Data Sources (Ziff-Davis Publishing Co.) a directory of hardware, communications and software, includes a section on disk, tape and memory.

Directories and textbooks

Several books deal with management and use of hard (Winchester) disks: *The Hard Disk Companion* (Prentice-Hall) by P. Norton and R. Jourdain, and *The Quick Reference Guide to Hard Disk Management* (Microsoft Press) by V. Wolverton. *Hard Disk Smarts* (John Wiley) by C. A. Bosshardt discusses what you need to know to choose and use a hard disk.

Floppy Disks and Microcomputers by F. Rouard, is a technical explanation of floppy disks, in English, provided by a French manufacturer. It offers a mass of technical detail, including magnetic recording and formatting.

A number of textbooks dealing with the subject of computer equipment generally also include details of storage devices. *The Principles of Computer Hardware* (Oxford, Oxford University Press) by A. Clements, is intended primarily for computer-science students. The chapter on computer memory includes semiconductor, ferrite-core, thin-film, magnetic bubble, magnetic recording, disk drives and tape transport. *The Microcomputer Handbook* (Collins) has contributions from experts in the field, electronics companies as well as universities. It includes chapters on memory chips and memory storage devices (disks, drives, tape, hard disks and optical drives). There is a directory of manufacturers and a glossary of terms.

The *Computer Users' Year Book* and *Microcomputer Users' Yearbook* are standard reference books for equipment, software suppliers and computer installations in the UK.

Trade literature

Manufacturers' journals, such as the *IBM Journal of Research and Development*, *Philips Technical Review* and *Philips Journal of Research*, provide reviews of the technology. The *Hitachi Review* is devoted to articles about technological areas in which Hitachi equipment is prominent or in which the company has an interest. Each issue concentrates on a particular technology, such as

92 Information and data storage

erasable optical disks, opto-semiconductor devices, computer peripheral products, disk drives, etc.

A great deal of product information can be found in the trade press. Most of these journals operate on a controlled circulation basis, with free subscriptions offered to certain categories of professional readers. They carry a great deal of advertizing and most offer a reader enquiry service, so that further information on specific products can be had from the manufacturer or supplier. *Computing Equipment* offers news on new products and regular features on all aspects of computing hardware and software, including storage devices (external drive, hard disks, DAT-based, tape systems, tape back-up, etc.). *PC-Tech Journal* (which is not affiliated to IBM) covers new products and developments in the PC field, including disks and disk drives.

A large number of magazines offer information on office and business equipment, including computers and computer peripherals. *Office Equipment News* and *Office Equipment Index* are both newspaper-style magazines covering all kinds of office equipment, but with regular features on storage devices—magnetic and optical media, disk drives, hard disks, etc. Similar ground is covered by *Business Computing and Communications* and *Business Systems and Equipment*, with the emphasis on business users, medium and large companies in particular. *What to Buy for Business* takes a different approach to the usual magazine style; each issue is devoted to one particular type of equipment, with supplier profiles, in-depth 'Which'-like evaluations of products, and advice on choosing and buying equipment. Computer equipment is a regular topic, with updates and new reports issued whenever necessary.

Dr Dobb's Journal is aimed at the professional programmer, with software and programming its main interests. It occasionally includes useful features on memory from the programming point of view—memory management, memory compaction, and so on.

Conferences

The IEEE Computer Society holds an annual international conference, COMPCON. This is a well-established and long-running series, with 1988 seeing the 33rd conference. Another regular event is INTERMAG (International Magnetics Conference). Proceedings of both are published.

The Head/Media Technology Review Conference, held in the USA in conjunction with COMDEX, the Computer Dealers' Exposition, meets annually to discuss developments in drive technology. The fourth meeting was held in 1988.

Semiconductor storage

Semiconductor memories are an integral part of computers and microprocessor-based systems. There are two basic types: those that can be both written to and read (RAM), and those that are permanently or semi-permanently programmed and can be read only (ROM). MOS (metal oxide semiconductor) memory devices have become the major growth area of the 1970s and 80s, and are used in the production of dynamic and static RAMs (Random Access Memories), volatile devices which lose their memory if the power is turned off, and in the production of ROMs (Read Only Memories), EPROMs (Erasable Programmable ROMs) and EEPROMs (Electrically Erasable Programmable ROMs), which are non-volatile. C-MOS, with its advantages of low power consumption, high noise immunity and operation over a wide power supply range, has become one of the most prominent semiconductor technologies.

State-of-the-art reviews and newsletters

Coverage of semiconductor technology is necessarily technical and seems to be better served by journals than by newsletter format, although there are some exceptions.

Electronics and Wireless World offers articles and news on all aspects of electronics, circuits, broadcast and semiconductor technology. A special feature is the Industry Insight, a series of features on the working of the electronics industry, which presents both the technical and market viewpoint. *Computer Design* is a U.S. newspaper-format newsletter, published twice-monthly, which offers news items on all aspects of computer systems, including semiconductor memory. The *IEEE Circuits & Devices Magazine* is published bimonthly and communicates technical information to members of the societies that make up IEEE Division I. While it is aimed at this technical community, its articles are of broad interest and widely understandable. A lot of space is dedicated to news of the various societies.

Journals

The journals in this field have a highly technical bias. *Microelectronics Journal* (BEP Data Services) aims to promote the interchange of knowledge between scientists and engineers concerned in the various fields of silicon and hybrid device technology and design, including semiconductor memories. The emphasis is on presenting research papers. There is also a section for abstracts of relevant articles.

Solid-State Electronics (Pergamon Press) also has a strong technical research bias. Solid-state and semiconductor devices for the storage and transfer of information represent a particular interest.

The *IEEE Journal of Solid-State Circuits* (IEEE Solid-State Circuits Council) and the *IEE Proceedings on Circuits, Devices and Systems* (IEE) both present technical research papers.

Semiconductor manufacturing requires ultra-clean environments and complex interactions of chemical, physical, electrical and mechanical processes. The problems of manufacturing complex microelectronic components are addressed by the quarterly journal *IEEE Transactions on Semiconductor Manufacturing*.

Rapid publication of up-to-date information is provided by two journals. *Electronics Letters* (IEE) is published fortnightly in the UK. Short, technical research papers, preceded by abstracts, report on recent experiments and developments. A similar format is adopted by the monthly *IEEE Electron Device Letters*, published in the USA.

Microprocessors and Microsystems (Butterworths), presents technical papers from both academic and industrial contributors on the design, development, evaluation and application of microprocessor-based systems. The coverage is chip-level to system-level architecture design. Pan-European coverage is offered by *Microprocessing and Microprogramming (the Euromicro Journal)* (Elsevier).

Secondary sources

The monthly *Electronics and Communications Abstracts* (Multi-Science Publishing Co.) includes abstracts of major periodical literature, conference proceedings, unpublished reports and book notices. There is a section on semiconductor materials, devices and phenomena.

Directories and textbooks

A good, detailed overview of the field is provided by *Semiconductor Memories* (John Wiley), by B. Prince and G. Due-Gundersen. This book examines the history of memory development, the technical processes involved in producing semiconductor memories, the technology of RAMs and ROMs, and the development of C-MOS. This is a thorough analysis and includes questions of reliability and packaging. Each chapter ends with a bibliography.

The Handbook of Semiconductor and Bubble Memories (Prentice-Hall) by W. A. Treibel and A. E. Chu, provides a good introduction to memory devices and discusses their architecture, operation and applications. It is intended as a handbook for practising technicians and engineers and is also of use as a reference book for computer-science specialists, programmers and hobbyists. Each chapter ends with a series of suggested 'assignments', so that the handbook can also be used as a textbook for students.

A detailed study of C-MOS is provided by the *Users' Guidebook to Digital C-MOS Integrated Circuits* (McGraw-Hill) by E. R. Hnatek. This is a technical guide to how C-MOS works and what it is used for. There is a detailed chapter on semiconductor memories.

Textbooks which cover computer systems in general also offer sections on semiconductor storage. *The Principles of Computer Hardware* by A. Clements and the *Microcomputer Handbook* edited by J. A. McCrindle both include chapters on semiconductor memory devices.

Trade literature

As with other storage media, manufacturers' journals, such as the *Hitachi Review* and *Philips Technical Review* provide useful reviews of the technology. New product information can be found in the trade press. These magazines carry advertizing and offer readers' enquiry services. The US magazines *Electronics* and *Electronics Design*, both from the same publisher, include computer storage and semiconductor memories in their coverage. *Electronic System Design Magazine* is a systems design publication serving computer and systems manufacturers, systems integrators, components and peripheral manufacturers, and commercial users. *Computer Design*, with the same name and from the same publisher as the newsletter, is a twice-monthly trade magazine covering system design, development and integration, with coverage of various types of semiconductor memory device.

Conferences

The Electronic Components Conference (ECC) and the IEEE International Electron Devices Meeting are both long-standing conferences in this field. Japan's International Conference on Solid State Devices and Materials is now also an international event, with English as the official language. Also of interest is the American Chemical Society's International Symposium on Polymers in Information Storage Technology.

CHAPTER SIX

Transmission of information

J. STROUD

Introduction

The theme of this chapter is transmission of information. Many attempts have been made to define information so it is not necessary to repeat the process here. However, it is useful to consider what we mean by 'transmission'. Dictionary definitions include *'passing on* [a message]', *'communicating'* and *'being a medium for'*. The last is perhaps the most useful in the context of this chapter, as it concentrates largely on the media used to communicate information. This also fits in with a description used by Robert Cole in his book *Computer Communications*—'to transfer information three components are needed: a sender, a receiver and a suitable medium'.

Recent developments in data and telecommunications have provided new ways of transmitting information over both short and long distances. This chapter examines some of the sources of information available, which help to define the jargon, so much a feature of the subject area.

The chapter is divided into a number of sections devoted to different methods of transmitting information. Whilst the topics are discussed in separate sections there are inevitably areas of overlap. This introductory section briefly describes the relationship of the topics covered.

Perhaps the most frequently heard term related to the transmission of information is 'network'. Whilst this term can be used to describe groups of people and many other types of network, in this context it is used to refer to networks of computers and related devices. Computer installations began as centralized systems with no real power for the end user, then the personal computer enabled users to become independent. However, it was not long before independence became isolation and the desire to become part of a network emerged. Whilst this might seem to be going back to the earlier centralized systems, more of the devices in today's networks have their own processing power and so are no longer dependent on the 'main' computer.

In this chapter we consider both local area networks (LANs) and wide area networks (WANs). Whilst developments in technology make it more difficult to distinguish between what is local and what is wide area, for the purposes of this work a local area network is taken to be within one building or site whilst a wide area network might be across a city, a country or the world.

An increasingly important building block of both local and wide area networks is the use of fibre optic cable. Fibre optic cable provides a means of transferring information at very high speeds in much less space than conventional cable and is therefore likely to make a very great impact on future telecommunication networks.

Another example of the technology available for transmission of information is direct broadcasting by satellite. Satellites have been in use for some time for weather forecasting and other applications and now the ability to direct information such as television pictures into people's homes is being developed. Whilst many predicted that computers would bring about the paperless office, if anything the amount of paper has grown. A prime example of the continuing need for written confirmation of information is facsimile transmission. More commonly known as fax, this technology enables a document to be fed into a machine in one place, sent down a telephone line and reproduced at the destination in a matter of seconds, including diagrams and other images.

The key to being able to transmit information is the need for both parties to be able to understand each other. In the world of computing and telecommunications this is not as easy as it sounds and consequently a great deal of work has gone into developing international standards. Much of this work has been focused on Open Systems Interconnection (OSI), a seven-layer reference model, which attempts to identify the stages involved in passing information from one computer system to another. This is described in more detail later in this chapter.

One of the OSI standards already agreed advocates the use of packet switching techniques. Rather than each device sending whole messages in turn, thus causing delays if a message is long, the data is split into packets and mixed with data packets from other devices, thus reducing the number of lines required and enabling the data to travel at speeds greater than the originating device is capable of. Packet switching is often referred to as X.25, which is the number of the standard agreed by the CCITT (International Telegraph and Telephone Consultative Committee) and has now been adopted by the International Standards Organization (ISO) as one of the OSI group of standards.

Whilst computers and telecommunications have grown up as separate areas, developments in technology have led to an increasing overlap between them. One example of this convergence is ISDN (Integrated Services Digital Network). Gradually public telecommunications networks are becoming digital (able to cater for data as well as voice) and this brings with it the possibility not only of greatly improved telephone communication but also of high-speed data and other services over the same network. ISDN is the phrase commonly used to describe these developments.

The final kind of networks considered in this chapter are information network systems also known as Value Added Networks or Electronic Data Interchange (EDI). A number of companies are making their computer networks available to transmit and process information for others. One of the earliest examples of this was the electronic transmission of orders and invoices between car manufacturers and component suppliers.

Most of the terms necessary for an understanding of the areas covered by this chapter are defined in the relevant section as they come up. However, it is perhaps helpful to define two terms, which are vital for an appreciation of data and telecommunications, at this stage. In its most basic form, information is a series of signals which travel along the communications channel. These signals can be either analogue or digital. Analogue signals are continuous in nature, such as speech. Digital signals, on the other hand are discrete, having only a limited set of values, such as ON and OFF. Computers work by this means. Until recently the public telephone network was entirely an analogue system and therefore, for computer traffic to travel on the network, the digital signals had to be converted into analogue ones by means of a modem. The gradual conversion of telecommunications networks into digital environments provides much greater flexibility for information transmission and the many new opportunities, which form the basis of this chapter. For a general appreciation of the field of information technology and communications in particular, Pitman have published a very good series of introductory guides, for example, the *Business Guide to Communications Systems*, which covers most of the topics included in this chapter and many others in a very readable way.

General sources of information

State-of-the-art reports and newsletters

An excellent starting point for anyone wanting to get an appreciation of the state-of-the-art of transmission of information in language easy to understand is *Telecommunications for Information Management and Transfer*, edited by Mel Collier. It is the proceedings of the first international conference on the subject held at Leicester Polytechnic in April, 1987. The papers include reviews and updates of local and wide area networks, satellite communications and facsimile transmission, as well as many other aspects of telecommunications.

For those who wish to explore the subject more deeply, *Networks for the 1990s* is an interesting review of networking, covering most of the same technologies as this chapter, including ISDN and the progress being made in various countries, Open Systems Interconnection (OSI) and Value-Added Networks.

In a different format are the *Library and Information Briefings*. Published by the British Library, in association with the Library and Information Technology Centre on a variety of subjects, the briefings include analysis of current developments and reading lists. Briefings available so far include OSI and Value-added Networks.

Newsletters seem to appear every day in this field, varying from freesheets issued by suppliers to very expensive specialist newsletters. Amongst those of general relevance are *Advanced Information Report*, which readers may recognize more readily as *CTI (Communication Technology Impact)*. The first issue under the new title includes an article on the state of play in European Telecommunications. *Comms File* is a relative newcomer on the scene and provides useful, down-to-earth advice on achieving success in communications. Also worth a mention in this section are the occasional items on transmission of information in daily newspapers. Interesting articles can often be found in the computing pages of *The Times* and *The Guardian*, and the *Financial Times* publishes special supplements in this area from time to time.

Journals

As with newsletters, journals also proliferate. Amongst those circulated free to those working in communications are *Network*, which includes useful articles on how organizations are putting networks into practice and *Communicate*, which caters more for voice communications.

Amongst the subscription journals worth investigating is *British Telecom World*, formerly known as the *British Telecom Journal*. The last issue under the old title (June 1988) was a 'network special', with the emphasis on optical fibres. (*British Telecom World* is now circulated free of charge to certain people and is more general in nature. However, it is a useful indicator of current trends.) *Telecommunications* covers communications world-wide and is a mixture of short news items and longer articles and *Data Communications* (McGraw-Hill) is a magazine of information networks and communications technology, which has a U.S. bias.

Apart from the general purpose journals, another useful source of information are the professional journals such as *Accountancy*, which occasionally include articles on the relevance of various technologies to the particular profession.

Secondary sources

The major organization involved in providing secondary sources is Inspec. The INSPEC database, available from most of the major database hosts such as Dialog and Data-Star, includes the contents of *Computer and Control Abstracts*, *Electrical and Electronics Abstracts* and *IT Focus*. *IT Focus* contains abstracts of articles concerning information technology and is also available in printed form. Another electronic source of information is COMPUTER DATABASE, which includes the telecommunications area and is also available from the major database providers. *Computing Journal Abstracts* (NCC), a monthly, is a useful printed source of information. These secondary sources are applicable to all of the topics covered in this chapter.

Directories and textbooks

Amongst the directories available, one of the most useful is *The Communications Users' Year Book*, which lists the major suppliers of equipment and services by subject. There are also introductory articles describing the latest trends in the particular subject area. Another valuable source is *The Datacomms Book*, which provides a similar function in listing communications equipment and services but also includes communications sites (actual users). There is a large number of textbooks covering transmission of information including *A Practical Guide to Computer Communications and Networking* and *Computer Networks—Protocols, Standards and Interfaces*, which both cover most of the topics in this chapter.

Trade literature

A number of the companies providing equipment and services realize the complexities of the technology and publish booklets explaining the jargon. These vary in quality. One worth a mention is the *CASE Pocket Book of Computer Communications*. Suppliers also produce newsletters and journals, of these, *Telcom Report*, published by Siemens is worth a look.

Organizations

There is a large number of organizations concerned with information technology in one aspect or another. Amongst the major ones specializing in transmission of information are the Telecommunications Managers Association (TMA), originally specializing in voice communication but now broadening its scope as the impact of ISDN, fibre-optics, etc. develops. Apart from publications and courses, there is an annual conference and exhibition. The Institution of Electrical Engineers runs a variety of events related to methods of transmission of information. As might be anticipated, some concentrate on the theory rather than the application of the technology but others are more practically based. The Institute of Information Scientists is now placing more emphasis on using the various technologies available to transmit information to users and run occasional courses and seminars to bring members up to date. The Institute also publishes a newsletter jointly with Aslib, on information technology, called *IT Link*.

In the USA, perhaps the most important organization in this area is the IEEE (Institute of Electrical and Electronics Engineers), which has a number of subgroups all of which have regular meetings and publish journals and other material.

On an international level, there is the International Telecommunication Union (ITU), an agency of the United Nations. It has a number of sub-sections including the CCITT (International Telegraph and Telephone Consultative Committee), which is responsible for many data and telecommunications standards.

LANs and WANs

As more computers are installed there is an increasing desire and need for them to be able to communicate with each other, the result being computer networks. Whilst the boundaries are increasingly blurred, there are basically two broad categories of computer network—local area networks (LANs) and wide area networks (WANs).

As explained earlier in this chapter, the usual definition of a local area network is that it is within one building or site and owned by one organization. There are a variety of stimuli for local area networks. At its simplest, PC users may want to share printing facilities. Another common desire is to rationalize computer cabling, with the added bonus that the devices on the network can share resources and information. There are three popular LAN topologies: star; ring; and bus. Star configurations tend not to be favoured as all the devices are dependent on the centre. Bus networks link devices in a straight line. The most popular bus network is Ethernet, originally developed by DEC, Intel and Xerox but now accepted as an international standard. As its name suggests, the devices in a ring network are connected together in a ring. IBM's Token Ring network follows this principle, although it is not strictly a physical ring.

Apart from the shape of the network, the access method which controls the way data travels around the network is also important. There are two major access methods. The first is known as Carrier Sense Multiple Access with Collision Detection or CSMA/CD. In simple terms each device listens for traffic on the network before transmitting. If no one else is transmitting it will send its message otherwise it will wait a random interval and try again. If two devices attempt to transmit at the same time this will be detected and both will back-off for a random length of time and then re-transmit. The random nature of this method means that it is not possible to guarantee when a station will be able to transmit. The second major access method is token passing. In this case a token travels around the network stopping at each station in turn. A device may only transmit when in possession of the token. Ethernet networks use CSMA/CD whilst IBM's Token Ring uses token passing.

LANs are often considered in two groups—smaller, personal computer networks such as those based on Novell's Netware and larger general purpose networks, which link mainframe, mini- and microcomputers, such as Digital's Decnet. Both large and small LANs can have either Ethernet or Token Ring topologies. To obtain more details of the types of local area network available and how they work *Local Area Networks: Issues, Products and Developments*, by Cheong and Hirschheim and *Local Area Networks* by Kirk Gee are good introductions.

Whilst local area networks allow devices in the same building to communicate, wide area networks can be national or international. In this case private circuits (sometimes known as 'leased lines') are rented from a supplier such as British Telecom or Mercury, which provide links between computers in different towns and cities. Until recently these networks have been predominantly analogue (intended to cater for voice communication) requiring the use of modems to convert signals into a suitable form. Digital links are now available, which can carry voice, data and video traffic at higher speeds. The availability of high-speed circuits such as Megastream and sophisticated multiplexors (which can divide the circuit into a number of channels) have enabled a number of private networks to be developed which carry both voice and data communications.

The variety of computer systems available has led to a mass of communications protocols as each supplier has developed their own methods of sending data between devices on wide area networks.

Examples of these include IBM's Synchronous Data Link Control (SDLC) and ICL's CO3 protocols. The existence of these different protocols inevitably causes problems when equipment from two or more different suppliers needs to exchange information. Protocol converters are available to translate between the most popular protocols. However, these are often difficult to use, requiring users to use combinations of keystrokes to represent instructions to the other computer. This situation is now beginning to improve with the development of open systems. This subject is covered later in this chapter. *The Handbook of Data Communications* (NCC) is a good starting point for those wanting to gain an understanding of the basic principles of telecommunications and the different protocols involved.

State-of-the-art reviews and newsletters

A useful starting point for determining the state-of-the-art of local area networks is the *LAN Jungle Book—a Survey of LANs* written by W. Scott Currie of Edinburgh University Computing Service. Apart from this, a number of commercial companies produce surveys of LAN use. *User Ratings of Local Area Networks*, part of a report on PC communications by Datapro provides some interesting insights into recent trends in the use of LANs.

In the field of librarianship and information management there are two reports worthy of attention. The first, by Mel Collier (*Local Area Networks: the Implications for Library and Information Research*) defines LANs and suggests how they might be applied in libraries. The second, *Applications of Local Area Networks for Information Management: a Practical Evaluation*, by Copeland, Flood and Haynes describes a research project funded by the British Library Research and Development Department. The practical implications of running a LAN are described, as well as comment on the likely impact on information management within organizations. Whilst the technology referred to in these reports is now somewhat out of date, the issues raised remain valid.

In the field of wide area networks, one of the best state of the art reviews is *Corporate Communications Networks* by Lane of the NCC.

There are a variety of newsletters available. Most of those concerning LANs tend to originate from the USA such as *The Localnetter* and *Local Network Systems Report*. The former tends to be of a technical nature, whilst the latter is more general in its approach. *Netlink* (Aslib) is a UK-based publication, originally intended to cover LANs only but is now concerned with all aspects of networking, specifically its application in the field of information management.

Journals

Perhaps, surprisingly, the most valuable journals dealing with LANs and WANs are those circulated free to those working in the communications field, such as *Network* and *Communicate* already referred to in the general section of this chapter. Another useful one is *Communications*. For those interested in PC networks, probably the best sources of information are the personal computer journals, which often review LAN products. Examples include: *Personal Computer World*; *Practical Computing*; and *PC Magazine*.

Directories and textbooks

Perhaps because it is a more self-contained area, there seem to be more directories of LANs than WANs. Amongst these, a particularly useful one is *Local Area Networks: a European Directory of Suppliers and Systems*. This lists manufacturers and products, including technical data. *The Local Area Networking Directory: Hardware, Software, Systems, Services and Suppliers* does a similar job for the USA. One useful feature of this directory is the inclusion of a section on LAN standards groups. The Pitman series of textbooks on information technology has already been mentioned; another publisher with a similar series is Blackwell Scientific. One of the books in this series is *Practical Data Communications: Modems, Networks, Protocols* which covers both local and wide area networks.

There is a large number of textbooks specifically on LANs. Three have been selected as good starting points. *The Data Ring Main* by Flint is recognized as a valuable introduction to the subject, and as well as describing the technology, the author also discusses the implications of LANs. For those needing a book which will give practical guidance, *Choosing a Local Area Network* by Gandy is a useful place to start. This book includes case studies of LAN installations and advice on preparing specification and tender documents. Meanwhile for those interested in building their own LANs from scratch, *Introduction to Local Area Networks with Microcomputer Experiments* by Reiss is a fascinating description of various laboratory experiments demonstrating some of the characteristics of LANs. Potential readers should be warned that some knowledge of computer programming is necessary to get the best out of this work.

Amongst the textbooks concerned with wide area networking is Ron Bell's *Private Telecommunications Networks: Design and Implementation for Business*. As the author is a prominent member of the Telecommunications Managers Association, this book primarily deals with voice networks but there are more general sections relevant to data transmission. With the advent of ISDN, the nature of wide area networks is likely to change dramatically, some even ceasing to exist. For an appreciation of the impact of digital communications on wide area networking, Richardson's *Exploiting Digital Communication* is a good introduction.

Trade literature

Networking is one area where suppliers catalogues tend to be more informative than usual. Nearly all catalogues of LAN products include descriptive articles as well as product listings. *The Networks Guide* supplied by Digital is a particularly good example. Also useful, is Data Translation's catalogue, *The Definitive Guide to Networking*. Rather than catalogues, IBM produce small booklets describing their products, including one on the *IBM Cabling System and Token Ring Network*. Another useful service which IBM provides its larger customers is access to its product information databases, known as DIALIBM. It is not the most user friendly system but can be more informative than ringing round a variety of sales representatives.

Conferences

The most important UK conference concerning networking is Blenheim Online's Networks, which is usually held in June of each year. An exhibition runs alongside the conference, at which all of the major suppliers are usually represented. Its U.S. counterpart is LocalNet.

Organizations

Whilst there is a number of professional associations concerned with computer networks, perhaps the most valuable are the user groups, which cater for users of specific products. These include the Net/One user group and the Novell Netware User Group. The IBM PC User Group also has an active LAN Special Interest Group. All of these provide an invaluable forum for exchange of ideas, as do the more informal groups set up by suppliers such as BICC's Information Exchange meetings and IBM's Networking Club.

Optical fibre technology

The use of optical fibre technology for information transmission is a relatively recent trend. Whereas conventional cabling systems use electrical signals to convey information, fibre optic cable uses light. Electrical signals are converted into laser pulses. These light pulses can then travel along optical fibres (made of glass). They are then converted back into electrical signals at the other end. Optical fibres are usually around 0.1 mm diameter and so are much smaller than conventional cable. Fibre optic cables have a much greater bandwidth than other cables and can therefore send much larger amounts of information at very high speeds. In the UK, British Telecom are replacing much of their network with optical fibres, particularly to large cities. Apart from high speed, there are other advantages in the use of optical fibres. They are much less prone to electrical interference and cannot be tapped into readily.

One very interesting application of optical-fibre technology is at the Charing Cross and Westminster Medical School. Optical fibres are being used as the backbone for an interactive cable television system linking six university hospitals. This is reported on in *Telecommunications for Information Management and Transfer* referred to in the general section of this chapter.

Journals

Journals specializing in optical fibre technology tend to concentrate on the technology rather than its application. Amongst these are the *Journal of Optical Communications and Fiber and Integrated Optics*.

Directories and textbooks

One of the best textbooks on optical fibre technology which describes it at an introductory level is *Understanding Fibre Optics* by Hecht; similarly readable though a little older is *Fiber Optics* by Lacy. On a slightly more technical level is *Optical Fiber Transmission Systems* by Geckler.

Conferences

Regular conferences specifically concerned with fibre optics tend to be held in the USA and include the International Fiber Optic Communications and Local Area Networks Conference and Exhibition and the International Symposium on Fiber Science and Technology. There is however, an annual European Conference on Optical Communication organized by Verband Deutscher Elektrotechniker.

Organizations

Again we must look to the USA for organizations working with fibre optics, such as the Society of Fiber Science and Technology and the Optical Society of America. In the UK, probably the organization with the most expertise in optical fibre technology is the IEE.

Direct broadcasting by satellite

The concept of satellite communication was first thought of about 40 years ago. Initially, very large receiving dishes were required to receive signals from satellites and it was not possible to restrict the area of earth able to receive the transmission. There is now a generation of satellites which are more powerful and have special directive antennae. It is therefore possible to receive signals with a much smaller dish and to restrict the area in which signals can be picked up. This type of satellite is ideal for broadcast television. After a slow start, satellite television is beginning to take off and there is the promise (or threat?) of access to hundreds of different channels catering for every taste.

Probably the best place to start in understanding direct broadcasting by satellite is *The Beginners' Guide to Satellite Television* (Penguin).

State-of-the-art reviews and newsletters

For a regular state-of-the-art review of satellite broadcasting, a good place to start is with the proceedings of the satellite communications and broadcasting conferences, for example Satellite Communications and Broadcasting '89.

Journals

One of the most useful journals in this area is *Space Communications and Broadcasting* (North-Holland), which concentrates on the application of the technology, whereas the *International Journal of Satellite Communications* is more technical in its approach.

Directories and textbooks

Along with the Penguin guide mentioned earlier, *Satellite Television: a Layman's Guide*, is a good basic introduction and includes a discussion of the progress being made in other countries such as the USA and Canada. For more technical detail on planning a satellite broadcasting service, *Satellite Broadcasting Systems: Planning and Design* by Slater and Trinogga is a valuable source. If however, you are more interested in satellite communications generally, then the best starting point is Bleazard's *Introducing Satellite Communications*.

Conferences

Blenheim Online organize two annual conferences in Europe on Satellite Communications and Satellite Broadcasting. The one on broadcasting is usually held in June and the one on communications in December.

Organizations

The major organization concerned with satellites is the International Telecommunications Satellite Organization (INTELSAT). In the UK, the Department of Trade and Industry is responsible for the granting of licences to broadcast by satellite.

Facsimile transmission

Whilst the basic idea of facsimile transmission has been around for over 100 years it is only in the last 20 years that standards have been available for facsimile machines. The CCITT is the body responsible for these standards. The latest standard is known as

Group IV. As Group IV fax is intended for use with high-speed digital networks, there are few of these machines in use at present. Most conform to the earlier standards of Group II and III (which work with analogue communications).

Facsimile transmission has become a major means of communication in business, as the price of fax machines has come down and the quality improved. The British Library has been particularly active in researching the applications of fax. The Document Supply Centre has carried out extensive experiments with Group III and IV fax as a more effective means of distributing documents to customers.

Apart from fax machines themselves, there is also a trend to use PCs for facsimile transmission. Scanners and laser printers are needed, which makes the cost prohibitive unless these are already owned. This is an area which is likely to develop in the future.

State-of-the-art reviews and newsletters

As previously explained, one of the organizations most involved with facsimile transmission is the British Library. Part of the work funded by them is described in a report entitled *Facsimile in Libraries Project* by Lucy Tedd. Fax is becoming an increasingly important tool in local government and is the subject of a report by LAMSAC (the body which used to advise local authorities on information technology), *Facsimile Transmission in Local Authorities*. Apart from these specialist reports, the best sources of information describing the latest developments is *What to Buy for Business*, which takes fax as one of its regular themes.

Journals

Coverage of fax in journals tends to be in the more general communications journals such as *Communicate*, which occasionally devotes a special issue to fax. The increasing trend for turning PCs into fax machines by inserting extra cards, means that another useful source of information on developments in facsimile transmission is the PC magazines.

Directories and textbooks

Most of the directories available tend to be listings of fax numbers and these include *The Fax Book* (British Telecom), *The Official Facsimile Users' Directory* and *FAX/Net Electronic Mail Source Directory*.

Amongst the textbooks available are *Facts on Fax* by Robinson and *Text Communications—the Choices* (NCC).

Trade literature

One of the major producers of fax machines is NEC, who regularly publish a short newsletter describing their products, called *Faxtalk*.

Conferences

There is an annual conference called Eurofax run by the Institute for Graphics Communication of Amsterdam. There is also a What Fax exhibition held in London.

Open systems interconnection (OSI)

As has previously been explained, most computer suppliers have tended to develop their own network architectures and protocols, leading to problems when there is a requirement for two different types of equipment to communicate. This potential problem was perceived in the late 1970s and the concept of Open Systems Interconnection was born. Partly because of the lengthy process involved in developing international standards and some inevitable unwillingness on the part of suppliers, it took until 1988 for sufficient workable OSI standards to appear which could be put to practical use.

This is another reason why 1988 should be a significant stage in the development of OSI. As part of its aim for an open internal market in Europe in 1992, the European Commission issued a *Decision (87/95/EEC)* in 1987 forcing public sector bodies in EEC countries to procure information technology, which meets international and European standards from February 1988. There were some derogations, or escape clauses, but its effect was to make public sector bodies at least prepare a strategy for migrating towards OSI compliant systems and to spur suppliers to make available suitable equipment.

So what is OSI? At the heart of OSI is a seven-layer reference model (*ISO 7498–1984, BS 6568: Part 1: 1988*) which outlines the activities necessary for two computer systems to communicate fully. Other standards then fit into the various layers. The seven layers are:

7 Applications
6 Presentation
5 Session
4 Transport
3 Network

Transmission of information 111

  2 Data link
  1 Physical

For those not familiar with the function of the various layers, a brief description is given below.

PHYSICAL LAYER

This layer is concerned with standards specifying the requirements for a physical connection between devices including the size and shape of the plug and the necessary electrical signals, an example of this is the V.24 or RS232 standard.

DATA LINK LAYER

The data link layer allows for error and flow control between the two ends, for example the ISO 8802/2 standards for Logical Link Control.

NETWORK LAYER

The network layer is concerned with routing and addressing, for example in ISO 8208 for X.25 packet procedures.

TRANSPORT LAYER

The transport layer is the final one concerned with transporting data between open systems ensuring that it arrives in the form which can be made use of by the destination system.

SESSION LAYER

This layer is responsible for managing the exchange of data by applications and synchronizing dialogue between them.

PRESENTATION LAYER

As most applications require data to be in a particular format for manipulation it is the presentation layer's job to arrange this.

APPLICATIONS LAYER

The application layer is the one which performs the information processing such as file transfer and electronic mail. Standards in progress include X.400 and MOTIS for message handling and FTAM File Transfer and Access Management.

State-of-the-art reviews and newsletters

Since the EEC Decision concerning OSI compliance there has been, not surprisingly, great interest in how far suppliers have been progressing with OSI. There have recently been several studies reviewing which suppliers are doing what. The first is by the CCTA (Central Computing and Telecommunications Agency), a body which advises central government on information technology, *Open Systems Interconnection—CCTA's Expectations and Suppliers' Implementations*. A second study was undertaken by the NCC (National Computing Centre) and is rather less accessible as it forms part of a much larger volume, their *OSI Programme for Local Government*. The Department of Trade and Industry has been heavily involved in promoting OSI. One of its publications is *Open Systems: the Technical Case for Open Systems Interconnection*, which is a guide to companies on how best to respond to open systems.

Another useful review is the final report of an *OSI Opportunity Study* carried out by EOSYS for four county councils. For those wanting an overall review of the subject, then perhaps the best place to start is the issue of *Library and Information Briefings* (LITC) on OSI.

The newsletters available specifically on OSI tend to be the expensive kind such as the *Open Systems Newsletter* and *SI Report*. The first is published by Technology Appraisals and includes very readable accounts of the main trends in OSI. The second is published by Online Publications and does basically the same job.

Journals

Journal coverage of OSI tends to form part of those concerned with communications generally, which have already been mentioned elsewhere. *Computers and Standards* (Butterworths) also includes articles on OSI.

Directories and textbooks

There is a number of services available which provide information on OSI standards. The British Standards Institute has a publicly available database known as STANDARDLINE. Meanwhile Omnicom publishes an index of OSI standards in printed form. Omnicom also provides a document service for people requesting copies of specific standards.

A rather different type of publication is the CCTA's *Government OSI Profile* or GOSIP (pronounced Gossip). GOSIP is a listing of current OSI standards with guidance on their use in preparing requests for tender.

For a basic understanding of the concepts of OSI a useful start is *What is OSI?* by Pye of the NCC. A more detailed description of how the OSI seven-layer model works is given in *OSI Explained*, one of the Ellis Horwood Series on *Computer Communications and Networking*. The book is quite theoretical and still leaves some explaining to be done but does provide valuable guidance. Quotations from A. A. Milne help to lighten the subject. Once in a position to work towards open systems, two further textbooks provide valuable guidance—*Building an Open System* and *Migrating to OSI*.

Conferences

Blenheim Online, as one of the major conference organizers on information technology, runs a regular conference on Open Systems usually in March/April in London. This is a good opportunity to catch up on the latest developments. The proceedings are published to coincide with the conference.

Organizations

The major organization involved in OSI standards is the International Organization for Standardization (IOS), which is formed from a number of national standards bodies including the British Standards Institution. The other international body involved in developing OSI standards is the CCITT (International Telegraph and Telephone Consultative Committee).

Apart from the CCITT, the Institute of Electrical and Electronic Engineers (IEEE) is also responsible for standards which have been adopted by ISO as part of the OSI group, such as Ethernet and Token Ring. There is a large number of organizations which have sprung up concerned with OSI, not least groupings of suppliers, for example the Standards Promotions and Applications Group (SPAG), which represents European Suppliers and COS (Cooperation for Open Systems), which represents suppliers worldwide. There are also other official bodies concerned with the implementation of OSI standards such as the CCTA, the Department of Trade and Industry, and EUROSINET, which encourages demonstrations of interworking between suppliers and the NCC.

Packet switching technology

Packet switching is one of the most efficient methods of transferring data around large computer networks. The principle behind it is that data are put into packets so that several messages can be transmitted on one circuit thus reducing the delay seen by the users. A necessary part of the packet is identification giving the destination of the data. The X.25 protocol is the international standard for packet switching. X.25 works at three levels of the ISO seven-layer model. At the physical layer, the standard connection should conform to the X.21 recommendation. This is a digital standard so the X.21bis standard can be used as an intermediate for existing analogue interfaces.

At the datalink layer the Higher Data Link Control Protocol (HDLC) is used. This performs three functions—establishing the link with the same level at the remote site, transferring packets securely and disconnecting the link without loss of information. At the network layer the same functions are performed but between two host computers.

The X.25 protocol is used by most of the national public data networks including British Telecom in the form of PSS (Packet Switchstream). The best introduction to PSS is *First Steps in Packet Switching*, which is given away free by British Telecom. Another important X.25 network is JANET, the Joint Academic Network, which links British universities. University libraries find it particularly valuable for accessing other information sources.

State-of-the-art reviews and newsletters

Reviews and periodicals, which deal specifically with packet switching technology are not easy to find. However, there is a newsletter for users of the JANET network called *Network News* produced by the Joint Network Team.

Journals

Computer Networks and ISDN Systems is an international journal on telecommunications and networking, which includes coverage of packet switching technology.

Directories and textbooks

Textbooks available covering packet switching technology can be divided into two groups. The first consists of general works on networking, which include chapters on packet switching and the second, books specifically on the technology. A good example of the first is *A Practical Guide to Computer Communications and Networking* by Deasington. The same author is also responsible for a useful textbook specifically on the X.25 protocol, *X.25 Explained: Protocols for Packet Switching Networks*. For guidance on PSS and its use in practice then Lane's *Packet Switchstream—a User's Guide* is a valuable tool.

Trade literature

British Telecom provides a variety of information describing their products. For those who have grasped the content of *First Steps in Packet Switching*, BT also publishes a *Technical Guide to Packet Switchstream*.

Organizations

The major organization concerned with packet switching is the CCITT, which regulates the X.25 standard. User views can be channelled through users groups such as the JANET User Group.

ISDN

The Integrated Services Digital Network (ISDN) is the future as far as public telephone networks are concerned. The basic idea is that voice, data, video and other services will be able to travel along the same channels without the need for special conversion equipment such as modems. The international standards for ISDN are still being developed.

There are expected to be two categories of ISDN. The first is known as Single-line ISDN and is expected to provide subscribers with two bidirectional channels operating at 64Kbps (usually known as 'B' channels) and one 16Kbps channel for control purposes (known as the 'D' channel). This is often referred to as 2B+D. The second form of ISDN is Multi-line and provides 30 'B' channels and a 64Kbps 'D' channel. This can be achieved by using a 2 Mbps link similar to that used in British Telecom's Megastream Services.

Rather than wait for the international standards to be finalized, British Telecom developed its own services known as IDA (Integrated Digital Access). Currently only available in selected areas, such as major cities, this service is gradually being extended to the whole country. Examples of the kind of uses being made of the IDA services include advertizing agencies transmitting colour images of artwork to major clients, the British Library transferring documents via group IV facsimile and what has been called 'desktop conferencing' whereby data can be transferred between two computers whilst the users speak over the telephone. British Telecom has announced that the first phase of a new ISDN service is being launched during 1990. This conforms to the standards being produced by the European Telecommunications Standards Institute (ETSI).

State-of-the-art reviews and newsletters

A good, international state-of-the-art review of developments in ISDN is *Networks for the 1990s* published by Online Publications. It includes chapters on the progress being made with ISDN in a variety of countries. Slightly more specialized is *Integrated PBX Systems: an NCC State of the Art Report*, which looks at the relationships between ISDN, LANs and telephones systems. One useful feature of this report is case study material of companies who have already solved problems in this area.

ISDN Connection is an interesting newsletter for those familiar with the terminology of ISDN.

Journals

Like most aspects of communications, ISDN is regularly covered by journals like *Network* and *Communicate*. There is also an international journal more specifically concerned with developments in ISDN, *Computer Networks and ISDN Systems* (North-Holland).

Directories and textbooks

Amongst the textbooks available on ISDN, perhaps the best starting point is *The Integrated Services Digital Network from Concept to Application* (Pitman). The *Guide to ISDN* (NCC) by Lane is also useful.

Conferences

One of the most important annual conferences on ISDN is the International ISDN Conference organized by Blenheim Online. It is usually run parallel to the Networks Conference.

Organizations

The CCITT is the body responsible for ISDN standards. The standards will be implemented by the providers of telephone services such as British Telecom and the Deutsche Bundespost. Other organizations with an interest in the implementation of ISDN include the Telecommunications Managers Association, the Telecommunications Users Association and the Telecommunications Industry Association, which between them represent potential users and suppliers.

Information network systems

A number of large companies have developed communications infrastructures with spare capacity to enable them to carry information for other users. This facility has come to be known as VADS (Value-Added and Data Services). The term 'value-added' refers to services offered in addition to voice. A major portion of the VADS services available specialize in Electronic Data Interchange (EDI).

An example of this is Istel's EDICT service, which carries orders and invoices between those involved in the car industry. In 1986 the Department of Trade and Industry launched a project called Vanguard to promote the development of this kind of service in 10 different sectors including construction, educational supplies and wholesale food distribution. The major VADS suppliers (BT, IBM, INS, Istel and the Midland Bank) in the UK were heavily involved in the project from the beginning.

Standards are vitally important in this area to enable meaningful information transfer to take place. The Article Numbering Association has taken an active part in fostering the development of suitable standards, known as *Tradacoms* standards. Another important international standard is *EDIFACT* (Electronic Data Interchange for Administration, Commerce and Transport), which is concerned with the way data should be formatted to be meaningful between the trading partners.

Another area related to VADS is data broadcasting. As the name implies this refers to high-speed data broadcasting using conventional broadcasting media such as television and radio, although cable and satellite are also used. This is an offshoot of the teletext services such as Ceefax and Oracle. The Cable and Broadcasting Act 1984 enabled the BBC and IBA to launch commercial services known respectively as Datacast and Air Call. The process usually works by information providers supplying the data to the BBC or IBA so that it can be broadcast to subscribers alongside conventional TV signals. A decoder (like that used for teletext) is required to decode the information.

The availability of VADS is expected to increase over the coming years. However, it is interesting to consider whether the coming of ISDN will reduce the necessity for this kind of service.

State-of-the-art reviews and newsletters

A good introduction to developments in Value Added Network services is the issue of *Library and Information Briefings* on VANs. Meanwhile the best source of information on current developments in EDI is the *EDI Handbook*.

As the body responsible for licensing VADS providers, the Department of Trade and Industry has a major role in current awareness and has published a report of their Vanguard project, which includes a review of the present situation.

Journals

Apart from the general-purpose journals, which include articles on VADs from time to time, *Vanguard* is a bi-monthly journal, which specifically deals with VADs. Whilst bearing the name of the DTI project, it is an independent publication.

Directories and textbooks

For a good explanation of the acronyms in this area such as VADS, VANS and EDI and the various licences and standards, *What are VADs?* is a valuable starting point. This work does include some directory information but it is not as up to date as *The VANs Handbook*.

Conferences

The major annual conference in this area in the UK is called Electronic Data Interchange: the UK National Conference on Paperless Trade, and is sponsored by a number of the organizations with an interest in this topic, including the Article Number Association, The EDI Association (EDIA) and SITPRO (the Simpler Trade Procedures Board).

Organizations

Some of the organizations involved in this area have already been mentioned such as the Department of Trade and Industry and the Article Numbering Association. There is a number of organizations specifically concerned with EDI including the EDI Association and EDICON (EDI for the UK construction industry). Fans of *Star Wars* may also be interested in the United Nations Joint EDI Task Force known as JEDI. Users of the major VADS networks are represented by user groups, such as the Tradanet User Group.

References

Bell, R. *Private Telecommunications Networks*, Communications Educational Services Ltd, 1987.
Bleazard, *Introducing Satellite Communications*, NCC, 1985.

The CASE Pocketbook of Computer Communications.
Chang, C. and Hitchcock, D. (Editors), *The VAN Handbook*, Online International, 1987.
Cheong and Hirshheim, *Local Area Networks: Issues, Products and Developments*, John Wiley, 1983.
Chilton, P. and Bird, J. *Text Communication—the Choices*, NCC, 1988.
Collier, M. *Local Area Networks: the Implications for Library and Information Research*, BLRDD LIR Report No. 19, 1984.
Collier, M. (Editor) *Telecommunications for Information Management and Transfer: Proceedings of the First International Conference held at Leicester Polytechnic, April 1987*, Gower, 1988.
Collier, Y. (Editor) *Local Area Networks: a European Directory of Suppliers and Systems*, Online, 1985.
The Communications Users' Year Book, NCC.
Computer Networks and ISDN Systems, North-Holland.
Computer Networks—Protocols, Standards and Interfaces, Prentice-Hall, 1986.
Copeland, J., Flood, S. and Haynes, D. *Applications of Local Area Networks for Information Management: a Practical Evaluation*, BLRDD Research Report No. 5879, 1987.
County Council Consortium OSI Opportunity Study of Information Technology Facilities, Eosys, 1987.
Currie, W. S. *The LAN Jungle Book—a Survey of Local Area Networks*, Kinesis Computing Ltd, 1984.
The Datacomms Book, VNU Business Publications.
Datapro Report on PC Communications, Datapro, 1988.
Deasington, R. *A Practical Guide to Computer Communications and Networking*, Ellis-Horwood, 2nd edn, 1986.
Deasington, R. *X.25 Explained: Protocols for Packet Switching Networks*, Ellis Horwood, 1986.
The Definitive Guide to Networking, Data Translation.
DTI Vanguard: EDI and X.400 Study, HMSO, 1988.
Facsimile Transmission in Local Authorities, LAMSAC, 1986.
The Fax Book, British Telecom.
Fax/net Electronic Mail Source Directory, Pergamon Press, 1986.
First Steps in Packet Switching, British Telecom.
Flint, D. *The Data Ring Main*, John Wiley, 1983.
FOC/LAN 87 Proceedings of the 11th International Fiber Optic Communications and Local Area Networks Conference and Exposition, October, 1987, Information Gatekeepers Inc.
Gandy, M. *Choosing a Local Area Network*, NCC, 1987.
Gaskell, P. *Migrating to OSI*, NCC, 1987.
Geckler, S. *Optical Fiber Transmission Systems*, Arctech House Inc., 1987.

Gee, K. *Local Area Networks*, NCC, 1982.
Gifkins, M. and Hitchcock, D. *The EDI Handbook: Trading in the 1990s*, Blenheim Online, 1988.
GOSIP UK Government OSI Profile, CCTA Version 3.1, HMSO, 1990.
Green, D. *Business Guide to Communication Systems*, Pitman, 1987.
Handbook of Data Communications, NCC, 1982.
Hecht, J. *Understanding Fibre Optics*, Howard W. Sams and Co., 1987.
Henshall, J. and Shaw, S. *OSI Explained: End-to-end Computer Communication Standards*, Ellis Horwood Series in *Computer Communications and Networking*, Ellis Horwood, 1988.
IBM Cabling System, IBM Token Ring Network. A Reference Book to Select the Proper Components for your IBM Cabling System, IBM Token-Ring Network Installation, IBM.
Integrated PBX Systems: an NCC State of the Art Report, NCC, 1987.
ISDN Connection, Technology Appraisals.
Jennings, F. *Practical Data Communications: Modems, Networks, Protocols*, Blackwell Scientific Publications, 1986.
Lacy, E. A. *Fiber Optics*, Prentice-Hall, 1982.
Lane, J. E. *Corporate Communications Networks*, NCC, 1984.
Lane, J. E. *Integrated Services Digital Network (ISDN)*, NCC, 1987.
Lane, J. E. *Packet Switchstream: a Users' Guide*, NCC, 1987.
Library and Information Briefing VANS, British Library and Library Technology Centre, 1988.
The Local Area Networking Directory: Hardware, Software, Systems, Services and Suppliers, Networks Systems Press.
Local Networks Systems Report, Network Systems Press.
Macpherson, S. *What are VADs?*, NCC, 1987.
Maybury, R. *The Beginners' Guide to Satellite TV*, Penguin, 1987.
Networks and Communications Buyers' Guide, Digital Equipment Company.
The Official Facsimile Users' Directory, FDP Associates, 1986.
Open Systems Interconnection—CCTA's Expectations and Suppliers' Implementations, HMSO, 1986.
Pearson, P. *Satellite Television: a Layman's Guide*, Argus Books, 1987.
Pye, C. *What is OSI?*, NCC, 1988.
Reardon, R. (Editor), *Networks for the 1990s*, Online Publications, 1987.
Reiss, L. *Introduction to Local Area Networks with Microcomputer Experiments*, Prentice-Hall, 1987.

Richardson, A. *Exploiting Digital Communications*, NCC, 1988.
Robinson, *Facts on Fax*, S. Davis Publications, 1986.
Ronayne, J. *The Integrated Services Digital Network from Concept to Application*, Pitman, 1987.
Satellite Communications and Broadcasting 87, Online International, 1987.
Slater, J. N. and Trinogga, L. A. *Satellite Broadcasting, Systems, Planning and Design*, John Wiley and Ellis Horwood, 1985.
Slonim, J., Schobenbachm, A., Bauer, M., Macrae, L. J., Thomas, K. A. *Building an Open System*, Van Nostrand Reinhold, 1987.
Technical guide to Packet Switchstream, British Telecom.
Tedd, L. *Facsimile in Libraries Project*, BLRDD LIR 57.
Vanguard, Marathon Videotex Ltd.

CHAPTER SEVEN

Information Technology Applications

H. RAMSDEN

Introduction

The applications of information technology are many and the major ones are covered in this chapter. There are many sources, however, which cover a range of applications and some of these are listed below. One of the best books on this topic is Cawkell's *Handbook of Information Technology and Office Systems* (North-Holland, 1986). The *Annual Review of Library and Information Science* (Elsevier) is another source worth consulting. Journals which cover a variety of applications include *Information Media & Technology* and *Electronic Publishing Abstracts* (Pergamon) which is also available online as the EPUBS database, together with many library/information science orientated sources. In general, journals are the best source of general information and trade literature for all these applications, particularly the PC magazines such as *Practical Computing*, *PC User* and *Personal Computer World*.

Artificial intelligence

There have been various definitions of artificial intelligence (AI) and its different components, but perhaps one of the simplest is Minskie's definition that

> '*artificial intelligence is the science of making machines do things that would require intelligence if done by men*'.

The applications include natural language processing, speech synthesis and recognition, vision, robotics and expert systems.

A useful state-of-the-art review is Ennals' *Artificial Intelligence* (Pergamon, 1987). The *Annual Review of Information Science and Technology*, vol. 22 (Elsevier, 1987) also includes a paper on AI and information retrieval, which makes interesting reading. There are a number of both newsletters and journals in this field, whose emphasis varies. *Artificial Intelligence Business* is a fortnightly UK newsletter, while *A.I. Week* is a monthly US newsletter formerly known as *Applied Artificial Intelligence Reporter*. Of the more erudite journals, *Artificial Intelligence* has been published since the early 1970s and is the most authoritative technical journal on the subject. *Artificial Intelligence Review* and *Applied Artificial Intelligence* are both new journals aimed largely at professionals working in the field. A number of journals which address specific areas within the AI field include the *International Journal of Pattern Recognition and Artificial Intelligence*, the *International Journal for Artificial Intelligence in Engineering* and *Robotica*.

There are three major conferences on AI, the proceedings of which are also useful sources of information. The International Joint Conference on Artificial Intelligence has been held biennially since 1969 (odd years), while the European Conference on Artificial Intelligence is held biennially in even years. Alvey, now the Information Engineering Directorate, holds an annual conference and the American Association for Artificial Intelligence has held annual meetings since 1980. There have also been recent conferences and symposia on AI applications in manufacturing systems, medical imaging, economics and information retrieval.

Online sources in this field are not as plentiful as other sources of information. There are four which cover AI, of which several are also available as hardcopy sources. The Turing Institute produces the database ARTIFICIAL INTELLIGENCE and the hardcopy *Turing Institute Abstracts in Artificial Intelligence*. Other useful online databases include ARTIFICIAL INTELLIGENCE NETWORK and ARTIFICIAL INTELLIGENCE ONLINE. FUNDESCO is a Spanish database covering information science, including AI.

A number of specialist dictionaries and other guides exist in the AI field. These include the *Dictionary of Artificial Intelligence and Robotics* (John Wiley, 1986) by Rosenberg and the *Wiley Encyclopedia of Artificial Intelligence* (John Wiley, 1987) by Shapiro. The *Artificial Intelligence and Expert Systems Sourcebook* (Chapman and Hall, 1986) by Hunt is a glossary of terms. Organizations involved in AI are good contacts for information and Scotland is a strong force in AI research. One of the major institutions in this field, the Turing Institute based in Glasgow, carries out a full range of AI training and information dissemination to industry and Edinburgh is also represented, by the Artificial Intelligence

Applications Institute. In the USA, the American Association for Artificial Intelligence is important and the Association of Computing Machinery has the Special Interest Groups on Artificial Intelligence (SIGART).

Directories of AI people and companies include the *International Directory of Artificial Intelligence Companies* (Artificial Intelligence Software, 1987), and the *Sourcebook on Artificial Intelligence—Products and Vendors* (Graeme Publishing Corp.) which is largely devoted to the USA. Textbooks in this field abound, many of them recently written, and they vary in complexity from the beginner's guide to the highly technical. Examples of the former are *The Hitch-Hiker's Guide to Artificial Intelligence* (Chapman and Hall, 1985) by Forsyth and Naylor and *Artificial Intelligence: a Personal, Commonsense Journey* (Prentice-Hall, 1986) by Arnold and Bowie. Those directed at a specific audience include *Machine Intelligence and Related Topics: an Information Scientist's Weekend Book* (Gordon and Breach, 1982), by Michie and *A Management Guide to Artificial Intelligence* (Gower, 1986), by Maney and Reid. At the technical level, there are several series on artificial intelligence produced by various publishers, including Ellis Horwood and Addison-Wesley. Barr and Feigenbaum's *Handbook of Artificial Intelligence* (Addison-Wesley, 1986) in three volumes is the 'bible' of AI, while Rich's *Artificial Intelligence* (McGraw-Hill, 1983) is both coherent and thorough. *Artificial Intelligence: Principles and Applications* (Chapman and Hall, 1986), edited by Yazdani, describes both the applications of AI and the principles behind them, the contributors being active researchers in their particular fields.

Expert systems

Expert systems is a specific field within artificial intelligence and as such, many of the sources listed above will have details of, or information about, expert systems. Kemp in *Computer-based Knowledge Retrieval* (Aslib, 1988) defines an expert system as

> '*a device which allows the identification and retrieval and application of a particular answer or problem-solution among many which may be available by appearing to ask the appropriate questions of the users of the system; it also enables and simplifies the entry and validation of appropriate data*'.

Expert Systems: the International Journal of Knowledge Engineering is one of several journals specific to this area and is a combination of both learned articles and news about the industry. A more recently-established journal, *Knowledge-Based Systems*, contains refereed papers and aims to provide a forum for debate about the implications of knowledge-based techniques for interactive computer systems design. *Knowledge Engineering Review* is the journal of the Expert Systems Specialist Group of the British Computer Society, while *Expert Systems/AI in Business* explores how business can make use of new technologies. A monthly newsletter, *Expert Systems User*, covers all aspects of the expert systems and artificial intelligence market for users and potential users of these systems.

Expert systems feature at many of the conferences devoted to AI, but the British Computer Society (BCS) Expert Systems specialist group also holds an annual conference in December of each year, and regular meetings on specific topics. Bibliographic information about expert systems is largely contained in the AI online databases listed above, particularly the Turing Institute's ARTIFICIAL INTELLIGENCE, but information about the software may be contained in the variety of online databases on software, such as MENU. Bigger and Coupland compiled *Expert Systems: a Bibliography* (IEE, 1983) from the INSPEC database, and although now dated, this is a good starting point. Other specialist guides include the National Computing Centre's *Guidelines for Information Management*, no. 119 '*Expert System Guideline*' and no. 125 '*Getting Started in Expert Systems*'. The Turing Institute and Artificial Intelligence Applications Institute (AIAI) cover this area, and in addition the Knowledge-Based Systems Centre, a unit of the Polytechnic of the South Bank, specializes in technology transfer in knowledge-based systems. The BCS Expert Systems specialist group is active in publishing as well as holding meetings.

The main directory for this field is the *CRI Directory of Expert Systems* (Learned Information, 1986) which has abstracts and references to every expert system written up and published in English. It is thus not a fully comprehensive directory of all systems. Software shells for expert systems can be traced through a variety of annual directories, including the *Software Users' Year Book* (VNU Business Publications) and the *PC Year Book* (VNU Business Publications).

There are fewer textbooks in this area, but there is still quite a range. Introductory books include *Introductory Readings in Expert Systems* (Gordon and Breach, 1982), edited by Michie and *The Guide to Expert Systems* (Learned Information, 1985) by Goodall, the latter being a complete introduction to what the systems are, what they can do, and how to build them. More detailed introductions are provided by *Expert Systems: Principles and Case Studies* (Chapman and Hall, 1984) edited by Forsyth, which is aimed at computer users unfamiliar with the latest research and is an introductory handbook for readers interested in how the systems work, and *Expert Systems: Concepts and Examples* (NCC, 1984) by Alty and Coombs, which is an overview aimed at the computing professional or IT student and is neither academic nor confined to narrow research fields. Technical books include *Machine Learning: Applications in Expert Systems and Information Retrieval* (Ellis Horwood, 1986) by Forsyth and Rada, *Expert Systems Technology: a Guide* (Abacus Press, 1985) by Johnson and Keravnou and *Intelligent Information Systems: Progress and Prospects* (Ellis Horwood, 1986) edited by Davies. A recent report commissioned by the DTI, *Expert Systems in Britain*, is intended to encourage awareness of and debate about expert systems.

Database systems

The wide variety of database systems ranges from simple microcomputer-based systems to complex mainframe ones, but the basic principle behind them is that they store and manipulate data in some way. The type of system also varies, from general database management systems (DBMS) through information/text retrieval systems to the specialized applications such as spreadsheets and library systems, to name two. A good overview of the range and variety of systems is given in the introduction to Kimberley's *Text Retrieval: a Directory of Software* (Gower, 1987) where the differences and similarities are explained. Cawkell also covers microcomputer software in his *Handbook of Information Technology and Office Systems* (see Introduction).

Information about database systems can be divided into the theoretical and the practical, and the journals in this area reflect this. Journals such as *Database*, *The Electronic Library*, *Library Hi Tech*, *Library Micromation News*, *Program* and *Vine* have news and reviews of information/text retrieval and library systems, with some detail of the more general systems commercially available. In some cases, users write about systems developed in-house. A wider variety of systems can be found in microcomputer-orientated journals such as *PC User*, *Personal Computer World* and *Practical Computing*, while the more specific systems can be found in journals such as *Unix Systems*, devoted to one particular type of operating system. The theoretical aspects of the design and use of database systems is covered by journals such as *Information Processing & Management* and *Information Systems*. Newsletters which may be useful in keeping up to date with developments include *Computers and Libraries* recently relaunched as *C&L Applications* and *IT LINK* incorporating *Automation Notes*.

There is an increasing number of conferences and exhibitions devoted to the computer industry, of which many will have details and demonstrations of database systems. Information industry conferences such as: Computers in Libraries, the International Online Information Meeting (IOLIM), and the Institute of Information Scientists' Text Retrieval conference are all held annually and are useful sources of information. An annual exhibition of library and information systems is also held at Cimtech, based at the Hatfield Polytechnic.

A number of databases list software available for specific functions or types of hardware. These include BUSINESS SOFTWARE DATABASE, COMPUTER EXPRESS, DIRECT-NET, ENGINEERING & INDUSTRIAL SOFTWARE DIRECTORY, IR-SOFT, MENU—THE INTERNATIONAL SOFTWARE DATABASE and ONLINE MICROCOMPUTER SOFTWARE GUIDE AND DIRECTORY. Of the specialist guides and directories in this area, many list software and some are also available online. Kimberley's *Directory of Text Retrieval Software* (see above) covers all types and sizes of machines, while Dyer and Gunson's *A Directory of Library and Information Retrieval Software for Microcomputers* (Gower, 1988) is limited to micros and is also available online as the IR-SOFT database. In the specialist application market, Leeves' *Library Systems: a Buyers' Guide* (Gower, 1987) describes library automation systems in detail. Other organizations often have their own directories of specialist software. Software specific to particular operating systems is also covered, by the *Unix Systems 1988 Yearbook* (Eaglehead Publishing, 1988) and *The Unix Systems Products & Services Catalogue* (/usr/group/UK, 1987) and software for other systems such as PICK are covered by similar sources. Other sources of information include *The Software Users' Year Book* and *The PC Year Book* (VNU Business Publications, annual).

Organizations working in this field include Aslib, the Institute of Information Scientists, the Library and Information Technology Centre and more generally, the National Computing Centre and the Computing Services Association. The Office of the Data Protection Registrar is now also an important source of advice on the legality of storing and using personal information. These organizations and the many journals are also useful sources of trade literature.

The standard technical text on database systems is Date's *An Introduction to Database Systems: Vols I & II* (Addison-Wesley, 1983). Another is Ullman's *Principles of Database Systems* (Computer Science Press, 1980), which as the title suggests describes the principles behind these systems and how they work. Kemp's *Computer-based Knowledge Retrieval* (Aslib, 1988) is another very useful source. James' *Document Databases* (Van Nostrand

Reinhold, 1985), Laurie's *Databases: How to Manage Information on your Micro* (Chapman and Hall/Methuen, 1985) and Kruglinski's *Data Base Management Systems: a Guide to Microcomputer Software* (Osborne/McGraw-Hill, 1983) offer more practical advice on using such systems.

Electronic mail

Electronic mail is, as the name suggests, an electronic form of communication between terminals on a computer network. It can be interactive, but often is not, with messages being left in 'mailboxes', for users to read when they next log on. There are both public and private systems. E-mail, as it is sometimes known, is much further advanced in the USA than in the UK or Europe.

There are few newsletters or journals specifically dedicated to E-mail, but useful journals include the U.S. *EMMS—Electronic Mail and Micro Systems* newsletter and the more general *Communicate*, *Comms Monthly*, *Comms File* and *Advanced Information Report* (formerly *Communication Technology Impact*). *Practical Computing*, *PC User* and *Personal Computer World* are also of occasional interest, with details of services available to micro users.

Conferences are another area where there are few events devoted solely to E-mail, but it is often a topic included in networking, online, general computing and office automation conferences. Two of the online databases on the subject of electronic mail are simply concerned with the people using the systems. PEOPLE IN ELECTRONIC MAIL SYSTEMS contains about 5000 E-mail addresses of Europeans involved in IT research and management, while the US NATIONAL E-MAIL WHITE PAGES contains address information for over 20 000 E-mail users. Various NewsNet databases contain the full text of journals or newsletters covering this and other areas; these include DATA CHANNELS, PR HI-TECH ALERT and YANKEENET. UK E-mail services are also listed in the *Britline* directory (EDI, 1988).

Various yearbooks of the communications industry include sections on, or articles about, E-mail systems and services and very often give an overview of recent developments. Examples are *The DataComms Book* (VNU Business Publications, annual), the *Telecomms Users' Handbook* (Telecommunications Press, 1986), *The Communications Users' Year Book* (NCC, annual) and the more general *Computing Services Association Official Reference Book* (CSA, annual). The *NCC Guidelines for Computing Management* include two in these field: no. 103, *X.400—Electronic Mail Standards* and no. 108, *Using an Electronic Mailbox*.

There is a number of organizations involved in E-mail, including the various host systems and software suppliers. Telecom Gold is probably the best known in the UK, while the BCS Office Automation specialist group may also be a useful contact. Directories in this field include the various yearbooks listed above, several of which have details of suppliers and their equipment. General telecommunications directories may also be worth checking, for example the UK *Telecomms Equipment & Services Directory* (Telecommunications Press, 1986) and the U.S. *Telecommunications Systems & Services Directory* (Gale Research, 1985, and 1987 supplement).

There are few textbooks on E-mail itself and many are now rather old; more often this subject is given a chapter or so in a book devoted to office automation, networking or communications. However, there are a few worth mentioning. *Electronic Mail: a Revolution in Business Communications* (John Wiley, 1984) by Galbraith and Connell, discusses what E-mail is and how it is used in business, including the benefits of doing so. Simpson's *Planning for Electronic Mail* is no. 2 in Gower's *The Office of the Future* series (Gower, 1982) and contains a variety of papers on different aspects of planning, choosing and using E-mail systems. *Electronic Mail Systems—a Practical Evaluation* (NCC, 1981) by Welch and Wilson is more technically detailed, giving an in-depth analysis of the various criteria to consider when choosing a system and sets out the evaluation procedure to be followed. Several other books have been published by John Wiley, including Trudell's *Options for Electronic Mail* (1985) and Mayer's *The Electronic Mailbox* (1987).

Cable TV

The difference between cable TV and broadcast TV which we currently receive is that cable TV is delivered through cables, normally buried underground, while our current system is broadcast over the airwaves. This means that access to cable TV can be much more easily controlled, since participating viewers need to be connected to the cable system. It also means that the volume of material, in terms of the number of channels, can be much greater, dependent on the capacity of the cable. Satellite TV, in contrast, is still broadcast, but needs a satellite dish to capture the information, which may be sent from another continent. Again, the volume of information transmitted can be much greater than in the simpler system we use at present, though control over those participating is more difficult to police than for cable TV.

Cable TV is a relatively new development in the UK, where the majority of TV is still broadcast, but it is much more widespread in the USA. Cable systems have the added attraction that information can be passed in both directions, unlike broadcast systems, and this has led to the growth of home shopping services. The Cable & Broadcasting Act 1984 established the UK Cable Authority to promote, licence and regulate the UK cable industry.

A very good overview of cable systems and markets is given by Cawkell's *Handbook of Information Technology and Office Systems*. Several newsletters cover the field, including *New Media Markets*, which includes news of the cable industry in the UK and US, *Cable Television Business*, which is devoted to the U.S. cable industry and *Cable & Satellite Express*, which covers the UK. There is a small number of journals devoted exclusively to the cable industry. *Cable Television Engineering* is the quarterly journal of the UK Society of Cable Television Engineers and is a technical journal covering the engineering aspects. *Cable & Satellite Europe*, in contrast, is a more 'newsy' journal with details of the industry in Europe. U.S. journals include *Cable Product News*, *CableAge* and *CableVision*.

Two conferences cover the cable TV field. Cable '83 and Cable '84 were the 1st and 2nd European Conferences on Satellite and Cable TV, held in London, while the international Cable '85 was held in Brighton. The proceedings of all three were published by Online Publications. The International Conference on New Systems & Services in Telecommunications, held triennially in Liege, Belgium (1980, 1983, 1986) also covers cable to a lesser extent.

The online databases on the cable TV industry largely consist of the full text of newsletters; these include *Communications Daily*, *Fiber Optic News*, *International Cable & Satellite TV News*, *PR Hi-Tech Alert*, *Satellite TV Newsletter*, *Telecom A.M.* and *Video Week*. Two databases give profiles of the cable TV systems available in the USA, these being CABLEPROFILE and CODE (CABLE ON-LINE DATA EXCHANGE). The FINANCIAL TIMES BUSINESS REPORTS FILE database has summaries of the business news from *Media Monitor*, including news of cable TV. There is also a number of useful yearbooks for this field. The *Television & Cable Factbook 1988* (TV Digest) is in two volumes, the cable and services volume and the stations volume, and covers the U.S. cable industry in depth and Canada in less detail. An international directory of licensing authorities is also included. The *Blue Book of British Broadcasting: a Handbook for Professional Bodies and Students of Broadcasting* (Tellex Monitors, 1987) covers the UK broadcasting industry and includes a section on cable and satellite. Details of the Cable Authority are given, together with a description of the various services and the companies providing them. *Electro-Media 86/7* (formerly *The Electronic Media Directory and New Media Yearbook*) published by CMP also includes a section on satellite and cable, listing services and suppliers. Finally, *Cable and Satellite Yearbook* is an annual industry directory published by Cable and Satellite Europe.

There is a number of organizations involved in the cable TV industry. The Cable Authority is the licensing authority for the UK and details of franchise-holders can be obtained from them. Other organizations include the Cable Programme Providers Group, the Cable Television Association, the Society of Cable Television Engineers (in both the USA and UK), the Joint Committee for Cable Audience Research and to a lesser extent the International Institute of Communications.

Apart from the yearbooks listed above, which have directory sections, there is a number of other directories. *Who's Who in Cable and Satellite* (Selection Communication Consultants) and *The Interval—Membership Directory* (Society of Cable Television Engineers) are both lists of people working in the industry. *Cable Communications—Directory and Buyers' Guide Issue* (Ter-Sat Media Publications) covers primarily the USA and Canada, while the *International Directory of Telecomms* (Longman) gives details of equipment suppliers and telecommunications operating companies, including cable broadcasting equipment. The *Satellite Communications—Satellite Industry Directory Issue* (Cardiff Publishing Company, USA), despite its name, does cover cable TV.

The majority of textbooks, as would be expected, are American. Kenney's *Cable for Information Delivery: a Guide for Librarians, Educators and Cable Professionals* (Knowledge Industry Publications, 1984) looks at the technology and the legislation, but concentrates chiefly on its use in and for libraries. The series *BCTV: Bibliography on Cable Television* has been published annually by Communications Library since 1975. *New Media: Communications Technologies for the 1990s* edited by Shorrock (Online Publications, 1988) covers a number of new technologies, including cable TV.

Viewdata/videotex

One of the main problems with this area is the considerable variation and possible confusion over terminology. Videotex is the general term for alphanumeric and graphic data presented as a still picture on a video display; in broadcast form it is called teletext and it is known by a variety of system names in different countries, e.g. Oracle and Ceefax in the UK. Viewdata was the term originally applied to the Post Office service, but they were unable to register it as a proprietary name and hence viewdata became a generic term applied to this type of telephone-based information retrieval system. The Post Office service later became Prestel, a similar system in France is Minitel. With the international growth of these systems, videotex became the accepted term, though both are widely used in the industry. One term which is sometimes confused with this field is teletex, the CCITT standard for text and message communications, which is intended to replace telex.

Commentaries and reports on the technologies, markets and state of the art are to be found in the *Videotex Industry Year Book* (Spicer & Pegler, 1987). An older, but more thorough, review of the industry is Veith's chapter on 'Videotex and Teletext' in the *Annual Review of Information Science and Technology*, vol. 18, 1983 (Knowledge Industry Publications, 1983).

A variety of newsletters and journals covers the field. In the UK, *New Media Markets* (Financial Times Business Information) is published fortnightly and covers videotex, with news of the industry and developments, while *Videotex Viewpoint: the Magazine for Business Users of Videotex, Teletext and Cabletext*, published quarterly by Marathon Videotex, has information on new services, conferences, companies, contacts and a buyer's guide. Others worth investigating include *Videotex Travel Update*, *Videotex Notes*, *Telelink* and *Connexions* (incorporating The Prestel Directory). European developments are covered by *Videotex International* (Transtex International) which is published fortnightly, while in Canada, *Videotex World* (Tele-Direct) is published quarterly. The USA has a number of publications including *International Videotex Teletext News* (Arlen Communications), *Viewdata/Videotex Report* (LINK Resources) and *Link-Up* (Learned Information) all published monthly, and *VideoPrint* (International Resource Developments) published fortnightly.

A number of conferences are held on this topic and the proceedings are published chiefly by Online Publications or Marathon Videotex. Videotex International, an annual event, has so far been held in Europe, while the USA is served by its own event, Videotex '86, etc. Videotex User '88 has also been held. This is another area on which many subject specific groups may hold their own seminars or conferences or which may feature as part of the programme in a wider conference.

Most of the online sources in this field are full text newsletters, including VIEWDATA/VIDEOTEX REPORT, INFORMATION INDUSTRY, INTERACTIVITY REPORT and WORLDWIDE VIDEOTEX UPDATE. Other information or communications orientated databases, such as PR HI-TECH NEWS, E-PUBS, YANKEENET and FANATEL also cover this area to some extent. Specialist guides on videotex/viewdata range from the obviously appropriate *Videotex Industry Year Book* (Spicer & Pegler), which covers mainly the UK, and the *Videotex Teleservices Directory* (Arlen Communications Inc.), which covers the USA, to the less obvious such as *The DataComms Book* (VNU Business Publications), the *Telecomms Users' Handbook* (Telecommunications Press), *Electro-Media 86/7* (CMP) and *The Communications Users' Yearbook* (NCC), all of which nonetheless contain sections on videotex or viewdata, with details of suppliers and equipment. The obvious organization in this area is the Videotex Industry Association, which represents UK firms providing videotex products and services.

As well as the guides listed above, which act as directories in many cases, in the USA *Videotex Marketplace* (Phillips Publishing) gives details of suppliers, trade associations, lawyers, networks and standards. Early in the history of this technology, a number of books were published on Prestel, its history and development. Nicholson and Consterdine's *The Prestel Business* (Northwood Books, 1980) and Oliver, *et al.*, *So You Want to be a Prestel Information Provider?* (Aslib, 1982), which was subtitled 'a manual of practical advice for providing local community information on Prestel', are, as the titles suggest, intended to explain what the technology is and how to make information available through it. There are also those books which look at the applications and use of videotex in business. Examples of these are Naughton, *et al.*, *Viewdata—The Business Applications* (Communications Educational Services, 1986), Aldrich's *Videotex: Key to the Wired City* (Quiller Press, 1982), Fedida and Malik's *Viewdata Revolution* (Associated Business Press, 1979) and Mayne's *Videotex Revolution* (October Press, 1982). By the mid-1980s the growth of videotex and viewdata was such that surveys of its use were deemed necessary. Yates-Mercer's *Private Viewdata in the UK* (Gower, 1985) reviewed the status of private viewdata in the UK, particularly from the viewpoint of who was using it, how they were using it and for what. The Videotex Industry Association commissioned a position paper by Aldrich, *The UK Videotex Market: Interactive Videotex* (Videotex Industry Association, 1986), to define and position the UK videotex industry within the UK information industry, for those both within and without the industry. Shorrock's *New Media: Communications Technologies for the 1990s* (Online Publications, 1988) looks at videotex among other technologies, and the impact it is likely to have over the next decade. For those choosing and using viewdata systems, Firth's *Managing Viewdata Systems* (John Wiley, 1984) and *Viewdata Systems: a Practical Evaluation Guide* (John Wiley, 1982) are likely to prove useful.

Office automation

There can be few people who have not come into contact with some form of office automation and the impact it has had on the lives of office workers and others who perform clerical routines has been considerable. Two recent reviews make it clear how great the impact has been. Chapter 8 of the *Annual Review of Information Science and Technology*, vol. 23, 1988 (Elsevier, 1988), by Thomas H. Martin, entitled 'Office Automation' is '*a status report on the interplay between a dream and reality*', which looks at the background, work and social impacts, planning, technology and trends. The *Yearbook of Science & Technology* (McGraw-Hill, 1987) has a section on office automation by Paul Wallich which is a comprehensive coverage of recent events and research.

There is a surprising number of journals and newsletters devoted to this subject, many of which have 'Office' in the title. *FinTech 2: Electronic Office* is one of the series from the FT Business Information Service on the business aspects of new technology, published semi-monthly. This one covers office automation, with news of products, user groups, PSS, PCs, take-overs, OCR etc. *The Office: Magazine of Information Systems and Management* is published monthly and has a variety of short articles on PCs, artificial intelligence, comms, electronic mail, equipment, product information and literature. *Modern Office Technology* (previously *Modern Office Procedures*) is published monthly in the USA for those interested in business and information systems management. It has short articles on a variety of aspects of office automation, plus news, people, literature, events and product news. *Office Magazine*, published monthly on controlled circulation, is not exclusively devoted to office automation, but has a lot on the subject. Each issue has a special feature on one aspect, e.g. comms, word-processing, computers, copiers, stationery. Otherwise there are no articles as such, concentrating on news, product launches, trade literature and so on. *Office Equipment Index*, published monthly on controlled circulation to managers and executives, is exclusively product information and is therefore very good for trade literature. *Buckley's Guide to Office Automation*, published ten times a year, is an easy-to-read colourful introduction to all new technology available for the modern office, and is aimed at chief executives and senior directors in the UK.

Online databases are limited and in most cases, information must be sought in more general files. The full text of some journals is available online, including the FT's ELECTRONIC OFFICE. Others include TECHNOLOGY WATCH on Electronic Information Systems, FIBER OPTIC NEWS on NewsNet, and ORGANIZATIONAL MARKETING and VIRTUAL MANAGEMENT which are available through ISYS Information Services. SB-I is a bibliographic database of French literature on computer science and related fields including office data processing.

The main specialist guides to this field are *Wharton's Complete Office Automation Guide* (Wharton Publishing Ltd) which has reviews and articles on a range of aspects, suppliers and addresses and *Kelly's Automated Office and Business Equipment Directory* which is published annually by Kelly's Directories and is free to selected companies. It lists British companies who are actively engaged in the manufacture or distribution of business equipment.

The British Computer Society, Office Automation Specialist Group, which aims to act as a forum for people interested in office automation, enables members to make contact with others with similar ideas and to exchange information and experience. It is independent from, but sponsored by, the BCS, circulates a monthly newsletter to members and holds meetings from September to May.

Many of the books on this subject were written in the late 1970s and early 1980s as the possibilities of automating procedures became less a dream and more a reality. Gower has been one of the more prolific publishers, with an early series entitled *The Office of the Future*, edited by Alan Simpson. Simpson also edited *New Developments in Office Technology* (1984) which as in the earlier series is a compilation of papers, largely contributed by suppliers in the industry. *Office Automation, Organization and the Nature of Work* by Wainwright and Francis (1984) has a number of case studies from different organizations. Gower also published a number of books in conjunction with Philips Business Systems, including Jarrett's *The Electronic Office: a Management Guide to the Office of the Future* (1984), Blaazer and Molyneux's *Supervising the Electronic Office* (1984) and Heigl's *The Electronic Office and You: a Guide to the New Technology for Secretaries and Office Staff* (1985), which show the diversity of audience at which such books were aimed. The National Computing Centre started earlier, publishing Price's *Introducing the Electronic Office* (1979) and Pritchard and Wilson's *Planning Office Automation: Elec-*

tronic Message Systems (1982) and *Office Technology Benefits* (1983). More recently Collins has published *The Automated Office: Information Technology and its Effect on Management and Office Staff*, by Bate and Burgess (1985).

The effect of office automation on information work and vice versa has not been ignored. In 1985, Wilson produced *Library and Research Report 31* for the British Library, entitled *Office Automation and Information Services: Final Report on a Study of Current Developments*. In 1987, the proceedings of the Institute of Information Scientists Text Retrieval '86 Conference was published by Taylor Graham, entitled *Information Handling Techniques for the Office: Full Text Rules OA?*, which was edited by Hills.

Office Trade News, published ten times a year, together with the other journals and directories, is a valuable source of trade literature for this field, covering office equipment dealers throughout the market.

Word processing and desktop publishing

One aspect of office (and home) automation which perhaps has made a greater impact than any other is word processing. The ability to store and manipulate documents in this way has had a profound effect on many working practices and this trend is continuing, with more sophisticated lay-out and manipulation of text in the form of desktop publishing (DTP). DTP is broadly the use of desktop equipment to produce documents which formerly would have been typeset and printed. It is also now possible to create, transmit and read a document in electronic form without ever having a hard copy.

An introduction to the fundamentals of DTP can be found in the form of an article by Kathy Lang in the *PC Year Book 1989* (VNU Business Publications, 1989) and a more in-depth assessment can be found in several issues of *Critique: Critical Reviews of Information Technology* (Aslib, 1989).

Several journals devoted to word processing have come and gone, often being incorporated into others on office automation. Existing ones include *Word & Information Processing* and *Which Word Processor & Office System?*, while for DTP, journals include *Desktop Publishing*, *Desktop Publishing Magazine* and *Desktop Publishing World*. *ICL Desktop* and *PIRA Desktop Publishing Commentary* are also produced by these respective companies. General PC magazines are very useful sources of information on both topics; these include *Practical Computing*, *Personal Computer World* and *Which Computer?*

The *PC Year Book* covers hardware and software for DTP and word-processing and gives details of DTP bureaux. *The Desktop Publishing Directory and Buyers' Guide* (Spicer & Pegler, 1987) has an introductory section describing DTP and giving a market overview, and goes on to list available systems in terms of both hardware and software. Bureaux and other supporting systems are also included. *Wharton's Complete Office Automation Guide* (see Office Automation section) has a section covering word processors, both stand-alone and multi-user. The BCS Office Automation Specialist Group is a useful contact in this field and PIRA have their own DTP advisory unit.

Many books have been published on these subjects, including Gibson's *Wordprocessing and the Electronic Office* (Council for Educational Technology, 1983), Flood's *Processing Words: the Information Manager and Word Processing* (Aslib, 1987), Carson's *Desktop Publishing and Libraries* (Taylor Graham, 1988) and Grout, *et al.*, *Desktop Publishing from A to Z* (McGraw-Hill, 1986).

CHAPTER EIGHT

Information policy and statutory control

D. HAYNES

Introduction

Information technology has had a profound effect on legislation and government policy particularly in the industrialized countries. Advances in telecommunications have prompted intergovernmental cooperation especially for the development of standards. Data about individuals held on computer has led to concerns about abuse of data and protection of privacy and there has been a round of legislation in the last ten years to address these issues. Considerable resources are expended in developing new products and services and in many cases it was found that existing legislation for protecting intellectual property was too ambiguous or simply did not deal with information technology. Finally, concerns about computer security and unauthorized access to computer systems, known as 'hacking', look as though they will lead to new legislation criminalizing hacking.

In this chapter we look at some of the key sources on various aspects of statutory control. Chapter fifteen deals with UK government publications in more detail. Chapter eleven covers organizations including government agencies and inter-government bodies.

Information policy

There are two main aspects to information policy. They are: the policies governing information technology; and those which regulate information itself. In this section we will look at both. Official information policy is usually codified in government legislation. Examples are: the UK Data Protection Act 1984 and the copyright legislation in the USA and Europe. A lot of government effort is directed at improving the uptake of information technology, and at improving international trade. *International Informatics Policy: From Participation to Regulation* (Logica, 1988) takes a look at government policy for computing and communication in six industrialized countries: France; Germany (Federal Republic); Japan; Sweden; the United Kingdom; and the United States. It discusses the general influences which have affected government policy especially where there have been shifts in policy emphasis. The report deals extensively with trade and economic policy and looks at deregulation of markets, and privatization of large nationalized companies. Each country is dealt with in a separate chapter and topics covered include: research policy; regulatory policy; competition policy; promotional policy; employment policy; education policy; trade policy; and procurement policy.

There are a number of sources of information on international information policy. General organizations such as The Royal Institute of International Affairs and UN agencies such as ACCIS and WIPO are useful sources. Publications such as the *ACCIS Newsletter* are a good means of finding what issues are topical. Two other sources are: *National Information Policies: Problems and Progress 1988* by John Gray; and *National Information Policies: a Review of Policies in 17 Industrialized Countries* (FID, 1989) by M. W. Hill.

In the USA the following documents are authoritative sources: *Federal Information Research Policy* (1987); and *Informing the Nation: Federal Information Dissemination in an Electronic Age* (US Office of Technology Assessment). Prior to this there is *Understanding US Information Policy: The Infostructure Handbook* (Information Industry Association), edited by F. W. Horton Jr. It is in three volumes and includes a comprehensive directory of interested bodies in the USA. It also gives an overview of U.S. information policy. The emphasis is on information policy rather than IT policy. Recently the Special Libraries Association of the United States called on President Bush to implement national information policy.

In the United Kingdom, the *CICI Newsletter* published by the Confederation of Information Communication Industries (CICI) is a useful general source. CICI represents the information industry and has many of the key IT organizations in the UK. Its members include groupings such as the Publishers' Association, Aslib, and various broadcasting and communications companies.

A number of other journals touch on IT policy among other

things. Newsletters such as *Advanced Information Report—an International Newsletter for Information Professionals and End Users* (formerly *Communications Technology Impact*) and published by Elsevier contains short articles with occasional news of policy reviews. *Information World Review* (Learned Information) and its U.S. sister paper *Information Today* (Learned Information), both include items on policy in Europe and the USA.

In the UK, the Central Computer and Telecommunications Agency (CCTA), a division of the Treasury is responsible for IT policy in government. It provides a source of expertise and guidance in implementing information technology in central government departments.

The Department of Trade and Industry is also responsible for IT policy, and an Information Engineering Directorate was set up in the wake of the Alvey Programme of research. The DTI sponsored IT82, a government publicity campaign to make people more aware of the benefits of information technology. More recently the House of Commons Trade & Industry Committee produced a two-volume report, *Information Technology* (HMSO, 1988). This document contains 116 findings including 52 recommendations. It also has a lot of useful statistical summaries comparing the UK with other industrialized countries.

Patents and copyright

Protecting the intellectual property of inventors or authors has presented major problems for the computer industry. Authors of software are particularly vulnerable to pirating of their products. Makers of semiconductor chips have faced similar problems, because of the lack of clear definitions of what is being protected. Data compiled to make a database is subject to limited protection and this is another area of concern. One of the dilemmas facing legislatures and intergovernmental bodies is determining whether copyright protection or patents are more appropriate for protecting computer programs and computerized databases.

There have been recent moves to bring copyright laws up to date so that they adequately address issues such as ownership of software rights and database rights. Some national laws have been extended to take into account electronically published material, either as online databases or on CD-ROM.

The Berne Convention provides the basis for international copyright law. The World Intellectual Property Organization (WIPO) based in Geneva is a United Nations agency and provides a useful source of information on international agreements on patents and copyright. For more specific information on patents as a source of information see Chapter fourteen.

International sources

The International Guide to Official Industrial Property Publications (London, British Library SRIS, 1988) by B. M. Rimmer is a good starting point for information on relevant legislations and guides published by official bodies. The main part of the text is organized by country and it covers patents, designs and trade marks.

The Patentability of Computer Software: an International Guide to the Protection of Computer-Related Inventions (Deventer, Kluwer, 1985) by H. W. A. M. Hanneman looks briefly at the mechanisms available for the protection of software before looking at the relevant national laws and case law history in the major industrialized countries. There are separate chapters on: the United States; Canada; the United Kingdom; Australia; France; the Federal Republic of Germany; Austria; Switzerland; Japan; the Netherlands; and Europe. Each chapter has a short bibliography and provides a useful entry point into the literature.

Another international view is taken in C. J. Millard's *Legal Protection of Computer Programs and Data* (London, Sweet and Maxwell, 1985) which covers several countries. The issues covered include: copyright; patents; trade secrets; criminal law; privacy and data protection; and transborder data flows. It cites legislation and specific cases in Canada, the United Kingdom and the USA. Although it is quite old, the book provides a useful guide to relevant laws, especially for the protection of intellectual property. It discusses some of the arguments current 10–15 years ago and which have led to some of the more recent legislation. This is a particularly good source for older legislation in Canada, the United Kingdom and the US. For instance it cites the Computer Software Copyright Act 1980 and the Semiconductor Chip Protection Act 1984 in the USA.

USA

A very good general summary of the situation in the USA is to be found in *Computers, Data Processing and the Law* (West Publishing Company, 1984) by S. L. Mandell. The orientation of the text is legal and it cites many specific cases to illustrate its points. It has a dual role as a college text and as a guide to companies who are purchasing or supplying services. It looks at protection of software under patent and copyright laws and also at computer crime. Practical advice on contracting is also given. *Intellectual Property Rights in an Age of Electronics and Information* (U.S. Office of Technology Assessment, 1986) looks at the impact of communication and information technology on intellectual property systems. *Computer Law* (New York, Wiley, 1984–) by M. D. Scott is perhaps the most detailed guide to U.S. law in this area. It covers software protection, computer contracts, criminal law and the Semiconductor Chip Protection Act 1984. The guide is ring bound and is continuously updated. The last update was in 1987.

A commentary on the Semiconductor Chip Protection Act is also provided in *The Semiconductor Chip Protection Act of 1984* (New York, Law and Business Inc., 1984) and is based on a seminar chaired by J. A. Baumgarten.

The Board of Copyright Clearance Center USA is responsible for distributing copy fees to copyright owners and is another potential source of information.

United Kingdom

For a general guide to laws in England and Wales, but not dealing specifically with Information Technology, *Protecting and Exploiting New Technology and Designs* (London, E. & F. N. Spon, 1987) by K. Hodkinson is a concise guide. It contains summaries of relevant laws including the Copyright (Computer Software) Amendment Act 1985. This of course has been superseded by the Copyright, Designs and Patents Act 1988.

Blackstone's Guide to the Copyright, Designs and Patents Act 1988 (London, Blackstone Press, 1989) by G. Dworkin, and R. D. Taylor provides a comprehensive and exhaustive legal guide to the new copyright act in the UK. It has a section on special topics including chapters on computer technology and on cable and satellite broadcasting. The book also contains a complete copy of the 1988 Act.

Clarion is the newsletter of the Copyright Licensing Agency in the United Kingdom. It is a four-page newsletter appearing quarterly and gives updates on recent events and on world events.

Data protection

Many of the leading industrialized countries now have data protection acts. Sweden was the first country to enact laws in this area in 1973. Other industrialized countries have since followed suit, often prompted by concerns about trans-border data flows.

There are generally two issues which are addressed in whole or part by the various national acts:

- Privacy and security of information held on individuals
- Freedom of access to information

For a good overview of data protection and privacy around the world, *Data Privacy and Security: State of the Art Report 13:6* (Maidenhead, Pergamon Infotech, 1985) provides a good starting point. The report contains invited papers followed by a detailed analysis and an annotated bibliography with 151 references. Although the report is now quite old, it contains useful background on the origin of many of the data privacy acts, currently in force around the world, and it identifies many of the key issues which are relevant today. The invited papers are by contributors from several countries. This is one of the most complete and wide-ranging sources on this topic.

Prior to the Data Protection Act 1984 in the UK, the Privacy and Security Division of the NCC (UK National Computing Centre) published *Privacy in the Computer Age* (Manchester, NCC, 1982) by G. L. Simons. This provided some of the ground work for the 1984 Act. The Office of the Data Protection Registrar publishes a number of guidelines to help organizations register and to help data subjects (individuals who are the subject of data held on computer) to obtain access to records on them. *Data Protection Law* (London: Sweet and Maxwell, 1988) by S. Chalton and S. Gaskill provides an extensive commentary on the Data Protection Act 1984. The guide contains a copy of the Act and has a detailed index. It provides a legal viewpoint on the Act even to the extent of being organized like a legal document with paragraph numbers rather than page numbers.

Trans-border data flow

The UK Data Protection Act arose partly in response to the need to continue trading electronic information with other countries. In order to avoid restrictions which might be applied to this type of trade, the UK has to ensure that similar standards of privacy and security apply to personal data. Publications such as the *Transnational Data Report* and *Government Information Quarterly* provide regular updates on trans-border data flow. International agencies such as the Organization for Economic Cooperation and Development (OECD), the Council of Europe and the European Community can be useful sources of information.

Hacking and computer security

There has been a lot of concern expressed recently about hacking into computer systems. Hacking is defined as gaining unauthorized access to computer systems, usually through a public network. Perhaps the most widely read book on the topic is Hugo Cornwall's *The Hacker's Handbook* (London, Century Communications, 4th edn, 1989). The book is well written and provides a good introduction to telecommunications and network technology as well as going into some of the details of how to hack. This is essential reading for those wishing to protect their computers against unauthorized access. There have been moves in a number of countries to make unauthorized access to computers a criminal offence. If hacking is used to perpetuate a fraud, by changing the contents of a database entry or to trade commercial or national secrets then the appropriate criminal laws apply. If no offence has been committed and it can be proved that there was no conspiracy to commit an offence it is difficult to prosecute under UK law (current situation in 1990).

Computer security is a recurring topic of discussion in the computer press and the following periodicals have covered this topic recently: *Communicate*; *Communications Management*; *Computer Weekly*; *Computing*; *Datalink*; *Datamation*; *Mini-Micro Systems*; *Software*; and *Telecommunications*.

Software licences

Software is usually covered by licences which any purchaser has to agree to. Normally software suppliers sell licences to use software, rather than selling a copy of the software. With the licence comes a copy of the software and the associated manual. There are usually strict conditions about unauthorized copying of the software and alteration of the programs. Further information on software licensing can be obtained from FAST (Federation Against Software Theft) which is sponsored by the major British software houses. In the US the Software Publishers' Association represents the interests of US software producers.

International trade

There is a lot of excitement about the European Single Market, which is due to come into effect by the end of 1992. This has had a dramatic effect on international trade, both within the community and outside. When the Single Market is in operation, common standards will apply across the community and there should be no artificial barriers to trade between member states of the EC. The DTI in the UK has set up a publicity campaign to educate businesses about the Single Market and to provide information. The Small Firms Service, available in each of the regions in the UK also provides an information service on the Single Market.

The European Commission itself is a major source of information on the Single Market and can provide guidance on:

- Trading laws and regulations
- Customs and documentation
- Training and qualifications

Major trading partners with the community such as Japan and the US have also been gearing up to the Single Market, when trade tariffs will apply to products which are of less than 60% EC origin. This is to prevent components being imported duty free into a European country for assembly in a community country for sale there.

PART II

Sources of Information

CHAPTER NINE

Machine-readable sources

G. TURPIE

Introduction

The term 'machine-readable sources' may conjure up images of computers processing reams of computer tape. Not a very romantic image and yet the development of machine-readable sources represents one of the major breakthroughs in the control and exploitation of information. The information explosion of recent years brings with it huge problems of management and control of not only published sources of information but also less formally produced documents. Whereas fifty years ago a card catalogue might have been adequate for providing access to information, this is not the case today. Pressures of space and time have caused libraries and information centres to look at alternative ways of providing an information service.

It is ironic that the first machine-readable information sources were developed primarily as an efficient means of producing paper publications rather than improving information-retrieval techniques. The first machine-readable database corresponded to the very large abstracting and indexing services such as *Index Medicus* produced by the National Library of Medicine in the US. The delays and costs of producing these paper-based publications by manual methods led to the development of computing techniques to produce the monthly issues. Indexing the contents became a much simpler process and this provided an information source which could be searched by machine.

The first computerized information sources were available in the late 1960s. These were clumsy affairs and had to be searched by a method known as 'batch-searching'. The instructions to the computer were run overnight and the enquirer had no direct access to the system while the search was in progress. As more powerful computers and more sophisticated techniques developed, it became possible to search databases interactively. This was a tremendously important step in terms of information retrieval, because it meant that an enquirer could alter the search whilst online to the computer—or in other words, whilst the computer was carrying out the search. This development led to the availability of commercially-produced online databases. Online databases are now one of the main forms of publicly available information in machine-readable form.

Today, libraries not only access commercially produced sources in electronic form but also build up their own internal databases using proprietary software. These very often correspond to the library's catalogue, and are usually developed to deal with their own particular information requirements. Many organizations, particularly academic libraries make their catalogues available to users via terminals. These are known as OPACs (Online Public Access Catalogues) and in many ways reflect the development of commercially available online databases. In this chapter, however, only commercially available machine readable sources will be considered.

The term 'machine-readable sources' therefore refers to collections of information held in some form of computerized or electronic format. This includes computerized databases whether held on mainframe, minicomputer or microcomputer. It can also refer to databases published on floppy discs and distributed in this way to customers. The most recent widely available development in electronic publishing is the CD-ROM or compact disc read only memory. The CD-ROM uses optical storage technology to store data on a disc which can be searched using retrieval software.

There are four clear advantages to providing information in machine-readable form. Firstly, storage of data using computer technology offers retrieval by retrieval software. Software can thus be used to manipulate the information into the format most suitable to the enquirer. Secondly, computer technology offers the facility to handle large amounts of data and to retrieve information in a much shorter time than is possible with non-computerized databases. There is a third advantage to computerized storage of information and it applies particularly to time-sensitive information (e.g. stock-exchange figures). Any database held in machine-readable form can very easily be kept up to date. And finally, a fourth advantage is the ability to search for information by several criteria at once. An example of this would be the retrieval of references to the literature in a particular subject, appearing in a specific year and published in the French language.

Electronically-published databases have been regularly used by the library and information profession since the 1970s when many of the large scientific and medical abstracting services became available as online databases. Online databases are the most widely available type of electronically-published information source. It is estimated that there are now over 4000 online databases, publicly available throughout the world. For this reason, the chapter will deal mainly with online databases, their availability and exploitation.

Online databases

A database is any collection of information. An online database is any collection of information stored on a remote computer which is accessed using a telecommunications link. It is possible therefore to access online databases situated all over the world, providing that a telecommunications link is available. Online databases are produced by many types of organization ranging from research associations to commercial publishers. Access to online databases is very often through a host organization which provides the hardware to mount the database and the software to retrieve information from the database. The host will also market the database and provide training courses, search manuals, etc. to help customers make the most use of the services. Hosts may provide access to one or more specialized databases or to many hundreds. To obtain access to databases marketed by a host, it is necessary to approach the host to request a password to the service.

Charging for the use of online databases is usually based on a fee per hour connected to the database and prices range from £60 to £120 per hour. There is also a charge for the information retrieved as a result of the online search and this is usually referred to as the print charge. Recently, there has been a move away from time-based connect hour charging to a charging system based on the amount of information retrieved from the database. The host ESA–IRS is a pioneer in this area. Price lists are available from the online hosts but there is also a very useful publication, *The Online Cost Chart* produced by Martin Woodrow.

Online databases can be accessed using a microcomputer with a modem. Many microcomputers are sold with internal modems, but separate units are also available. The modem simply acts as a device which transfers the information on a microcomputer screen into signals to be transmitted down the telephone line. In addition

152 Machine-readable sources

a piece of communications software is also necessary to access remote databases. Further details about the equipment can be obtained from the Information Resources Centre at Aslib (the Association for Information Management) and also from the Library and Information Technology Centre. Many computer shops will also be able to offer assistance.

There are several good general guides to searching online databases. A short, concise introduction to the subject is provided by a publication entitled *Going Online* (Aslib, 1988) by Helen Starkey and Beverley Thwaites. Another book which looks more specifically at the process of searching is *Online Bibliographic Searching: a Learning Manual* (1982) by Chen and Schweizer. Finally a new edition of *Online Searching: Principles and Practice* (1990) by Hartley, Tedd, Large and Keen provides a good up-to-date introduction to online databases in their most general sense.

Databases specific to information technology

Online databases fall into three main categories according to the type of information contained. These three types are generally referred to as:

- Bibliographic
- Factual (also called directory or non-bibliographic)
- Full-text

Bibliographic databases provide references to published material, often with abstracts. This includes journal articles, textbooks, monographs, conference papers, research reports, and so on. Bibliographic databases are useful for identifying published documents. However, if the original paper needs to be consulted then it usually has to be obtained from the original publisher or from a library. Factual databases contain information such as addresses, technical and scientific data, or numerical information. Full-text databases contain the full text of the original journal or newspaper article.

Online databases in the field of information technology fall into three categories:

- General databases covering the subject of information technology and research in the field
- Databases carrying specific information on software packages
- Databases on information technology applications

Machine-readable sources

GENERAL COVERAGE

INSPEC. The major bibliographic database covering information technology is INSPEC, which is produced by the Institution of Electrical Engineers. It is divided into four main areas:

- Physics
- Electrical engineering
- Computers and computing technology
- Information technology

The last two areas are those of particular interest here. The section on computers and computing technology covers:

- Artificial intelligence
- Computer theory
- Hardware
- Software

Hardware is defined as including computers themselves, their circuitry, storage, peripheral equipment and networking. Software includes application programs, software engineering system and techniques. Applications of computing include expert systems, word processing, desk-top publishing, computer-aided analysis and design, communications and instrumentation.

The information technology section of the INSPEC database is particularly aimed at the non-technologist and provides information on applications of information technology in the following fields—business, banking and insurance, leisure and media, marketing and retailing, as well as many others. There is also coverage of office automation and this refers to topics such as facsimile transmission, electronic mail, teleconferencing, viewdata and word processing.

INSPEC contains almost three million references to the literature, dating back to 1969. The database is updated every month by approximately 16 000 records. The primary coverage of the database is journal articles and papers presented at conferences. However textbooks, reports and dissertations are also included and the coverage is international.

Each record in the database contains an English-language title and descriptive abstract, together with full bibliographic information (journal or source title, author's name and affiliation and details of the language of the original publication).

Classification codes (corresponding to the sections in the equivalent printed abstracts journals) are used in INSPEC to structure the records contained in the database. There is also an *INSPEC*

154 Machine-readable sources

Thesaurus which indicates the preferred indexing terms. This kind of language control enhances the retrieval by bringing together synonyms under one term. The Institution of Electrical Engineers publishes several titles to improve the use of the INSPEC database. These include a very comprehensive *INSPEC User Manual*, *INSPEC Classification 1988* and the *INSPEC Thesaurus*. Over 4000 international journals are scanned to produce the INSPEC database and a list of these journal titles is published as *List of Journals*. This list provides the journal title, the address of the publisher and the date when the journal was first abstracted in the INSPEC database.

The database corresponds to three published abstracting journals produced by the Institution of Electrical Engineers: *Computer and Control Abstracts*; *Electrical and Electronic Abstracts* and *Physics Abstracts*.

INSPEC is considered one of the most comprehensive sources of information in information technology, especially on the research side. It is often a good first port of call for information on a subject in this area because of the comprehensive coverage. INSPEC is available through the major online hosts (see Table 9.1).

TABLE 9.1 Major online hosts

Name of Database	Hosts through which it is available
ARTIFICIAL INTELLIGENCE	The Turing Institute
THE BUSINESS SOFTWARE DATABASE	BRS, Data-Star, Dialog, ESA-IRS, Knowledge Index
THE COMPUTER DATABASE	BRS, Data-Star, Dialog, Knowledge Index
ELECTRONIC PUBLISHING ABSTRACTS	ORBIT Search Service
INSPEC	BRS, CISITI, Data-Star, Dialog, ESA-IRS, FIZ Technik, JICST, Knowledge Index, ORBIT Search Service, STN International, TECH DATA
MENU—THE INTERNATIONAL SOFTWARE DATABASE	CompuServe, Dialog, Knowledge Index
MICROCOMPUTER INDEX	Dialog, Knowledge Index
MICROCOMPUTER SOFTWARE AND HARDWARE GUIDE	Dialog, Knowledge Index

COMPUTER DATABASE. The COMPUTER DATABASE, produced by the Information Access Company in California, is an excellent general source of information on computers, the computer industry and many related fields of information technology, including

Machine-readable sources 155

telecommunications and the wider field of electronics. This is a bibliographic database and thus provides references to the literature together with abstracts. The sources abstracted for this service are international and include journals and newsletters as well as conference proceedings and books. Interestingly, it also covers product evaluations and company information about organizations in the industry. The database is primarily aimed at those working in the industry or those who require information on computers for their own sphere of work.

The database deals with many specific topics ranging from computer games to operating systems. It covers many aspects of information technology including hardware, software and computer peripherals as well as aspects of the companies within the industry.

Although the database is international in its scope, there is a bias towards information from the US. However because the US is such an important producer of IT as well as a consumer, the COMPUTER DATABASE is relevant internationally. It can be accessed on many of the major commercial host systems. (See Table 9.1.)

MICROCOMPUTER INDEX. The MICROCOMPUTER INDEX is another database produced in California. It provides abstracts of magazine articles contained in fifty microcomputer magazines published in Australia, the UK and the US. The magazines are popular titles such as *Practical Computing*, *PC World* and *Byte*. General articles, book reviews, product reviews and individual software specifications are included in the database.

MICROCOMPUTER SOFTWARE AND HARDWARE GUIDE. The MICROCOMPUTER SOFTWARE AND HARDWARE GUIDE is the online equivalent of the *Software Encyclopedia* (Bowker). It is similar to the *Computer Users' Yearbook* in the UK and provides details including prices, specifications, supplier details of software packages available in the US together with information on hardware compatible with the software.

The MICROCOMPUTER INDEX and MICROCOMPUTER SOFTWARE AND HARDWARE GUIDE services are both available through Dialog and the special Dialog service, Knowledge Index.

SOFTWARE PACKAGES

MENU. There are several databases which provide information solely on software packages. The first one, and most comprehensive in terms of coverage which should be considered is MENU— THE INTERNATIONAL SOFTWARE DATABASE produced by the

International Software Database Corporation. It contains information on commercially-available software for microcomputers, minicomputers and mainframe computers. The software is both for business and home applications. Information on each package is represented in a standard record format and includes details of: application; hardware; price; and supplier. It is also possible to order packages online. The database is international in its coverage and corresponds to the following hard-copy publications:

The Software Catalog—Business Software
The Software Catalog—Health Professions
The Software Catalog—Microcomputers
The Software Catalog—Minicomputers
The Software Catalog—Science and Engineering

BUSINESS SOFTWARE. The BUSINESS SOFTWARE database is produced by Information Sources in California and as its name suggests, it provides descriptions of software packages which have business applications. Approximately 9000 packages are described and these include micro-, mini- and mainframe computer packages. Information on each package includes: a description of the package; details of the producer; the price; and the number of packages sold. The description includes information on hardware requirements, the program language and a description of the documentation available. The coverage of this database is primarily the US, however, some non-U.S.-produced software is included. The database corresponds to part of the *Business Software Directory*.

COMPENDEX. This is the major engineering database and as such it contains a certain amount of information on computers and communications engineering. This database is produced by Engineering Information Inc. and contains references with abstracts to the literature which is primarily in the English language. References date back to 1970. Although not primarily aimed at information technology this database would be worth accessing for information on computer hardware and telecommunications research and applications. It is accessible through the major online hosts including Dialog, Knowledge Index, ESA-IRS, Orbit, STN and BRS.

PTS PROMT. This is another database which is also worth considering, produced by Predicasts. It is primarily a business database but it does provide access to information on new technologies and products. Information is given in the form of citations with abstracts and refers to newspapers, newsletters, international trade journals and press releases. The database is available through BRS, Data-Star and Dialog.

INFORMATION TECHNOLOGY APPLICATIONS

There are a number of databases which specialize in specific areas of information technology. Although these are often not available through the major online hosts, they should always be considered as possible sources of information. Two such databases are discussed below.

ARTIFICIAL INTELLIGENCE. One of the more interesting of the specialized IT databases is ARTIFICIAL INTELLIGENCE produced by the Turing Institute in Glasgow. Access to it is limited to members of the Institute, although library staff at the Institute can carry out searches on your behalf. The database contains over 35 000 references to the literature on artificial intelligence. Each citation also has an abstract of the original article. The subjects covered include: expert systems; knowledge representation; machine learning; robotics; and human–computer interaction. The Institute also publishes a hard-copy version of the database called *The Turing Institute Abstracts in Artificial Intelligence*.

ELECTRONIC PUBLISHING ABSTRACTS. Another specialist bibliographic database is ELECTRONIC PUBLISHING ABSTRACTS which is produced by PIRA the research association for the paper and board, printing and packaging industries. Its main emphasis is electronic publishing but it also covers most aspects of information technology including: input/output technologies; communications technologies; processing; storage technologies; and information retrieval and publication. Specific technologies covered include: CD-ROM; videotex; videodisc; and cable TV.

The coverage of journals scanned is international. ELECTRONIC PUBLISHING ABSTRACTS is available on the Orbit Search Service in the US. A search manual has been produced to aid searching, along with a list of journals abstracted for the service.

Using online databases

Using online databases may seem complex. In fact, it can be very easy to carry out simple online searches. It is only when you want to employ the full range of search commands available that searching becomes more difficult. Added to this is the lack of standardization of search commands, which means that each host has developed its own command language. There is variation both in the names and the purposes of the commands. In the late 1970s an initiative was taken to develop the Common Command Language, or CCL and several hosts offer this as an alternative to their own search languages.

The principles of online searching apply to all computer databases whether they are online or not. The searcher inputs a series of commands via the keyboard and the retrieval software acts on these commands to obtain the required information. Thus if you wished to find out recent references on the application of expert systems in medicine, you would simply input the following keywords:

EXPERT SYSTEMS
MEDICINE

The software would then retrieve all the records in the database which contained those words. The records can then be displayed or printed in a variety of formats. This is a very crude search and you could refine it for instance by using a truncation character so that both 'expert systems' and 'expert system' are retrieved. You could also employ alternatives for the word 'medicine' such as 'hospital', 'doctor', 'diagnosis' and so on. It may be that the records which you obtained from the first crude search would suffice, in which case you would not need to refine the search. However, to take the example further, if you wanted to obtain information on all the references to research papers on expert systems in medicine, you would need to expand the search to ensure that all the relevant references are retrieved.

This example demonstrates that there are a great many levels at which a search may be carried out, any of which may be acceptable to the enquirer.

In many organizations searches on bibliographic databases are carried out by non-information professionals for their own needs. Research has shown (Dutton, 1989) that this is most often for a quick, crude search to obtain a few references on a particular topic. When an exhaustive or more difficult search was required, the scientists in this study tended to ask the library service to carry out the search on their behalf. However it must be that many scientists are quite used to carrying out their own searches on numerical databases.

Complex searching does require training and continued practice. However, for occasional searches, it is often possible for end-users to carry out quick searches quite satisfactorily.

Finding out more about online databases

PUBLISHED SOURCES

The databases described above are those which are particularly relevant to information technology. It should be remembered however, that there are now several thousand commercially-available databases, a small proportion of which deal with information technology. There are also a number of databases of peripheral interest to information technology and these should not be neglected as a source of information, especially in the application-specific areas.

The most satisfactory way of obtaining an overview of database availability is to consult one of the many database directories now available. The most comprehensive of these is the *Directory of Online Databases* published annually with quarterly supplements by Cuadra/Elsevier and known as 'Cuadra'. It provides an excellent coverage of online database produced by organizations throughout the world. To be included in Cuadra, the database must be publicly available. This directory also has a number of very good indexes. It is now available as an online database through several of the major host systems.

Another directory worth consulting is the *Database Directory* produced by Knowledge Industry Publications and the American Society for Information Science. It concentrates on databases produced in the US and Canada with only a few services from other countries included. This directory is also available online from the host BRS.

A third directory which is worth mentioning here is the *DIANE Guide* which is produced by the European Information Market Development Group, an initiative of the European Economic Community. It is only available online through the European host ECHO.

All of these published database directories provide a brief description of the database coverage together with information on the database producer and through which host or hosts the database is available. Contact addresses are also given but often these are the main offices of the companies and it is always worth checking to see if an office or representative is available locally.

The directories are an excellent way of achieving a good overview of availability; however to find more information you will need to consult more detailed information produced by the database producer or host.

As noted earlier, the number of online databases is growing and there are over 4000 now available. There is a steady turnover with new databases appearing on the market whilst others are being taken off. Even older, more established services such as INSPEC are subject to changes in the coverage, the journals abstracted or the hosts on which the service is available. It is therefore essential for regular users of online services to keep up to date with the latest developments.

There are a number of newsletters and journals which provide news reports and articles on online databases. Newsletters such as *Online Newsletter*, *Monitor*, *Information World Review*, *Information Today* and *Online Notes* provide general information on what is happening in the online industry. There are also several specialized newsletters such as *Online Business Information* which deal with services in specific subject areas.

As well as these there are many journals which carry longer articles which look at particular issues in the online field. These are useful for obtaining critical reviews of online databases. Journals fulfilling this task include *Online*, *Database* and *Online Review*.

UNPUBLISHED SOURCES

Although all of these previously-mentioned published sources provide excellent coverage of the online scene, it can be more entertaining to consider other methods of keeping up to date. Many countries now run annual online conferences and exhibitions—in the US there are two major shows every year. Exhibitions provide an opportunity to meet database producers and the host organizations. If you take some questions along to the exhibition they are often willing to demonstrate the benefits of their systems using your question. You can then compare results from different services and you will also have obtained the answer to your question free of charge. Exhibitions are a good way of finding out about new developments, new databases or new search commands. Again you have the opportunity of trying out new services or features at no cost to yourself—you may even find yourself being given a free gift or the opportunity of winning some free search time!

Attending conferences, which often go hand-in-hand with an exhibition, offers a very convivial way of meeting fellow online searchers. A more formal way of meeting others would be to join an online user group. These can be local or national and often publish newsletters.

INFORMATION FROM THE HOSTS AND PRODUCERS

In addition to the published and unpublished sources just mentioned, the hosts and producers of online databases also provide information. The host provides a variety of information which includes both published information in the form of search manuals and newsletters and informal methods such as telephone helplines.

Training

It is important to obtain adequate training. The hosts themselves run training courses; alternatively, many of the library and information professional organizations run similar courses. None of these courses is specific to the needs of information personnel and professionals working in other areas will find them helpful.

Many commercial organizations are actively encouraging their staff to carry out their own online searches. In these organizations, the library and information staff will usually run training courses in-house for interested staff.

In addition to this trend, there are several commercial services specifically aimed at the end-user or non-information professional. One of the best known of these is EasyNet, which provides entry into several hundred databases. Payment is debited from a credit-card account. Another service, Istel, provides access to a number of databases directly and also into the EasyNet system. Payment is by monthly subscription.

Online search services

There is an alternative to accessing online databases yourself. Many libraries now operate online search services. In addition, many of the specialist database producers also offer an online search service. The advantage of this type of service is that you do not need to have the passwords, the equipment or the experience to carry out an online search. It is also particularly helpful if you do not search very often or if you wish to search a database with which you are not familiar, either in terms of the subject or the online host on which the service is held.

There are several directories of libraries or individual information consultants who offer this service. A European one which is available through the online host ECHO is called BROKERS-GUIDE. It provides details of more than 600 information brokers working the European Economic Community. The ECHO host can be accessed free of charge.

In the UK, Aslib produces a directory called *UK Online Search Services* which lists individuals and libraries which offer online search service. In the US, the *Online Database Search Services Directory* provides similar information.

Databases on CD-ROM

The CD-ROM or 'compact disc read-only memory' is an increasingly important medium for machine-readable sources of information. Although online sources are an excellent medium for information, there are disadvantages. Some of these are a direct result of the technology—'online' means that the database has to be accessible via a telephone link and it can be expensive to retrieve information. Their advantage is that they are capable of handling very large amounts of data, databases can be updated very quickly (which is important for timely data) and the searching software is extremely powerful.

The CD-ROM offers different advantages. The CD-ROM is loaded on a microcomputer, so there is no telephone link. CD-ROMs can also be updated fairly frequently, depending on the decision of the publisher. However, at present the CD-ROM is better suited to information which does not need to be updated more frequently than quarterly or possibly monthly. The information needs to be able to fit on to one disc which means that the large databases such as INSPEC are not suitable since several discs would be needed. However, some of the larger databases are being published as subsets on CD-ROM.

An information source on CD-ROM is usually paid for by annual subscription; once you have the CD-ROM you can access the source as often as you wish and at no additional cost. Updates are provided periodically as part of the subscription. In this respect, CD-ROM is similar to traditional publishing. Because there are no connect charges, the user can practise easily and become proficient without any cost penalty.

Many of the information sources available on CD-ROM correspond to online services already mentioned, although the name of the CD-ROM version is often different. The CD-ROM version also often corresponds to a section of the online database, usually, but not always, defined by date.

COMPENDEX. This engineering database is available in a CD-ROM version from Dialog. COMPENDEX PLUS corresponds to the online version of the service and is updated on a quarterly basis.

SOFTWARE-CD. This is the equivalent of the BUSINESS SOFTWARE online database produced by Information Sources Inc. In this case, the CD-ROM version is equivalent to the online one. It is updated twice a year and has been developed by SilverPlatter Information.

COMPUTER-SPECS. This is a CD-ROM publication which provides details of computer products. The information is compiled by the

GML Corporation. Included in the listing are details of mainframes, minicomputers, microcomputers, operating systems, communications equipment, terminals and other peripherals. The information provided includes the name, model and manufacturer. This product has also been developed by SilverPlatter and is updated twice a year.

In addition to these specific information technology products, there are many other CD-ROMs which provide general information. BOOKS IN PRINT PLUS is the CD-ROM version of *Books in Print*, a directory of English language titles currently in print. The directory is produced by R. R. Bowker. Book titles on aspects of information technology can be identified easily by using the excellent retrieval software of the CD-ROM version. WHITAKERS is the CD-ROM version of *British Books in Print* and books published in the UK can be found using this product. Finally, ULRICHS PLUS corresponds to the *International Directory of Periodicals* (Bowker). This is an excellent means of identifying periodicals and magazines providing coverage of information technology areas.

There are many books which deal with the technology and applications of CD-ROMs. A very comprehensive treatment of the subject is given in *CD-ROM: Fundamentals to Applications* edited by Charles Oppenheim. There is also a magazine entitled *LaserDisk* which provides reviews of CD-ROM products and details of new products available on the market.

There are also several directories which provide details of available CD-ROM publications. These are the *CD-ROM Directory* and *CD-ROMs in Print 1990*. In 1990 a new publication, the *Directory of Portable Databases* (Cuadra/Elsevier) was launched as a sister publication to the *Directory on Online Databases* (Cuadra/Elsevier). The new directory covers databases available on CD-ROM, diskette and magnetic tape.

Conclusion

Accessing machine-readable information sources requires some skills, but the possibilities for retrieving information and then for manipulating it locally are enormous. Online databases provide access to a wide range of international sources, many of which could not otherwise be identified.

The developments in the area of machine readable publications have been enormous over the last decade and the move towards online systems more suitable for the non-information professional to access coupled with the development of the compact disc technology offer the information seeker much easier, cheaper and direct access to information.

Appendix

Database producers

ARTIFICIAL INTELLIGENCE
The Turing Institute
George House
36 North Hanover Street
Glasgow G1 2AD
UK

The BUSINESS SOFTWARE DATABASE
Information Sources Inc.
1173 Colusa Avenue
P O Box 7848
Berkeley
CA 94707
USA

COMPENDEX
Engineering Information Inc.
345 East 47th Street
New York
NY 10017
USA

COMPUTER DATABASE
Information Access Corp.
362 Lakeside Drive
Foster City
CA 94404
USA

ELECTRONIC PUBLISHING ABSTRACTS
PIRA
Randalls Road
Leatherhead KT22 7RU
UK

INSPEC
Institution of Electrical Engineers
Station House
Nightingale Road
Hitchin SG5 1RJ
UK

MENU—THE INTERNATIONAL SOFTWARE DATABASE
International Software Database Corp.
P. O. Box MENU
Pittsburgh
PA 15241
USA

MICROCOMPUTER INDEX
Learned Information Inc.
143 Old Marlton Pike
Medford
NJ 08055
USA

MICROCOMPUTER SOFTWARE AND HARDWARE GUIDE
R. R. Bowker Company
245 W 17th Street

New York
NY 10011
USA

PROMT
Predicasts
8–10 Denman Street
London W1V 7RF
UK

CD-ROM addresses

R. R. Bowker
Borough Green
Sevenoaks
Kent TN15 8PH
UK

SilverPlatter Information Ltd
10 Barley Mow Passage
London W4 4PH
UK

Bibliography

Armstrong, C. and Large, A. *CD-ROM Information Products—an Evaluative Guide and Directory*, Gower, 1990.
The CD-ROM Directory, TFPL, 3rd edn, 1988.
Connory, M. (Editor), *Online Database Search Services Directory*, 2nd edn, Gale Research Publications, 1987.
Desmarais, N. *CD-ROMs in Print 1990*, Meckler, 1989.
Dutton, B. End-user Searching—What are the Implications?, *Aslib Proceedings*, 41(4), April 1989, pp. 149–157.
The Laserdisk Professional, Online 1988–, bi-monthly, $86 p.a. (11 Tannery Lane, Weston, CT 06883, USA)
Oppenheim, C. (Editor), *CD-ROM: Fundamentals to Applications*, Butterworths, 1988.

CHAPTER TEN

Secondary sources and reference works

D. HAYNES

Introduction

Secondary sources are guides to information sources. Rather than giving us the information we may need, they tell us where to look. Secondary sources include literature guides, abstracting and indexing journals, and bibliographic databases. There is a number of general guides to secondary sources and they provide a good starting point for more detailed information. Directories such as the *Directory of Directories* (Gale Research) are geared to a particular type of source, rather than a specific subject area. The *Directory of Directories* has a strong emphasis on U.S. sources. The American Library Association publishes the *Guide to Reference Books* which has a section on computers.

Standards are covered in *Access to Standards Information: How to Enquire or Be Informed about Standards and Technical Regulations Available Worldwide* (ISO 1986).

Current British Directories (CBD Research Ltd) is a bibliography of directories of UK and Ireland. It includes an extensive subject index and a publishers index. CBD Research also publishes *Current European Directories*, which covers continental Europe. Alan Armstrong and Associates used to publish *The Top 3000 Directories and Annuals*, which has now sadly ceased publication. It was broadly based on a survey of the most popular reference works in a number of libraries and information units in the UK, and the coverage of directories was international. The indexes are clear and well presented.

Another general source worth investigating is *British Sources of Information. A Subject Guide and Bibliography* (Routledge & Kegan Paul) by Paul Jackson.

Guides to the information technology literature are not very common. A notable example is the *Computing Information Directory* (Pedarco) compiled and edited by Darlene Myers Hildebrandt. It is probably the most comprehensive guide of its kind to the computing literature and provides a useful indication of the scope of the literature. It is divided into sections dealing with particular sources and is intended as a guide to librarians setting up a library for computing. The directory has useful notes on how to select relevant items and acquisitions policies for building up different types of collection. The chapter on journals lists over 1800 English-language journals. Many of the titles listed are defunct, and this is indicated. There are also notes on the coverage and names of former titles of the journals listed. The ACM and IEE Computer Society are listed as key publishers of core journals in computing. The emphasis is very North American, although some UK and European sources are included. Publishers of computer titles are identified and include: Academic Press; Springer-Verlag; John Wiley & Sons; Prentice-Hall; Elsevier; North-Holland; Yourdon; McGraw-Hill; and Pergamon Press. Some of the main abstracting services are also identified including: *Electronic Publishing Abstracts*, *IT Focus*, and *Telecommunications Alert*.

Directories

General

General directories of direct relevance to information technology include the *Information Technology Yearbook* (Century), published annually.

The Confederation of Information Communication Industries (CICI) produces the *CICI Directory of Information Products and Services* (Longman) which provides a guide to services and products in the information industry including broadcasting and libraries. It is also available online on CICI-NET and as a gateway to services such as Telecom Gold.

McGraw-Hill recently published two new titles in its *Science Reference Series: Communications Source Book* and the *Computer Science Source Book*. The *Communications Source Book* covers telecommunications and provides a comprehensive overview of the state of the business and associated technologies. The *Com-*

168 *Secondary sources and reference works*

puter Science Source Book also has over 120 articles on computer and science and data processing. It covers many aspects of information technology including computer architecture and systems applications.

Computing Decisions (Kemps Group Ltd), edited by the National Computing Centre, identifies 6000 suppliers of hardware and software products in over 150 classifications. The *Computers and Computing Information Resources Directory* (Gale Research) covers the USA.

Computing Services Association Official Reference Book and Buyers Guide (Computing Services Association) provides an analysis of computing developments worldwide.

Regional

The *Asian Computer Directory* (Computer Publications Ltd) provides a comprehensive, up-to-date source of information on the computer industry in Asia. The 1986 edition has over 12 000 listings. It gives profiles of more than 7500 companies which have installed computers and 5110 companies which supply services, products to the computer industry and computer organizations.

Electronics

Components which go to make up computers are covered in the electronics directories. A good source for suppliers in the UK is *DIAL Industry: Electrical, Electronics, Computers, Instrumentation*. The *Electrical and Electronics Trades Directory* (Peter Peregrinus) also covers UK companies (4000) and has a comprehensive index of all organizations. It is in seven sections: Manufacturers; Manufacturers' Representatives; Wholesale Distributors; Associations; Electrical Undertakings; Trade Names; and Products and Materials.

For details of UK distributors of electronic components the *Distributor Survey* (1985) by Karen Packham and Alasdair Reid, provides a useful source.

Electronic Engineering Index (Technical Indexes Ltd) published three times a year is a comprehensive guide to manufacturers of electronics components and equipment. The index is compiled from suppliers' full technical literature.

European directories include *Électro annuaire électricité—électronic* (Paris, Société nouvelle d'éditions publicitaires) is a comprehensive directory of manufacturers and suppliers of electrical and electronics goods and components in France. It is in three sections with a listing of suppliers by region, a subject index and a trade name index. The *Electro Electronics Buyers' Guide* (German

Secondary sources and reference works 169

Electrical and Electronics Industry) contains an index to products with 12 000 headings. Suppliers are listed under 62 main manufacturing groups and 2400 product groups. Trade names and company profiles are given.

The *European Electronic Component Distributor Directory* (Elsevier) covers 17 European countries. Three thousand distributors are included, listing 7500 component manufacturers. Active and passive components are both covered in the *Surface Mount Components* directory (IFS Publications/Clementson/Nu-Markets Ltd). Entries are by country and the coverage is worldwide.

The *Electronics and Instruments Directory* (Morgan-Grampian) includes sections on UK companies, UK agents for foreign firms, trade names, associations, diary of events, buyers' guide, and distributors.

Microcomputers

Microcomputers are covered in *The Bowker Complete Source Book of Personal Computing* which contains details of over 1100 personal computers and peripheral items such as printers, disk drives and acoustic couplers, all with full specifications and latest prices. About 3700 software programs are arranged by hundreds of applications from accounting to household management to word processing. Annotated listings of 3500 current books, periodicals, associations, publications and online databases and a list of companies are included.

Datapro Research Corporation publishes several specialist directories, notably: the *Datapro Directory of Small Computers*; the *Datapro Directory of Software*; and the *Datapro Directory of Online Services*.

The *Computer Users' Yearbook* (VNU Business Publications) comes in three volumes and is a valuable reference guide for computer professionals. It includes listings of computer equipment, services and suppliers and contains details of major UK installations.

Software

If you need to find out about software products, the *Software Users' Yearbook 1990* (VNU Business Publications) provides a comprehensive guide to software available in UK. It is published in four volumes. The first two volumes contain useful background information and Volumes 3 and 4 list actual software products. Volume 1, on suppliers and services, contains master profiles of all companies listed in the directory. It lists the products and services under each company and also includes associations in the UK.

There are supplier profiles on 2200 companies and then a listing of training courses, by subject. The recruitment section indicates the number and location of staff among major employers. The consultants listing is indexed by industry, application, operating system and by manufacturer. There is also an A–Z of products. Volume 2 deals with system software and provides an alphabetic listing of software under seven headings. It also contains supplier details indexed by category, manufacturer, and by operating system. Volume 3 deals with industry specific software and the products are listed under 12 categories and are comprehensively indexed. Volume 4 covers general applications software, listed under seven headings and indexed by application.

Educational software in the US is covered by *Educational Software Directory: A Subject Guide to Microcomputer Software* (Libraries Unlimited).

Engineering and Industrial Software Directory (Engineering Information Inc.) contains information on over 3000 programs designed specifically for engineering and industrial applications. Each entry draws a comprehensive profile of the software described, including a list of available published reviews.

Communications

Communications is a growing area and is covered by a number of directories. The *Communication Yearbook* (Sage Publications) covers all aspects of communications from communications between people, to mass communication and covers many interdisciplinary fields of study. *Communications* (Macmillan Press) on the other hand lists organizations involved in telecommunications using a classification scheme to identify those organizations' activities. The *Communications Management Yearbook* (EMAP) is published in association with the Telecommunications Managers' Association. It lists equipment and suppliers and includes advice on European regulatory bodies governing telecomms standards.

Jordan Information Service publishes *Britain's Data Communications Equipment Suppliers* which provides market analysis and financial and trading profiles of 100 leading companies in this area.

Data Communications Product Directory deals with the U.S. market and lists over 2500 data communications products in 24 product categories. The *DataComms Book* (VNU), covers data communications telecommunications and office automation. It is in six sections: systems; services; suppliers guide; software; sites; and supplier details. Local area networks are covered by *The Local Area Networking Sourcebook* (Phillips Publishing Inc.). It covers manufacturers and distributors, software, business and technical services, standards and it gives detailed descriptions under many of the entries in the directory. Most of this information comes direct from the suppliers.

The *Television and Cable Factbook* comes in two volumes and covers the U.S. television, cable and electronics industries. The listings are given by state for each of the three categories covered.

Computer Graphics

There is a number of directories on computer graphics including the *Computer Graphics Directory* (PennWell Publications). It is a guide to the location of hardware, software and services in the computer graphics industry listing over 2000 companies, organizations, bureaux and conferences, and with editorial commentaries. The *Directory of Computer Graphics Suppliers* (Technology & Business Communications) is more limited covering vendors for products from 400 computer graphics companies in North America. There is also an international vendor section.

Butterworths *CAD International Directory* is a buyers' guide to software, workstations, displays, plotters, turnkey systems, consultancies, bureaux and organizations in the area of computer-aided design.

Automated Manufacturing

The *Process Engineering Directory* (Morgan-Grampian) is a guide to over 50 000 products provided by nearly 3000 companies and indexed under 4000 product headings. The *Automated Manufacturing Directory* (Morgan-Grampian) is devoted to computer assisted manufacturing and covers services and systems provided by over 500 companies in the UK.

Expert Systems

The *CRI Directory of Expert Systems* (Learned Information) is a directory with abstracts and references on every expert system which has been written up and published in English.

Market Information

For a guide to market research reports *Market Research: A Guide to British Library Holdings 1989–90* provides a good starting report. It includes a list of market research reports with a subject index and list of publishers.

Quarterly statistics are produced by the Statistics Office in a series of bulletins. Of particular relevance to information technology are *Business Monitor PQ 3301. Office Machines, Business Monitor PQ 3303 Electronic Data Processing Equipment, Business Monitor PQ 3454 Electronic Consumer Goods and Miscellaneous Equipment*; and *Business Monitor PQ 3453 Electronic Subassemblies and Active Components*. The Business Monitors include details of sales by UK manufacturers in numbers of units and value, and HM Customs and Excise figures on imports and exports.

Infotech publishes a series of market reports looking at different sectors. An example is *Financial Comparison and Directory. Market Sector: Distributors and Dealers of Computer Equipment*.

Britain's Computer Industry (Jordan Information Services) is a market summary and financial and trading analysis of the major companies in the industry.

IRD published the *Directory of Plans, Executives, Policies for PCs, Office Automation, Datacom and Electronic Mail* in 1985. It contains plans for procurement of microcomputers and software and resulted from a survey of 1000 major U.S. corporations. Names, addresses and purchasing responsibilities of 3500 executives of these companies were also listed. It is an expanded version of *Electronic Mail Executives Directory*.

Dictionaries

Information technology is a convergence of several technologies, some of which are very specialist. It is a discipline particularly prone to proliferation of new terms and acronyms. This is a characteristic of any rapidly developing field where new concepts are developed and the existing terminology very quickly becomes inadequate or too cumbersome to use.

There are a number of general dictionaries including the *Penguin Dictionary of Computers*, the *Dictionary of Computing* (Oxford University Press) with 4000 terms and the *Dictionary of Computers, Information Processing and Telecommunications* (John Wiley). ISO have published *Data Processing Vocabulary*, although this is a little long in the tooth now, having been published in 1982.

Electronics and Computer Acronyms (Butterworth) contains explanations of acronyms and abbreviations used in computers, data telecommunications, electronics, fibre optics, hardware, microcomputers, microprocessors. It has 2500 entries and covers information technology in its widest sense.

Electronics is covered by the *Dictionary of Electronics* (Butterworth), which is a concise technical reference guide for all those concerned with any aspects of electronics. There are also some multilingual dictionaries covering electronics. The *Dictionary of Electronics* (Kluwer) is an English/German/French/Dutch/Russian dictionary. Plenum Press publishes the multi-lingual *Dictionary of Electronics and Electrical Engineering*, which covers English/Japanese/German/Russian.

The *Arabic Computer Dictionary* (Routledge & Kegan Paul) is compiled by Multi-lingual International Publishers Ltd.

Microcomputers are covered in the *Macmillan Dictionary of Personal Computing and Communications*, compiled by Dennis Longley and Michael Shain.

The *Dictionary of Printed Circuit Technology* (Elsevier) is an English/German dictionary. Elsevier also publishes the *Dictionary of OptoElectronics and Electro-Optics* and this is a multilingual dictionary covering English, German, French, and Spanish.

Image technology is covered by the *Dictionary of Image Technology* (Focal Press, 1988).

Robotics and computer integrated manufacturing have become popular subjects lately and there is continuing interest shown in this area. The *Dictionary of Robotics* (Macmillan) goes some way towards satisfying the need. Elsevier publishes the *Dictionary of Advanced Manufacturing Technology* and John Wiley publishes the *Dictionary of Artificial Intelligence and Robotics*.

Abstracts and indexing journals

There are two main types of abstract, the indicative abstract and the informative abstract. The indicative abstract aims to tell the reader what the item abstracted is about. The scope of the article and the topics covered are indicated. The informative abstract is usually longer and contains more detail about the substance of an item, including a summary of any results or findings. Reading an informative article is often sufficient and can preclude the necessity of reading the original. This type of service is more expensive to provide and is relatively rare. At the other extreme there are a number of services which provide basic bibliographic information, with no abstract. These services often depend on detailed subject indexes to provide access. Many of the services covered in this section are also available electronically as online databases or as CD-ROMs. The advantages of the printed versions are transportability (you can scan an issue of an abstracts journal on the train, for instance) and the capability for browsing, an option often denied to users of online services. The online versions allow for more flexible retrieval of items and selection of items using several

174 Secondary sources and reference works

several different criteria. For more details of online databases and CD-ROMs, see Chapter nine on machine-readable sources.

Producers of abstracts services come at information technology from different angles. The Institution of Electrical Engineers in association with the Institute of Electrical and Electronics Engineers produces one of the most comprehensive services, *Computer & Control Abstracts*, under its Inspec imprint. This is available online as the INSPEC database and is described in detail in Chapter eleven. The IEE publishes a number of abstracts services through Inspec. The information scientists at Inspec scan and abstract a wide range of journals and produce more than 70 000 abstracts a year. Bibliographic details only are published in *Current Papers on Computers and Control*, which is a monthly compilation. The papers are arranged in classified order according to the Inspec classification. *Current Papers in Electrical and Electronics Engineering* is a sister journal with over 80 000 items a year and containing just bibliographic details of items in classified order. There is no index, providing alternative routes for subject access. *IT Focus* is an abstracts service dealing specifically with information technology from the Inspec stable.

Inspec also publishes a series of *Key Abstracts*, which are subsets of *Computer & Control Abstracts*. Over 4000 journals are scanned and indicative abstracts appear in classified order. This service is intended for those with specialized interests who do not want to subscribe to the whole of *Computer & Control Abstracts*. Individual titles cost £60 per annum or £950 per annum for all the sections. Titles in the *Key Abstracts* series include:

Computer Communication and Storage
Business Automation
Optoelectronics
Telecommunications
Artificial Intelligence
Machine Vision
Robotics and Control
Software Engineering
Computing in Electronics and Power
Electronic Circuits
Microelectronics and Printed Circuits
Semiconductor Devices

A more modest abstracts journal is *Computer Abstracts* (Technical Information), published in Jersey, which covers articles and papers in periodicals as well as conference proceedings, U.S. government reports and books. It is highly selective and tends towards the learned journals. The turnaround is slow with a typical time-lag of nine months between publication of the original article and the abstract appearing. They publish about 300 items a month.

Computer Contents (ISI) is a compilation of tables of contents from computer, electronic and telecommunications magazines, journals and transactions. It appears twice a month, with a three- to four-month time lag between publication of the original and the publication of the contents pages. This service enables subscribers to rapidly scan through a selection of titles. This kind of browsing facility complements the highly-directed searching offered by the well-indexed abstracts services.

General sources such as *Current Contents. Engineering Technology & Applied Science* cover diverse topics including computer science and technology, data processing applications, electronics, optics, robotics, and telecommunications. Each issue lists the journals which are covered in that issue. The Contents pages appear very rapidly, normally within one week of publication of the original periodical. There is a title word index and an author index. This is an effective current awareness service and offers the information in a browsable format.

The *ACM Guide to Computing Literature* is an annual bibliography of the computing literature. There are several detailed indexes, including a keyword index, category index and proper noun index. The subject index gives titles and refers to the main entry which contains the bibliographic details. The 1988 issue of the *Guide* has more than 18 000 items in it.

The *Data Processing Digest* is a monthly service for computer professionals. It contains digests of articles from a range of computer, business, industrial and professional publications. Turnabout is relatively rapid at two months. It is highly selective with perhaps 20 items an issue. Each item is summarized in half a page, and is highly informative.

Cambridge Scientific Abstracts publishes the bimonthly *Electronics and Communications Abstracts Journal*. There are approximately 1500 indicative abstracts per issue. It covers: electronics systems and applications; electronic physics; electronic circuits; electronic devices; and communications.

Telecomms Abstracts (TechGnosis/NCC) is a small specialist abstracts journal, which contains informative and indicative abstracts and has a turnaround of about two months. It covers electronic mail, local area networks, and micro to mainframe communications.

Classification schemes

Classification schemes provide a useful model of the disciplines which make up information technology and can show the relationship between these disciplines. They are a useful tool for locating relevant literature and should not be overlooked. All libraries use some kind of classification scheme to determine the shelving order of books. Two widely used schemes are DDC (Dewey Decimal Classification) and UDC (Universal Decimal Classification). UDC was originally based on DDC, although the two classifications have diverged considerably. Intended to cover the complete range of human endeavour, they are both used by general libraries, such as public libraries and some academic libraries. UDC is published continuously in parts as an international standard ISO 1000.

Two of the world's great libraries, the Library of Congress and the British Library, have both devised their own in-house classifications, and indeed Library of Congress classification is used in a number of general libraries.

Specialist libraries have for a long time devised their own classifications. The general classifications provided by UDC are often not specific enough to distinguish between specialist titles. The result is that a lot of titles may come under one heading. The general schemes can also be rather cumbersome when it comes to notation, especially for the specific subject areas which can result in very long codes for specialized topics.

Many of the abstracts services have their own specialist classification schemes. This is usually used to determine the headings under which individual items appear.

CHAPTER ELEVEN

Organizations libraries and referral services

R. POYSER

Introduction

The aim of this chapter is to give an overview of the types of organization which provide information including libraries and referral services. Organizations exist within much wider international political/economic frameworks and here organizations ranging from the multi-national companies and agencies of the United Nations down to the small independent software houses will be considered.

Gaining a good understanding of the structure and arrangement of organizations is an important step in deciding where to look for information. Here this is portrayed in a hierarchical manner, beginning with international agencies, followed by government organizations and national libraries. It then focuses on professional and trade associations, academic institutions and finally private companies.

Tapping the information that may be available from these organizations can be much enhanced by accurate query profiling, relating the complexity of a query to the type and personnel of the organization involved. It is appropriate at this point to refer to a few rules to adopt when approaching any organization:

- State your purpose clearly
- If a query is complex, write a briefing note first to the person concerned and then begin further discussion
- Use the correct forms of address politely
- If you must visit in person, notify in advance your intention
- Remember that information may not always be free

International agencies

International agencies can be large multi-facetted organizations that implement policy decisions made by member nations. There are also a number of agencies which do international work. A third category is the multi-national private companies whose interests and scope are large enough to become international in character.

The United Nations, the British Commonwealth, the Organization for Economic Co-operation and Development (OECD) and the European Community (EC) are examples of large international organizations with interests which encompass information technology. It is the committees, sub-groups and agencies of these organizations that are the sources of information. They implement policy decisions taken by the parent organizations, produce publications and collate data. International agencies can be a source of international standards, codes of practice, technical reports and patents.

Types of information

This is a list of suggested pathways to information which could be tried.

Information type	Source
Information about people	Professional associations, embassies and information centres, large multi-national companies (which may act as referral agencies)
Education	UNESCO, British Council, other information centres, Association of Commonwealth Universities
Research	UNESCO, Commonwealth (GTAD and the Science Council)
Financial	UNCTAD, GATT, OECD, EC, CTO, UN
International Standards	EC Regulations, ILO, ITU, IEC, EPO

Locating organizations

The *Europa World Yearbook* is useful for locating international organizations. It contains a large section on the United Nations and its agencies, the European Community organizations, the

British Commonwealth and other intergovernmental organizations. There is a selected coverage by subject of other major international organizations that do not fall into the above categories. The main body of the directory is a country-by-country analysis that includes details of chambers of commerce, industrial associations and major governmental ministries.

Specific international agencies

UNITED NATIONS

The United Nations Organization is the largest body for international cooperation. The policy is decided by the United Nations Council and various agencies act on the directives of the UN.

Regional Commissions

The Regional Commissions support research into technology transfer and through various committees improve statistical and review work in key economic areas. Publications of the ECE (Economic Commission for Europe) which are of importance include: *Economic Bulletin for Europe*, *Economic Survey of Europe*, and *Annual Review of Engineering Industries and Automation*.

UNCTAD

UNCTAD (United Nations Conference on Trade and Development) promotes international trade, particularly that of Third World countries. It cooperates with GATT (General Agreement on Trade and Tariffs) and together they publish a number of directories.

International Telecommunications Union (ITU)

The ITU is a UN agency which promotes cooperation between national telecommunications agencies and develops standards. It is a source of information on technical standards, traffic routing data and technical developments. The ITU promotes technical development and harmonization. It has various committees, a library and archives. The library at the ITU headquarters in Switzerland has a collection of 20 000 volumes, 700 periodicals, press cuttings and several databanks. The service is intended for researchers and ITU member states.

ASSOCIATION OF COMMONWEALTH UNIVERSITIES

The Association of Commonwealth Universities provides information about Commonwealth educational institutes. There is also a professional group called the Commonwealth Association of Science Technology and Mathematics Educators. The Commonwealth Telecommunications Organization is another potential source of information.

OECD

The Organization for Economic Cooperation and Development (OECD) has a Committee for Information, Computer and Communications Policy.

EUROPEAN COMMUNITY (EC)

Information generated by the EC and its agencies can be traced using the press and information office of the Commission of the European Communities or by using either a European Documentation Centre (EDC) or a European Referral Centre (ERC). These are designated centres for the dissemination of EC information with EDCs providing in-depth information and ERCs mainly at a basic level. A listing of these organizations is given in the *Directory of European Documentation Centres* (Association of EDC Libraries).

Notification of the progress of EC directives and projects in computing and information technology is contained in the supplement to *Euroabstracts* (European Commission), called *DG XIII Innovation and Technology Transfer* (European Commission). DG XIII is responsible for information services and commissions research projects and studies of direct interest. In particular they have commissioned research into information technology applications, as well as doing surveys and feasibility studies within Europe.

OTHER ORGANIZATIONS

Other organizations which provide technical information include:

- The European Patent Office in Munich, which grants European patents. Its official journal is the *European Patents Bulletin*.
- The International Electrotechnical Commission (IEC) in Geneva coordinates the unification of national electrotechnical standards. It produces a catalogue of publications.
- The Intergovernmental Bureau for Informatics in Rome is a United Nations body covering informatics and acting as an advisory body to over 40 participating members. It publishes *Agora* and *IBI Newsletter*.

Organizations libraries and referral services 181

- The European Association for the Transfer of Technologies, Innovation and Industrial Information is based in Luxembourg and promotes exchange of innovation and industrial information in the EC. It was formed by the Commission of the European Community. The association maintains a database on technology transfer, which is available to members.
- The International Federation for Information Processing based in Geneva promotes research and exchange of information in information processing.

National organizations

Introduction

This section deals with those government departments whose areas of activity cover information technology. The work of such government departments, ministries, research institutes, government laboratories and regional organizations and centres provide a rich resource in information. The USSR, USA, Japan and the European countries are fertile areas for information on computing and here the most relevant institutions are highlighted.

Government organizations are major sources of information within their areas of responsibility. Either individuals or groups within such organizations have information or their associated library and information services. That information can exist in many forms: personal knowledge; written memoranda; papers; published work; and computer data. The different types of information generated by governmental organizations are shown in the table below.

Organization	Type of information generated
Parliament or Congress	Acts; Bills; Command Papers; White Papers; Green Papers; debates; Statutory Instruments
Government and non-government departments	Reports (annual, serial and investigative); statistics (published and unpublished form); pamphlets; publicity material; periodicals; abstracts; catalogues; bibliographies; codes of practice; manuals; regulations and forms; patents and product specifications; consultative papers; memoranda; ephemeral papers.

182 *Organizations libraries and referral services*

In the UK many government publications are available from HMSO (Her Majesty's Stationery Office). Official publications are covered in further detail in Chapter fifteen.

National Information Centres

A number of countries run national information centres as part of their diplomatic missions overseas. Notable examples are the Japan Information Centres and the United States Information Service Reference Centres. The British Council plays a similar role for the United Kingdom, although it is an independent organization and does not normally have diplomatic status. The role of these organizations is to promote the cultural, scientific and technical achievements of their respective countries. They provide a useful point of access to information services in their countries.

SOVIET UNION

In the USSR, all research institutes are under the wing of the Academy of Sciences, itself part of a ministry. Access to the information of the 136 libraries of the Academy is available via the library of the Academy of Sciences in Leningrad. VINITI is the acronym for the All-Union Institute for Scientific and Technical Information and it is a part of the Academy of Sciences of the USSR, providing scientific and technical information.

UNITED STATES

Organizations of value in the US are: the Brookhaven National Laboratory, NASA and the National Bureau of Standards. This last organization is divided into several departments, two of which, the National Engineering Laboratory and the Institute for Computer Sciences and Technology, are very important information providers. The National Technical Information Service (NTIS) is a part of the U.S. Department of Commerce and it provides an information service covering scientific and technical information from over 50 countries. It maintains a comprehensive list of over 1.5 million titles.

JAPAN

In Japan, the Ministry of International Trade and Industry or MITI, administers the Agency of Industry and Technology which in turn controls over 30 institutions. Four of these produce relevant information: the Electrotechnical Laboratory, the Industrial Research Institute, the Institute for Future Technology, and the Applied Science Research Institute. The Japan External Trade

Organization, and the International Economic and Trade Information Centre in Tokyo are also useful sources.

FRANCE

In Europe there are a number of centres of excellence, particularly in France, Germany and the UK. The Centre National de la Recherche Scientifique (CNRS) is the main governmental research institute in France, controlling 1500 laboratories and research centres. CNRS information is available from the Institute de l'Information Scientifique et Technique de CNRS in Paris. Information on telecommunications is available from the research centre of the PTT at the Centre National d'Études des Télécommunications, CNET.

GERMANY

In Germany, the Frauenhofer Society for the Advancement of Applied Research (Frauenhofer Gesellschaft zur Förderung der Angewandten Forschung) contracts out research on behalf of government and industry. The Max-Planck Society for the Advancement of Science (Max-Planck Gesellschaft zur Förderung der Wissenschaften) controls 61 research institutes and is a member of the Wissenschaftsrat, or Science Council.

UNITED KINGDOM

Obtaining information from government organizations is not impossible, just tricky. First of all we must be clear what we mean by government organizations. These must include the prime progenitors of legislation in the United Kingdom, the House of Commons, and the associated second chamber, the House of Lords. Following on from them, in a sort of pecking order, are the government departments that are the main instruments for giving effect and power to the legislation passed by the two chambers. These departments work through local authorities, statutory bodies and government sponsored organizations. There are also a number of non-departmental public bodies that exist as autonomous organizations such as the National Economic Development Office. They tend to be of three types: executive; advisory; and tribunal. Each body exists to further government policy in specific areas and there are now approximately 1600 in existence.

Finally, there are separate government departments for the regional areas of the British Isles: the Scottish Office; the Welsh Office; the Northern Ireland Office; and the Isle of Man and Channel Islands Office.

In the UK, the following government bodies are useful sources of information: Department of Trade and Industry; Department of Education and Science; Health and Safety Executive; and the Science and Engineering Research Council.

Department of Trade and Industry (DTI)

The Department of Trade and Industry is responsible for the development of trade and industry, research, science and technology. It is a very large government department, composed of various divisions, executive bodies, advisory bodies and committees. There are also several government laboratories run by the DTI. The Patent Office and the British Standards Institute both come under the auspices of the DTI, as well as various committees, organizations and research bodies that are directly funded by them. The DTI also has eight regional offices which are listed in the *Directory of British Official Publications* and in *Whitakers' Almanack*.

The publications produced by these organizations in the form of reports, recommendations, statistics, patents, standards and current-awareness bulletins, are a useful source of information. Although issued by a variety of divisions within the DTI, they are available from the central library at Ashdown House. The library issues a weekly *Additions to Libraries* list and an annual catalogue is available. Some priced publications can be bought from HMSO, others via the departments and from the DTI itself. Unfortunately, some publications are restricted and only available to interested commercial organizations for internal circulation.

The stock of Ashdown House Library covers: industrial policy; development, manufacturing industries; science and technology; information technology; and telecommunications. It also has complete collections of DTI publications. It is open to the public by appointment only; loans are via the British Library.

Areas worth exploring for additional information are the various libraries and information services supporting the DTI, its subsidiary bodies and governmental laboratories, for example the CCTA (Central Computer & Telecommunications Agency) which is a part of the Treasury and advises government departments on information technology. Where access is restricted it may be given if there are no other suitable sources. The following is divided into three subject approaches for information from the DTI's various divisions: general information including patents and standards; information on telecommunications; and information on computing and IT.

General Information

Information may be obtained from the Telecommunications Division of the DTI: pamphlets, codes of practice, publicity literature and newsletters. Although not a part of the DTI, OFTEL (Office of Telecommunications) supervises telecommunications activities in the UK and maintains a small library. Priced publications are available from the library service.

Computing and IT

The two major sources of information are the Manufacturing and Information Technology (MIT) Division and the Information Engineering Directorate (IED). Both departments produce codes of practice, publish publicity literature and liaise with organizations and firms in order to develop the UK's market position in computing and IT. MIT division deals with the applied side of IT focusing on the public procurement of IT, online, medical electronics, IT security and standards, OSI, information services publishing and capital electronics (such as ground radar). IED on the other hand specializes in the non-applied fields of software engineering, software standards, programming, quality control and electronic components. IED is jointly responsible with the DTI, and the Science and Engineering Research Council (SERC), for the Joint Framework for Information Technology (JFIT). JFIT is a major research programme in computing and IT that replaced the Alvey Programme. It is a source of information on DTI/SERC and European-funded research programmes and it publishes a newsletter, *JFIT News*, detailing current developments, conferences and forthcoming events.

Finally, there are two government laboratories with libraries containing significant collections in computing. The National Engineering Laboratory library contains some literature on automation and computer-aided design and manufacture. The National Physical Laboratory covers, among other areas, computer science. Access may be restricted. Reports and publications from all government libraries and research establishments may be obtained from the Technology Reports Centre.

Overseas Technical Information Unit (OTIU)

This is a service provided by the DTI that helps UK industries to keep in touch with technological developments overseas. Reports, etc. are free. Enquiries are via PERA.

Department of Education and Science

Within this department the National Council for Educational Technology is one of the most important sources of information on the impact of information technology on education. It acts as a forum for exchange on new technology and the curriculum, organizing conferences, workshops, publishing papers and a house journal (*NCET News*) and arranging training programmes. The DES has two divisions devoted to aspects of information technology—the Health and Safety Executive and the Science and Engineering Research Council.

Health & Safety Executive (HSE)

Through a network of 20 area offices and several laboratories, this statutory body deals in all areas of health and safety within the workplace. It enforces standards and gives advice to industries. It has published reports on VDU hazards and guidance notes on ergonomic design of IT products. HSE publications are useful sources of information and include reports, pamphlets, guidance notes and a newsletter. Most of these are published by HMSO. Free publications are available directly from HSE. A publications' catalogue is available and current information is displayed on Prestel.

Science and Engineering Research Council (SERC)

This is one of five research councils funded by the Department of Education and Science. It supports basic research in science by means of research grants and work in its own institutions plus encouraging collaboration in research among institutions of higher education and industry. It operates through four boards and divisions, one of which covers microelectronics and computer applications.

SERC produces an annual report and a bulletin. Publications of some of the establishments of SERC are sold by HMSO as well as being available directly from SERC. Two of the research institutions covered by the SERC have libraries with relevant material. They are: Rutherford Appleton Laboratory in Didcot; and the Daresbury Laboratory in Warrington.

National Electronic Council

This is a government-funded body that advises schools, government and industry trying to promote the use of electronics and information technology. It publishes the *National Electronics Review* and various monographs such as *Girls in IT*.

National libraries

The national libraries of the US, Germany, United Kingdom, Japan and France are of particular importance because the quality of their collections in computing and information technology reflects the leading role of those countries in this area. The size and breadth of such collections means that they are able to provide bibliographic information, inter-library loans, online databases and information services to industry, government and the general public. They can be used as a library of last resort when all else fails. Unfortunately, it is difficult to obtain current knowledge on the provision of information services in other national libraries. It is perhaps best to contact them by letter, telephone or fax in the first instance.

Specific libraries

USA: LIBRARY OF CONGRESS

The largest national library in the world is the Library of Congress based in Washington. It has a collection of 80 million items, provides reference and bibliographical services and maintains a national referral centre database covering all subjects.

JAPAN: NATIONAL DIET LIBRARY

Modelled on the Library of Congress, the National Diet Library is the largest library in Japan, acting as a deposit library, producing bibliographic information and maintaining an information centre. The library has a section devoted to science and technology, covering books, dissertations, reports and subscribes to 20 000 serial titles.

GERMANY: DEUTSCHE BIBLIOTHEK

Because of its federated constitutional nature, Germany is slightly different in that it has three Universal Libraries which act as the national library: the Staatsbibliothek Prussischer Kulturbesitz (Berlin), the Bayrische Staatsbibliothek (Munich) and the Deutsche Bibliothek (Frankfurt). It is the last of these three libraries that holds the most comprehensive collection in science. The German national libraries contain most of the publications produced in the two former German states.

188   *Organizations libraries and referral services*

FRANCE: BIBLIOTHÈQUE NATIONAL

The French national library, the Bibliothèque National, which holds over 9 million items, has a centre for public enquiries, the Bibliothèque publique d'Information based at the Pompidou Centre in Paris.

USSR: LENIN STATE LIBRARY

Many of the East European countries are poorly developed in the field of computing and are generally regarded as lagging 5–10 years behind the West. Nevertheless the Lenin State Library in the Soviet Union is important because of its size; it has a collection of 30 million items and it supports an enquiry, loan and reference service for the USSR.

UK

The British Library

The British Library is the national library for the UK. It is a legal deposit library and a copy of every publication published in the UK is deposited in the British Library. There are extensive collections at the Document Supply Centre at Boston Spa, currently numbered at over 4.5 million documents. There are also specialist collections in the divisional libraries of the British Library, notably the Science Reference and Information Service in London.

British Library Document Supply Centre

The Document Supply Centre is a lending library, covering all subject fields and providing a loan and photocopying service to organizations. It is the ultimate back-up for all libraries in the UK. Its stock in 1988 was:

- 4.5 million books and periodicals
- 2 million technical reports
- 54 000 serial titles
- All British Official publications from 1962
- All UNESCO publications from 1954
- All EC publications from 1973

The Document Supply Centre does loans to approved organizations using printed requisition forms. UK local public libraries all have access to this service, and there is a charge for loans made in this way. Individual organizations can purchase loan requisition forms and can order via various online services, notably Dialog's DIALORDER service.

Science Reference and Information Service (SRIS)

The Science Reference and Information Service has one of the most comprehensive collections in modern science and technology, including patents, trade marks and designs. It is open to any member of the public and it operates an enquiry service for those who cannot visit the library in person. Other facilities include:

- Business Information Service
- Japanese Information Services in Science, Technology and Commerce
- Online computer search services
- Photocopying
- Linguistic help

The scope of SRIS includes business, scientific and technological literature. There is a large collection of British and foreign patents, trade directories and trade literature. There are 30 500 current periodicals, 1400 abstracts journals and approximately 200 000 books.

Official Publications Library

The Official Publications Library is another source of potentially useful information. Based in the British Museum, access is permitted for holders of a readers' ticket, which is normally issued on application by bona fide researchers.

UK National Libraries

The National Library of Scotland and the National Library of Wales serve similar functions to the British Library, but with an emphasis on their own particular regions. Each library may have useful collections in computing and literature as well as large reference collections.

The National Library of Scotland is a depository library under copyright legislation. It receives all British and Irish publications including all HMSO publications and parliamentary papers, a proportion of UN publications and other international bodies' publications sold by HMSO. It has approximately 4.5 million volumes. Access to the reading room is permitted for reference and research work which cannot easily be carried out elsewhere. Tickets can be obtained on application. The Scottish Science Library is a department of the National Library of Scotland.

The National Library of Wales is a legal depository library for British and Irish publications as well as a selection of UN publications. It contains approximately 3 million volumes. Access to the reading room is allowed to holders of readers' tickets. Applications for readers' tickets should be made to the Secretary of the Library.

UK Public Libraries

The public library service is run by the local authorities in the United Kingdom. Many public library services also cater specifically for their local business communities. Some library services have large reference collections with significant collections in computing and information technology. Birmingham, Liverpool, Manchester and Sheffield all operate such services and membership is open to anybody living or working in these urban areas. They offer online search services, access to large reference/trade directories and major collections of patents, trade specifications and EC publications.

Some local authorities have set up business information services which offer help to organizations, usually on a membership basis. Two of the best-known are, HERTIS in Hertfordshire and HATRICS in Hampshire.

Trade associations, research associations and learned societies

The associations, professional and learned societies provide the following services:

- Databases
- Current awareness
- Online search service
- Translations
- Document delivery
- Referral

They may run information bureaux or libraries with reference and sometimes loan collections. They usually subscribe to a core collection of journals and printed abstracts and indexes. Many of the associations have developed their own internal databases, some of which are now commercially available.

In addition to the information services many of the organizations described may be able to offer consultancy, referral services and training. Aslib for instance maintains a comprehensive training programme employing experts in a whole range of subjects in information management. EUSIDIC, the European Association of Information Services, sponsors research and has produced a number of reports.

There are a number of professional bodies that exist in order to promote a wider and deeper knowledge in their particular subject field. The British Computer Society is an example of a learned society, the National Computing Centre is a trade association and the Scientific Documentation Centre Ltd is a research association.

There is a lot of overlap in the work done by these organizations. Both the BCS and the NCC are involved in training although the BCS is the nationally recognized professional examining body.

Each type of organization collects information that reflects its members' interests and this produces different exploitable sources of information. Overlap between the work of these organizations helps to promote connections in each organization's databanks and in the personal relationships between organizations. These informal and formal connections are of immense value in the search for information. Organizations are after all collections of people in the pursuit of a common aim. Information can only be obtained by making the right connections with people in organizations and getting access to the network of knowledge that exists there. The best connections are made when one knows the role of an organization for then one can reasonably predict what type of information they may provide and what sort of access you may get to their collection.

Locating information services

The following directories can be useful in locating information services: *Aslib Directory of Information Sources in the UK*, *Encyclopedia of Information Systems and Services*, *Inside Information*, and *Higher Education Resources for Industry*.

More organizations can be found by using the following guides: *Aslib Shorter Guide to Institutions*, *Directory of British Associations*, *Directory of European Industrial and Trade Associations*, *Industrial Research in the United Kingdom*, and *Yearbook of International Organisations*.

Other directories are: *European Research Centres, a Directory of Organisations in Science, Technology Agriculture and Medicine*; *National Trade and Professional Associations of the United States*; and *Pan European Associations, a Directory of Multi-national Organisations in Europe*.

Current Research in Britain, a four-volume work, details

research in higher education. *Industrial Research in the UK* is a comparable work that details research in industry. It covers industrial firms, research associations and laboratories, consultancies, government departments and laboratories, trade associations, learned and professional associations.

Unfortunately the indexing of directories tends to be very general and index entries under computing or information technology are often not very detailed.

Going further afield, the *Directory of European Industrial and Trade Associations* is useful for Western Europe (excluding the UK). The *Directory of British Associations* covers UK organizations. The *Yearbook of International Organisations* is good for other countries even though its size is daunting and the indexing system complex. In the subject index, Computing and Information Technology comes under Informatics, code W4350. Looking up this section gives a list of institutions and international organizations in computing. Alternatively you can look up such institutions under the entry for each country.

There are other more general guides and directories that may be of use. These include: *Kompass, Kelly's Manufacturers and Merchants Directory, Anglo-American Trade Directory*. There are certain pitfalls associated with using directories. The most important one is the fact that directories age. Names and addresses change and directories can get out of date very quickly. Alternative sources of information include telephone directories. Institutions change both in character and in identity. This can affect their information services and their availability.

Trade associations

The trade associations are usually centred around a particular industry or technology and their role is to promote their members products in a variety of ways:

- Liaison with national and international organizations
- Catalyzing mutual cooperation between organizations involved in the marketing of the products
- Promoting wider knowledge of the product outside immediate professionally-related organizations
- Dealing with the media
- Training

Membership is often very mixed with representatives from suppliers, producers, franchise agencies, users, professional organizations and government.

Organizations libraries and referral services 193

The trade associations provide information such as annual reports, brochures and membership lists. They often compile their own statistics, which may be published as yearbooks for instance. Some of the trade associations produce their own databases, a few of which are commercially available. A major area of activity for trade associations is the organization of conferences, seminars, exhibitions and training programmes. Many also publish their own journals.

The trade associations usually offer only limited services to non-members, who may have to pay for use of information. It is always best to contact them before visiting the library or information unit.

Trade associations represent the interests of groups of manufacturers. ECTEL, for instance, represents the telecommunications and electronics industry in Europe, where technical and commercial standards are negotiated for the European Community. TEMA, the Telecommunications Engineering and Manufacturing Association, is the UK's local representative of ECTEL.

Two other European trade associations are the Committee of European Associations of Manufacturers of Electronic Components (CEMEC), based in Italy, and the European Conference of Associations of Telecommunications Cable Industries.

There are also larger comprehensive associations that deal with all business subjects where computing and IT forms a small but significant part, for example the CBI, the Design Council and the European Association for the Transfer of Technologies, Innovation and Industrial Information, which is based in Luxembourg.

CONFEDERATION OF BRITISH INDUSTRY (CBI)

This is the leading association supporting British industry with considerable influence in national affairs. It publishes reports, holds conferences, seminars, and has contacts with government departments such as the DTI. The library covers all areas of interest to employers including industrial affairs, economic policy, industrial relations, wages, company law and European aspects of industrial policy.

The following is a list of some of the most well-known of the trade associations with information services.

ASLIB

Aslib is a membership organization that provides a comprehensive information service covering IT, information management, online services, training, referral and advisory services. It supports a number of special interest groups including the Aslib Informatics

Group and the Aslib Computer Group. Services are intended for members but non-members may use the information resources centre on payment of a fee.

ASSOCIATION OF THE INSTRUMENTATION, CONTROL AND AUTOMATION INDUSTRY IN THE UK (GAMBICA)

GAMBICA is the trade association for the instrumentation, control and automation industry in the UK. It arranges conferences, meetings, exhibitions and provides information services to its 150 members. It also produces a product guide and an annual report.

BRITISH MICROCOMPUTER MANUFACTURERS GROUP (BMMG)

BMMG is a trade association helping to develop microcomputer manufacture in the UK. It currently has 21 members. It organizes meetings and exhibitions. There is also an information service. The association produces a quarterly newsletter and a biannual guide to members and products.

BRITISH RADIO AND ELECTRONIC EQUIPMENT MANUFACTURERS ASSOCIATION

This association is concerned with the production of domestic radio and television receivers, tape recorders, record players, video recorders and CD players. It publishes an annual report and a yearbook. Statistical and technical enquiries are referred on to appropriate authorities.

BUSINESS EQUIPMENT TRADE ASSOCIATION (BETA)

This is a trade association which is also a member of the European Association of Manufacturers of Business Machines and Data Processing Equipment and the European Federation of Importers of Office Machines. Product divisions cover every aspect of equipment and special committees determine international standards. Activities include exhibitions and trade missions; it also organizes the London Business Equipment Show. The information service covers general information on the industry's products, plus names and addresses of suppliers of business equipment in the UK. BETA also has a newsletter and publishes various monographs.

COMPUTER RETAILERS ASSOCIATION LTD (CRA)

The CRA is a trade association representing manufacturing industry. Its activities include meetings, exhibitions and user groups. It runs an information service for its 53 members and publishes a buyers' guide.

COMPUTING SERVICES ASSOCIATION (CSA)

The Computing Services Association is a trade association helping to increase the market for computing services in the UK. Activities include conferences, meetings, research, education and training, and an information service. It has a number of user groups including: bureaux services, consultancy, systems and software, telecommunications, privacy, statistics, and microelectronics. It publishes a newsletter, *Datalink*.

COMPUTING AND COMMUNICATIONS INDUSTRY ASSOCIATION (CCIA)

This is an American association of computer vendors, software and service houses, leasing and maintenance, telecommunications, equipment and service providers. It provides information to CCIA members, and has information on effects of Federal policy on telecommunications and computing. The association produces quarterly reviews on technological, economic and marketing developments.

CONFEDERATION OF EUROPEAN COMPUTER USERS ASSOCIATIONS (CECUA)

The Confederation Européene des Associations d'Utilisateur des Technologies de l'Information (CECUA) is based in Belgium and defends the interests of computer consumers in the EC. It organizes meetings, exhibitions and working groups. The library service will answer questions.

CONFEDERATION OF INFORMATION AND COMMUNICATION INDUSTRIES (CICI)

CICI is a co-ordinating, voluntary body strengthening the UK role in information industries and expanding international and domestic markets. Activities include: conferences; meetings; and study groups. They have working parties on legal environment, public affairs, market development, technology, statistics, and distance learning. It has approximately 30 members. Its information services include CICINET on Telecom Gold, which gives market information, news, etc. This service is accessible to the public. CICI also produces a newsletter, *Electronic Online*.

196 Organizations libraries and referral services

CONSTRUCTION INDUSTRY COMPUTING ASSOCIATION

This is an independent professional association promoting the use of computing in the construction industry. It has 365 members in the UK and 30 overseas and is affiliated to the BCS, the Federation of Master Builders and the International Federation of National Construction Computer User Groups. The Association organizes meetings, exhibitions, evaluations of software, and it publishes the *Computer Newssheet* and evaluation reports.

ELECTRONIC ENGINEERING ASSOCIATION

The Electronic Engineering Association is the trade association for manufacturers of electronic equipment. It influences the government via parliamentary committees, discussions and participation in government initiatives, like the National Economic Development Council. On the educational front, it is involved with the Training Agency. It has a computing and IT division which involves itself with the EC and in research programmes like ESPRIT and RACE.

EUROPEAN ASSOCIATION OF INFORMATION SERVICES (EUSIDIC)

EUSIDIC is an international platform for information producers, hosts, online users, and all other groups interested in the handling, production and dissemination of information in an electronic form. Publications include *Newsidic* and the *Eusidic Database Guide*. It also sponsors research projects and has produced a number of reports.

EUROPEAN COMPUTING SERVICES ASSOCIATION

The European Computing Services Association promotes and protects the computing services industry in member countries. It collects statistics, has working groups and runs a biennial conference.

EUROPEAN COMPUTER MANUFACTURERS ASSOCIATION (ECMA)

ECMA is an organization that studies and develops (in conjunction with other national and international organizations) methods and procedures that help to standardize data processing systems and equipment.

EUROPEAN INFORMATION INDUSTRY ASSOCIATION (EIIA)

EIIA was formed from the amalgamation of EURIPA and EHOG in 1989. Membership is open to individuals and organizations. It is

Organizations libraries and referral services 197

an association of electronic database producers, operators, computer hardware and software firms and other organizations involved in the delivery of electronic information products. It promotes the European information industry and tries to influence relevant governmental and non-governmental bodies. It organizes seminars, symposia and publications.

EUROPEAN TELECOMMUNICATIONS AND PROFESSIONAL
ELECTRONIC INDUSTRY (ECTEL)

ECTEL represents the interests of industries in the fields of industrial policy and in the technical and commercial spheres of common interest. On technical matters the primary ECTEL influence is in the fields of telecommunications and information technology standards and in the harmonization of equipment requirements for new standards. This is a conference body and as such represents ECTEL member associations at a European level. Access is therefore via member associations.

FEDERATION OF MICROSYSTEMS CENTRES

The Federation of Microsystems Centres is a trade and employers' association providing impartial advice to users and intending users of small business computers. Activities include conferences, meetings, study groups, open-access workshops, education and training. An information and consultancy service is provided. It currently has 16 members.

NATIONAL COMPUTING CENTRE LTD (NCC)

This is a non-profit organization backed by industry and the government. It directs technical programmes, products and services helping to make the fullest utilization of information technology. It promotes standards, codes of practice, education and training, and has a large publishing programme. The information service covers all aspects of computing equipment, programmes, services, consultancy, training, standards and codes of practice. It has databases on computer-aided engineering, manufacturing and construction, software, telecommunications and data communications equipment and suppliers. There is also a computer services index on companies supplying hardware and software. The Centre produces *Computer Journal Abstracts* and publishes *Computer Installations Record*, and the *Interconnecting Applications Handbook* series as well as various monographs and videos.

NATIONAL ELECTRONICS CENTRE

This is a trade association with 70 members covering computing and information technology. It offers a range of services including product demonstrations, conferences and training. It publishes *National Electronics Centre News*.

TELECOMMUNICATIONS ENGINEERING AND MANUFACTURING ASSOCIATION (TEMA)

TEMA is the prime trade association for the telecommunications industry in the UK. It promotes the standardization of telecommunications equipment and apparatus and helps to expand the development of modern telecommunications. TEMA is a member of ECTEL, the European association.

Other trade associations are based in the following countries:
- European Association for Microprocessing and Microprogramming (EUROMICRO) (France)
- European Association of Manufacturers of Business Machines and Data Processing Equipment (EUROBIT) (Germany)
- European Electronic Component Manufacturers Association (EECA) (Belgium)
- European Association for Computer Graphics (Netherlands)
- European Association for Theoretical Computer Science (EATCS) (Germany)

Research associations

The research associations exist to communicate knowledge about a particular subject, usually by providing an information service to its members or profession. There are research associations supported by membership schemes, such as PERA and SDC Ltd, and research associations organized as private companies or as contract research companies, for example QMC Industrial Research.

The particular strengths of research associations lie in the large databases and libraries needed to support their research work. Some of these databases are commercially available online. This can be a rich source of information particularly in the fields of knowledge involved in the cutting edge of the technologies. Due to the nature of their work they are more likely to be able to appoint experts in particular fields of knowledge and may be a good source for referrals to other people or institutions.

ERA TECHNOLOGY LTD

This is an industrial research association geared towards the electricity industry. It has a comprehensive information service and includes in its coverage: computing technology, electronic engineering, cables, radio frequency technology and materials science. It publishes *ERA Technology News* three times a year, a reports list, and a translations list.

INTERNATIONAL ELECTRONIC PUBLISHING RESEARCH CENTRE (IEPRC)

IEPRC is a part of Pira and is a non-profit organization researching applications of electronic technologies to the publishing process. Activities include evaluating and testing of systems, software and equipment, seminars, conferences and training. Pira also produces an abstracts journal, *Electronic Publishing Abstracts* corresponding to the IEPRC's area of interest. The corresponding database is EPUBS. Pira provides information to members and to non-members for a fee.

NETHERLANDS ORGANIZATION FOR APPLIED SCIENTIFIC RESEARCH (TNO)

TNO specializes in database management, CAD/CAM, artificial intelligence and software development tools. It also provides an advisory and consultancy service.

PRODUCTION ENGINEERING RESEARCH ASSOCIATION (PERA)

PERA provides an information service for its 900 members. It has a technical library, databases and an internal database of databases. PERA also provides consultancy services for members and non-members. It also organizes, on behalf of the DTI, overseas information collected from embassies. This information is communicated to members by OTIS (Overseas Technical Information Service). PERA also houses Comcentre which is the UK centre for communications standards, machine protocols and CAD systems.

QMC INDUSTRIAL RESEARCH

QMC Industrial Research is an example of a private company attached to an educational institution, Queen Mary College (a part of the University of London). It specializes in CAD, human–computer interaction and electronic materials.

SCIENTIFIC DOCUMENTATION CENTRE (SDC)

This is a non-profit research association with approximately 3 million records on file covering, among other things, computing technology. Services include weekly information services on technical and scientific subjects, periodicals, photocopying, bibliographies, company information, analysis in conjunction with laboratories and translations, especially Eastern European languages. The Centre also provides abstracting services. Non-members can use the information services for a fee.

TURING INSTITUTE

The Turing Institute in Glasgow is an example of an independent commercial research laboratory which specializes in artificial intelligence.

Learned Societies and the Professions

Professional organizations promote their members' interests. As well as information on their subject areas, they may have information networks, lists of experts and research groups as well as publishing conference proceedings and periodicals. The International Association for Maths and Computers in Simulation and the International Federation for Information Processing are examples of such international professional associations.

The learned societies exist to promote knowledge in their chosen subjects among their members and the public by providing a variety of services including information services. This usually consists of a library with journals, reports, abstracts and papers. The societies are increasingly providing SDI services as well as publishing their own journals. They maintain competency in the subject by organizing conferences, exhibitions, and sitting on working parties.

The British Computer Society and the Association for Computing Machinery (USA) are the two most important national and international societies in computing and information technology. Both look after the interests of their members by a worldwide network of information, providing professional support through a system of publishing, training, and organizing conferences and seminars. There are other societies of importance, such as the Institution of Electrical Engineers and the Institute of Electronic and Radio Engineers. To a lesser extent the more general societies can be a source of information, such as the Industrial Society. There are also international societies such as the International Federation for Information Processing.

Internationally-important societies include the Gesellschaft für Mathematik und Datenverarbeitung (National Research Centre for Computer Science) and the All-Union Council of Scientific and Engineering Societies in Moscow. This is a coordinating council for all of the Soviet Union. The Information Processing Society of Japan (IPSJ) which has similar interests to the British Computer Society and the Association for Computing Machinery, publishes journals and transactions and organizes conferences and special interest groups.

ASSOCIATION FOR COMPUTING MACHINERY (ACM)

This is the largest international educational and scientific society servicing the computing community. It organizes seminars and conferences, education of its members via in-service training and professional examination, and maintains a comprehensive publishing programme.

The association's major organizational units are the 31 Special Interest Groups (SIGs) which concentrate on narrower subject areas within the field of computing. For example SIGSOFT deals with software. The SIGs organize their own conferences and also publish their own newsletters. The subject scope of ACM includes: computer and information processing including applications in management, business, programming, systems design, systems engineering, research, education, consulting, operations, sales and marketing, personal computing, computer-assisted learning, and computer-aided design. ACM is a membership organization but non-members may purchase ACM publications. Publications include: *Communications of the ACM*, *Journal of the Association for Computing Machinery*, *Computing Surveys*, *ACM Transactions on Mathematical Software*, *ACM Transactions on Database Systems*, *ACM Transactions on Graphics*, *ACM Transactions on Programming Languages and Systems*, *ACM Transactions on Office Information Systems*, *ACM Transactions on Computer Systems*, *Computing Reviews*, *ACM Guide to Computing Literature*, *Collected Algorithms from the ACM*, *Topics in Computer Education*.

The *ACM Guide to Computing Literature* is an important secondary source. It lists all the items reviewed in *Computing Reviews* plus all the papers from ACM Conferences as well as other references to the subject by other societies and bodies.

BRITISH ASSOCIATION FOR THE ADVANCEMENT OF SCIENCE (BAAS)

Founded in 1831, BAAS promotes general interest in science. It organizes meetings, conferences and lectures.

BRITISH COMPUTER SOCIETY (BCS)

The British Computer Society is the professional body for computing in the United Kingdom and has over 28 000 members. It is affiliated to the ACM, IFIP and the National Computer Users' Forum. One of its main roles is to provide a professional qualification for computer specialists. To this end, it has a two-part professional examination each year. It organizes conferences, seminars and exhibitions and supports over 43 special interest groups covering topics such as advanced programmers, computer arts, expert systems, Fortran and robotics.

The scope of the society is computers and their applications, data processing, management of commercial data processing, programming and programming languages, and computer electronics. The BCS's collection is a part of the IEE library, which is open to the public. Publications include: *Computer Newsletter*, *Computer Journal*, *Computer Bulletin*, monographs and conference proceedings (via Cambridge University Press), special bibliographies (via IEE).

INSTITUTE OF ELECTRICAL AND ELECTRONIC ENGINEERS (IEEE)

The IEEE is the largest of the professional societies covering electronics, computing and information technology. It is based in the US and has numerous special interest groups. The institute also publishes a large number of professional journals ranging from the academically-orientated learned journals to newsletters and glossy magazines. It also organizes many conferences and symposia. The IEEE runs a current-awareness service about Japan. SDI services and retrospective searches are available as well as advisory services related to software provision and a service including abstracting and indexing for external organizations. Services are available on a fee basis, printed services by subscription.

INFORMATION PROCESSING SOCIETY OF JAPAN (IPSJ)

The IPSJ is a membership organization with similar aims to the BCS and ACM. It has a number of special interest groups and organizes conferences. It also publishes the *Journal of Information Processing* (quarterly, in English), and *Transactions of the Information Processing Society of Japan* (monthly, in Japane e).

INSTITUTE OF DATA PROCESSING MANAGEMENT

The Institute of Data Processing Management is the professional association for data processing managers, with 4000 individual members in the UK and 1000 overseas. It also has some corporate members. The institute has a number of special interest groups and it organizes conferences, seminars and training courses. It publishes the *Information Management Journal* and the *Information Management Yearbook*.

INSTITUTE OF ELECTRICAL AND ELECTRONICS INCORPORATED ENGINEERS (IEEIE)

This is a professional society for electrical and electronics engineers and technicians. Activities including training, professional exams, conferences and professional groups. The Institute publishes *Electrical & Electronics Incorporated Engineering*, *Electrotechnology* and various technical monographs.

INSTITUTE OF INFORMATION SCIENTISTS (IIS)

The Institute of Information Scientists is a professional association promoting the principles and practice of information provision and its dissemination and management. Activities include conferences, exhibitions and meetings, training and professional exams. It has a number of special interest groups. Publications include *Inform*, *Journal of Information Science* and *IT Link* (a joint publication with Aslib).

INSTITUTION OF BRITISH TELECOMMUNICATIONS ENGINEERS

The institution promotes the general advancement of electrical and telecommunications science and their application.

INSTITUTION OF ELECTRICAL ENGINEERS (IEE)

The IEE is a learned society covering all fields of electrical engineering. It is the parent body of Inspec. It also incorporates the Institute of Electronic and Radio Engineers (IERE). The IEE has an extensive library which includes the British Computer Society's collection. It covers electrical, electronic and control engineering, computer science, and information science. The library provides a number of information services including an online search service. Publications include: *Computer Aided Engineering Journal*, *Electronics and Power*, *Electronics Letters*, *Proceedings of the IEE*, *Software Engineering Journal*, *Electronics Engineer*, *Radio and Electronics Engineer*, *Electronics and Communications Engineering Journal*.

Inspec

Inspec is a department of the Institution of Electrical Engineers (IEE). It provides one of the most comprehensive abstracting and indexing services covering information technology. The subject areas are: physics; electronic and electrical engineering; computers; control engineering; and information technology. Inspec produces the INSPEC online database and publishes *Computer and Control Abstracts*, *IT Focus*, *Key Abstracts*, and *Current Papers on Computers and Control*, all of which are excellent sources.

INTERNATIONAL FEDERATION FOR INFORMATION PROCESSING (IFIP)

Based in Switzerland, IFIP is a federation of professional and technical societies concerned with the theoretical and applied aspects of information processing. It has official relationships with UNESCO and WHO. It promotes cooperation, research and the dissemination of information in the field of information science and technology. Publications include *Computers in Industry*, *Computers and Security*, and *Information Bulletin*.

NUMERICAL ENGINEERING SOCIETY

Linked with the Institute of Production Engineers and the Institution of Mechanical Engineers, the Numerical Engineering Society is a common interest society covering numerical control, flexible manufacturing systems, CAD/CAM and robotics. Its collection is part of the PERA library. Publications include *Numerical Engineering Journal* (part of *Computerised Manufacturing*) and a biennial buyers' guide to products and services in numerical engineering.

Academic institutions

Academic institutions are potentially a rich source of several types of information:

- Libraries, databases
- Academic staff, consultancies, etc.
- Specialist research groups
- Departments associated with, or supporting, the new industrial liaison units now springing up in educational establishments, sometimes known as 'science parks'

Universities, polytechnics and institutes of higher education have access to specialists who can provide information of use to computer professionals. The largest institutions are the universities and polytechnics, and the type of work associated with them is reflected in their library and database collections and the type of academic staff they employ. The role of the polytechnics is to teach and do research in practical vocational subjects, whereas universities tend to concentrate more on advanced research and teach pure rather than applied subjects. However these distinctions are becoming increasingly blurred. Polytechnics may have better links with industry and are more used to providing access to external users.

The *Commonwealth Universities Yearbook* lists universities in the Commonwealth by country. It also provides indexes by institution name and by subject. The *World of Learning* lists universities and polytechnics and selected colleges by faculty and school name, but only selected institutions in the larger countries. Another useful international guide is the *International Handbook of Universities* (Macmillan). National guides exist for most countries and these generally give more detailed information. The *Education Yearbook* lists all institutions in the UK. The *Japanese Colleges and Universities Handbook* details all institutions in higher education in Japan and a further example is the *American Universities and Colleges Guide*. These directories may allow users to pinpoint international centres of excellence.

Documents

All academic institutions maintain libraries to support their work. Significant collections of information technology literature range from 2000 volumes upwards and 4000 volumes is considered a respectable collection. At the end of this section you will find a list of institutions with significant collections in computing and information technology.

Academic libraries also contain collections of computing journals and abstracts. Many of them subscribe to learned journals published by the ACM (Association for Computing Machinery) and the IEEE (Institute of Electronic and Electrical Engineers). These are definitive but expensive publications to obtain. Other commonly-available sources include: *Computer and Control Abstracts* and the COMPUTER LIBRARY database (on CD-ROM). They are also very expensive.

Data collections

Academic libraries may be able to help you access the online databases. In the United Kingdom many academic libraries are members of JANET (Joint Academic Network) which allows access to member institutions, various online databases and to some online library catalogues.

Each institution provides computer services to staff and students and there will be various sets of data mounted on each institution's internal database, that may be of use. For example, Lancaster University maintains a database on IT and education (also available via JANET).

Personnel

Librarians are skilled information workers who can help you to find information within their own collections or locate other centres of information that could be of use.

Academic staff are a source of expertise in their fields of research and the library or faculty office will probably hold a list of experts, enabling you to go directly to the most relevant person or department. Many academic staff now offer consultancy and advice to firms and individuals or they may be part of a research group such as the Scottish Human–Computer Interaction Centre at Heriot-Watt University.

Increasingly campuses support science parks where new technologies and processes are linked to the expertise of academic staff, quite often in purpose-built accommodation. Both Aberystwyth Science Park and the South Bank Technopark are examples of these organizations, now numbering 33 in the UK. These may be further sources of additional information.

Computing staff may be able to offer consultancy or advice. They will also be experts on the operations of their own computer systems. You can find out what type of system they have by referring to Volume 3 of the *Computer Users' Yearbook*, which lists major computer installations.

Locating research groups and consultancies

Current Research in Britain, *Industrial Research in the UK*, and *Higher Education Resources for Industry* are all useful directories for locating research groups and consultancies in the UK. The online alternative is the national database, BEST (British Expertise in Science and Technology). Further detail about experts can be found in Chapter 18.

Current Research in Britain is a large four-volume work detailing all major research projects in higher education, and provides a subject index. Chapter 4 of *Industrial Research in the UK* lists all substantial research being carried out in universities and polytechnics. Alternatively, one can now use *Higher Education Re-*

sources for Industry, which details research, consultancy and training in all institutes of higher education.

Obtaining access to academic facilities

ACADEMIC STAFF

Consultancy and other forms of help may have to take second place at certain times of the year, especially during examination periods. Staff can usually be contacted through the faculty or school office via the faculty officer or perhaps a secretary.

LIBRARIES

It is best to write first and provide a reasonable explanation of why you need access to their collection. Some libraries may not allow external users or you may have to pay for loan facilities. Address your enquiries to the Head of Library Services or through the Librarian.

Manufacturers, software houses and suppliers

Ways of obtaining information from companies associated with selling, supplying and manufacturing computers and information systems will now be discussed. Looking for information in this area can be confusing owing to the complex nature of computer systems. A computer can have the hardware and software provided by different companies or it can be a system provided as a complete package via a service bureau. Either way, to solve one problem you may have to contact several organizations.

Companies exist in all shapes and sizes but can be roughly divided into the following categories:

- Hardware manufacturer (original equipment manufacturers or OEMs)
- Systems house or service bureau
- Distributor
- Software supplier
- Consultancy service
- Computer shop

A service bureau is a company that deals with a complete system, often specializing in particular fields, for example, banking payroll systems.

Distributors and retailers are unlikely to answer complex queries and it is often necessary to refer to the original producer of the software or hardware. Smaller software producers may not have the resources to adequately support users.

Within organizations you will need to contact a variety of departments. The customer relations department, technical support and service are three commonly used designations for the functions which deal directly with the public.

Locating organizations

Locating organizations is relatively easy, though a note of caution is appropriate at this point. Most manufacturers and suppliers can be found using a combination of directories. However directories soon go out of date and you may have to resort to telephone directories or directory enquiries for more up to date information. The most useful directories include: *Communications Yearbook*, *Computer Users' Yearbook*, and *Computing Decisions*. More specialized directories cover a smaller market segment but give greater in-depth coverage and are particularly suitable if an enquiry is very specific. The following directories are excellent sources of information within their own areas: *Software Users' Yearbook*, *Software Encyclopedia*, *CADCAM Association Yearbook* and *Electronics and Instruments Directory*. Two other specialist directories of use are the *International Computer Graphics Directory* and the *International Directory of Telecommunications*.

Foreign companies can be located using the various Kompass trade directories that are available for most countries, or information may be obtained from the relevant diplomatic mission or chamber of commerce.

Software

If you are looking specifically for software and related applications, such as consultancies, the best directories to use are the *PC Yearbook* for IBM PC and IBM PC-compatible software and the *Software Users' Yearbook*. The *PC Yearbook* details all the hardware and software for IBM PC microcomputers and their clones. The vast bulk of the directory is a listing of 3500 software products, an A–Z of software, a software suppliers' index and an index of products designed for a specific industry (e.g. CAD/CAM). This is very useful if all you want is a listing of IBM software. Each entry gives in full the release date, supplier and cost with a brief description. There is also a separate section on desk-top publishing giving full supplier and cost details and a detailed review of each package.

The *Software Users' Yearbook* is an enormous four-volume

Organizations libraries and referral services

work, offering information on 2080 listed companies and 9000 products. It has sections on training, consultants and technical authors. It is very well indexed, hence its size, but it does mean you can search under a variety of headings including: software name, manufacturers, product category, operating system. Volume 1 is an index giving full supplier details. The other volumes give full descriptions of the types of software, referring back to Volume 1 for supplier details. Volume 2 deals with systems, Volume 3 industry-specific applications and Volume 4 general applications. This directory is extremely valuable for searching for all types of software.

The *Software Encyclopedia* restricts itself to microcomputer software and brief descriptions of publishing companies and is therefore able to offer a much bigger listing of 20 000 software packages. Published in two volumes, it gives a classified listing by applications of the software divided and filed under 14 major micro systems. Systems covered include: Atari, IBM, UNIX and Apple Macintosh. Each entry gives clear simple descriptions of the software including price, version and operating system.

An alternative way of finding the most current information on software is to use online electronic databases or CD-ROM databases. Given below are a few of the most well known.

Online	CD-ROM
BUSINESS SOFTWARE DATABASE	COMPU-INFO
COMPUTER DATABASE	COMPUTER LIBRARY
ISIS SOFTWARE DATABASE (German)	SOFTWARE CD
MENU—THE INTERNATIONAL SOFTWARE DATABASE	
MICROCOMPUTER INDEX	
MICROCOMPUTER SOFTWARE GUIDE	
MICROCOMPUTER SOFTWARE DIRECTORY (SOFT)	

Hardware

For hardware in general, the best directory to use is the *Computer Users' Yearbook*, Volume 1, which describes 471 mini and mainframe systems and numerous microcomputers. There is a large section on peripherals. Volume 4 is a handy classified guide to equipment suppliers and services. If your requirements veer more towards networking and digital communication you will find the *Communications Users' Yearbook*, and to a lesser extent, the

International Directory of Telecommunications, most helpful. The best directory for electronic components is the *Electronics and Instruments Directory*. Comprehensive information on IBM PC hardware is available in *PC Yearbook* which gives a machine listing of 200 IBM PCs, peripherals and a listing of 160 micro-to-mainframe products and local area networks. Approximately 240 companies supplying products in these areas are listed at the end of Section 1.

Large companies such as IBM are another source of information. Many of these supra-national companies have their own information services in many countries and can often provide information on foreign user groups, research establishments and experts. The *World Guide to Special Libraries* (Saur) provides a useful means of locating such organizations.

Services

All of the directories mentioned, apart from *Software Encyclopedia*, can be used to find information on computer services, such as recruitment and training, computer services bureaux, data preparation services, technical authors, consultants and systems houses. Volume 2 of the *Computer Users' Yearbook* has the largest selection. It lists, for example, over 900 consultants, including a special section on public relations consultants. The *Communications Users' Yearbook* is the next most useful directory. It includes a section on network management services.

IBM services are, of course, detailed in the *PC Yearbook* where over 100 maintenance companies are listed with details of contracts they can negotiate with individual firms. The directory also lists the top 50 IBM dealers.

Finally, the Institute of Purchasing and Supply publishes a range of model contracts and agreements suitable for hardware and software.

Private companies

Most large private companies maintain information services to inform their own staff about their organization and to collect external information and data in their own specialized field of technology or commerce. This information is usually located with the main company but can be associated with a research department.

Although access to the libraries of private companies is normally restricted it may be possible to use the expertise of individual members of staff within the organization.

If the company does not have the information or expertise they

Organizations libraries and referral services

are sometimes able to refer enquirers on to other organizations, so they are a useful source of contacts. Some companies have built up comprehensive databases, which although strictly for internal use, may be used to answer an enquiry from outside. The library or information unit is normally the focus for database services. As well as collecting regular publications, they may have good collections of trade literature, which is often difficult to get hold of. House journals are another source of information as are publications such as annual reports and statistics.

British Telecom's research laboratories at Martlesham Heath have a lot of information on telecommunications and will answer simple technical queries free. They also offer a consultancy service for more involved queries.

Manufacturers such as GEC Research Ltd, Lucas Research Centre, GEC/Plessey Telecommunications (GPT), Plessey Research, Thorn-EMI and IBM are examples of manufacturers with specific research centres dealing with various aspects of information technology and telecommunications. IBM, BASF, AEG, Siemens, Mitsubishi, Motorola, Sony and Intel all maintain libraries and information centres. They can be located using the *World Guide to Special Libraries* (Saur) and to a lesser extent *Centres and Bureaux, a Directory of Concentrations of Effort, Information and Expertise*. For U.S. organizations, the *Computer and Computing Information Resources Directory* is a comprehensive and easy-to-use directory.

MICROINFO

Microinfo Ltd publishes and acts as an agent for other information providers, notably NTIS (U.S. National Technical Information Service), the U.S. National Standards Association and the Japan Information Centre of Science and Technology. It also provides a translations service, SDI and current awareness. Microinfo is particularly good for U.S. information and information on optical disc systems.

Information brokers

Information brokers act as go-betweens for clients requiring information and the information sources and services available. Most brokers specialize in specific subject areas and some also specialize in particular types of source. For instance there are a number of brokers who specialize in doing online searches. Details of brokers can be found on the BROKERSGUIDE database available on ECHO. There is also a number of directories of information consultants and brokers published. Examples are Christine Smith's *Directory of Consultants* (British Library) and *Who's Who in the Information World* (TFPL). Other sources of consultants include the *Communications Users' Year Book*, the *Computer Users' Yearbook*, the *Electronics and Instruments Directory*, the *PC Yearbook* and *Higher Education Resources for Industry*.

CHAPTER TWELVE

Trade statistics and market information

J. DEUNETTE

Introduction

Trade and market information sources include official statistics, market research reports, publications of various research and trade associations and the national and specialist press. The information available varies from country to country and from industry to industry and the use of published guides to information is recommended.

A useful starting point for production and trade figures is the *Yearbook of World Electronics Data* (Elsevier), published annually from 1973 onwards. Its coverage includes leisure electronics and industrial and medical electronics as well as electronic data processing and telecommunications. The yearbook comes in two volumes; Volume 1 covers Western Europe and Volume 2 covers America, Japan, Asia and the Pacific. Each volume includes an overview, including foreign trade figures, followed by more detailed information for each country. The 1990 edition of Volume 1 was published in October 1989 and most of the statistics shown in it are for 1987 and 1988, plus forecasts for 1989 and 1990. Volume 2 appeared in 1990.

The country entries follow a standard format as far as possible, although the same type of data is not necessarily available from each country. Information in the country chapters includes the number of electrical and electronics companies, analyzed by product group where available, the main production activities in the country, the major companies based in that country, including subsidiaries of foreign companies and data on employment by the industry. There is a useful summary of activity in the country plus important recent events (updating will be necessary, however because of publication delays). For each country there is a list of national statistical sources and international sources relevant to that country. Statistics on EDP equipment production are not broken down but are given for whole machines and components or parts.

Statistics included in the yearbook are taken from the national and international statistical offices and converted to a comparable form as far as possible. Customs classifications have been changed over the years and this means that problems can arise when conducting historical research over several years. To alleviate this problem, the publishers also produce, on computer diskette, revised historical information which allows comparisons between different years.

Government statistics

The data collected varies from country to country and guides such as the *Yearbook of World Electronics Data* will lead the searcher to the appropriate statistical series for each country. For the UK, sales information is collected by the Business Statistics Office and published in the various *Business Monitor* series. Each *Business Monitor* covers a particular industry and presents statistics gathered by the government survey of manufacturers, the Quarterly Sales Inquiries. *Business Monitors* provide total UK manufacturers' sales analyzed by product group. These sales totals are shown as value (manufacturers' sales prices) and, for some products only, also by volume. Manufacturers employing below a certain number of staff are not obliged to participate in the survey and so statistics are usually indicative of trends and approximate levels only, being lower than the true total sales figures for many products. *Business Monitors* also provide import and export data from HM Customs and Excise. The *Business Monitors* are published quarterly and data for each quarter is published about four to six months in arrears. Each issue contains annual data for the last few quarters and full years. Subscription to each *Business Monitor* series costs £15.*

Business Monitor PQ1003, Electronics and Information Technology (Manufacturing Components) is a new series including a combination of data from other *Business Monitor* series, such as *Business Monitor PQ3302, Electronic Data Processing Equipment*, and *Business Monitor PQ3441, Telegraph and Telephone Equipment*. *Business Monitor PQ1003* commences with first quarter 1988, which appeared in 1989. However, since data are drawn

---

* All prices quoted in this chapter are for 1990.

from other BM series, the 1988 issues are able to cover annual UK manufacturers' sales back to 1983 and quarterly sales from 1987.

The analysis of UK manufacturers' sales by value includes, among others, the following product categories: mainframe computers, minicomputers, microcomputers other than home computers, home computers, high-speed storage units, low-speed storage units, VDUs, printers, other input/output units, modems and multiplexers, miscellaneous peripheral units, computer memory boards, other parts, hardware maintenance, public telephone exchange equipment, private telephone exchange equipment, switching equipment, transmission equipment, subscribers' telephone apparatus including cellular telephones, radio communications equipment and TV receivers (capable of receiving viewdata, capable of receiving teletext and capable of receiving both). All the statistics in *Business Monitor PQ1003* are by value rather than volume; a limited amount of data on sales volumes can be found in *Business Monitor PQ3302*.

Business Monitor SDQ9 covers the computing services and shows total billings to clients by the software, consultancy, training maintenance and database services. *Business Monitor PQ3302* has a large overlap with *Business Monitor PQ1003* but includes software. The *Business Monitors* also provide foreign trade statistics, but in many cases the breakdown into products by the trade statistics is quite different from that used in the sales statistics, giving for example imports and exports of complete processing units, central storage units, etc.

Overseas Trade Statistics of the United Kingdom (HMSO) is published monthly, price £255 per year. The official trade statistics for the UK and for other countries can be consulted at the Export Market Information Centre, in the Department of Trade and Industry. This centre also provides help free of charge with enquiries concerning foreign markets.

TRADSTAT is an online database providing world trade statistics. In many cases trade statistics can be obtained online several weeks or months before the printed collections can be seen. The database also has the advantage that it allows presentation of the data in a choice of several report formats. TRADSTAT is produced and provided online by Data-Star, either on subscription or on a payment for usage basis, with a small sign-up fee.

Yearbooks from trade associations and commercial publishers

The amount of data available from the various national trade associations varies greatly from country to country and from sector to sector. *Yearbook of World Electronics Data* gives some guidance to useful associations. A particularly comprehensive publication is *Facts and Figures on the Japanese Electronics Industry*, compiled annually by the Electronic Industries Association of Japan, and in English. This yearbook can be purchased from the Overseas Public Affairs Office of the Electronic Industries Association of Japan. Each annual volume provides an overview of the electronics industry in the year prior to publication. Statistics are provided for three groups of products—consumer electronics, industrial electronics, and electronic devices and components. For each of these product groups, production, export, import and employment are compared for Japan, the USA, Western Europe as a whole and the NIEs (newly industrializing economies). Each of the three industry sectors is then treated in more depth. For example, in the industrial electronics sector, Japanese production and exports are analyzed by category into mainframe computers, PCs, word processors, facsimile machines, copiers, desktop calculators, mobile communications equipment, printers, etc.

Japan Electronics Almanac (Dempa Publications) ($40) is an annual summary of the electronics industry in Japan. Subject coverage includes consumer electronics, industrial electronics, electronic components and devices, business trends of electronics companies, the information processing industry (software, VANs, etc.), semiconductors, microprocessors, computers, terminals and peripherals, telecommunications, office machines and office automation equipment. Profiles of the top 100 electronics companies in Japan are provided.

Informatization White Paper (formerly *Computer White Paper*) concerns the Japanese information industry and market. It includes information services industry sales by type of service and sales by sector of end user, also trends among users of information and telecommunications services. It is produced by the Japan Information Processing Information Center and is available from the Fuji Corporation.

Data on the U.S. industry, sales, production, exports and imports are provided by *Electronic Market Data Book*, published by Electronic Industries Association, 2001 Eye Street NW, Washington DC 20006, USA. [Tel (202) 457 4900. Price $88 + $12 air mail.] This annual publication covers consumer electronics, communications equipment, computers and industrial electronics (e.g. CAD, CAM, CAE, word processing, desktop publishing), electronic components, government electronics, electronics related products and services. The section on communications includes data on fibre optics, satellite communications, facsimile, microwave transmission, common carrier business, telephones and answering machines, cable television, cellular radio, PBX Centrex and key systems, data communications, modems, LANs, VANs, teletext and videotex, land mobile radio, and integrated services digital networks.

The Electronic Industries Association also publishes *Electronic Trends* monthly and *Electronic Foreign Trade*, also monthly.

Market research reports

A large number of market research organizations are active within the broad area encompassed by information technology. Many specialize in specific technologies and products but there are a few which offer a very wide coverage. Some of the largest in terms of the range of subjects covered are as follows.

IDC

International Data Corporation (IDC) and its subsidiary, Link Resources Inc., produce research reports covering the USA, Western European and world markets. IDC has offices in 20 countries in Europe, Asia and America. IDC reports include the *Eurocast* series of European research reports. Thirty of these were published in 1989, covering topics in the areas of multi-user computer systems, personal computer systems, printers, Unix, software and services, terminals, distribution channels/VARs, LANs, also the DP market forecast and spending patterns. In addition, IDC ran nine European Continuous Information Services in 1988 offering telephone enquiry services, preliminary research data prior to publication in Eurocast reports and bulletins. IDC UK produces a series of reports on UK markets, covering mainly software, services, vertical markets and personal computers.

Dataquest

Dataquest is a company belonging to the Dun and Bradstreet Corporation. With headquarters in California and offices in Massachusetts, New Jersey, Tokyo, London, Paris and Munich, the company specializes in electronic high-technology market research. Over 25 industries are covered, within the broad areas of: semiconductors; information systems (computers, telecommunications, office systems and software); peripherals (printers, electronic publishing, storage systems, terminals); office equipment; and industrial automation. For each industry, Dataquest produces updated loose-leaf reports, research bulletins and conferences and offers an enquiry service and access to its research library. Various other reports and newsletters are also published. Geographical coverage varies according to the report, but Dataquest monitors markets and industries around the world.

Romtec

Romtec plc specializes in computer industry market research and consultancy. Subjects include microcomputers, minicomputers, mainframes and peripherals, software and computer services. Research concentrates primarily on UK markets but there are also services covering German, French and other European markets and the U.S. market. Some of the specialized reports are researched by partner organizations in Europe and elsewhere. Research covers the three areas of: vendors and products (including sales and market shares, etc.); end users; and distribution channels. Reports take the form of standard surveys and multi-client studies. Romtec also offers continuous monitoring of segments, confidential research, focus groups, directories and an information service. Most of the reports are updated annually or biannually. There is also a set of forecast reports covering various UK, European and U.S. markets. For the UK, there is a *Monthly Sales Monitor* (£650 per month) and a *Quarterly Trends Review* (£1350 per quarter). *Romtec Review* (£450 per year) is a newsletter on the microcomputer marketplace.

UK markets covered by past research reports include: business micros; monitors; desktop publishing; portable terminals; and third party maintenance. Other reports by Romtec include the *U.S. Forecast 1984–1993* and the *European Markets for PCs and SBSs 1988–1992*. Directories include micro dealers in the UK, France and West Germany and OEM resellers. This is not an exhaustive list of reports and over 30 titles are published each year.

Many of the reports are produced annually and have quarterly or semiannual updates. Prices for the main volumes are mainly in the region of £600 to £1000 and several products are available in diskette form as an alternative to printed copy. Romtec also offers report generator software for production of listings analysis and mail-shots, also a modelling package.

Logica

Logica is a UK research publisher which specializes in telecommunications markets in Western Europe. Among the many important publishers of market research reports covering the USA, world and, in many cases European-wide markets, some of the most prolific are Auerbach, Business Communications Co. Inc., Creative Strategies Research International, Frost and Sullivan and the U.S. Department of Commerce. Two further European-based publishers which cannot be omitted are Admerca, covering world and Western European markets and some individual countries, and IPI, covering world, Western European, U.S. and Japanese markets. Addresses for these publishers are shown at the end of this chapter.

Besides the many companies offering original market research, which is necessarily expensive, there are services based on desk research which provide a basic introduction and industry/market overviews. For a very wide range of UK markets, ICC publishes three series of reports. These are *Key Note Reports*, *ICC Business Ratio Reports* and *ICC Financial Surveys*. *Key Note Reports* are intended as overviews of markets and industries and form a good basis for research. They are priced at £135 per report (1989) and include data on sales, market shares, companies active in the market and recent trends, etc. Titles relevant to IT are: Microcomputers; Online Databases; Videotex; Telecommunications; Word Processors; and Office Software. New editions are published at approximately 18-month intervals. The reports are also available online in full text via Dialog, Profile, and Data-Star. ICC FINANCIAL SURVEYS and ICC BUSINESS RATIO REPORTS both provide financial data on companies active in UK industries, with overview and comment. *ICC Business Ratio Reports* cost £225 (1989) and relevant titles include: *Computer Equipment Manufacturers*; *Computer Equipment Distributors*; *Computer Services*; *Computer Software*; *Electronic Equipment Manufacturers*; and *Telecommunications*. Relevant *ICC Financial Surveys* include: *Computing and Data Processing Equipment* (£185); and *Telecommunications Equipment Manufacturers and Distributors* (£185).

The above list can only indicate some of the companies active in this area. There are various guides to published market research which cover the reports of these and other publishers. One of the most comprehensive directories for IT subjects (as well as other subjects) is *MarketSearch: International Directory of Published Market Research*. This is produced by Arlington Management Publications Ltd in association with the British Overseas Trade Board. The directory is published annually with a semiannual update and purchasers have access to a telephone enquiry service to check on updating material received throughout the year. The 1989 main volume listed 17 000 reports from 684 publishers. Entries are very brief, showing classifications of subjects (accessed via an alphabetical product index), title of report, publisher, frequency of publication, price and countries covered by the report.

Other guides to published market research include *Findex* and *Marketing Surveys Index*. *Marketing Surveys Index* (Marketing Strategies for Industry) is available as a monthly updated loose-leaf directory or online via the Profile service. *Findex Directory of Market Research Reports, Studies and Surveys* is published in New York by Find/SVP and is also available online via the Dialog Service.

The national and specialist press

IT market research is well reported in the national press and the computer journals worldwide and a large amount of information on market sizes, sectors, manufacturers' market shares and trends and user opinions can be traced in these readily available sources. With a large number of relevant newspapers and journals available in each country, the best method of research is via the online services, such as INFOMAT, TEXTLINE, PROFILE, and the PTS range of databases.

INFOMAT and TEXTLINE both summarize newspaper articles from several countries, providing English summaries of foreign language items. INFOMAT also contains summaries of articles from a wide range of trade journals, while TEXTLINE has a full text subfile on computers and includes coverage of some newswire services. The producers of the INFOMAT database also offer *Electronic Publishing Alert*, a fortnightly current awareness bulletin containing records from the INFOMAT database. Despite its title, a large proportion of the coverage of this bulletin relates to microcomputer and workstation markets and electronic storage media. There is also coverage of database services in various forms. Full text of the articles is not available on INFOMAT, although the producer does run a photocopy service. INFOMAT can be accessed via several of the major online hosts, including Pergamon Financial Data Services, Data-Star and Dialog. Charging via all these services is based on usage, connection time plus output, with no subscription. TEXTLINE is available directly from the database producer on either a subscription basis or a usage basis.

INFOMAT, produced in the UK, is owned by Predicasts Inc, of the USA whose many other databases include PTS PROMT, summarizing information on markets and technology worldwide. The two databases complement each other to a large extent, although there is overlap. While PTS PROMT is a larger database covering a very wide range of publications of many types, including press releases and reports for example as well as periodical articles, sources from the USA outnumber sources from the rest of the world. INFOMAT gives fuller coverage of markets in individual European countries in many cases as it has the advantage of a much fuller local press coverage. Ideally, both should be used for many searches. PROMT can be accessed via Data-Star and Dialog and other online services.

PROFILE covers most UK newspapers in full text within hours of publication, as well as several newswires from around the world and business and media magazines. Source coverage concentrates on the UK but there are several U.S. sources and some from other countries, including Japan. A small proportion of foreign language material is covered in the McCarthy Online subfile. There is very little indexing for most articles on PROFILE and searches can sometimes be difficult to define in natural language. The database is of greatest value when there is a precise search topic which can be unambiguously defined. PROFILE can also be used as a fast method of retrieval of the full text of an article that has been identified by other means. It can be accessed directly from its producer on a payment for usage basis; there is also a subscription option.

Online databases can be used to provide continuous monitoring of a particular market sector but there are newsletters which cover certain subjects in a more readable manner. The two types of information are complementary for many needs. Financial Times Business Information Ltd produces a series of newsletters. Among these are *Telecom Markets*, *Electronic Office*, *Advanced Manufacturing* and *Mobile Communications*. Each newsletter appears twice a month. The subscription for *Electronic Office* and for *Advanced Manufacturing* is £366 per year for each title. For *Telecom Markets* and *Mobile Communications* it is £435 each. Alternatively, all items in the newsletters can be retrieved in full text online from the FTBR database, made available by the Profile and Data-Star services. The online database combines all the FT newsletters, although it is possible to restrict the search to one newsletter. Online access is useful for those who do not wish to be committed to an annual subscription (e.g. Profile charges £1.40 per connect minute). Regular users would find the printed versions cheaper to use and easier to scan but, although the newsletters do include regular indexes, the online format can be searched more easily for specific terms or names embedded in the text. Each fortnightly newsletter is about ten pages long and contains company and product news and usually some items providing market statistics. Coverage is international but with strongest coverage of the UK and the USA.

New Media Markets is another of the Financial Times newsletters with a similar format to the *FinTech* newsletters. It includes coverage of cable and satellite television and videotex as well as other media. Subscription is £423 per year for 24 issues and it is available online in the same way as the *FinTech* newsletters. *Media Monitor* has similar subject coverage to new media markets, but unlike the other FT newsletters it comprises abstracts of articles published in newspapers and media magazines rather than original articles. It is available online, alongside the other newsletters, and on subscription.

Trend Monitor (Aslib/TMI) began publication in 1988 and provides a concise and readable summary of trends in IT. There are separate bulletins for *Computing*, *Communications*, and *Media* and there is a fourth bulletin entitled *Hybrid Digital Telemedia* which covers topics not easy to classify elsewhere, such as computer and video conferencing, teleworking and data broadcasting. Each part covers both technical and market developments of its subject and each part appears twice per year. The information is summarized from about 150 British and American publications. There is little European coverage, excluding the UK, but there are plans to extend coverage to include some European publications. As a six monthly publication, *Trend Monitor* does not provide a replacement for the online search in terms of currency but it has the advantage that it provides an authoritative summary of developments, with references for further reading. *Computing*, *Communications* and *Media* cost £95 or US$195 each and subscriptions include *Hybrid Digital Telemedia*. There are substantial discounts for subscriptions to two or more parts.

Government services

Government run services may provide free or subsidized help to exporters researching foreign markets. The British Overseas Trade Board's PRODUCT DATA STORE is a source of market data and product data which has been developed as an aid to British exporters. A large amount of input comes from the commercial sectors of British embassies in many countries. This is supplemented by facts extracted from UK and non-UK journals and trade magazines and from reports of associations, banks, companies and government organizations outside the UK. All types of product are covered and output can range from a few lines to several pages. The PRODUCT DATA STORE is searchable via a computerized index which identifies documents on the markets and countries of interest. Documents are then viewed in the form of microfilm with prints available as required. Use of the PRODUCT DATA STORE is free and open to representatives of British exporters via a personal visit. It is located at the Department of Trade and Industry.

Product data

A large amount of data on new products can be obtained by scanning the computer, office equipment and telecommunications magazines, many of which have extensive product review sections with reader enquiry services. Consumer oriented publications, such as *Which Computer?* (EMAP) are useful for comparisons of the features, prices and performance of different manufacturers' products. *Which Computer?* (EMAP) is published monthly and covers a wide range of peripherals as well as computers.

Directories and specialized trade literature services are useful for more extensive searches. Directories are also discussed in Chapter 10. Coverage is limited here however to a few of the larger, more general sources and to those directories which give a reasonable amount of detail about the products, rather than being primarily directories listing manufacturers.

General product directories, covering all industry sectors for a particular country, are usually easy to locate in reference libraries and are often the best available sources of information. However, where a reliable specialized trade directory exists this is likely to provide a fuller and more up-to-date coverage of the industry concerned. In the fast-moving sectors encompassed by the term 'Information Technology', directories need to be updated at least annually. Guidance can be obtained from such publications as *Directories in Print* (Gale Research) covering the USA and *International Directories in Print* (Gale Research) covering the rest of the world. They are both published annually. Other sources are: *Current British Directories, 1988* (CBD Research); *Current Asian and Australian Directories* (CBD Research); *Current African Directories* (CBD Research); and *Current European Directories* (CBD Research).

An example of a well-respected and general directory is the U.S. source, *Thomas Register of American Manufacturers* (Thomas Publishing Co.). This is published annually and the 1989 edition runs to 23 large volumes covering manufacturers of all types of products. Volumes 1 to 14 list products in alphabetical order with manufacturers' addresses, Volumes 15 and 16 list manufacturers alphabetically and Volumes 17 to 23 provide a collection of manufacturers' trade catalogues, cross-referenced from the other two main sections. (Not all manufacturers provide catalogues.)

Among UK trade directories, the *Computer Users' Yearbook* (VNU) is a well established and up-to-date source with a very wide coverage of products marketed in the UK. It contains information on computers, peripherals, accessories, supplies, consultants and system houses, computer service bureaux, data preparation services as well as many other types of information relevant to the computer industry and computer users. Details of specific equipment models are necessarily brief and are presented in the form of comparative charts. The 1990 edition, published in December 1989, runs to four volumes and over 2000 pages and costs £109.50.

VNU also publishes *Software Users' Yearbook*, covering over 8300 software packages with their suppliers, *Data Comms Yearbook* and *PC Year Book*, this last covering hardware, software, services and support for IBM and compatible micros.

The *Communications Users' Yearbook* (Manor House Press/ NCC) gives details of telex, fax and videotex equipment, LANs, VANs, X25 packet switches, modems, multiplexers, networking equipment, cellular telephones and radio paging equipment from UK manufacturers and suppliers.

Among the many national and international directories of online databases, one of the longest established, *Directory of Online Databases* (Cuadra/Elsevier), is arguably still the best and most comprehensive. Coverage is worldwide, although some databases which can only be accessed locally are excluded. The directory costs $175 in the USA and $205 elsewhere. Subscription includes one main volume and one update in the year. *Directory of Online Databases* is also available online on the Data-Star service.

Online databases provide the publisher with the opportunity to update a directory more frequently and several software directories are now available in this form. So far these are mainly of U.S. product coverage or have a stronger coverage of U.S. products. BUSINESS SOFTWARE DATABASE, available via several of the host services, is produced by Information Sources Inc. and updated monthly. It contains details of over 11 500 mainly U.S. produced programs for business or professional use, including programs for microcomputers, minicomputers and mainframes. The database corresponds in part to the printed directory, *Business Software Directory*. *Engineering and Industrial Software Directory*, produced by Engineering Information Inc., is made available online by Data-Star. It contains information on more than 4200 programs produced in the USA, Canada, Mexico and the UK. ONLINE MICROCOMPUTER SOFTWARE GUIDE AND DIRECTORY is produced by Online Inc. and hosted by BRS. It covers 5700 packages for microcomputers and is updated monthly. Coverage is international. MICROCOMPUTER SOFTWARE AND HARDWARE GUIDE is produced by Bowker and hosted online by Dialog. It corresponds to the printed *Software Encyclopedia* but is updated monthly. It gives details of 34 000 microcomputer programs available in the USA.

Technical Indexes Ltd provides product catalogues in microform. This is a service for which the manufacturers pay and so not all manufacturers will necessarily contribute. Seven industries are covered and these are as follows: Electronic engineering; Engineering components and materials; Process engineering; Manufacturing and materials handling; Laboratory equipment; Information technology; Construction and civil engineering.

Technical Indexes also publishes Product Data Books, which are printed product indexes with manufacturers' addresses and references to the product catalogues on microform. The *Information Technology, Computer and Communications Index* is one of these Product Data Books and is published twice per year. It is free to subscribers to the microform service and costs £44 per year to others. It also includes a 'What's New' section describing new products.

The Technical Indexes microfilm service is available for reference at the Science Reference and Information Service.

Trade literature provided by companies includes product catalogues and brochures, house journals and annual reports. Several public and institutional libraries have collections of trade literature, notably the British Library's Science Reference and Information Service.

Datapro Research Corporation publishes a range of reports on data processing and office equipment and services, including for example, microcomputers, online services and software. These contain a large amount of product data in a directory format.

Stockbroker research

Stockbrokers' research reports mostly cover individual companies but may also cover whole industry sectors. There are two online databases which cover these often neglected sources. Both INVESTEXT and the ICC INTERNATIONAL BUSINESS RESEARCH DATABASE can be used both to identify suitable reports and to provide the full-text or extracts of the text online, according to the user's requirements. ICC INTERNATIONAL BUSINESS RESEARCH DATABASE also contains the full-text of the Key Notes industry reports and the full texts of many company reports. It is available online via Dialog, and Data-Star also offers the STOCKBROKER RESEARCH database from ICC. INVESTEXT is available via Dialog. The difference between INVESTEXT and the ICC services is that INVESTEXT, the larger database, covers reports from U.S. financial research and banking companies while ICC INTERNATIONAL BUSINESS RESEARCH and ICC STOCKBROKER RESEARCH concentrate on European stockbrokers' reports. However both are international in coverage. A hardcopy directory of stockbroker research reports is published by ICC, entitled *ICC Directory of Stockbroker Research* and priced £48.

Addresses

Admerca, Postfach 5, Arostrasse 25, CH8008, Zurich, Switzerland

Arlington Management Publications Ltd, 87 Jermyn Street, London SW17 6JD, UK

Aslib/TMI, 3 Tower Street, Portsmouth PO1 2JR, UK Tel. (0705) 864714. Fax. (0705) 828009

Auerbach, 6560 North Park Drive, Pennsauken, NJ 08109 4374 USA;
 also at: Thomson Organization, Bourne House, 34 Beckenham Road, Beckenham, Kent, UK

Business Communications Co. Inc., 9 Viaduct Road, PO Box 2070C, Stanford CT 06906, USA Tel. 203 325 2208.

CBD Research Ltd, 15 Wickham Road, Beckenham, Kent BR3 2JS, UK Tel. 081-650 7745

Creative Strategies Research International, 2900 Gordon Avenue, Suite 100, Santa Clara, CA 95051, USA Tel. 408 245 4750

Cuadra Elsevier, 655 Avenue of the Americas, New York, NY 10010, USA Tel. (212) 989 5800

Datapro Research Corporation, Delran, NJ 08075, USA Tel. 604 764 0100

Dataquest, 13th Floor, Centre Point, 103 New Oxford Street, London WC1A 1DD, UK Tel. 071-379 6257. Fax 071-240 3653

Data-Star, Plaza Suite, 114 Jermyn Street, London SW1Y 6HJ, UK Tel. 071-930 5503

Dempa Publications Inc., Drususstrasse 7, 4000 Dusseldorf 11, West Germany;
 also at: 11-15 Higashi Gotanda 1 Chome, Shinagawa-ku, Tokyo 141, Japan

Trade statistics and market information 227

Dialog Information Retrieval Service, Learned Information, Woodside, Hinksey Hill, Oxford OX1 5AU, UK Tel. (0865) 730969

Electronic Industries Association of Japan, Overseas Public Affairs Office, Tokyo Chamber of Commerce and Industry Building, 2–2 Marunouchi 3-chome, Chiyoda-ku, Tokyo 100, Japan Tel. 03 213 1071. Fax 03 213 1078

Elsevier Advanced Technology Group, Mayfield House, 256 Banbury Road, Oxford OX9 7DH, UK Tel. (0865) 512242

EMAP Business and Computer Publications Ltd, Abbots Court, 34 Farringdon Lane, London EC1R 3AU, UK Tel. 071–251 6222. Fax 071–608 2696

Export Market Information Centre, Department of Trade and Industry, 1 Victoria Street, London SW1H 0ET, UK Tel. 071–215 5444

Financial Times Business Information Ltd, 30 Epsom Road, Guildford, Surrey GU1 3LE, UK Tel. (0483) 576144

Frost and Sullivan, 106 Fulton Street, New York, NY 10038, USA;
also at: 4 Grosvenor Gardens, London SW1W 0DH, UK Tel. 071–730 3438

Fuji Corporation, Han-ei Daini Building, 6F, 10-1, Shinjuku 1 chome, Shinjuku-ku, Tokyo 160 Japan

Gale Research, Book Tower, Detroit, Michigan 48226, USA

HMSO, PO Box 276, London SW8 5DT, UK Tel. 071–873 8499

ICC Business Ratios Ltd, Field House, 72 Oldfield Road, Hampton, Middlesex TW12 2HQ, UK Tel. 081–783 0922

ICC Financial Surveys Ltd, 28–42 Banner Street, London EC1Y 8QE, UK Tel. 071–253 9736.

IPI, Norde Ringvej 201, 2600 Glostrup, Denmark Tel. +45 2 632044.
also at: IPI Inc., 465 Convention Way, Suite 1 Redwood City, CA 94063, USA Tel. 415 364 9040

Key Note Publications Ltd, Field House, 72 Oldfield Road, Hampton, Middlesex TW12 2HQ, UK Tel. 081–783 0755

Link/IDC European Research Centre, 2 Bath Road, Chiswick, London W4 1LN, UK Tel. 081–995 8082

Logica Ltd, 64 Newman Street, London W1A 4SE, UK Tel. 071–637 9111

The Manor House Press Ltd, 404–406 Holloway Road, London N7 6QA, UK

Marketing Strategies for Industry (UK) Ltd, 32 Mill Green Road, Mitcham, Surrey CR4 4HY, UK

Pergamon Financial Data Services, Achilles House, Western Avenue, London W3 0UA, UK Tel. 081–992 3456

Profile, Sunbury House, Sunbury on Thames, Middlesex TW16 7AH, UK Tel. (0932) 785566

Reuter Textline, Reuters Ltd, 85 Fleet Street, London EC4P 4AJ, UK Tel. 071-250 1122

Romtec plc, Hattori House, Vanwall Road, Maidenhead, Berks SL6 4UW, UK Tel. (0628) 770077. Fax (0628) 785433

Science Reference and Information Service, 25 Southampton Buildings, London WC2A 1AW, UK

Technical Indexes Ltd, Willoughby Road, Bracknell, Berks RG12 4DW, UK Tel. (0344) 426311

Thomas Publishing Company, One Penn Plaza, New York, NY 10001, USA Tel. 212 695 0500. Fax 212 290 7362

US Department of Commerce, International Trade Administration, Office of Trade Information Services, PO Box 14207, Washington DC 20044, USA

VNU Business Publications, 32-34 Broadwick Street, London W1A 2HG, UK

CHAPTER THIRTEEN

Research

D. HAYNES

Introduction

The 1980s saw the start of several major research programmes as the industrialized countries started jockeying for a leading position in information technology. The three major groupings for IT research are the US, Japan and Europe. Japan now produces more than 50% of the world's microprocessors and has dominated the market for consumer electronics for some time. The US is the centre of innovation and until now has had a lead in supercomputers, although Japan is now a serious competitor in this market. European research has concentrated on innovative technologies such as new semiconductor materials and on telecommunications.

Research programmes

All three groupings are keenly aware of the importance of research for future products and innovations. In the USA, much of the research into IT is tied up with defence and many of the innovations with miniaturization of electronic components arose directly out of the space programmes. Although government provides a lot of the funds for research, much of the research is actually carried out in the private sector. Corporations in the private sector have established research associations so that they can pool resources. Notable examples (described below) are: Microelectronics and Computer Technology Cooperative (MCC); Semiconductor Research Corporation (SRC); Computer-Aided Manufacturing International (CAM-I); and the System Development Foundation (SDF). In the public sector there is the Defense Advanced Research Project Agency (DARPA).

In 1982 the Japanese government established the Fifth Generation Computer project, and this was followed closely by the UK's Alvey Programme. Both programmes of research were intended to support research effort to enable the development of new products. In its *Framework Programme of Community Activities in the Field of Research and Technological Development (1987 to 1991)* the European Community earmarked 1600 million ECUs for information technology and 550 million ECUs for communications research, out of a total of 5396 million ECUs for the period (*Official Journal of the European Communities* No. L 302/5, 24 Oct. 1987). The ESPRIT-II Programme is a major part of the information technology research activity. A number of information services have arisen around these programmes.

Japan: Fifth-Generation Computer Project

The Japanese Ministry of International Trade (MITI) announced a ten-year research programme in 1982. This arose directly out of a three-year study within MITI. The objective of the programme is to develop a computer capable of inference, logic, natural language processing and able to converse directly with human beings. The idea of the fifth-generation computer has become widely accepted. *Fifth Generation Computers* (edited by R. K. Miller) reviews a number of programmes with one chapter per programme. Fifth-generation computers are defined as those based on symbolic inference and using parallel processing. The Japanese Fifth-Generation Computer Project is funded by the Japanese government to the tune of £500 million and is intended to stimulate cooperation between the private sector and the universities.

North America

MICROELECTRONICS AND COMPUTER TECHNOLOGY COOPERATIVE (MCC)

This is an association of 19 major U.S. corporations set up in 1982. Its particular areas of research interest are:

- Development of new architectures
- Software technology
- CAD for VLSI chips
- Component packaging

SEMICONDUCTOR RESEARCH CORPORATION (SRC)

Based in North Carolina, SRC is funded by 12 major U.S. corporations and works through 30 U.S. universities. The corporation funds research in: micro structure science; design science; and manufacturing systems.

DEFENSE ADVANCED RESEARCH PROJECT AGENCY (DARPA)

DARPA started in 1984 with the aim of developing supercomputers for defence and civilian applications. It had a budget of $500 million over a period of five years. The particular areas of research undertaken include:

- Artificial intelligence
- Software development
- Computer architectures
- Expert systems for aircraft

COMPUTER AIDED MANUFACTURING INTERNATIONAL (CAM-I)

CAM-I is a non-profit membership organization formed in 1972. It has a worldwide membership in both the public and private sectors. Its research interests include:

- Geometric modelling
- Process planning
- CAD/CAM
- Computer-aided quality assurance
- Robotics

THE SYSTEM DEVELOPMENT FOUNDATION (SDF)

SDF was organized by the Rand Corporation in 1956 and has an annual funding of $37 million. It is a non-profit organization and does research into the following areas:

- Robotics
- Information science
- Man-machine interface
- Non-von Newmann computation

Europe

EUROPEAN STRATEGIC PROGRAMME OF RESEARCH AND DEVELOPMENT IN INFORMATION TECHNOLOGY (ESPRIT)

ESPRIT is a jointly funded research programme with contributions from the EEC and private industry. It has a budget of $1.5

billion and includes the following areas:
- Advanced microelectronics
- Software technology
- Advanced information processing
- Office systems
- Computer integrated manufacture (CIM)

The first phase of ESPRIT funded 226 projects and was completed in 1988, when phase 2, ESPRIT-II was launched. ESPRIT-II is known as the Technology Integration Project and is intended to develop some of the pre-competitive research lines established in phase I. The areas covered in ESPRIT-II are:

- Microelectronics
- Peripheral technologies
- Information processing systems
- IT application technologies

EUREKA

EUREKA was established in 1985 to improve technological co-operation in Europe. The programme has 19 European countries participating in it including EEC and EFTA members. Within the EUREKA programme there are a number of projects, some of which are IT related: Eurobio (information technology applications in manufacturing); Eurocom (telecommunications); and Euromatic (manufacture of electronic components and software products).

FORECASTING AND ASSESSMENT IN SCIENCE AND TECHNOLOGY (FAST)

FAST is a strategic research programme to analyze scientific and technological change so that the EC can determine new priorities for research and development. It has a secondary role of fostering cooperation among forecasting centres in the EC. The present programme of research is the third programme which started in 1988 and is due to finish in 1992.

R&D IN ADVANCED COMMUNICATIONS FOR EUROPE (RACE)

This is a programme to develop integrated broadband communications to provide Community-wide services by 1995. The main part of the programme runs from 1987 to 1991. It is divided into three parts:

- IBC development and implementation strategies

- IBC technologies
- Pre-normative (standards) functional integration

ALVEY PROGRAMME

The Alvey Programme was a £350 million five-year programme of research funded by the UK government. It was designed to encourage cooperation between universities and the private sector and in particular to encourage the development of new products from innovations in information technology. Research projects were divided into the following categories:

- Microelectronics
- Software engineering
- Knowledge-based systems
- Man-machine interfaces

The Programme has now come to an end and the UK Department of Trade and Industry has set up an Information Engineering Directorate to carry forward the work of the Alvey Programme.

Research in the private sector

Many of the major manufacturers in IT and telecommunications have considerable research establishments, geared towards fundamental research, development of new products and improvement of existing ones. Many of these firms have been involved in government-funded research programmes and there is ongoing contact with the academic world. A lot of the research which goes on in companies is commercially sensitive and it can be difficult to find out what is going on until the research has reached an advanced stage. Firms such as IBM, Plessey, Siemens and ICL produce their own research publications, which give their scientists an opportunity to publish their research findings. Details of in-house research journals can be found in Chapter 16 on periodicals. Notable titles include: *IBM Journal of Research and Development*; *IBM Technical Disclosures*; *ICL Technical Journal*; *Philips Technical Review* and *British Telecom Technology Journal*.

Another clue to research activities is patents. Searching patents is a highly skilled operation and it is not always obvious where to look. However most patents will indicate the organizational affiliation of the person filing the patent, or the assignee, usually the company for which the inventor works. Patents are dealt with in Chapter fourteen.

Conference proceedings are another important clue to the

research activities of companies. Proceedings usually give the affiliation of the author of the paper. The journals literature and especially the learned journals are another avenue worth exploring.

Listings of research in progress

There are very few research listings specific to information technology. Most are geared to a country or funding agency. In the UK the best known of these is *CRIB (Current Research in Britain)*, published by the British Library. Some of the listings are available both as databases and as published bulletins, yearbooks or directories.

There is often a considerable time-lag between starting a project and seeing the first publications arising from it. Research listings provide a useful service—a way of finding out what people are doing now. Even so there can be delays in reporting commencement of research projects, and the projects themselves may well be over before the listing has appeared.

Projects which are part of a research programme are often listed in progress reports by the organizers of the programme. Some of the programmes have annual research meetings, where participants have an opportunity to report any progress made with their research. It is best to contact the programmes directly to see if this kind of information is available.

Databases

Machine-readable sources of information including online databases are dealt with in Chapter nine. Another useful reference work is the *Directory of Online Databases* (Cuadra/Elsevier), which is published annually with quarterly updates, and the *Directory of Portable Databases* (Cuadra/Elsevier) which comes out twice a year.

Most of the databases identified, covering IT research are nationally or regionally oriented rather than subject oriented. Some are even more specific, covering research funded by a particular agency or research within an institute. The following databases are national and regional research databases.

Specific databases

FORKAT

BMFT-FÖDERUNGSKATALOG is produced by the Federal Ministry for Research and Technology (BMFT) in the Federal Republic of Germany. It contains details of 6000 research and development projects supported by the Ministry and is available on STN International. The Ministry also produces an equivalent printed annual research catalogue *BMFT-Föderungskatalog*.

CSIRO RESEARCH IN PROGRESS

CSIRO RESEARCH IN PROGRESS is produced by the Commonwealth Scientific Industrial Research Organization (CSIRO) in Australia and contains details of research funded by CSIRO. It covers a very wide range of subjects including information science and is limited to Australia. CSIRO also publishes the *Directory of CSIRO Research Programs*.

CRIB

CURRENT RESEARCH IN BRITAIN (CRIB) is produced by the British Library Document Supply Centre and contains details of 75 000 current research projects in the UK. This includes research conducted in academic institutions, in the public sector, and in the private sector. The online database is available on Pergamon Financial Data Services (PFDS). The British Library Document Supply Centre also publishes a printed directory in four volumes. The one on physical sciences is likely to be of most direct interest.

MINERVA

MINERVA contains details of research projects at more than 200 U.S. universities and research establishments. The service is part of the Electronic Editions of *The Spokesman-Review* and the *Spokane Chronicle* (Cowles Publishing Company).

FEDERAL RESEARCH IN PROGRESS

This database is available on Dialog and contains details of research projects funded by the U.S. government in all subject areas. Certain parts of the database are available only in the US. The database is produced by the National Technical Information Service (NTIS).

IEC

IEC is the equivalent of the printed *Directory of Federally Supported Research in Universities*. It is produced by CISTI and is accessible to users in Canada. It covers research in universities funded by the Canadian government through its 36 funding agencies. The database is in English and French and contains 150 000 records; 15 000 new records a year are added to the database.

JICST

JICST (The Japan Center of Science and Technology) is a Japanese-language online service. It has two files on research: JICST FILE ON CURRENT SCIENCE AND TECHNOLOGY RESEARCH IN JAPAN and JICST FILE ON GOVERNMENT REPORTS IN JAPAN. The first one is a referral database with details of basic and applied research funded by the government. The second one is a bibliographic database with references to research reports arising from government funded research projects.

THE SCITECH REPORT

This is available both as a printed journal and as a full-text database on the NewsNet service. It covers developments in pure and applied science and includes new products. Computer hardware and software and novel technologies are also covered.

SSIE CURRENT RESEARCH

This is another database produced by NTIS in the US. It covers research funded by the Federal Government and includes the physical and engineering sciences.

Other types of database list research projects sponsored by or conducted in a specific organization. Examples are SITRAFO and the National Bureau of Standards databases.

SITRAFO

SITRAFO covers research in progress at two universities: Universität Karlsruhe and the Université Louis Pasteur. The database is available on STN International and is in English and French.

NATIONAL BUREAU OF STANDARDS BULLETIN

This bulletin is available as a full-text database on NewsNet and is produced by the U.S. National Institute of Standards and Technology. Its coverage includes research into computers and electronics.

Research 237

INSIDE R&D

This is available on Dialog and Data-Star as part of the PTS Newsletter database and on NEXIS. INSIDE R&D is a weekly disclosure bulletin which covers a wide range of subjects including several information technologies. The emphasis is on research results with licensing potential.

CRIP

There are very few sources which look at IT research specifically. CRIP (*Compendium of Australian Research in Progress*) is one example. The *Compendium* contains details of research on computers and computer applications, including software, electronic components, peripherals, graphics, systems and communication networks. The online equivalent, CRIP (*Computing Research in Progress*) is produced by CSIRO (Commonwealth Scientific Industrial Research Organization) and also includes details of research projects completed over the last five years. Both the directory and the database contain details of the project title, methodology, organizations, instigators, source of funding and subject terms. The *Compendium* and the database are updated annually.

IT PROJECTS

Another source dealing specifically with IT research is IT PROJECTS, which is a database on the ECHO online service in Luxembourg. It is produced by the European Commission and covers publicly funded research projects on information technology in Europe. The database is updated quarterly.

Chapter nine on machine-readable sources goes into detail of databases which cover information technology. Most of these are bibliographic databases and do not give details of research projects; their focus is usually on published papers, which may arise from research projects. Notable databases are INSPEC and COMPENDEX. EABS and its hard-copy equivalent *Euro Abstracts* (European Commission) covers publications resulting from research funded by the European Commission. A large proportion of the funding available has been allocated to information technology and telecommunications related areas.

Another secondary source worthy of note is *Index to Scientific Reviews* (ISI) which is published twice a year. The main entries are listings of review articles appearing in scientific journals and arranged by author. The publishers have developed the concept of *Research Front Specialty Index*™ to identify clusters of articles covering the same research area. This is done by analyzing the citation patterns of the articles. A core cluster of cited articles is used to define a research area, and any article citing one of the core cluster will appear in the *Research Front Speciality Index*™. This means that having identified a paper of interest you can then find other reviews covering the same research area. Each review has a weighting depending on the number of papers from the core cluster quoted.

As in other ISI publications, there is a *Permuterm*™*Subject Index* which refers to author name and to *Research Front Speciality*™. The corporate index is arranged geographically starting with U.S. states followed by the rest of the world by country, and by organization.

Theses and dissertations

Theses and dissertations are a valuable source of innovative research. A lot of academic research is geared to pushing forward the frontiers of our understanding of the world and a great deal of the basic research done in universities is subsequently applied in the development of new products and technologies. There are two useful guides to dissertations and theses, one covering the US and the other the United Kingdom.

Index to Theses

Index to Theses has been published by Aslib since 1950. Recently abstracts have been added to the main entries and this provides probably the most comprehensive guide to theses in the UK. The full title is *Index to Theses Accepted for Higher Degrees by the Universities of Great Britain and Ireland and the Council for National Academic Awards*. It is produced quarterly by Aslib and covers approximately 9000 theses accepted each year. The main entries are arranged by 11 main subject headings including electrical engineering. The second level of classification includes the following headings:

K1 Electrical Engineering
K2 Communication Engineering
K3 Physical Electronics
K4 Computing Science and Technology
K5 Control Theory and Engineering

There is a third level of heading, so that if you were interested in Computer Hardware for instance you could look under heading

'K4c Computer Hardware'. There is no specific heading for information technology and any of the headings listed above might contain relevant material. The subject index is very specific, normally with only one or two items per index term. There is also an author index.

Dissertation Abstracts International

Dissertation Abstracts International (University Microfilms Inc.) is published in three sections, of which two are relevant to information technology. Section B (Science and Engineering) covers dissertations accepted by North American universities for doctoral and post-doctoral degrees. This is published monthly. Section C (Worldwide) (formerly European Abstracts) was expanded to worldwide coverage in Spring 1989. This section is published quarterly. The main entries contain bibliographic details of the dissertation, the awarding institution, and translated title where appropriate. The majority of entries also have an abstract as well. The entries are arranged by subject heading. Relevant headings include: Information Science; Electronics and Electrical Engineering; and Computer Science.

UMI also offers a document supply service for those dissertations they have on microfilm. Ordering details are given in the main entries. UMI publishes an annual cumulation of *Dissertation Abstracts International* and *American Doctoral Dissertations*, the *Comprehensive Dissertation Index Supplement*.

British Reports Translations and Theses covers grey literature and includes details of doctoral theses. This is a bibliographic index, with no abstracts and corresponds to the online database SIGLE, available on Blaise-Line. A more detailed description of this source appears in Chapter ten on secondary sources.

CHAPTER FOURTEEN

Patent information

T.S. EISENSCHITZ

The nature of a patent

A patent is a bargain between an inventor and the state. The inventor receives a limited-time monopoly to prevent others exploiting the invention. This is the most public and visible aspect of the patent grant. However, the main purpose of the system is to facilitate the spread of knowledge of technological advances. In return for the monopoly on the invention, the inventor has to deposit a written description of the idea for the public. This description must be in sufficient detail for someone skilled in the art to be able to carry out the invention.

The monopoly lasts for around 16 to 20 years depending on national law, but the information continues to be available and useful indefinitely. In most countries specifications are published and available for sale or for consultation in specific libraries. Increasingly, patents are being searched online in bibliographic or full-text databases for both technical and commercial/marketing purposes.

Patents are instruments of national or regional law and one grant establishes the bargain over one or a small group of countries. Therefore patents appear in families of similar documents relating to protection in a number of territories. They are held together and defined under the International (Paris) Convention signed in 1883. The Convention identifies as a key characteristic of patents the date, country and number which relate to the very first application of the series and are called collectively the 'priority data'. The defining characteristics of patentable inventions are that they should embody knowledge which is new and not obviously deductible from that already known. These two criteria are called 'novelty' and 'inventive step' or 'non-obviousness', respectively. The priority date supplies the time limit for judging these characteristics (Eisenschitz, 1987). Inventions must also be useful, but this is not a strong constraint. Broadly speaking, any saleable product must be useful to the buyer, and this satisfies the criterion.

Next we look at different systems available for obtaining a patent. The details of any one nation's law are best looked up when required. There are a number of compilations in existence (e.g. *Patents Throughout the World*). Finally the documentation and information derived from patents and applications of that information are explored.

How to apply for a patent

There are three major systems of patent administration. These are: deferred examination; traditional patents; and the COMECON system. Anyone can apply for a patent and companies or individuals may be patentees. (For a survey of patent problems see Phillips, 1985).

Patent grant procedure usually involves an examination of the contents of a written specification in comparison with the laws and practice of the country concerned in order to check that the invention satisfies all requirements of patentability. Major considerations are novelty and inventive step, and for these purposes a search of the prior art is carried out.

Deferred examination

The essence of deferred examination is that the prior art search is carried out in advance of the examination. The applicant is given time to consider the results of the search and then requests substantive examination. The specification is published twice; once after the prior art search and again simultaneously with the grant. In this way details of all inventions are published whether or not a patent grant ensues. The deferred examination system is now in widespread use. Most European countries use it as do Australia, Japan and many others.

The traditional patenting system

This was the predominant means of granting patents until superseded by deferred examination. Once a patent application is received, the examiner embarks on the full examination and carries out the prior art search as part of this process. Only one document is published and this is after the specification has been accepted by the examiner. This may be simultaneous with grant but is more likely to be followed by an opposition period as this is the first opportunity for public comment. Grant then follows after any objections have been dealt with or at the end of the fixed period.

The UK Patents Act 1949 provided for the traditional type of patenting system. Quite a number of ex-colonial countries inherited such systems on independence and a number still use them. In particular the U.S. system is of this type. U.S. patents last for 17 years from the date of grant, subject to renewal fees being paid.

The COMECON system

This system is used by the USSR and its CMEA partners. It is a dual arrangement. Foreign applicants receive an ordinary patent of the traditional type. National inventors are given an inventor's certificate which confers recognition and an appropriate reward. Exploitation is left in the hands of the state. The two types of document are arranged in a single numerical sequence when published and are made equally available through patent libraries and information services. Within the current negotiations for revision of the Paris Convention there is pressure to include inventors' certificates in its scope.

Contents of the specification

Patent documents are highly standardized. This is a great help to readers as the basic contents and lay-out are very similar in all cases. The three main divisions are into the front page, the body of the specification, and the claims.

The front page

A modern front page of a British patent is shown in Figure 14.1. It contains the title, abstract and drawing and bibliographic details mainly added by the Patent Office. Each item is labelled with a number on the left-hand side. Thus the application number is 21. These are INID (international numbers for the identification of bibliographic data) numbers allocated by WIPO (the World Intellectual Property Organization) which concerns itself with international standardization. They are the same in all countries and intended as field labels for computer processing. More generally, they indicate to a searcher which names and numbers are

Patent information 243

(12) UK Patent Application (19) GB (11) 2 200 225 A

(43) Application published 27 Jul 1988

(21) Application No 8727714

(22) Date of filing 26 Nov 1987

(30) Priority Data
(31) 8701564 (32) 24 Jan 1987 (33) GB
8716852 17 Jul 1987

(71) Applicant
Lucas Industries Public Limited Company

(Incorporated in United Kingdom)

Great King Street, Birmingham, B19 2XF

(72) Inventor
Neil Andrew Cooper

(74) Agent and/or Address for Service
Marks & Clerk
Alpha Tower, Suffolk Street Queensway,
Birmingham, B1 1TT

(51) INT CL⁴
G05B 23/02

(52) Domestic classification (Edition J)
G3N 288A 288B 375 381 GK2
U1S 1883 1987 G3N

(56) Documents cited
GB A 2045968   GB A 2000327   EP A 0190664
US 3834361

(58) Field of search
G3N
Selected US specifications from IPC sub-class
G05B

(54) Computer control of an apparatus

(57) An apparatus 112 (e.g. a gas turbine fuel control) can be controlled by either of two computers 113, 114 in respective lanes A, B connection of the computers 113, 114 to the apparatus 112 being controlled by switch devices 119, 121 in respective input-output buses 118, 120 of the computers 113, 114. The switch devices 119, 121 are responsive to control signals generated by a logic arrangement 132 in response to faults in either computer 113, 114. The logic arrangement 132 includes a latching bistable device (150, 151; Fig 4) which maintains the switch devices 119, 121 in their last operated state, in the absence of a subsequent fault in the currently controlling computer.

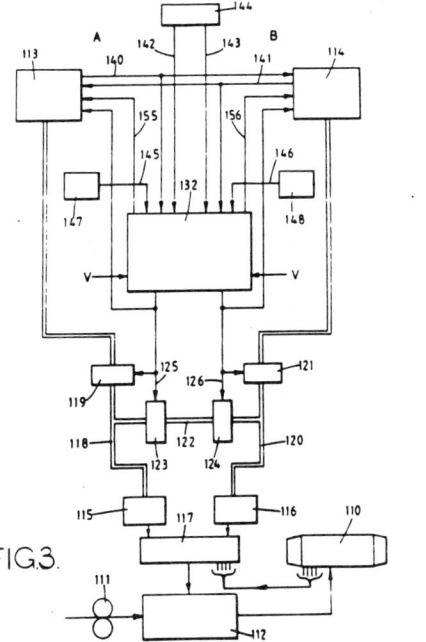

FIG.3.

Figure 14.1

which if the specification is in an unfamiliar language. The title alone is often too brief to be helpful, but is informative if combined with the abstract. Provision of a drawing is optional and depends on the nature of the invention.

Two classifications are given, the domestic and the international. The field of search is also given and this is in terms of the domestic classification. The international classification is administered by WIPO and all adherents put its symbols on patents to aid multi-country searching (WIPO, 1985). Many countries use only the one international classification, having no separate domestic system. The British and U.S. classifications are two of the major national schemes left. Documents found in the search are listed but under the European and PCT systems these are at the back of the specification and give details of degree of relevance and which claims are affected.

Other entries include details of the applicants, inventors and their agents. Application date and number are given and also the priority date, number and country. Priority data is valuable beyond the one patent as it determines the members of the family and the time available for Convention applications.

The body of the specification

This part is to contain the disclosure to the public. It starts with an introduction which sets out the background and prior art of the invention. It is usually quite brief in case further prior art is discovered which changes the perspective of the invention. A few countries, notably the US, require a complete disclosure of the prior art as known to the applicant. Even in this case disclosure can be made to the office on a form and not discussed on the specification. There follows the specific description of the invention. This will be firstly in general terms and then elaborated in examples.

The claims

These set out the inventive aspects which are to be protected and stake the legal claim. Claims run in sequences starting with the most general formulation and then narrowing as specifics of the actual operation are included. There may be more than one sequence for an invention and its applications. The applicant wishes to claim widely so that an infringer cannot make an insignificant change and yet circumvent the patent. The examiner is concerned to ensure that no part of the prior art is included in the claims on the one hand, and that they do not wander off into flights of fancy on the other. A great many claims are submitted so that a lesser number may survive; it is not permissible to widen the scope of claims once entered. They can only be maintained or narrowed. These then are the sections of a patent specification.

Specifically IT-related inventions

Patents are concerned with technical concepts which may still need development into products. In IT areas some of the technical areas patents will cover are as follows: electrical circuits, methods of manufacture of electronic components and of whole systems and generally all kinds of equipment, its construction and interconnections and new things to be done with it. Software is not patentable in most countries, but degree of strictness is variable and software can be patented if it can be presented as a part of a mechanism, an integral part of the functioning of an apparatus.

Disclosure in a patent is at the level of an expert in the art. For many IT patents this means they will be quite complex and only give details of the actual advance, but where there are leaps in technology then the patents are very informative. A patent for an early IBM computer is four volumes thick and contains full details of circuitry and the flows of logical argument (GB 1 108 800). More recently it was decided in court that the level of expertise to be addressed for developments in colour TV was that of the entire research team, not just one person (Valensi, 1973).

One of the best ways to indicate the subject matter of these patents is to review the main classification schemes. Nowadays an information searcher is likely to be using a computer and to rely on keywords, but with patents one needs to be careful, since they are written in abstract terms so that the appended classifications are still important searching aids. Free text in full text searching should be seen as an adjunct to the classifications not a replacement. This is even more true when there are only abstracts available.

National/international classification

UK patents

In the UK classification, the two main sections to note are:

G   Instrumentation
H   Electricity

Within these are various headings such as:

G3N   Automatic electric control systems
H4F   Pictorial communication

These are the working levels and within them terms give the details. When combined with the indexing schedule for uses and applications, U1S, both technological and product information should be available (Patent Office, annual).

International Patent Classification (IPC)

The international classification, IPC, uses the same sections as the UK (WIPO, 1990). The main divisions are classes and subclasses. Examples are:

G06   Computing, calculating and counting
G06F 15/40   Electric digital computers for information retrieval

The IPC is not very detailed having reached only its fifth edition. Being international makes for some ambiguities but is very important as most countries include its symbols and the international searching authorities use it.

U.S. patents

The U.S. classification is rather differently structured but has essentially the same kinds of labels on its classes, for instance Class 369 is dynamic information storage and retrieval. This will have many subdivisions being a very detailed classification (USPTO).

With all the classifications there is an index of ordinary words (i.e. uncontrolled terms) to start off with and then it is a matter of finding the most appropriate of the detailed terms. It is essential to look in as many places as possible for possible terms. Combining keywords with classifications is the most comprehensive strategy and gives some assurance that important aspects have not been overlooked.

The availability of patent literature

Patents are usually held separately from other forms of literature and form their own libraries. Because of this, they have often been overlooked by researchers who tend to think almost entirely in terms of the journal literature. Other than looking directly at the patents it is the abstracting journals which will give new users the necessary guidance around their subject.

Ultimately the best service is given by those organizations that specialize in patent information and give complete coverage in one or many countries. These are described in the discussion below on searching.

Some of the literature-based database services cover patents as well. Of particular relevance are: the COMPUTER DATABASE on Dialog, and CHEMICAL ABSTRACTS. INSPEC does not cover patents at all. Coverage is not comprehensive and it is important to look out for the cut-off points for subject coverage and for country coverage. Most database producers have their own classification and indexing systems, which may not reflect the patent classification assigned by the patent authority. Patents from countries with non-Western European languages or with problems of availability of documents tend to get left out. Despite these problems, a reasonable coverage of main countries may be given. Because important patents are likely to have equivalent publications in major trading countries, good coverage need involve only a few of them such as the USA, West Germany and the UK. The problem then, is to find out which are the major countries for any technology. Although patent literature is so vast and repetitive, it is possible to get good coverage by looking at a few key countries (Eisenschitz, 1984). For example, in a study of British patents (Mann and Hellyer, 1980) of 32 electrical patents abstracted, the three main journals were: *Plastics Abstracts*, *Electrical and Electronics Abstracts* and *Chemical Abstracts* with 11, 7 and 4 abstracts respectively. The biggest problem with use of these journals for patent information is to be sure where the boundaries are drawn in respect of their selection policy.

An argument against using patent literature is that any worthwhile information will be reproduced in more accessible form in journal articles. For electrical patents, reproduction of one patent in one article is around 10% (OTAF, 1977). However, it seems that when entire research projects are considered as delineated by groups of patents, then the overlap with articles is much higher (Eisenschitz, Lazard and Willey, 1986). Articles can cover any aspect of the project and the overlap with patents is not one-to-one. However many of the operational details are given in patents and nowhere else and patents are rarely cited in journal references. This reflects the fact that articles and patents are written for different purposes and therefore at different stages of the lifetime of a project. Results from a group of British pharmaceutical patents give an overlap of 60%, much higher than any previous studies. Other subject areas could be expected to generate lower overlaps as the scientific interest of patent contents is very variable. In a food processing study the total overlap was only 25%. No survey involving IT patents has been done as yet. In an unknown number of cases the main reason for lack of journal publication will be commercial value irrespective of scientific concerns. The encouraging point is that in areas of great interest, the overlap is high. A problem is that patents are rarely cited in journal references so that it is difficult for a researcher to locate them. It remains true that many of the operational details are given in patents and nowhere else.

Searching

One can search for patents using general literature services or using those specific to patents. The value of general services has been discussed above. They are useful in that the patent search is integrated with the searches for all other forms of literature. Nevertheless, for completeness of subject coverage and width of country coverage, the specialist services are required.

Most of the general and the specific services are available online so they can be accessed as and when required. There are also many more searchable items available online so that one is not restricted to those indexes provided by the database compiler.

Specialist services

All countries maintain their own integral collection of national patents and appropriate indexes. Most countries also collect the patents of selected other countries and hold these as single-country collections too. The Dutch national patent collection comprises patents from many countries which are all classified in the same scheme and searchable as one file. This collection forms the basis of what is now the searching branch of the European Patent Office at The Hague.

With online systems it is much easier to have a single integrated collection, as is the case with the Derwent and INPADOC databases, described later. There are also a number of single country services which being online are more usable than the printed versions. The online services make bibliographic information and sometimes abstracts available. Drawings, the claims and the body of the specification usually have to be consulted in hard copy (WPI, 1985).

Single-country services

For many years only U.S. patents were available as a database of their own. More recently, French, European, and PCT databases have been made available. A UK patents database will be available soon.

USA

U.S. patents have been printed using computer technology since 1971 and tapes of the full texts of U.S. patents from that date are leased to any organization prepared to pay for them. These are only complete from 1975 onwards as there were still some unsolved problems relating to diagrams. The Orbit service in the USA offers a separate U.S. database of front page information in a file set up by Derwent Publications. The full text is not provided but all claims are given. Missing documents pre-1975 have been added back to 1971. They also provide a file called COMPUTERPATS covering all U.S. computer patents from the beginning of the industry. The earliest patent dates from 1942. These have specially written, very detailed abstracts. Another U.S. producer, IFI Plenum, has U.S. patent bibliographic details mounted in a file called CLAIMS. This file extends back to 1950 for chemical patents and is unique in its extent of backlog. All other patents including electrical extend back to 1963. It is mounted on Dialog, Orbit, and STN International. The only U.S. full-text file available at present is LEXPAT. It goes back to 1975 and is mounted by Mead Data Central who own LEXIS and NEXIS and are therefore experienced in handling full text.

FRANCE

The French Patent Office has created a set of databases of French patents since 1969 and also all European patents. These are called INPI and are mounted on the French host, Questel.

JAPAN AND CHINA

A problem for patent searchers in all fields arises when one finds Japanese patents with no equivalents and needs to know whether they are relevant. Readers of Japanese are scarce (outside Japan) and Japan seems to produce many more patents than other countries. Orbit provides a file called JAPIO which contains abstracts of Japanese unexamined patent applications. There is also an Orbit file called CHINAPATS which covers documents from the new system in China.

Multi-country services

There are two sets of services. Inpadoc covers 56 sources of patents (Piltch and Wratschko, 1978) and Derwent Publications covers 33 (Dixon and Oppenheim, 1982). Inpadoc's strength is its very wide coverage but it gives bibliographic information only and reproduces what the various national patent offices provide it with. Derwent covers fewer countries but nearly all the material is produced by their own staff so that the product is closely tailored to its users. The two markets are complementary.

INPADOC—THE INTERNATIONAL PATENT DOCUMENTATION CENTRE

Inpadoc is a private company set up by the Austrian Government in association with WIPO. Any patent-issuing authority can become a member; there are currently 56 of them. They send their weekly or monthly records to the Centre in Vienna where they are entered without modification into the computer. This is used to produce the computer database plus a series of indexes printed on COM microfiche. Patent offices of member states have access to all the output. There are also obligations on the offices to provide free access to most of the indexes to fulfil WIPO's aims of technological development through access to information and products. Other organizations can subscribe to the output. Most records go back to 1968 but it is best to check the starting date for each country if in doubt.

The database consists of purely bibliographic details, there are no abstracts. All words, numbers and dates are searchable. It is available by direct line from Vienna. INPADOC is also hosted by Orbit, Dialog and STN. It is updated weekly. On Orbit, Derwent accession numbers have been added to all records to enable cross file searching. This is particularly useful in that it allows an abstract to be consulted. The COM indexes arrange the patents as follows:

- in IPC order
- in applicant/patentee order
- in inventor order
- in numerical order for each country
- giving all previous family members

Patent information 251

The weekly collection is published together as a *Gazette*; quarterly, annual and five-yearly cumulations of each index are published separately. The index of family members is not freely available in libraries. All the others are, but this one is charged for to allow the company to recoup costs. For recent publications, the family will be available freely in the *Gazette*.

For subject searching INPADOC is only of moderate use as there is only the International Patent Classification available as a guide. However for comprehensive family searching there is no rival. Families are sought by priority data and there is a recursive algorithm so that multiple priorities may be followed through. Non-convention equivalents (see below) cannot be found in this system. Another valuable command is the 'GET' command on Orbit. Once a set of references has been created it enables time series and ranked lists to be produced. These are valuable for purposes of commercial intelligence as similar work and active firms or inventors can be identified. Uses of the information will be discussed later.

DERWENT PUBLICATIONS LTD

Derwent covers 33 sources of inventive information. There are 29 countries, the EPO and WIPO-PCT and also two defensive publication journals (these journals publish brief accounts of inventions for the purpose of establishing a publication so that no one can apply for a patent later): *Research Disclosures* and *International Technological Disclosures*.

All patents are entered onto the Derwent computer. If a new document is an equivalent it is noted and the patent number added to the database. Additional information is added if appropriate. This includes designated states, examiners' search reports and additional assignees. A new abstract is written for some of the more important countries. If the document is a basic (i.e. the first of the family to be handled by Derwent), then it is given an informative title, abstract and indexing terms by Derwent staff with the aim of bringing out the information of use to industrial searchers as well as the inventive information useful to patent offices.

The product consists of bibliographic details and abstracts. There is a complete database and various printed products containing the information repackaged in a variety of ways for different user groups. Once the database is prepared it costs little to print in a different format for small groups of users, the true costs are of course hidden in the preparation required to enable this variety of printing. The database on pharmaceutical patents goes back to 1963 and other chemical areas started at various dates up to 1970. All other subjects started in 1974.

ELECTRICAL PATENTS INDEX (EPI) started in 1981 and is modelled on CHEMICAL PATENTS INDEX (CPI). It is indexed to a high level and is divided into six main sections:

> Instrumentation, measuring and testing
> Computing and control
> Semiconductors, and electronic circuitry
> Electronic components
> Communications
> Electrical power engineering

Not all countries are included in EPI. Lists are published and if in doubt a user should check for inclusion and starting date.

All other matter has only a rather simple classification applied to it and the file is called WORLD PATENT INDEX. Online the entire collection is called WPI. Anyone can access it, but only subscribers to the hard copy have access to the full indexing online.

National classification codes are not available, instead the general Derwent classes and the International Patent Classification terms as applied by the national offices are used. Equivalents searching is by Derwent accession number which means that only members of the immediate family can be traced. Although there are fewer countries than for INPADOC, related priorities are listed and you can search directly on priorities to get the extended family. The WPI file was closed in 1980 and a second file WPIL opened for the latest input. WPI remains open for subsequent family members as these have to be checked and assigned the same accession number, much more cumbersome than using the priorities.

The one item of family searching in which Derwent does excel is that of non-convention priorities. This seems to be a contradiction in terms, but what it means is an application made outside the 12 month limit but before there are any publications of applications or patents in the family. In many countries, as long as there is no publication the application would still be patentable and it clearly belongs to the same family. They are difficult to trace as their priority details are different. Derwent makes an effort to include them in families, something which Inpadoc cannot do. Note that in the larger more active patenting authorities such as the USA and European countries, prior art is defined to cover pending applications for novelty purposes so that this possibility does not arise. Non-convention applications occur particularly where developments are rapid over a long enough time scale to open up possible markets after the time limit has expired. This is mainly in pharmaceuticals, otherwise they are rare.

The statistical package

Derwent has organized its statistical functions into a package to be run on a microcomputer called PATSTAT-PLUS and first described by Oppenheim (Oppenheim, 1983). It is very powerful, allowing for a number of cross-correlations as well as basic ranking and time series. PATSTAT was developed for use with Derwent's WPI files but has recently been extended to accept data from its U.S. Patent Office files as well. The results of different analyses can be merged and edited.

On the Infoline host system, since merged with Orbit, a set is created and then statistical operations are carried out using the basic statistical command 'GET' on the mainframe computer. It ties up a lot of CPU time and has to be done at once following the search (Terragno, 1984). With PATSTAT-PLUS, the created set is down-loaded into the micro and then statistical operations can be undertaken at leisure. Although only selected required lines need be down-loaded, this can take a very considerable time and is a disadvantage of the system. DERWENT databases are available on the Orbit, Questel and Dialog hosts. Questel has its own additional online statistical software called Memsort so the Derwent package can be bypassed for quick analyses. The Infoline 'GET' command is now available on Orbit and is another online statistical package available with the DERWENT files.

Occasional and small-scale users may be better off with the online software where there is no additional outlay and one pays only for what one uses. For a large user, the Derwent software is much more powerful and versatile and analyses can be done at leisure when the occasion arises. There are also no delays arising from overused CPU time.

Use of the information

The main aim of the patent system has always been to transmit technical information. Apart from this, some commercial information is also transmitted by way of statistical analysis of numbers of documents. The two types of information have different users, and therefore patent information is now used as much if not more in strategic planning and marketing as in R&D and other technical departments. The monopoly protection granted to users is a by-product of the need for information to further technological development.

Technical information

In the IT industry, technical information can cover such things as construction of circuitry, arrangements into logical sequences to carry out tasks and apparatus like robots or TV sets and how they are constructed. Programs are only protected if they are part of an operation. On their own they are protected by copyright. Topological layouts such as the masks from which semiconductor chips are manufactured have their own form of protection. No information is revealed, but the main forms of legislation do provide that such a work is not infringed if reproduced by means of 'reverse engineering' for the purposes of analysis, research and further development (U.S. Code, 1984; Council Directive, 1986).

If specific details are wanted, then a patent can be very precise. However this can be a disadvantage if the searcher is looking for an answer to a general problem. In this case a range of patents may provide better information.

Techno-commercial information

Techno-commercial information can be yielded using the statistical analyses described above. Either a package is available or software is provided by the online host computer. Competitors can be identified by looking for those working in a way most similar to your own. The most active countries, companies and individuals will be revealed and the most productive technologies in a country or worldwide can also be identified.

Much research is being carried out on the use of patent statistics for commercial forecasting so as to make best use of these analyses. It has opened a whole new market of patent users. Recognition of this wide interest in patent statistics is evidenced by the recent development by the Battelle Institute of a package called PATENTS-PC which looks similar (at least on a brief assessment) to PATSTAT and analyzes the output of an online search of any patent database (Battelle Institute, 1987).

Intellectual property and the European Community

Membership of the European Community has distorted the application of intellectual property rights among member states. The main function of the European Community is to provide conditions for free movement of goods and services. Intellectual property rights are all national rights. They allow proprietors to prevent others from dealing in their products within national boundaries. This re-establishes the boundaries which the European Community is trying to abolish and is therefore in conflict. The European Community has resolved the problem by asserting that although intellectual property rights can be exercised in certain ways, their effect is limited so as not to override the principles of the Common Market (Korah, 1986). In practice this means that goods may be placed on the market for the first time as chosen by their owner, but once released into the European Community then competitors must be allowed to deal in them. Therefore competitors can buy in one country and sell in another, undercutting the local producer for instance. In these ways, some competition is enforced even within monopoly enterprises. Licensing agreements must be framed to take this into account. It is worth noting that European Community law takes precedence over national law where there is conflict. European Community law is enshrined in the Treaties, cases are reported in special series of law reports such as *Common Market Law Reports*. New European Community regulations and directives are notified in the *Official Journal of the European Community*. This is available online as a database called CELEX which is most easily available in the UK within the legal host, Justis. It is also available directly from the European Commission.

The 1992 European Single Market is of great significance to all of industry. It will demolish all barriers to trade within the European Community and this will encourage use of Community-wide brand names and even greater user of Community-wide patents.

References

Battelle Institute (1987), PATENTS-PC—A Method and Personal Computer Based Software for Analyzing Published Patent Data. Product brochure.

Council Directive (1986), *The Legal Protection of Topographies of Semiconductor Products, 87/54/EED. Official J. European Communities*, 27 June, No. L24/36.

Eisenschitz, T. S. (1984), The Student Research Programme into Patent Information at the City University London. *World Pat. Info.*, Vol. 6, No. 1, pp. 108–114.

Eisenschitz, T. S., Lazard, A. M. and Willey, C. J. (1986), Patent Groups and their Relationships with Journal Literature. *J. Info. Science*, Vol. 12, No. 1, pp. 35–46.

Eisenschitz, T. S. (1987), *Patents, Trade Marks and Designs in Information Work*. Croom Helm, Beckenham.

Jalloq, M. C. (1982), *Use of Patent Literature by Academics*, British Library R&D Report No. 5770.

Korah, V. (1986), *EEC Competition Law and Practice*, 2nd edn, ESC, Oxford.

Mann, H. and Hellyer, A. (1980), Coverage of UK Patent

Specifications by Abstracting Journals, *World Pat. Info.*, Vol. 2, No. 1, pp. 27–28.
Oppenheim, C. (1983), A Micro Computer Program for the Statistical Analysis of Patent Databases. *World Pat. Info.*, Vol. 5, No. 4, pp. 209–212.
OTAF (1977), *Patents as a Technological Resource*, 8th OTAF Report, U.S. Department of Commerce, pp. 23–27.
Patent Office, *UK Classification Schedules* (annual editions), Department of Trade and Industry, London.
Patent Office (1986), (a) *Patents as a Source of Information.* (b) *Introducing Patents.* (c) *Annual Report of the Comptroller.* Department of Trade and Industry, London.
Patents Throughout the World. Trade Activities Inc., New York.
Phillips, J. (ed.) (1985), *Patents in Perspective*, ESC, Oxford.
Piltch, W. and Wratschko, W. (1978), INPADOC—A Computerised Patent Documentation System. *J. Chem. Inf. Comput. Sci.*, Vol. 18, No. 2, pp. 69–75.
Shenton, K. (1987), personal communication.
Terragno, P. J. (1984), The GET Command. *World Pat. Info.*, Vol. 6, No. 2, pp. 69–73.
USPTO U.S. Patent Classification Schedules, U.S. Patent and Trademark Office (continuous revisions), Virginia, USA.
U.S. Code (1984), *Protection of Semiconductor Chip Products*, Section 302, Title 17, Chapter 9.
Valensi v. *British Radio* (1973), Reports of Patent Cases, 337.
WIPO (1985), *PCT Applicant's Guide*, WIPO, Geneva.
WIPO (1990), *International Patent Classification Schedules*, 5th edn, WIPO, Geneva.
WPI (1985), Online Patent Information. *World Pat. Info.*, Vol. 7, Nos. 1/2.

Addresses

Derwent Publications Ltd
Marketing Manager
Rochdale House
128 Theobalds Road
London WC1X 8RP
Tel. 071–242 5823/6

Inpadoc
Moellwaldplatz 4
A-1041 Vienna
Austria

Pergamon-Orbit-Infoline
Head of Sales and Marketing
Achilles House
Western Avenue
London W3 0UA
Tel. 081–992 3456

CHAPTER FIFTEEN

Government publications

P. RAGGETT

This chapter examines some sources of information about government publications. Part 1 looks at material issued by the UK Parliament, government departments and various official bodies. In the second part we will look at sources for obtaining information emanating from a couple of major international organizations.

Part 1: British government publications

All publications issued by Parliament are published and sold by HMSO through its publishing arm HMSO Books. Non-parliamentary material can be published by HMSO Books or issued by the official departments themselves. HMSO Books only publishes priced items: the departments are free to make a decision about publishing an item through HMSO or through other channels—usually by some in-house method. About half of non-parliamentary items are published by HMSO and half by the departments themselves.

HMSO publications

HMSO publishes about 8000 new items each year and all these appear in the lists and catalogues which HMSO issues.

- The *Daily List* (ISSN 0951–843X) lists all new parliamentary, non-parliamentary, statutory instruments and agency material published each day which is sold by HMSO. Annual subscription is for daily posting or for weekly batches posting.

The *Daily List* appears every day on PRESTEL—lead frame 50040.
- The *Monthly Catalogue* (ISSN 0263-7197) lists all publications issued that month (except Statutory Instruments). There are four sections: the first lists parliamentary publications by their parliamentary number; the second classified section lists parliamentary and non-parliamentary material arranged under the corporate heading of the sponsoring body; the third lists Northern Ireland publications; and the fourth the agency material. This last category consists of publications of mainly international organizations for which HMSO acts as an agent. The monthly catalogue cumulates into the *Annual Catalogue* (ISSN 0951-8584).
- The *List of Statutory Instruments* together with the *List of Statutory Rules of Northern Ireland* (ISSN 0267-2979) is issued monthly and cumulates into an annual volume.
- There is an annual *HMSO Agency Catalogue* which lists that year's material which is sold by HMSO on behalf of those organizations for which it acts as an agent.
- *HMSO in Print on Microfiche* (ISSN 0267-1727) lists all HMSO titles that are currently in print and is updated quarterly.

HMSO also issues other subject catalogues of which some have particular relevance in the IT field.

Sectional Lists list publications currently in print organized by the sponsor department. All the lists contain references to some publications in the IT area, but of particular interest are:

No. 2—Education and Science which contains references to publications sponsored by the Department of Education and Science.

No. 32—Treasury and Allied Departments which contains references to publications sponsored by the Central Computer and Telecommunications Agency.

PUBLICITY CATALOGUES

In addition to the above catalogues, HMSO issues a series of free subject catalogues which list a selection of titles in a specific subject area. The *Science and Technology Catalogue* includes titles on information technology and on office systems.

ON-LINE SOURCES

HMSO's bibliographic database has been mounted on British Library's Blaise-Line service and on Dialog. This gives public

Government publications

access to over 120 000 catalogue records covering HMSO and agency publications from 1976 onwards.

HOW TO OBTAIN HMSO PUBLICATIONS

There are HMSO Bookshops in London, Edinburgh, Belfast, Bristol, Birmingham and Manchester as well as 40 agents throughout the UK. Publications can be ordered direct from HMSO Books at:

> HMSO Publications Centre
> PO Box 276
> London SW8 5DT
>
> Tel: 071–873 0011 (enquiries); 071–873 9090 (orders)
> Fax 071–873 8463

There are booksellers acting as HMSO agents in most countries.

Non-HMSO British government publications

About 50% of non-parliamentary material is published by the departments themselves and not through HMSO. Many of these publications are important policy documents or research studies but a proportion are ephemera such as press notices or short memoranda.

Departments have an agreement to deposit one copy of everything they publish with Chadwyck-Healey Ltd who microfiche many of them and sell microfiche copies of out of print items. All deposited publications are listed in Chadwyck-Healey's *Catalogue of British Official Publications not Published by HMSO* (COBOP). This is issued bimonthly with an annual cumulation. Chadwyck-Healey also issues a keyword index to COBOP on microfiche which is updated bimonthly. Enquiries about COBOP should be addressed to:

> Chadwyck-Healey Ltd
> Cambridge Place
> Cambridge CB2 1NR
> Tel: (0223) 311479

Three government departments which are particularly concerned with developments in IT are the Central Computer and Telecommunications Agency (CCTA), Department of Trade and Industry (DTI) and the Department of Education and Science (DES). Information about non-HMSO publications issued by these departments can be obtained direct from their respective libraries. The CCTA Library produces a list of departmental publications which is updated monthly. This and CCTA Press Notices are obtainable from:

> The Librarian
> CCTA Library
> Riverwalk House
> 157/161 Millbank
> London SW1P 4RT
>
> Tel: 071–217 3331

Information about DTI publications can be obtained from:

> The Library
> Department of Trade and Industry
> 1–19 Victoria Street
> London SW1H 0ET
>
> Tel: 071–215 4477

They are also listed in *Business Briefing* which is obtainable from:

> Association of British Chambers of Commerce (Subscriptions Department)
> Business Briefing
> Border House
> High Street
> Farndon
> Chester
> CH3 6PK
>
> Tel: (0829) 270714

A list of DES publications is issued monthly which is cumulated into an annual list. Further information from:

> The Library
> Department of Education & Science
> Elizabeth House
> York Road
> London SE1 7PH
>
> Tel: 071–934 9140

The addresses and telephone numbers of all government libraries are listed in *Guide to Government Department and Other Libraries*, price £30, published by:

> British Library Science Reference & Information Service
> 25 Southampton Buildings
> Chancery Lane
> London WC2A 1AW
>
> Tel: 071–636 1544

CATALOGUE OF UNITED KINGDOM OFFICIAL PUBLICATIONS
(UKOP) ON CD-ROM

Before 1989 there was no single source which contained bibliographic references for both HMSO and non-HMSO official publications. HMSO and Chadwyck-Healey have jointly produced a database of official publications on compact disc (CD-ROM): UKOP contains the bibliographic records for HMSO's parliamentary and non-parliamentary material, official publications which appear in Chadwyck-Healey's COBOP, and publications of international organizations for which HMSO acts as the UK agent. The database contains records from 1980 onwards and the disc is updated quarterly. Users can search by keyword taken from the subject and title fields, by corporate heading and by the parliamentary number. For the first time the division between documents published by HMSO and those published independently by more than 500 government organizations is removed. Powerful retrieval software, allowing Boolean combination of search terms, means that, where previously librarians and researchers had to consult several printed lists and catalogues, now an official publication can be located in seconds. Records can be down-loaded from the CD-ROM to produce bibliographies, which can be added to a library's in-house catalogue, or for ordering purposes.

An annual subscription to UKOP can be ordered from HMSO or Chadwyck-Healey at the addresses given above.

Part 2: International official publications

The major international organizations publish a great deal about information technology each year. Her Majesty's Stationery Office acts as the UK sales agent for the following organizations:

    United Nations
    European Community
    Organization for Economic Co-operation and Development
    Council of Europe
    Customs Co-operation Council
    Food and Agriculture Organization
    General Agreement on Tariffs and Trade
    International Atomic Energy Agency
    International Monetary Fund
    United Nations Educational, Scientific and Cultural Organization
    United Nations University
    World Health Organization

Information about the publications of any of these organizations can be obtained from:

>Agency Enquiries
>HMSO Books
>PO Box 276
>London SW8 5DR
>Tel: 071–873 8372

It is worthwhile examining the sources of information about the United Nations and the European Community.

United Nations (UN)

An outline of what is published by the UN and its specialized agencies is given in *Publishing in the United Nations and its Related Agencies*, price £2. It is a useful overview of the confusing maze of the UN and its related organizations. Each entry gives subject areas covered, information about the publications and the address of each organization's headquarters. Publications catalogues are issued by each of the organizations and are obtainable on request from the HQ addresses.

Amongst the indexes and reference works which list UN publications is *UNDOC: Current Index (United Nations Document Index)*. This gives a comprehensive coverage of UN documentation including full bibliographic description with subject, author and title indexes. Issued since 1979, there are four issues yearly with an annual cumulation on microfiche. A subscription to *UNDOC* is obtainable from HMSO.

UNDOC is complemented by *Current Bibliographic Information* (CBI) which provides a current awareness listing of materials about the United Nations issued by worldwide trade publishers, governments and institutions. It covers both books and articles selected from about 900 periodicals. It has been issued monthly since 1971.

A useful free publication for librarians who work in UN depository libraries is a booklet entitled: *United Nations Documentation* (1981). This is available from:

>External Relations Officer
>Dag Hammerskjold Library
>United Nations
>New York, NY 10017
>US

The *Yearbook of the United Nations* gives an overview of the UN's activities for that year, including developments in science and technology. A drawback is that the yearbook tends to take some years to collate and publish.

An important semi-annual publication on information technology is *Advance Technology Alert Systems (ATAS) Bulletin* produced by the United Nations Centre for Science and Technology for Development. The aim of *ATAS* is to survey and provide discussion about innovations in new technology and their use in development planning processes. Each issue is concerned with one aspect of technology. Topics covered have included Microelectronics-based Automation Technologies of Development and New Information Technologies and Development.

UN ON-LINE DATABASES

The UN's Advisory Committee for the Co-ordination of Information Systems (ACCIS) publishes a *Directory of United Nations Databases and Information Systems, DUNDIS* (ISBN 92 9048 295 8). The directory is also produced as an online database, DUNDIS, which is available on ECHO (European Commission Host Organization). DUNDIS lists the information sources and services produced by the organizations and agencies which make up the United Nations Organization. This includes libraries, information services and databases and provides an authoritative guide to UN information.

The number of UN databases runs into three figures but two which are particularly concerned with information technology are:

(i) The database of the holdings of the GENERAL INFORMATION PROGRAMME DOCUMENTATION CENTRE which was established in 1980.
(ii) UNISIST PROGRAMME is the database produced by UNISIST—an inter-governmental programme of international co-operation in scientific and technical information.

Further information about these databases can be obtained from:

UNESCO
7 Place de Fontenoy
F-75700 Paris
France
Telex: 204461 Paris

European Community (EC)

The European Community (EC) consists of several institutions, the main ones being: European Economic Community (EEC), the European Parliament, the Council of Ministers and the European

Commission. The EC produces many publications each week but the chief day-to-day publication, available from HMSO, is: *Official Journal of the European Communities* which appears in two main series: (i) L series (ISSN 0378–6978) which lists EC legislation and (ii) C series (ISSN 0378–6976) which lists information and notices from the EC. Subscription to the L and C series of the *Official Journal* can be for the paper edition or for the microfiche.

The European Commission issues a series of working documents known as a *COM doc*. These can cover all aspects of EC work and inevitably this includes much on information technology. The *COM docs* number about 400 a year and an annual subscription can be for the paper edition (ISSN 0 254–1475) or for the microfiche. Both editions come complete with hard-copy indexes.

It is possible to obtain a global subscription to EC documents which comprises: *COM docs*, Committee Reports of the European Parliament and the Reports of the Economic and Social Committee.

The Commission is divided into a number of Directorate-Generals (DG), each charged with specific areas of interest. The two DGs which are particularly concerned with information technology are DG-X, whose brief is Information, Communications and Culture and DG-XIII, whose brief is Telecommunications, the Information Industry and Innovation. There is a considerable overlap of interest between these two.

DG-XIII produces an annual report on the European Strategic Programme for Research and Development in Information Technology (ESPRIT) as well as a review of progress made during ESPRIT's first two years: *ESPRIT: the First Phase—Progress and results, 1984–1986*, price £5.90 (ISBN 92–825–6916–0).

ON LINE DATABASES

The EC has around 20 databases most of which are on the ECHO online service. They cover European law, scientific and technical research, the environment, development projects, external trade, community statistics and grey literature.

Law and legislation

Parliament issues some 4000 publications each year, all of which are published by HMSO and are listed in HMSO catalogues. These parliamentary publications include those papers issued by the Government in formulating its legislative policy.

GREEN PAPERS

Before presenting a formal bill to Parliament, the government or a department may issue a 'Green Paper' for consultation purposes. A Green Paper sets out proposed Government legislation and invites comments from interested parties. About half of the Green Papers are presented to Parliament and are therefore published by HMSO and half are issued by government departments as departmental papers. This is where the CATALOGUE OF UNITED KINGDOM OFFICIAL PUBLICATIONS (UKOP) on CD-ROM is so useful; as its database contains bibliographic references to both HMSO and non-HMSO publications, without UKOP it is necessary to search HMSO catalogues and Chadwyck-Healey's *Catalogue of British Official Publications not Published by HMSO* to trace Green Papers.

If a Green Paper is presented to Parliament it will appear as a 'Command Paper'—literally by command of Her Majesty the Queen. These are numbered consecutively from 1–9999 regardless of session or year, with a prefix which is currently 'CM'.

WHITE PAPERS

Having considered all the submissions to a Green Paper, the Government will issue a 'White Paper' which is a firm statement of intended government legislation and policy. This will be published by HMSO as a command paper—an example is *Broadcasting in the 90s—Competition, Choice and Quality* which is paper number CM 517. This sets out the Government's policy on broadcasting some of which, at the time of writing, has come to fruition and some of which is still the subject of discussion. Interested parties can still make a formal response to policy set out in a White Paper.

BILLS

To enact its policies, the Government must pass laws, the first stage of which is to present a bill to Parliament. These are numbered sequentially within each parliamentary session with the prefix HC or HL to indicate whether the bill originated in the House of Commons or the House of Lords. The first reading of a bill is a formal presentation to the House; it is at the second reading that the bill is debated and a vote taken. It is usual then for the bill to be scrutinized by a Standing Committee which examines the bill clause by clause and proposes amendments to them. Every day that Parliament sits a report of the Parliamentary Debates known as *Hansard* is produced. The *House of Commons Debates*

(ISSN 0309–8826) and the *House of Lords Debates* (ISSN 0309–8834) are available as single issues or by annual subscription.

The bill then passes to the other chamber—i.e. to the House of Lords if it originated in the Commons or to the Commons if it originated in the Lords. The bill is debated again and amendments proposed or in some cases the whole bill may be defeated by vote.

Having passed through both Houses the bill is given a third reading and, after it has received royal assent, it becomes an Act of Parliament. Acts are numbered consecutively within a calendar year with a chapter number. Thus the Criminal Justice Act 1988 is Chapter 33 of 1988.

STATUTORY INSTRUMENTS

An Act of Parliament does not cover every detail of the legislation with which it deals. Instead it confers on the relevant Minister the power to enact the legislation through Statutory Instruments (SI). These bring parts of an act into force and a Statutory Instrument can be issued if there is to be a minor change in the legislation.

SIs are numbered consecutively each calendar year; there are usually about 2000 SIs issued each year. The normal designation is by year and number: SI 1989/227. To see the legislative process in action it is possible to trace the progress of a piece of law from initial proposals to the appearance of the final Act of Parliament. For example, during the 1970s it became obvious that technology was taking copyright into hitherto unexplored areas. The Copyright Act 1911 and the Copyright Act 1956 had, of course, not addressed themselves to the copyright problems of computer programs, electronic data storage or the copying of television programmes onto video tape.

In 1977 Lord Justice Whitford produced the report, Copyright and Designs Law (Cmnd. 6732). During the 1980s the Government issued three Green Papers concerned with copyright matters: Reform of the Law relating to Copyright Designs and Performers' Protection (Cmnd. 8302) 1981; Intellectual Property Rights and Innovation (Cmnd. 9117), 1983; and The Recording of Audio and Video Copyright Material (Cmnd. 9445), 1985.

These Green Papers and the Whitford Committee's report provoked a large number of responses from interested organizations. Having considered these responses the Government published a White Paper setting out its proposals for legislation, Intellectual Property and Innovation (Cmnd. 9712), 1986. There were many responses to this White Paper but finally the Government presented to the House of Lords in October 1987 the Copyright, Designs and Patents Bill (House of Lords Bill No. 12).

Government publications 267

The bill was then examined by a House of Lords Committee and the amendments proposed by the Committee were published as House of Lords Bill numbers 12a, 12b, 12c through to 12g. The bill then passed to the House of Commons where further amendments were made and it was then returned to the Lords as House of Lords Bill No. 125—notice that when returned to the Lords it had a different bill number. The amendments proposed after the Commons amendments had been considered were published as House of Lords Bill 125a, 125b, 125c and 125d.

Finally after all the months of amendments, debates and votes the bill received royal assent on the 15 November 1988 and became the Copyright, Designs and Patents Act 1988, Chapter 48.

SELECT COMMITTEES

Parliament has over the years evolved a number of Committees which oversee and report on aspects of Government policy and the work of each department. Two committees which produce reports on information technology-related matters are the House of Commons Select Committee on Education, Science and Arts and the House of Lords Select Committee on Science and Technology. These committees publish their reports as House of Commons Papers and House of Lords Papers, respectively.

A useful source of information is the *House of Commons Weekly Information Bulletin* (ISSN 0261–9229). This lists the current stage of progress for bills in that session, topics to be considered by Parliament in the following week and forthcoming business of the house. The *Bulletin* is available from HMSO.

INDEXES TO LEGISLATION

Bills, Acts and Statutory Instruments are listed in the HMSO catalogues, but there is a consolidated index to acts, *Index to the Statutes*. Having found the relevant act with its year and chapter number, it is possible to look it up in the *Chronological Table of the Statutes* which shows what part of the act is still in force. The corresponding volumes for Statutory Instruments are: *Index to Government Orders* and the *Table of Government Orders*. These volumes are published by HMSO.

ON-LINE SOURCES

Parliamentary and legislative material is listed on the HMSO file on Blaise-Line and Dialog and on the CATALOGUE OF UNITED KINGDOM OFFICIAL PUBLICATIONS (UKOP) on CD-ROM. Details of both these products are available from HMSO.

268 Government publications

Printed indexes to debates and parliamentary questions which appear in *Parliamentary Debates (Hansard)* are available from HMSO but the best source is PARLIAMENTARY ON-LINE INFORMATION SYSTEM (POLIS). POLIS lists parliamentary material and some non-parliamentary and EC publications, but its great strength is the on-line index to *Hansard*. By entering a topic or an MP's name, references to debates and Parliamentary Questions (PQ) are displayed at the terminal. Each reference gives the date, volume number of *Hansard* and the column where the debate or PQ can be found. The user then only has to turn to the relevant column in that copy of *Hansard* to find the text. Further details about POLIS can be obtained from:

Meridian Systems Management Ltd
18 Elmfield Road
Bromley
Kent BR1 1LR

Tel: 081-313 0178

CHAPTER SIXTEEN

Periodicals and conferences

D. HAYNES

Periodicals

Periodicals dominate the information technology literature. They are a well established means of communication and range from the learned journals to rapidly-produced newsletters. For the purposes of this chapter 'periodicals' are defined as publications which are issued more than once a year. Annuals and conference proceedings are dealt with separately.

There are a number of important collections of periodicals. The British Library's Science Reference and Information Service held 32 000 current serials in 1988–89 including 783 new periodicals. The British Library has a total of over 300 000 serial titles at the Document Supply Centre at Boston Spa. Details of these titles are available on CD-ROM, BOSTON SPA SERIALS. The CD-ROM is updated twice a year, with 35 000 new records added every year and 80 000 amendments annually.

The Library of Congress has produced an index, *Computer Periodicals Currently Received in the Library of Congress*. The second edition came out in September 1988. It lists 619 titles and includes a keyword index. Like all libraries the Library of Congress is selective and the list represents the key titles in computing and does not attempt to be comprehensive.

Periodicals fall into a number of different categories, which depend partly on the purpose of the publication and partly on the type of publisher. From an academic and scientific point of view the most important are the learned journals. Typically they are produced by learned and professional societies and are intended to report advances in our understanding of the technologies involved or to report new insights into the fundamental science underlying information technologies. In any guide of this type covering information technology, the subject scope could include: chemistry, optics, magnetism, electricity and electronics, and even some branches of biology. All of these topics are covered in part or in whole by other guides in this series.

As well as journals produced by the learned societies, there are the international journals produced by commercial publishers. This category shares many characteristics with the learned journals with the emphasis on original papers, refereed by recognized authorities in the field.

Progressing along the scale of publications we come to the professional journals which are more widely circulated and geared towards practising professionals rather than researchers and academics. Some of these are produced by the professional societies; the commercial publishers also play an important role here.

Then there are the trade and product journals and magazines aimed at the mass market of lay people. The market can be divided into two groups: business users of information technology products, and consumers. This type of publication attracts heavy advertising and the advertisements become an important source of information themselves.

Finally there are the newsletters which are either market-oriented or technology-oriented. In this sector there is often a premium on timeliness and some of the more specialist publications can be very expensive.

To summarize, the categories of periodicals in information technology are:

- Learned and international journals
- Professional (non-learned) journals
- Trade and product news
- Newsletters

Ways of identifying journals

There are a number of general sources of journal information. *Ulrich's International Periodical Directory* (Bowker) is one of the most comprehensive. In the UK there is also *Benn's Press Directory* which is more selective. The British Library recently brought out a CD-ROM, BOSTON SPA PERIODICALS, which lists over 300 000 serial titles.

One problem facing many researchers is the difficulty in identifying the most important or 'core' journals. There are a number of techniques which can be used to make this easier. If you have access to a special library which covers information technology, it may be sufficient to scan the shelves and the title list to identify possible titles. If there is a classification scheme for the journals, that is usually a more effective way of identifying titles. However these approaches do not necessarily give a good indication of the relevance or quality of the journals.

You can rapidly identify relevant periodicals by searching online databases or CD-ROMS. Large databases such as INSPEC have a good coverage of information technology and you can quickly acquire a large number of references. On some database hosts, ranking facilities are provided, so that journal titles can be ranked in order of the number of papers appearing in each title. For instance, a search on input technologies on INSPEC might tell us that there are 5000 items on the database of which about 800 were published in 1988. If you then rank the 800 items you might get a printout looking like the one in Figure 16.1. This tells us that *Proceedings of the SPIE* (International Society for Optical Engineering) is an important source, being quoted 37 times in the retrieved set. The next most quoted journal in the set is *Speech Technology* (20 times), followed by *Transactions of the Institute of Electronic Information and Communication Engineering* of Japan (9 times) and then the *British Telecom Technology Journal* (8 times) and the West German *Mikrocomputer Zeitschrift* (7 times).

Text Analysis Results	
Frq	Words/Phrases
37	PROCEEDINGS OF THE SPIE THE INTERNATIONAL SOCIETY FOR OPTICAL ENGINEERING
20	SPEECH TECHNOLOGY
9	TRANSACTIONS OF THE INSTITUTE OF ELECTRONICS AND INFORMATION COMMUNICATION ENGINEERS
8	BRITISH TELECOM TECHNOLOGY JOURNAL
7	MIKROCOMPUTER ZEITSCHRIFT
6	COMPUTER PROCESSING OF CHINESE ORIENTAL LANGUAGES
5	TRANS INF PROCESS SOC JPN JAPAN
3	J INST TELEV ENG JPN JAPAN
3	NEC TECH J JAPAN
2	ACTA AUTOM SIN CHINA

Figure 16.1 Ranked output from a search on INSPEC

A similar technique can be used to identify often quoted authors and identify the journals they publish in. The frequency to which an author is referred in other publications can be taken as an indication of that author's reputation. *Science Citation Index*, which is available online as SCISEARCH is the single most useful source for this type of searching.

Some of the secondary abstracting services provide lists of journals which they abstract from cover to cover. This indicates the titles which they consider of importance and this is a good way of identifying core journals, especially if you are using a specialist database. For example, Inspec and PIRA (which produces *Electronic Publishing Abstracts*) both publish lists of journals which they abstract.

Learned journals

The learned journals are research-oriented and contain original papers or authoritative reviews. The papers are refereed by acknowledged experts in the field. An editorial board is made up of senior academics, experienced researchers and other leading authorities. Within the broad category of learned and international journals there are three sub-groups, which are defined by the type of publisher which produces the journal:

- Journals from learned and professional societies
- Journals from commercial publishers and university presses
- Research journals from manufacturers

LEARNED AND PROFESSIONAL SOCIETIES

These are often qualification-granting bodies. In the area of information technology, notable publishers include the Institute of Electrical and Electronics Engineers Inc. (IEEE), the Institution of Electrical Engineers (IEE), and the Association for Computing Machinery (ACM). The learned journals often have the word 'Transactions' or 'Proceedings' in the titles.

The IEEE is one of the most prolific publishers of learned journals in any discipline. It is the pre-eminent publisher of learned journals covering information technology. As the discipline has grown, the IEEE has spawned a number of specialist journals. These journals are characterized by their rigorous approach. Papers submitted are refereed by leading experts in the area and only original papers are considered. Titles such as *IEEE Transactions. Acoustic, Speech and Signal Processing, IEEE Transactions on Automatic Control, IEEE Transactions on Communication, IEEE Transactions on Computers, IEEE Transactions on Consumer Electronics, IEEE Transactions on Electron Devices, IEEE Transactions on Pattern Analysis and Machine Intelligence, IEEE Transactions on Professional Communication* and *IEEE Transactions on Semiconductor Manufacturing* are examples.

In the UK, the Institution of Electrical Engineers (IEE) is the leading publisher of learned and professional journals in IT. The title *IEE Proceedings* is the main learned journal. It comes in 10 parts, of which the following are of direct relevance to information technology: *Control Theory and Applications (Part D)*; *Computers and Digital Techniques (Part E)*; *Communications, Radar and Signal Processing (Part F)*; *Electronic Circuits and Systems (Part G)*; *Solid-State and Electron Devices (Part I)*; *Optoelectronics (Part J)*. In addition special issues of *IEE Proceedings* are available separately. In the past there have been special issues on: artificial intelligence; systems on silicon; satellite communications; and optical signal processing.

A number of other notable journals are published by learned and professional societies. The British Computer Society publishes the *Computer Journal*, which contains refereed original papers on a wide range of topics including computing science. In the US the Association for Computing Machinery (ACM) publishes several titles including: *ACM Transactions on Graphics*; *ACM Transactions on Programming Languages and Systems*; *ACM Transactions on Computer Systems*; and *ACM Transactions on Database Systems*.

Learned journals in foreign languages can be inaccessible unless translations are available. For instance some of the learned journals from the Soviet Union are available in cover-to-cover translated into English six months after the original Russian language journals. Their titles include: *Cybernetics (Kibernetika)*; and *Automation and Remote Control* (*Avtomatika i Telemehkanika*). The *Transactions of the Institute of Electronic Information and Communication Engineering* (Japan) provides access to Japanese language material.

COMMERCIAL ACADEMIC JOURNALS

Many of the major international journals are published by commercial publishers with interests in many countries. The professional societies are usually nationally based although the larger ones are in effect international in scope. Some of the international journals have excellent reputations, especially those from specialist publishers. Elsevier publishes a number of titles under its North-Holland imprint. These include: *Artificial Intelligence*; *Computer Standards and Interfaces*; *Computer Networks and ISDN Systems*; and *Space Communication and Broadcasting*. Other publishers active in this field are: Butterworth Scientific who publish *Knowledge Based Systems*; Academic Press, *Journal of Computer and Systems Science*; and Pergamon Press, *International *Journal of Micrographics and Video Technology*, and *Solid-State Electronics*.

The research community is international and this is reflected in the make-up of the editorial boards and in the titles of the journals themselves. For instance we have the *International Journal of Electronics*, the *International Journal of Pattern Recognition and Artificial Intelligence* (World Scientific), and the *International Journal of Robotics Research*.

MANUFACTURERS' RESEARCH JOURNALS

Several of the major manufacturers publish their own research journals. These often contain high-quality research papers based on work done in the companies' own research facilities or work sponsored by the companies. Special issues on specific topics are a feature of this kind of publication and they can provide a good overview of a technology or application. IBM produces two journals: *IBM Journal of Research and Development*; and *IBM Technical Disclosures Bulletin*. Titles from other manufacturers include: *ICL Technical Journal*; *Philips Technical Review*; and *British Telecom Technology Journal*. They provide a vehicle for companies to report on research done by their staff or work sponsored by the company. They tend to focus on applications-oriented research, although some fundamental research is also undertaken.

Professional journals

The professional journals are directed at computer and information technology professionals rather than at academics and researchers. The type of papers which they publish tend not to be as rigorously refereed, if at all. This category includes magazines produced by the learned societies, as well as professional journals produced by commercial publishers. There are three sub-groups in this category:

- General journals
- Technology-specific journals
- Application-specific journals

As well as feature articles and technology reviews, the professional journals are a valuable source of information on products and professional and managerial techniques. They also feature regular columns by correspondents and events calendars.

General journals

General titles range from *British Telecom World* (formerly *British Telecom Journal*) to *Computer Bulletin*, produced by the British Computer Society, and *Computing Techniques*, which does a series of annual reviews on different topics each issue. *Critique: Critical Reviews of Information Technology* (Aslib/TMI) does a similar job, giving in-depth analysis of different topics. *Library and Information Briefings* is a series of single topic issues on various aspects of information technology and librarianship. Notable issues include the ones on: CD-ROMs; OSI and VANS; ISDN; and standards. Each issue gives an excellent introduction to the topic and often produces useful sources of further information. The briefings are cumulated annually into a single volume, with updates for each issue.

IEEE Spectrum is a wide-ranging journal with a good selection of articles. *Electronic Engineering* is a similar title based in the UK. *Communications of the ACM* is another UK journal with articles on a range of topics in IT. *Electronics and Wireless World* has news and articles on all aspects of electronics, circuits, broadcast and semiconductor technology. *Mini-micro Systems* focuses on hardware. *Andrew Seybold's Outlook on Professional Computing* is a monthly magazine reviewing hardware and software products in some detail. It also reports on major U.S. exhibitions. *IEEE Micro* covers all aspects of microcomputers.

Technology-specific journals

The full range of technologies in information technology is represented by specialist journals and magazines. Process control is an increasingly important area and journals on this also cover robotics, speech synthesis and artificial intelligence. *Sensor Review* is an example, which also includes news and product reviews. *Automation*, the journal of automated production does a regular survey on robots. *Speech Technology* covers linguistic aspects of speech technology and *Computer Speech and Language* covers speech synthesis and recognition.

Optical technologies used for mass data storage have become the subject of an increasing number of journals. *Optical Information Systems* from Meckler carries articles on the use and development of optical media. *Optical Engineering* is more technical in its approach.

Communications and network technology is covered by a range of titles including *Netlink* (Aslib) which covers all aspects of networking and especially its application to information management. *Communicate* deals mainly with voice communications, but also has significant articles on data communications, ISDN, and electronic mail. *Comms Monthly* covers electronic mail as does *Commsfile*, which has a lot of practical advice on communications.

Other specialist professional journals include: *Displays*; *Data Processing*; *Computers and Graphics*, which concentrates mainly on software; *Computers and Standards*, including OSI and *Cable Television Engineering*, a technical journal covering the engineering aspects of the cable television industry.

The learned and professional societies also produce a number of professional journals for rapid exchange of ideas, without going through the rigours of refereeing. These journals often have the word 'Bulletin' or 'Communications' in their titles. If we look at the ACM, it has a number of special interest groups (SIGs), which publish their own bulletins and newsletters. The articles in these bulletins tend to be shorter informative articles or communications. Examples include: *SIGSMALL/PC Notes*, published by the ACM Special Interest Group on Small and Personal Computing Systems and Applications; *SIGPLAN Notices* which covers programming languages; *SIGMOD* on the management of data; and *SIGOA Bulletin* on office automation. *SIGIR Forum* has contributed articles on information retrieval as well as abstracts from other relevant journals. *SIGCHI Bulletin* deals with computer and human interaction and consists of short articles and items. *SIGAT News* contains unrefereed working papers, news and current awareness on automation and computability theory.

The IEEE produces a number of magazines and journals in this category such as *IEEE Micro* (mentioned in the previous section) and *IEEE Expert* which covers intelligent systems and their applications and includes contributed articles from academics and the commercial sector. It is a valuable source of information about conferences in the area. *IEEE Electron Device Letters* provides rapid publication of short technical research papers on recent experiments and developments. *IEEE Control Systems Magazine* is a glossy magazine containing professional news, short academic articles and technical comments as well as a number of regular columns. The bimonthly *IEEE Circuits and Devices Magazine* also has some quite readable articles.

Electronics Letters produced by the IEE contains short technical research papers on recent experiments and developments. The emphasis is on applications rather than theory and novelty is an important element in the selection of papers published.

Applications-specific journals

There are a lot of applications-specific journals outside the information technology field. Automation and process control are covered in titles such as: *Production Engineer*; *Manufacturing Technology Horizons*; and the *International Journal of Production Research*.

The library and information field has yielded a lot of titles including: *RQ*, which includes features of library automation; *NFAIS Newsletter*, produced by the National Federation of Abstracting and Indexing Services in the United States; and *C&L Applications* (formerly *Computers and Libraries*), which covers all aspects of information technology applications to library and information work.

Journals from other professions increasingly feature IT applications specific to that area. A good example is *Accountancy*, which does regular features on information technology.

Trade and product news

The IT industry is served by a large number of newspaper format periodicals. Many of these are controlled circulation publications directed at particular parts of the industry. *Computer Weekly* and *Computing* are two UK titles directed at professionals in the computer and IT industry. They both contain short news items about the industry and developments within it. Because they are widely read they also carry a good selection of job advertisements. In themselves the advertisements are a source of information, because they provide an indication of the data processing activities of the companies placing the advertisements.

Other titles include *Systems International* which is aimed at systems designers, scientists and managers. It has a new products section. From Germany there is *Computing Today Journal*. A useful guide to events is *What's on in Computing*. *High Technology* is a good general magazine which is not IT specific but which covers a lot of IT material. It includes a good mix of news items, longer articles and product news.

In the electronics field, some of the general magazines often available free to those on the controlled circulation list include: *New Electronics*, which has news and features on all aspects of electronics and computer technology including microprocessors and digital design; *Electronic Systems Design Magazine*; *Electronics* (USA), which has a lot of advertisements for components as well as short articles and reviews; *Electronics and Computing Monthly*, which is aimed at enthusiasts; *Electronics Times* (UK) which contains industry and product news; *Electronics Weekly* (UK) which contains short articles and advertisements on all aspects of hardware, input and output devices and processors; and *Elektronik*, a German language magazine.

The popular computer magazines make up a lively part of the market. With the growth in sales and use of personal computers, a range of special and general magazines has emerged. *Personal Computer World*, *Practical Computing* and *Which Computer?* are all examples of well established magazines with product reviews and news of the computing industry. Recently *Practical Computing* and *Which Computer?* have turned their attention to small minicomputer systems as well as microcomputers. This trend is likely to continue as the distinction between mini- and microcomputers becomes blurred. Both *Byte* (USA) and *Mini/Micro News* straddle this divide already. *PC Magazine, PC User, Personal Computer Magazine*, can all be found on the shelves of newsagents and serve a large market of non-IT professionals.

What to Buy for Business does excellent comparative reviews of a wide range of office products including microcomputers and software. They apply carefully devised criteria to compare products and judge the products in terms of value for money. A similar, though less rigorous approach is taken by a number of different titles including *Which Computer?, Computer Decisions, Micro Decision, What Micro?, Which PC?*, and *Which Word Processor & Office System?*.

Computer Terminals Review is an authoritative product guide to the full range of computer peripherals such as keyboards, terminals and display screens. It is a ring-bound volume which is updated twice a year. Price information is also included. Peripherals are listed by type and then there is an alphabetical listing of individual products followed by a section on new products and finally a list of manufacturers. *What's New in Computing?* is a monthly guide to hardware, software and systems and has details of the latest data processing products as well as industry news and features. *What's New in Electronics?* serves a similar purpose for the electronics industry.

What to Buy for Business has already been mentioned as an office equipment guide. There are also a lot of glossy free circulation magazines directed at office managers, which mention a vast array of computer products and consumables. *Computing Equipment, Business Equipment Digest, Business Systems and Equipment, Modern Office Technology* (formerly *Modern Office Procedures*), *The Office, Office Equipment Index* and *Office Magazine* are all examples. They have a high proportion of advertisements to editorial material and text is mainly rehashed press releases from suppliers, and does not attempt to be objective or critical. The free circulation magazines depend on advertising revenue rather than subscriptions. The titles usually contain reader enquiry cards so that you can indicate which products you are interested in. The publishers then forward your enquiry to the appropriate suppliers.

Office automation is a widely used and abused term. It can mean anything from a word processor on a stand-alone microcomputer to a local area network with several different applications on it to a fully integrated system for text handling and processing and incorporating electronic mail, corporate databases, spreadsheets, text retrieval and word processing. *Buckley's Guide to Office Automation* provides an introduction office automation technology.

Automation, robotics and process control are areas with considerable overlap which are covered by the trade literature. *Assembly Automation*, *Automation News*, *Control Systems*, *Process Engineering* and *Industrial Engineering News* are all geared more towards engineers rather than information technologists. On robotics there is *Robotics World*, *Automation and Robotics Times* and the French language title, *Axes robotique*.

Information Media and Technology is a general magazine covering storage media especially optical discs and microform. *Infotecture*, a French language journal and its English language equivalent *Infotecture Europe* also covers optical memory as well as other aspects of information technology. *LT Electric World* (formerly *Language Technology*) covers IT applications in speech, word and text processing. This includes speech recognition, automatic translation and word processing systems. In fact its interests are so wide ranging that it is of interest to the general reader. As well as product and industry news there are occasional features on specific topics.

Networks and communications technology is covered by titles such as *Data Communications* (USA), which has a strong US bias; and *Network*, a free circulation journal. *Cable Age* and *Cable and Satellite Europe* and *Cable Vision* are more applications-oriented.

Graphics is covered by titles such as *Computer Images International* and *Computer Graphics World*. Storage media is covered by *Microform Review*, *Microfilm and Imaging Systems*; and *Optical Product Review*, which is U.S. based. *Mémoires Optiques* is an English language journal on optical disc technology and applications. *Electronic and Optical Publishing Review* (Learned Information), formerly *Electronic Publishing Review*, covers new products, company news, hardware and software development, product reviews and feature articles.

Several of the manufacturers produce their own glossy magazines featuring their products. *IBM UK News* for instance is a company magazine for employees, but it is of interest to outsiders, because of new products which the company might be developing.

Similarly *ICL Desktop* and *Hitachi Review* cover their respective companies' products.

Newsletters

There is a vast range of newsletters on the market. They are normally rapidly published, have very little advertising and pay more attention to currency and accuracy of data than to presentation. Some of them are very specific and have a limited circulation and consequently a high price.

Elsevier publishes an international newsletter, *Advanced Information Report* (formerly *Communication Technology Impact*) with news on all areas of the technology including data storage and transmission. *Monitor*, a monthly newsletter from Learned Information provides selective reports on the information market. *C&L Applications* is a general newsletter on information technology applications for information work. *Computer Design* covers all aspects of information technology. For an analysis of journal and press coverage of the industry there is *Computing, Communication and Media Trend Monitor*, and *Media Monitor*. *Informatics Daily Bulletin* is published daily.

In areas where there are new markets emerging and a proliferation of products there is often a significant increase in the number of publications available. Many of them emerge only to disappear again once the excitement is over. In recent years we have seen the growth of areas like cable television in the US, videotex in Europe and artificial intelligence applications.

A.I. Week (formerly *Applied Artificial Intelligence Reporter*) is a U.S. newsletter and *Artificial Intelligence in Business* is a UK-based newsletter covering artificial intelligence.

The cable industry is covered by *Cable & Satellite Express* (UK), *Cable Product News* (USA), *Cable Television Business* (USA). *International Cable & Satellite TV News* is more international in its coverage. A number of other titles have been mentioned in Chapter Eight.

Videotex is another area where newsletters have proliferated. Titles include: *Video Print* (USA); *Videotex Notes*; *Videotex Travel Update*; *Videotex/Viewdata Report* (USA); *Videotex World* (Canada); *Telelink*; *International Videotex Teletext News* (USA). Two more general titles which cover cable television as well are: *New Media Markets* and *Link-up* (USA).

Newsletters on communications, networks and electronic mail include: *EMMS—Electronic Mail and Micro Systems Newsletter*; *Connexions*; *Telcom Report*; *Communications and Fibre Optic News*. On standards there is *SI Report* and *Open Systems Newslet-*

ter which both cover OSI and are both highly priced. *ISDN Connection* deals with ISDN.

Optical storage media, especially CD-ROM, have recently exploded with a huge increase in the number of products currently available on the market. *CD-Data Report* is a monthly newsletter. *CD-ROM* (A. Jour) is a French language newsletter, the English-language equivalent being *CD-ROM International*. *Data Storage Report* from Elsevier is a more general title. There are two titles called *Optical Memory News*, one from Microinfo and the other from Rothchild Consultants. Interactive media including videodisc technology and compact disc interactive (CD-I) are covered by: *Videodisc Monitor* (USA), *Videodisc Newsletter*, *Videodisque* (France) and *CD-I News*.

Information World Review (Learned Information) and *Infoteture Europe* both cover the information industry in Europe. *Information World Review* focuses more on the information services industry than on information technology. *Information Today* (Learned Information) is the sister title for the US. *Information Hotline* (Science Associated International) is also U.S.-based and also covers information services rather than information technology. It has analytical reviews of current events in electronic information and provides a more considered approach. *Online Notes*, *Online Libraries and Microcomputers*, and *Library Micromation News* all deal with IT applications in library and information work.

Other titles worth mentioning are: *Behaviour and Information Technology*, *PIRA Desktop Publishing* and *Robot News* (Japan).

Financial and statistical newsletters provide important indications about the information technology market. The *FinTech* series of reports and the *Business Monitors* issued by the Department of Trade and Industry are important sources for the UK.

Conferences

Conferences are useful sources of up-to-date information. They range from highly specialized theoretical deliberations of academics and researchers to the more pragmatic and general events geared towards the lay-person. Conference organizers include professional institutions, academic institutions, government agencies and commercial conference organizers. Many conferences are regular events, usually annual or biennial. There are also many one-off meetings which may contain papers of interest to enquirers. Conferences are sometimes used as the venue for important announcements, both of theoretical advances and for new product launches. Conferences organized by learned and professional institutions often have a formal refereeing process analogous to the process used for learned journals. Indeed many of the institutions such as the IEEE and the ACM publish conference papers in their 'Proceedings'.

Many conferences and meetings have exhibitions associated with them. The exhibitions are a particularly valuable source of information on new products and services. They are a convenient way of gathering a wide selection of trade literature and they provide an opportunity to see many products at first hand.

Conference listings

There are several publications which list conferences and meetings. Notable examples are: *Proceedings in Print*; *Conference Papers Index*; *Index of Conference Proceedings Received*; and the *Directory of Published Proceedings*.

Index of Conference Proceedings Received (British Library) is a monthly list of the proceedings received by the British Library Document Supply Centre. Details of 18 000 conference proceedings are published in the index each year. The titles of the conference proceedings are listed under key terms taken from the titles. Where necessary titles are duplicated under different terms to ensure flexible subject retrieval. The *Index of Conference Proceedings Received* is also available as a database on Blaise-Line.

The *Directory of Published Proceedings* (InterDok Corporation) is published 10 times a year in New York. It covers science, engineering, medicine, and technology and lists proceedings by accession number. There is a combined subject/sponsor index and an editor index. Details of the publishers are also listed, to help readers to obtain copies of the proceedings listed.

Conference Papers Index (Cambridge Scientific Abstracts) is published seven times a year. It is also available as an online database, which is described below. Each issue has a subject index and each year this is consolidated into an annual index. Papers are listed under the conference details, which in turn are listed under broad subject headings. Individual entries contain an accession number, title, author, and organization. Currently about 60 000 papers a year are covered.

Proceedings in Print is an index to conference proceedings in all subject areas and all languages. Listings are under unique title of conference and entries include date and place of the conference, title of the proceedings and the publication details. There is a single index for corporate authors, editors and subject headings.

Databases

Many of the bibliographic databases include published conference proceedings in the range of publications scanned for information. Papers are often individually abstracted. Online searching provides a useful way of identifying relevant papers and by extension, relevant conferences. Useful databases for conference papers include: INSPEC; E-PUBS; and COMPENDEX.

The CONFERENCE PAPERS INDEX, produced by Cambridge Scientific Abstracts, is available on the Dialog search service, ESA-IRS and BRS and covers about 150 scientific and technical meetings worldwide every year. The database covers life sciences, physical sciences and engineering including electronic engineering. This is a particularly useful tool for retrospective searching and goes back to 1973.

CONFERENCE PROCEEDINGS INDEX is the database version of the *Index of Conference Proceedings Received*. It is produced by the British Library Document Supply Centre and is available on the Blaise-Line service.

Conferences by subject

Part I of this book gives details of conferences and exhibitions under specific topics, such as computer hardware and components. In this part of the book we have concentrated on general sources and have not attempted to duplicate the detailed information in Part I.

At this point it is worth noting Sylvina Penniston's *Index to Information Technology* (London, Taylor Graham, 1985) which provides an index to papers presented at major information technology conferences between 1979 and 1984. There is a strong emphasis on library and information science applications and it furnishes the reader with a practical indication of the main events in this area.

Conference organizers

The professional institutions and learned societies organize a vast range of conferences and meetings every year. The conferences tend to be academically oriented and provide an opportunity for research workers to publicize their findings to a critical audience. For instance the IEE (Institution of Electrical Engineers) in the UK publishes proceedings of about 15 major conferences a year. The IEE also organizes nearly 100 colloquia a year, many of which are published as digests.

The special interest groups of the IEEE and the ACM organize a wide range of specialist conferences. For instance the IEEE Computer Society organizes an annual international conference, COMPCON. Other conferences coming under the IEEE wing include INTERMAG, the International Magnetics Conference and the IEEE International Conference on Consumer Electronics. There are also regular meetings such as the IEEE International Electron Devices Meeting. Other conferences take place irregularly or are once-off conferences, which will be found through any of the indexing systems.

Many of the learned societies group together to organize international events. The International Society of Photo-optical Engineers (SPIE) is a particularly active co-organizer of events. Conference papers are published in the *Proceedings of the S.P.I.E.*

The commercial conference organizers are very active and tend to gear their events to practitioners. This a potentially large market and the emphasis is usually on practical applications and techniques and new products and services. Exhibitions are often organized in conjunction with the conference and in many instances they are open to non-delegates as well. In the United Kingdom there are several significant commercial conference organizers. Blenheim Online runs a number of conferences and exhibitions on the business implications applications of high technologies, especially information technology. Events include: Document Image Processing; Image Processing; Open Systems; CASE Symposium; European Telecommunications Policy Update; European Cellular & Mobile Communications; Networks; ISDN; Software Tools; IT in Government; The Electronic Publishing Show; and European Satellite Broadcasting.

IBC Technical Services Ltd runs a number of specialist seminars and product specific events in London and Amsterdam including: DEC Systems Architectures & Networks; Object-oriented Analysis; Managing the Transition to Relational Technology; UNIX/C; The Macintosh in Business; Hypermedia; and PC LANs.

Publishers such as Meckler have moved into the conference organizing business with OIS International, which is sponsored jointly with Cimtech and HDTV International. These European events correspond to the North American events Optical Information Systems and HDTV.

CHAPTER SEVENTEEN

Foreign language material

The foreign-language barrier to information on information technology

P. MAYORCAS

Introduction

Information technology is probably one of the most international of scientific and technical disciplines—as witnessed by the many references to international information sources elsewhere in this guide. Yet for very many years the field has been dominated by American, and therefore English technology, and library and information specialists (LIS) have been as guilty of parochialism as the experts they serve by neglecting the many sources of information on products and services which, in the 1990s, no-one working in this field can afford to ignore. For example, the impact of Japanese information technology has notably created a whole new growth market in Japanese language courses, and sources of information on Japan. The European Single Market, due to come into effect by the end of 1992 will give suppliers in the European Community a far larger market in which to operate. The radical political and economic changes in Eastern Europe will create further opportunities.

LIS workers need to be much better informed than is presently the case as to developments and practice in the developed and developing world: they need to know what fellow professionals have discovered about equipment—terminals, keyboards, modems, printers—and to know what services, techniques and software are being offered around the globe. Increasingly, there is a trend towards European solutions to information problems and companies need to be in a position to compete with their European competitors and work together with collaborators.

Information itself is surely an international commodity, with online bibliographic data whizzing around the world in global telecommunications systems and all manner of electronic information services supplying the financial, business and technical communities. And yet far more and better use could be made of other countries' resources: information services, library and informal, or personal networks. Judgements and decisions must be based on complete information and on the wealth of available knowledge worldwide.

The predominance of English as a language of communication cannot be denied. English is rapidly becoming the world's *lingua franca* and 80% of all information stored in the world's electronic retrieval systems is in English; it is the official or semi-official language in more than 70 countries, occupies an important position in a further 20, and serves as the mother tongue of about 310 million people, or more than 6% of the world's population.

However one of the effects of the Single European Market will be to make all sorts of people aware not only that other people in other countries do actually build computers, write software and design systems, but also that other people in other countries using other languages are producing a good deal of literature and support services for exploiting available technology.

There is also a growing awareness that, in order to conquer markets, suppliers of products and services need to provide product literature, user and maintenance manuals in the language of the country in which they hope to operate. The lobbying industry which is growing around the European Community institutions is generating a lot of material, much of which will be of great relevance to the information technology industry. Successful operators in the new economic order will need to learn far more about what is happening in their market sector than can be learned from what is written in English about foreign markets.

With so much material being either generated or required in languages other than English, the language barrier becomes an information barrier unless you know how to deal with it. The implications are a need not only for familiarity with and ability in foreign languages, but also familiarity with the sources of translated material and resources for obtaining and arranging translations and interpreting services.

The language barrier

The language barrier presents a number of aspects. Firstly, it is necessary to find out whether useful and important material exists, which can mean searching foreign-language sources, having first established where and what these sources are. Secondly, you need to be able to use that material once it has been found, either in the original language or in translation.

In order to have complete information on services and suppliers—of PCs, database software, online services—it is important to know what is happening not only in Europe to open up markets to products and services, but also throughout the world as more and more countries enter the technology race. The foreign language general and specialist press is a valuable source of information.

Establishing the existence of foreign-language material

Weekly popular periodicals

As is the case in the English-speaking world, a lot of the most up-to-date information about information technology is to be found outside the conventional learned journals in weekly and monthly publications, many of which are not yet part of the regular scanning, bibliographic and abstracting services; it is worth noting, however, that *Computer and Computing Abstracts* lists a number of the popular weeklies and monthlies in its list of scanned journals. It is a useful exercise to identify the relevant titles for the country or countries relevant to your work, and to find out how to obtain them.

It is impossible to mention all the titles which might be useful, but any good newspaper or press shop in the major towns and cities will stock a very full range of journals on computing, personal computers, telecommunications and systems. Titles worth noting for France are: *01 Informatique* (known as *Zéro-Un Informatique*); *Ordinateur Individuel Oi*; and *Informatique Magazine*. The U.S.-published *Datamation* has a special European section.

The popular scientific journal, *Science et Vie* also publishes a computing supplement, *Science et Vie Micro* which frequently carries long, review articles and special issues on single topics. And, as in the UK, many of the quality dailies publish a supplement devoted to computing topics. These frequently carry up-to-date news of innovations in equipment and services. *Le Monde*

Informatique is published by the Computerworld Group and provides a comprehensive weekly guide to technological and business development in France and the rest of Europe.

Foreign-language journals

It is probably realised by few that in addition to its vast stock of English-language books and periodicals, British Library's Science Reference and Information Service (SRIS) includes in its collection many foreign-language monographs and periodicals. This source of information should not be ignored and is relatively easy to use since foreign-language journals are classified within the main SRIS classification scheme and all foreign language material is shelved in the same place as English language material on the same subject (for example, everything on computers will be held at PN76). Different categories of material are identified as follows: B = books; P = periodicals; A = abstracting journals.

In view of their importance, separate lists are maintained for Japanese, Russian and Chinese journals.

Conferences and exhibitions

A further important source of information on what is happening at the international level are the many exhibitions, conferences and shows which are held throughout Europe, and all over the world, and it is certainly worth checking the international calendars and attending at least one overseas exhibition every year. A good source of such meetings is Aslib's *Forthcoming International Scientific and Technical Conferences*. It lists over 1000 conferences in a main list published in February, with a supplement in May and cumulative supplements in August and November. The *International Congress Calendar* is published by K G Saur. *Eventline Directory* (Elsevier/EventLine) claims to cover 13 000 events, conferences, conventions, symposia, exhibitions and trade fairs worldwide.

The range of exhibitors and products grows each year and these meetings provide an unrivalled opportunity to meet representatives of databases, documentary centres, research organizations literally from all over the world, to study their literature and make valuable personal contacts. Many suppliers produce literature in English but you are likely to acquire armfuls of literature in other languages, and may then need assistance in translating them. For example, the International Symposium on Information Technology Standardization held in Braunschweig, West Germany in July 1989 was an important meeting of people from the EC, the principal standardizing bodies, universities and major producers.

A major conference on ISDN in Europe in 1989 in the Hague, focusing on developments and assessments of interest to professional users of integrated networks in Europe, was jointly sponsored by the ICCC (International Council for Computer Communication) and the IFIP (International Federation for Information Processing). Similarly Data '90 in Brussels hosted both the 3rd Desktop Publishing Fair and the 2nd Fair on Professional Computing.

Conference proceedings

Important conference papers are often translated and included in the registers and indexes of translations and an even greater number appear in the relevant abstracting journals. Once you have identified the source, you can obtain the full proceedings and decide whether it is worth having a translation of some or all of the papers.

The *Index of Conference Proceedings Received* (British Library) is a monthly journal with a series of annual cumulations.

International organizations

Much of the literature from international organizations is bi- or multi-lingual, so if a foreign-language text comes your way, you should check whether an English-language version also exists.

The *World Directory of International Organizations* (Bowker-Saur), formerly the *Yearbook of International Organizations* (Union of International Associations/International Chamber of Commerce) is an important guide to international organizations, and to the correct original language title and official translated title.

Broadsheets

There is also a host of newsheets which give valuable information on business and company news, market developments, mergers, new products, public procurement. An example is *La Lettre des Technologies de l'Information*, published by Groupe Tests (which also publishes *01 Informatique*, *Data Decisions*, and *L'Ordinateur Individuel*).

Special areas

EC information

The SRIS Business Information Service has considerable holdings of material from all EC Member states, including general directories, market research reports, *Financial Times Surveys*, and business journals, both those published in the country and in the UK.

EUROPEAN COMMISSION

The Commission of the EC has done a great deal to promote the dissemination of information across language barriers and to this end has promoted:

- Publications and programmes which collect material in all European languages and disseminate this through periodic or occasional publications and/or through databases.
- Pan-European databases which provide all or part of the data in at least one other language.

Thus some French, German and Italian databases provide at least a title but sometimes an abstract as well as indexing terms in English (e.g. Pascal). English speakers can therefore search foreign-language databases in their own language. Once relevant documents have been identified, the user can check whether the full English translation exists either in the database itself, or via one of the translation registers.

Diane Guide is published by ECHO, the host service of the Commission of the European Communities and is also available on the ECHO host. It is an inventory of all databases and hosts in Europe and it provides a detailed list of the subject coverage of each database, a subject index, and alphabetical lists of all databases, with their addresses, and those of host services. The online version is updated monthly and is available in all Community languages.

I'M Information Management, incorporating *Euronet Diane News*, is a monthly journal which gives news and information about developments in database markets throughout Europe, much of which may not penetrate through to the English-language press. It is published as a special supplement to *Euroabstracts* (European Commission).

Euroabstracts

This monthly abstracts journal is prepared by ECOTEC and published by the European Commission. It includes abstracts of reports, papers and articles relating to EC Member states' research activity supported by the scientific and technical programme of the European Community. Abstracts of publications and patents appear in their original language and in English. It is a source of information on the unpublished results of research programmes and activities which are likely to prove elusive via the normal information channels.

The full texts are generally available from either DG XIII/B or the Office for Official Publications of the EC. There is a General section which includes documentation and information science, a Materials section and Mathematics and Computer section—all areas likely to be of interest to those concerned with information technology.

Euroabstracts is also available as an online database, EABS which is accessible free-of-charge via ECHO.

Eurobases

A number of documentary databases originally developed for internal use by EC staff are now available to the general public. One of the most important is CELEX (CE-Lexis) which is available as an online service through the Office of Publications of the European Community. It contains all European Community primary (Treaties, Agreements) and secondary (Directives, Decisions, Regulations) legislation as well as jurisprudence of the Court of Justice, all preparatory legislation and documents for Commission proposals, European Parliament opinions and resolutions, Economic and Social Committee opinions and the full texts of European parliamentary questions.

For most sectors, the full text is available and searching can be carried out on the full text as well as on the many, highly-detailed indexed fields. In theory, all documents are put up, and therefore searchable, in all official languages; in practice, it is taking some time to implement all the language versions and it is advisable to contact Eurobases for full information. There is an extremely practical printed register, or index, published annually, which can be used to trace legislation when only part of the reference is known; it also provides a concordance of all amending legislation to any instrument.

SCAD is another source which also exists in online and printed versions and provides over 90 000 bibliographic references to Community acts in English and French, official publications and public documents issued by the European institutions in English, French and German and selected periodical articles on EC matters in the original languages. Launched in 1983 it adds approximately 15 000 references per year and is updated weekly.

Further information is available from Eurobases. In the United Kingdom, the Small Firms Service has set up a Centre for European Business Information which can provide access to the EC databases.

Since the EC is particularly active in the area of telecommunications, information technology and the information market, these databases and printed journals could prove a fruitful source of advance information on political, regulatory and technological developments.

TED—or Tenders Electronic Daily–is the online version of the S supplement to the EC Official Journal; it lists invitations to tender for public works and supply contracts from twelve EC countries, and 62 African, Caribbean and Pacific States (ACP-countries) associated with the EC. Japanese tenders were added in March 1984. The database is available in eight of the official EC languages (Greek is not available).

Japanese information

A valuable source of translated material from Japan is produced in Japan itself—there are a number of journals which select articles from the Japanese technical literature. There are also cover-to-cover and partial translation journals.

The British Library has recognized the commercial value of the interest in Japanese literature and in addition to a conference and a series of publications to help disseminate information about what is published in Japan, SRIS runs regular seminars including Japan Information Sources both in and out of London. The Japanese Information Service in Science, Technology and Commerce was founded in May 1985 but the collections it exploits have been built up for well over a century, especially in the patents field. It is probably the UK's most concentrated source of directories, statistics and news on Japan.

The Service was set up to improve access to Japanese scientific, technological and industrial information—the enquiry service offers online searching including direct searches of Japanese databases, help with the language and document supply. It holds over 3500 Japanese scientific, technological and commercial journals and over 9 million Japanese patents and virtually all Japanese industrial property publications. It also holds market and industry surveys, company, business and trade information, conferences and reports, translation journals and translation indexes.

An International Conference on Japanese Information in Science, Technology and Commerce was held in London in 1987. The full proceedings were published in 1989, available from the Japanese Information Service.

The BL has also produced *Japanese Business Publications in English: a Selected Annotated List of Recent Publications held by the British Library*, 2nd edn, compiled by Sheila Edwards and

Karen Thompson in 1987. It lists statistics, market information and industry surveys, company reports, bibliographies, directories, trade and business and abstracting journals. It has an alphabetical index of titles and organizations and suppliers of literature published in Japan.

Another useful publication is *Journals in English, Scientific, Technical and Commercial Journals held by the British Library Science Reference Library and the British Library Lending Division* (1985) by Betty Smith and Shirley V. King which lists more than 1000 titles, with journals in subject keyword order and includes translated journals and journals with translations. All titles are available for loan from the British Library Document Supply Centre.

The University of Sheffield Japan Business Services Unit is a commercial enterprise within the University, and a leading centre of expertise on Japan and Korea in the UK. It offers a range of services to industry and commerce including translation and interpreting, the preparation of technical and commercial information on Japanese and Korean companies and markets, briefing sessions covering Japanese and Korean business etiquette and tailor-made language courses at all levels in Japanese and Korean (see below).

The Unit undertakes all types of translation—letters, promotional materials, technical manuals, patent specifications and scientific papers. It also provides interpreters for business meetings, technical discussions, courtesy visits, conferences and international exhibitions.

Chinese information

Another important source of information is China—the China Information Service was set up by Scientific Information Consultants, which in a joint venture with SRIS is publishing the *China Journals Catalogue* which lists essential information from over 1000 current scientific, technological and medical journals published in China and available at SRIS.

Scientific Information Consultants also offers a range of services as part of its China Information package including contents lists in English, and condensed English versions of a number of scientific, engineering and life sciences journals. These are published separately in the *China Science Series*, issue by issue, with the same frequency as the corresponding Chinese version. In addition to a table of contents, each issue contains an English abstract, figures, tables and bibliography for each article. Relevant titles include *Non-ferrous Metals—China* and *Journal of Electronics—China*.

Special appendices will be published occasionally containing news items, tables of contents of conference proceedings and collections of papers.

China Journal Contents is published in three separate series:

    Series A: Mathematics, Physics, Chemistry, Geology
    Series B: Engineering, Technology
    Series C: Medicine, Biology, Pharmacology

Both the Condensed English Versions of Chinese journals and *China Journal Contents* are available at SRIS.

The *International Guide to Official Industrial Property Publications* (2nd edn, 1988), by Brenda M. Rimmer with its explanations of specifications, official gazettes and indexes now includes a section on the People's Republic of China and is a comprehensive guide to searching in the principal countries of the world. It also has sections on international conventions.

Patents as a source of multi-lingual or foreign language material

Patents are a valuable source of information on international developments in new technologies. Most patent-issuing countries classify their patents using the *International Patent Classification*, which is published in English and French and may be purchased from Carl Heymanns Verlag KG. It can also be consulted at the Science Reference and Information Service (Holborn Branch). Patent Cooperation Treaty (PCT) and European applications are also classified using IPC.

When Patent Cooperation Treaty (PCT) applications reach the national phase, the applicant has to provide a translation of the description, the claims and any textual material in the drawings in the language of the designated countries.

SRIS interfiles translations with the main sequence of patent applications in the Foreign Patents Section (Chancery House). To distinguish them from ordinary applications, translations are annotated on the fiche and in the register as TRANS. Photocopy requests for PCT patents will receive the English translation in place of the original unless the request states otherwise.

EUROPEAN PATENT AND PCT APPLICATIONS

Under the European Patent Convention, a single European Patent application may be filed in any of the EPC countries giving simultaneous protection in those countries, including the UK. Similarly, it is possible to file an International Application under the Patent Cooperation Treaty and use this as the basis of separate national applications.

Both methods are more complex and costly than getting a UK patent alone, but may be cheaper and easier than filing individual national applications. And, it is now becoming increasingly important for companies to ensure that their invention is protected outside the UK.

The full text of an EPC application may be filed in any one of the three official languages (English, French or German), but patentees are obliged to provide an abstract written by an expert patent translator, in each of the three official languages. However, signatories to the convention can insist, as in the UK, that patents filed under the EPC are filed with a translation of the full text, or simply the claims in the language of the designated country. The accompanying abstract for PCT applications will be in English although the full text of the application may be in English, French, German, Russian or Japanese.

It is likely that an increasing number of foreign-language patents will prove of interest to information technologists. Consequently it is important to know what other language versions exist, and how to arrange for translations and/or abstracts to be done.

SRIS can provide the names of experienced translators and many patent agents have either in-house translators or a regular panel of freelance translators who they use for translation of patents and all related material both from and into the foreign language. It may be helpful to seek their advice since they are experienced in placing this kind of work with the most appropriate translator. The Patent Network of the Institute of Translation and Interpreting (see below) should also be able to supply the right translator for any particular job. While the standard of translation is extremely high, it is advisable, where the information is critical to a project, to obtain the original document as well.

The European Patent Office translators in Munich deal with all administrative documents connected with the European Patent scheme.

Foreign patents can be consulted in the Foreign Patents Reading Room of the British Library's Science Reference and Information Service (SRIS). British and EPC Patents can also be consulted at SRIS.

The complete collection of European patent applications is available on FIRST CD-ROM which provides a facsimile of the first page of each application. Searches can be conducted using the IPC classification and on words in the title in English, French or German. Further information is available from the European Patent Office's Patent Information Department (Gerhardstrasse 27, D-8000 Munich, Germany).

WORLD PATENT ABSTRACTS JOURNAL

In many countries patent applications are published without examination a few months after filing, so that patent literature may be a more up-to-date source of information on technological progress than journals. Rapidly publishing countries are Belgium, France, Germany, Japan, Netherlands, and the United Kingdom. The European and PCT Patent Applications are also published early.

Derwent Publications provides detailed English language abstracts with drawings, conveniently packaged by country or subject matter. The abstracts are made by highly-competent translators with expert specialist knowledge. The Derwent classifications codes which are likely to be of interest for information technology are:

P	General
P7	Pressing printing
S-X	Electrical
T	Computing and control
U-V	Electronic components, circuitry
W	Communications

JAPANESE PATENT INFORMATION

A remarkable initiative is the search service which SRIS offers on PATOLIS, the Japanese language database of Japanese industrial property information, produced by JAPIO (formerly JAPATIC). The database includes unexamined patent applications, trade mark applications, and designs as well as the standard patent applications.

The searches are carried out at INPADOC in Vienna, but are prepared with the assistance of an SRIS specialist who will also assist in converting the results which come in a mixture of Japanese and code.

Further information is available from the British Library, SRIS Foreign Patents Enquiry Desk.

GUIDE TO OFFICIAL INDUSTRIAL PROPERTY PUBLICATIONS

Many inventions are patented in several countries and for legal reasons their specifications are often published two or three times by each country. This results in some three-quarters of a million new specifications each year. The specifications and their associated official gazettes are published in the language of the patenting authority and although some degree of uniformity has been achieved in the presentation of specifications, expertise is needed to identify and select documents of likely interest.

This major directory of the collections of patent specifications, gazettes and abstracts available around the world is published by the World Intellectual Property Organization. The loose-leaf work comprises data sheets on individual library or information centres, and the publications available, as well as extensive indexes for each patent office, the list of institutions which hold its patent specifications and institutions which hold official gazettes. A similar publication is *Patent Information and Documentation in Western Europe* published by the Commission of the European Communities.

INSPEC database

One of the most useful online services in information technology is the INSPEC database which contains abstracts of literature published in some 63 languages. The *INSPEC User Manual* shows that the percentage of documents in the major languages on the database is as follows: English 83%; Russian 4.8%; German 4.4%; French 2.1%; Japanese 1.8%; and others 3.9%.

All INSPEC abstracts are in English; outside of the 83% deriving from original English documents, the database contains English abstracts for a small percentage of foreign language documents selected from a wide range of foreign-language journals and periodicals (a full list of the publications scanned is given in the *INSPEC List of Journals*). The abstracts are written by specialist abstract translators employed by Inspec.

In addition, the database publishes abstracts, again in English, of foreign-language articles which have been translated and which are available as full texts in English. It also contains a number of abstracts of articles taken from the cover-to-cover and selective translation journals.

It is not particularly easy to identify translations in the database. Abstracts are marked TRANS, but this information is not an index term and so it is not possible to search for translated documents. However it is possible to search on the country and language of publication, so users can identify what has been published in France or in Germany, and additionally what has been published in German or in French.

NTIS database

Similarly NTIS provides information on government-sponsored research and development activity in many of the industrialised nations including Japan, France and West Germany. The annual input of 18 400 items includes 7900 originating in languages other than English. The title and other bibliographic information are translated into English and both the English and foreign language title are searchable. Thus if you come across a notice of government-sponsored research in other countries, you may well be able to search for it—using title-words, and find the English translation—on NTIS.

Overcoming the language barrier and the DIY method

Language learning

Language training in the UK educational system is not as well-developed as it ought to be. Indeed it has undergone something of a crisis in recent years, and language departments in the higher education sector are under pressure. However, awareness of the importance of foreign-language skills is evident in new courses being offered at universities and polytechnics which combine technical subjects with languages.

German is still an important language for many of the scientific or applied disciplines, and is still very much a *lingua franca* in Eastern Europe; similarly Russian should be enjoying a re-emergence, while both Japanese and Chinese are going to be important languages in the twenty-first century.

There are ample opportunities for learning the more conventional Western European languages after school or university, though they may require some seeking out. Most adult education colleges offer evening and part-time courses which can lead to the examinations of the Institute of Linguists, the RSA (Royal Society of Arts), London Chamber of Commerce or Cambridge Proficiency. The level of instruction and examination ranges from pre-GCSE to degree level. The London Chamber of Commerce and Industry and other chambers of commerce are beginning to set up such language classes, as are the many LX-Centres [Languages (for) Export] which have been set up throughout the UK. Other specialist training centres such as Cranfield Institute of Technology are now offering language training specifically tailored to the needs of professional people and are including languages in their undergraduate courses.

Scanning foreign-language material

An alternative to learning the language so that one can speak it fluently, and/or translate whole documents, is to learn how to scan a text in a foreign language in order to extract the essential information, and perhaps decide whether it would be worth having a full translation done. There are courses and textbooks which can help the motivated learner to acquire enough knowledge of a language in order to be able to understand the content of the text.

In the 1960s and 1970s, technical colleges and universities such as PCL and City University ran regular courses in technical French or German, or beginners' German for chemists and scientific staff; these were designed to give participants a reading knowledge of a language so that they could understand texts within their own area of specialization. They have disappeared with the successive cuts in education and public funding. If you feel you would like such a course, persuade your company or your professional organization to run one. PCL and many other institutions will set up one-to-one or group courses tailor-made to your needs. If you are unsure where to start, then the Institute of Translation and Interpreting (ITI) or the Institute of Linguists (IL) can put you in touch with trained language teachers and translators who could help you to set up such courses.

Learning the more exotic languages—Japanese

One of the important sources of information in information technology is, of course, Japan, and the Japanese language immediately raises a major language barrier. According to IDS (see below), Japan publishes a total of around 9000 scientific and technical serials, many of them concerned with topics which come under the heading of information technology. Much of this is in the form of grey literature (reports, technical notes and specifications, conference proceedings and preprints) which is not available through the normal channels. In addition, Japan has 60 or so database companies providing about 700 services.

It is possible to learn Japanese for read-through and information purposes: of the two best-known courses only the one at Sheffield University survives; the PCL course was dropped due to lack of funding and interest. The Sheffield course, originally designed by the University's Centre of Japanese Studies and designated as 'Reading Scientific and Technical Japanese', is now run by Integrated Dictionary Systems Limited. Participants learn the alphabet and the rudiments of grammar and syntax so that they can decipher a title and an abstract to see whether the document or text is likely to be useful and worth full translation. The seven-week residential summer course requires no previous knowledge of Japanese and leads to independent reading ability. Entry requirements are a good command of English and preferably a knowledge of traditional English grammar. Students who successfully complete the course may sit the Examination for the

Certificate of Competence in Reading Scientific Japanese awarded by the University of Sheffield. The cost of approximately £800 covers tuition fees, a complete set of textbooks and the examination entrance fee. The course is also offered as a correspondence course lasting on average one year. Correspondence course students can spend up to two weeks on the residential course.

Recognizing foreign languages

One not-so-obvious point is to establish which language a foreign text is in; this can prove quite difficult in some cases. A very useful book, now unfortunately out of print, is Piette's *Guide to Foreign Languages* (Aslib). This is, or rather was, a guide to foreign language scripts and basic grammar and syntax for librarians and information staff. It was particularly useful for the less-commonly known European languages and for those written in non-Roman alphabets.

Standardized terminology

The many international standards and regulatory bodies publish regulations, standards, recommendations or nomenclatures and a great deal of accessory literature in at least two languages, sometimes with a multilingual glossary. Of special interest in the area of information technology are: CCITT, CENELEC, CEN, ISO and ITU. Unfortunately, much of this literature falls into the 'grey' category, but once you have established which organizations and which body of literature are of relevance to your work, it should be possible to get onto the appropriate mailing list, or find out where the material is regularly available.

Dictionaries and specialized reference works

It may be helpful to keep one or two reputable foreign-language dictionaries, in order to look up the occasional term, or for help in searching a foreign-language database.

The British Library SRIS has an important collection of technical dictionaries in all languages covering a wide range of subjects—it probably has one of the most comprehensive collections of foreign-language dictionaries and glossaries anywhere in the world. The fact that it is an official deposit library and also receives dictionaries from many overseas libraries accounts for a comprehensive and sometimes exotic collection of rare subjects and languages.

As well as the collection of general English language and foreign-language dictionaries (mono-, bi- and multi-lingual), the library houses an impressive collection of specialized subject dictionaries and reference works. While subject-based English language dictionaries are classified with the subject and held at the appropriate shelf location, they are also listed in the classified catalogue in the (160–199) dictionary sequence. Bilingual general and general technical dictionaries are shelved in alphabetical order of language in the range AA 102–159 (e.g. AA 152 = Swedish). The language codes are:

- E   English
- F   French and Romance
- G   German and Germanic
- S   Scandinavian
- R   Slavonic
- X   Oriental

Specialized technical and multilingual dictionaries are shelved by subject in the range AA 160–199. English reference works or general reference books with definitions or a glossary in foreign languages are classified at AA 186 but shelved at the appropriate subject classification location.

The microfiche classified catalogue reveals an astonishing wealth of works. However finding a particular dictionary requires some dedication: as with many classification schemes, there are some curious idiosyncrasies and material turns up in the most unexpected places.

The most useful class marks for information technology are likely to be:

- AA 161   Patents
- AA 162   Economics, commerce, operational research
- AA 163   Publishing, library and information science, including information theory, linguistics
- AA 187   Automation and control
- AA 190   Semiconductors
- AA 192   Telecommunications, radio, television
- AA 197   Mechanical engineering, heat refrigeration—includes materials (e.g. silicon and gallium arsenide)

Two examples, which indicate the specificity of this collection are: *Wörterbuch der CAD/CAM-Technologie* by S. Wajna (in German) and *Dictionary of Robot Technology* (in four languages—English, French, Russian, German) by Erich Bürger.

IEE has a reasonable collection of dictionaries in the area of information technology and ITI has a growing collection of general and specialized dictionaries. The Institute's journal *PTI* regularly reviews specialized dictionaries. A comprehensive catalogue of foreign-language dictionaries is available from the specialist publisher and foreign-language booksellers, Grant & Cutler (35–52 Great Marlborough Street, London W1V 2AY).

Terminology data banks

EURODICAUTOM

EURODICAUTOM is an online terminology databank containing scientific and technical terms, contextual phrases and abbreviations in all the official EC languages. The databank is used by terminologists and translators in the Community institutions and is also available to governmental and non-governmental organizations under the same conditions as for EC staff. EURODICAUTOM is also available to members of the general public through ECHO. The version marketed outside the Community institutions which does not include the Greek section can be accessed using either CCL or the GRIPS query language—both can give rise to some difficulties since the original query language and database were designed as a dedicated system over 20 years ago, and the databank does not offer many of the standard retrieval facilities (e.g. identification of number of records which match query, and refining of query, left-hand truncation, proximity criteria).

There is no charge for the use of the databank, although users do have to pay their own telecoms charges to the nearest local node, and so it is relatively cheap.

Currently, the database contains over 420 000 terms and contextual phrases and over 120 000 abbreviations, and is updated with approximately 2000 new items every month. While much of the terminology deals with Community legislation and key areas of Community policy such as agricultural and social affairs, there is a significant amount of terminology in the areas of computing, data processing, and telecommunications. The abbreviations section contains a wealth of important abbreviations and acronyms with their meanings and explanatory notes in all Community languages.

Once access to EURODICAUTOM has been arranged, it is worth looking at some of the other databases available on the ECHO host. ECHO holds regular information and training days throughout the European Community countries, and can also arrange individual seminars for groups of interested users (e.g. an online user group, an in-house information service).

TERMIUM

The Canadian Government's terminology databank TERMIUM is used by all Canadian government translators and provides French translations of standard English/American terms. The online version is not currently available in Europe, but the databank is available on CD-ROM and the Secretary of State has plans to market this version in Europe. A limited selection of terms has been included in the Swedish National Standards organization (TNC) service, TERMDOK and is also available on CD-ROM.

TEAM

Siemens of West Germany created this database for its own staff translators and freelance translators working for Siemens can also have access to the system. However, it is not available to the general public. Again a selection of terms has been included in PC-TERM, a PC-based terminology management and look-up product marketed in the UK by Siemens (UK) plc.

There are a number of other terminology databanks which are used by national standards organizations and research institutes which are not available to the general public but to which it may be possible to have access if your work brings you into contact with such bodies.

Obtaining translations

I'd like it in English, American will do.

Dr John Chillag, BLDSC

Even if you are able to read and understand the language, it may be necessary to have a fuller understanding of the text. In that case you will need to establish whether a translation already exists, and if not how a translation can be obtained.

Having full translations done is expensive but the money is well spent if you use a competent and reliable translator. But you should not waste a valuable translation budget on translations which may already exist. Much foreign-language material, and their translations, fall into the category of grey literature and are not readily traced through the standard secondary services.

There are two main types of information on existing translations—translation journals and translation registers (primary sources) and the related registers and indexes (secondary sources).

The major effort in collecting and translating foreign-language material was in the 1950s to mid-1970s when traditional science and technologies—metallurgy, materials science, mathematics and physics, chemistry—were of greatest interest. Since that time and the arrival of newer technologies, there has been a lessening interest in—or rather lessening appreciation of the value of—translated material. The cause for this is not certain. It could be the result of economies which have had to be introduced into library and documentation services generally. It could be that after the initial interest in activity across the Iron Curtain, it was perceived that research in Eastern Europe was of less interest than had once been thought and there was no longer an imperative need to monitor developments in the Eastern Bloc. Thus many of the guides and directories in the SRIS shelves on translation and abstracting journals are now out of date (e.g. *List of Books Received from the USSR and Translated Books* (BLLD, 1974)). It must also be related to the Anglo-centric nature of computer and information technology and the tendency for authors to seek to publish in English, in order to gain wider dissemination, or for academies and publishing houses to ensure that journals were published in translation. The best known of these in our field is *Informatika*. Whatever the reason, while there are several holdings and journals devoted to the collection and publication of translations articles from the literature of the traditional industries and technologies, it is extremely difficult to find any evidence of a serious and concentrated collection of such material in the area of information technology.

The purpose of translation registers is to:

- eliminate costly duplication of translation effort, freeing funds for translating new material
- disseminate information on available translations, thus avoiding duplication of translation effort
- provide copies of translations available from the collection centres or the original supplier of the information

Translation journals

Translation journals provide either cover-to-cover or selective translations of the foreign-language journal, often published by the original publishing house or by major American scientific publishers or professional associations.

Cover-to-cover is self-explanatory—every article, editorial and advertisement in the original journal is translated. Selective may mean a selection of articles from any issue, or more usually, a selection of articles from a volume or part-volume which are published in a single issue of the translated journal.

A guide to such translation journals held at the British Library

Document Supply Centre at Boston Spa is *Journals in Translation*, a compendium which is jointly published by the BLDSC and the International Translations Centre, Delft. The fourth edition, published in 1988, cost £40. It was first published in 1976 and lists journals which are translated cover-to-cover or selectively together with journals which consist of translations of articles collected from multiple sources. It includes multi-source translations serials published in the USA.

Journals in Translation replaced the lists of translation journals previously published separately by each organization: *Translation Journals* (ETC, up to 1974); and *Journals in Translation Lending Division*.

The Science Reference and Information Service also produces its own compendium of translation journals held at Holborn, published under the title *Journals with Translations*. The most recent edition was published in 1985. Both *Journals in Translation* and *Journals with Translations* are held at the Enquiry Desk of the Science Reference Information Service.

Translation registers and indexes

Translation registers record the bibliographic details of existing translated material, including the originator and location of the translation. They publish monthly and quarterly announcements, and occasional annual and quinquennial compendia.

British Reports, Translations and Theses (BRTT) is published by the British Library (previously *British Research and Development Reports*, published under that title until 1970). In addition to British report literature, it lists translations produced by British government organizations, industry, universities and learned institutions. It also covers unpublished translations from the Republic of Ireland. It is published monthly, and in 1989 cost £64 a year. All items listed in BRTT are available from the British Library Document Supply Centre.

Currently, all translations are also notified to the International Translations Centre in Delft, and can be consulted via the WORLD TRANSINDEX (WTI) database which contains 300 000 titles and is updated monthly. Titles held by BLDSC and BLSRIS are clearly marked.

The SIGLE database (Information System for Grey Literature in Europe) is run by the European Commission in Luxembourg: all material listed in BRTT excluding translations appears in the SIGLE database which is available in the UK via the BLAISE host service.

NATIONAL TRANSLATIONS CENTER (US)

The National Translations Center (NTC) in the US was formally established in 1953 after a seventeen-year association with the Special Libraries Association (SLA). The Center became a department of The John Crerar Library, University of Chicago, in 1971.

The NTC is a depository and information source for unpublished translations into English from the world literature of the natural, physical, medical and social sciences. NTC files contain information on approximately 1 000 000 translations, approximately 400 000 of which comprise the NTC translation collection.

Translations are deposited by over 100 scientific and professional societies, governmental agencies, industrial and other special libraries, colleges, universities and other institutions in the US and abroad, including the BLDSC. The Center also solicits information on translations available from commercial translators and other collections in the US and abroad. Index files are maintained by author, journal citation, report number, standard number and patent number.

NTC runs a subscription/service programme, such that those who produce and acquire large numbers of translations can join the Center in a programme which is mutually beneficial. The deposit of copies of translations to the Center will entitle the donors to receive information about the availability of other translations which they may need at no charge.

The NTC service was founded when librarians realized just how expensive it could be to have a custom translation done, and also that important translations were often being done simultaneously by different organizations. They decided, therefore, to produce a list of existing translations, pooled from various agencies. In 1969 there were 140 000 translations, 60% in Russian, 40% in other languages. A *Consolidated Index* of the monthly lists was published in 1969 (142 000 entries) when it was realized that even the lists were not solving the problem: quite frequently searchers did not find a translation and so recommissioned one.

NTC holdings as well as translations available from other sources are listed in *Consolidated Index of Translations into English 1969 (1953–1966)*, and now *Translations Register–Index*, a monthly, published from 1967 onwards. It is a byproduct of the NTC database and announces new accessions to the database. The index sections include an author, journal citation, patent and standard index. In the register section, translations are listed in subject categories. NTIS ONLINE subject classifications are used. Each translation carries an entry and an order number. Sources of availability are found in the Directory of Sources published with each issue. The index sections of *TR–I* are cumulated semi-annually and annually.

France's COST (Centre de Documentation Scientifique et Technique) has a directory of 300 000 references to translations made prior to 1977. Later references are held by WORLD TRANSINDEX.

Document supply

Once it has been established that a translation does exist, you will want to obtain it: the translation registers indicate whether the translation is available at one of the major holding centres or whether it has to be obtained from the originator of the translation. In fact, the British Library's Document Supply Centre with its total stock of 7 000 000 books, journals, reports and theses covering almost every subject in any language, stock of foreign language journals and stock of translation journals is probably sorely under-utilized as a source of foreign language material.

The SRIS library as the national reference library for science and technology, business and commerce and for patents, trade marks and designs has the most comprehensive reference collection in Western Europe and may be consulted without prior arrangement or readers' ticket. Other national libraries and information centres and professional bodies hold copies of translations.

CNRS, Belgium, is collecting translations of articles from East European and Asian languages.

Reliability of translation registers and indexes

In spite of this relative wealth of translated material and indexes thereto, they represent only the tip of the iceberg of potentially valuable material. Unfortunately, therefore the 'hit' rate is fairly low, and there is considerable overlap between the various registers particularly since they list not only individual translations, but also translations issued in the various translation journals. However, the routine for checking the registers is fairly straightforward, once known, and even one hit in a year can result in savings of translation cost and a great deal of time.

Using translation services

Once you have identified and obtained an article or document, you may be able to scan or read it in the foreign language and provide a summary for the end user, or you may need to arrange for a summary or full translation.

Abstracting and read-through (or summary) translation

You may not need a full translation but may need to check what the text is about, either to pass the information on or to decide whether a full translation is required. Many people think that providing a gist translation which gives just an idea of what the text is about is very easy and much quicker to do than a full translation. However, this is generally not the case; abstracting itself is a specialist task so to translate and abstract together requires a great deal of skill. The Institute of Translation and Interpreting (ITI) can provide information on translators who specialize in abstracting work. We have already mentioned patent abstract/services and those which monitor foreign-language journals and conference proceedings. Read-through services, where the linguists and the technical specialist look through the text together, are designed to help users gain an outline understanding of the content of foreign-language scientific or technical papers after which they can decide whether it is worth having a full translation made.

LINGUISTIC AID SERVICE

The British Library Science Reference and Information Service offers a Linguistic Aid Service free of charge to all users of the library. It is stressed that this is an 'information-only' service and not a translation service.

Many of the staff are fluent in a range of languages and can help enquirers to understand foreign business, scientific and technological documents. The enquirer will generally spend approximately 20–30 minutes studying the text with a member of staff who has a reading knowledge of the language in question. The linguist scans for key words and phrases which clarify the subject matter, prompted by the enquirer, and will interpret the content with the help of the enquirer's specialist knowledge which the linguist will probably not possess.

Captions or table headings often help to identify sections of a paper which contain the information required. Sometimes essential information is in a single paragraph: enquirers are encouraged to make use of the service even if they suspect that the problem will only need a few minutes assistance. The linguist works orally and will not provide written notes, and users may not record the session on tape.

Languages available are: Chinese, Dutch, French, German, Hungarian, Italian, Japanese, Polish, Portuguese, Russian, the

Scandinavian languages—Swedish, Norwegian, Danish—and Spanish. The Library is usually also able to help with other languages, especially those in the Slavonic group.

Having a full translation done

Any worker in the information technology field will need to know how to obtain reliable, high-quality translation and interpreting services at competitive rates. The most important thing to establish is exactly what the document is about in order to ensure that the best qualified person is chosen to translate it. This is not always easy for a non-linguist, so ideally you should speak directly to a translator who specializes in the area in question. With a few keywords and perhaps some bibliographic references, translators can usually establish whether the document is within their area of competence.

FINDING A TRANSLATOR OR INTERPRETER

The Institute of Translation and Interpreting (ITI) publishes an Index which lists the names, addresses, telecoms and language and subject specialization of more than 800 Fellows, Members and Associates of ITI who have been graded following a rigorous admissions procedure to establish their professional competence and experience. The Institute can provide advice on translators and interpreters, on dictionaries, on rates and salaries, and can also advise you on the best way of obtaining translations. It can also provide information on translator organizations in other countries, should you wish to find a mother tongue translator overseas.

In addition to the specialist language networks, the Institute has a number of subject specialist networks—these group translators who have built up an expertise in a particular discipline, often through direct work experience, and who have developed useful contacts with experts in the field. Of particular interest are the ITI Infotech Network and the ITI Patents Network mentioned earlier. The ITI Index and Networks Directories can be purchased from the Institute and should be available for consultation in specialist and major public libraries.

As a professional rule, translators work into their mother tongue, and it should generally be possible to find a specialist translator who works from one of the commoner foreign languages into English. For certain languages—including Slavonic and East European, the Scandinavian and Asian languages—you may only find foreign nationals who can translate from the foreign language into English. If possible such work should always be checked by an

English mother-tongue specialist. Where you require translation into the foreign language, you should endeavour to find the appropriate mother-tongue translator either in the UK or overseas.

If you are a regular user of translation services it is probably a good idea to develop a good relationship with a number of individual translators, or to negotiate a special arrangement with a translation company, or possibly to set up a staff translation department. It is also worth finding out if your company already has such a service either on site or at headquarters; it is surprising how many people do not realize that there is an in-house translation capability.

It is important to understand how translators work since misconceptions about how they convert text from one language to another can result in serious problems. It is erroneous to think that a translator can produce a translation much as a typist can copy type a document: nor is it simply a question of being good at foreign languages and knowing how to look up technical words in a dictionary and set them down in the right order. Even the most rigorous scientific and technical texts can be arbitrary and ambiguous in their use of language and if you, the user, are to derive maximum benefit from the information contained in the document you should ensure that the translator is given both adequate time and background help in order to provide you with a worthwhile product.

You should:

- brief the translator properly
- provide background material which applies to the area for which you require the translation
- be prepared to explain what you need the translation for and to answer questions on specialized terminology
- above all endeavour to develop a regular relationship with the translators you use—whether in-house staff or freelance—so that they get to know your work and have the chance to build up their own reading and specialized knowledge of the subject.

Beware the unnecessary translation

You may be asked to obtain a translation of an important standard or recommendation—be sure to check its origin, because if it has been published by one of the regulatory bodies then it is more than likely that a version in another language will already exist.

You should also beware of requests for translations of product literature—a few moments thought may suggest that there is very likely to be an original English version, especially for products manufactured in an English-speaking country, or where the parent country is in an English-speaking country. Some detective work may be necessary, but this is often cheaper than paying for a translation of a highly-specialized and lengthy text.

Is machine translation the answer?

A word of caution about machine translation is necessary. The daily and specialist press frequently carry uninformed reports of machines which will deal with the foreign-language problem once and for all. But the language industry is generally agreed that there will probably never be a universal translation machine for handling any and every kind of document in any and every field. Anyone familiar with the complexities of indexing—both manual and automatic—must have some understanding of how impossible it would be to construct a program which can interpret national language with all its complexities, ambiguities, and nuances, and of how unpredictable even highly-specific and highly-technical texts can be in their use of terms.

Dedicated computational linguistics specialists and computer scientists will nevertheless continue to search for the Holy Grail: there is something futuristic about the idea of machine translation which is likely forever to exert a fascination on journalists, researchers and certain managers in the language industry alike. However, the new realism which prevails in the machine translation industry itself has resulted in a quite dramatic shift from research on pure machine translation and machine-aided translation (MAT) programs to highly-interactive systems which depend on close interaction between man and machine to produce usable text. The main practical and economic advantages of MAT systems apparently relate to the elimination of multiple keyboarding, and the facility for passing from initial data capture to a first-class desktop-published product within the same technical environment.

In addition to the persistent problems of analyzing natural languages and generating a syntactically-correct target text, experience has shown that very expensive (human) pre-editing and constant dictionary development is required for machine translation systems to produce meaningful text. Potential users may have heard of the successful Canadian METEO project, which uses the highly limited syntax and vocabulary of weather reports to produce translations for the French-speaking population; similarly restricted language systems in which the dvocabulary, syntax and style are determined according to a set of rules are gaining currency for certain mass-volume multi-lingual projects. The advantage is that material written in a restrictive language may be readily comprehensible to non-native speakers and that a machine translation or language conversion program can be more easily written to produce the required language version at higher speed and lower cost than would be possible with conventional translation. This kind of computerized translation boilerplating (generally interactive since translators will vet the text as it is produced, or revise it after the first batch processed draft) is well tried and tested in certain areas of mechanical and aeronautical engineering. Multinational corporations such as Rank Xerox use it for the mass of literature required for installing, maintaining and repairing their office machines.

Producing foreign-language texts

This is no straightforward matter, since the world of word processing and desk-top publishing is still Anglo-centric. However, as the need for processing text in non-standard English and non-Roman alphabets grows, and as users begin to reject the compromises imposed by a limited character set, a range of multilingual word-processing software is beginning to appear on the market. Further information on multilingual word processing can be obtained through Sesame, an organization and publication run by John Clewes based at the British Library, Boston Spa.

A rather innovative piece of software is a Canadian product, no doubt developed with the Pacific Rim in mind, and Canada's large Chinese population. Tian Ma is a kind of computerized stenography system which allows a standard Western-type keyboard to be used for calling up Chinese pictograms and ideograms which can then be selected by the operator.

Further information on multilingual word processing can be obtained from the Institute of Translation and Interpreting.

References

J.A. Large. *Overcoming the Foreign Language Barrier.*
A Brief Guide to Centres of International Lending and Photocopying. IFLA, 3rd edn, 1984.

Addresses

Carl Heymanns Verlag KG
Steinsdorfstrasse 10
Postfach 275
Munich
Germany

DG XIII/B (Euroabstracts)
CEC
L-2920 Luxembourg
Tel. +352 4301 2883

Commission of the European Communities
Service Eurobases
rue de la Loi 200
Bruxelles B-1049
Belgium

ECHO
177 route d'Esch
L-1471 Luxembourg
Tel. 352 488041

Institute of Linguists (IoL)
24a Highbury Grove
London N5
UK

Institute of Translation and Interpreting (ITI)
318a Finchley Road
London NW3 5HT
UK
Tel. 081-794 9931; Fax 081-435 2105

Integrated Dictionary Systems Limited (IDS)
28 Star Hill
Rochester
Kent
ME1 1XB
UK
Tel. (0634) 46789

Japan Business Services Unit
The University of Sheffield
Sheffield
S10 2TN
UK

London Chamber of Commerce
Language Advisory and Referral Service
69 Cannon Street
London EC4N 5AB
UK

National Translations Centre
The John Crerar Library
University of Chicago
5730 South Ellis Avenue
Chicago, IL 60637
USA
Tel. +312 962 7060

London Languages and Export Centre
Polytechnic of Central London (PCL)
The Short Course Unit
35 Marylebone Road
London NW1 5LS
UK
Tel. 071 486 5811

Scientific Information Consultants
Eugene Gros
661 Finchley Road
London NW2 2HN
UK

Small Firms Service
2–18 Ebury Bridge Road
London SW1W 8QD
UK

Tests Publications SA
3 avenue de la Ferme Rose
Bruxelles B-1180
Belgium
Tel. 345 99 10

CHAPTER EIGHTEEN

Experts

M.J. CRAWFORD

Use of experts

An expert is a person with special skill or knowledge. Experts are especially good at problem solving. A major handicap for decision makers is that they may not even see a problem until it is too late. This chapter aims to describe situations where expert advice might be sought, the type of response an expert can be expected to give and finally, ways of identifying experts.

Expert advice can be obtained from an individual, a group of individuals, or a corporate body such as a research centre or agency. Experts might be academics or practitioners, commercial firms or government agencies. Special skill or knowledge exists in all of these sources and their advice may be available free or for a fee. The important thing to remember is that most areas of human endeavour have experts and seeking their advice can be worthwhile.

Any project or undertaking which involves a substantial investment of capital or time should be reviewed to consider if seeking expert advice would influence the decision or outcome. Money spent on expert opinion could well represent good value and result in savings in the long term. Given the large investment in capital and effort which goes into many IT systems, it seems only logical to seek the advice of an expert at an early stage.

Even when the project seems to involve known technology which has been successfully employed by others, the expert may know of new developments or refinements which would make the installation more advanced or more efficient than those currently in use. IT is a constantly changing field and what may have seemed theoretical a few years ago may be available now.

Companies seek expert opinion for all types of reasons—some of them the wrong ones. In some cases an expert is consulted as insurance in case something goes wrong with the project; the decision-maker will have someone to share the blame. In these cases, the advice of the expert is not really being sought but simply affirmation of a decision which has already been taken.

There is another aspect to this, however. It is possible to seek the opinion of an expert but then take some alternative course of action because of financial considerations, organizational policies or even because the expert failed to establish the benefits of his recommendations. There is no law which says that the advice of the expert has to be followed; naturally expert advice should be weighed thoroughly and not ignored lightly. A case in point might be an expert's recommendation for a state-of-the-art installation where a more mundane and proven package (at lower cost in most cases) might be appropriate in a given situation. The cheaper solution may be selected but only after considering all the ramifications of the decision.

Experts are normally good at diagnosing or predicting problems and should be called on when a problem exists or one is anticipated. The expert should be able to identify the likely cause(s) of the problem and suggest remedies or alternatives. The skilled expert sees many systems in the process of development and this accumulated knowledge can be applied to a problem which would take others much longer to analyze.

Finding an expert

There are many ways of identifying experts but chances are it will be necessary to communicate with several people before the expert is located. Because of the special characteristics of their knowledge, experts are often difficult to find. It may be necessary to locate a person or organization familiar with a subject field and who can then identify experts in that field. If some of the information sources cited in this chapter appear to be at a tangent to expertise, it is because they are a means of identifying someone who may know of an expert.

- Ascertain if there is a professional body in the field. Experts will often be known to the professional body and there may even be an advice service offered by the organization to match enquirers with suitable experts. The publications of

the organization are another way of identifying experts or centres of specialist knowledge.
- Ask people in firms which have dealt with similar problems. It is unlikely that a direct competitor will be a good source for this type of information, but suppliers or even clients may have experience with the problem or project under consideration and may be able to recommend an expert or warn about certain courses of action. Use the network system to benefit from the experience of others.
- It is possible to benefit from expert opinion without directly employing the expert involved. Research into the written material on a topic is one way of learning what the experts have to say about it. It is often possible to find reports, articles, written communications or conference proceedings which discuss a problem in detail and outline the possible solutions available.
- Use a directory or guide to locate people or organizations with special skills. The information sources mentioned in this chapter cannot be comprehensive but give an indication of the type of published sources which can be useful in locating an expert.
- Attend seminars, conferences in the field. Experts and consultants often speak on the lecture circuit and that provides a preview of their style. It may even be possible to find the solution to a problem through this means although generally a conference or seminar is not specific enough to answer individual cases.
- Magazines and journals have articles written by experts and news stories about consultancy contracts which have been commissioned or completed. These can provide an insight into the complexity of the problem, the timescale involved and (in some cases) the range of fees. It can also provide a source for a recommendation; contact with the client of a consultancy contract might reveal pitfalls or hazards in the area involved.

In addition to identifying experts in the field, a review of the published literature on a topic may also provide a basic insight into the scope of the problem or project and assist in the later evaluation of experts and their recommendations.

Experts know that their knowledge is their only asset and therefore are reluctant to record all they know in print. Apart from providing their specialized knowledge free of charge, there is also the fact that they may well know things which cannot be broadcast because of issues of confidentiality. Therefore, it might be possible to learn more by attending a seminar or presentation where the detailed proceedings are not published. In that sort of 'off the record' setting both experts and others attending the seminar are often more open and honest.

Working with an expert

A fundamental question is whether the expert is providing information for a fee or free of charge. In the former case it is easier to establish the ground rules and ask more direct questions. If the information is being provided free of charge or 'off the cuff', tact is required to work with the expert to get the best results.

Matthew Lesko, editor of *Information USA*, lists ten techniques for obtaining information from bureaucrats. Although the word 'bureaucrat' is somewhat loaded, the techniques are useful when obtaining information from anyone who is providing information at no fee.

1. Introduce yourself cheerfully.
2. Be open and candid.
3. Be optimistic.
4. Be humble and courteous; experts do not like their positions of authority questioned.
5. Be concise.
6. Don't be a 'gimme' (American for 'give me this' or 'give me that').
7. Be complimentary; give credit to the expert's insight or expertise.
8. Talk about other things; avoid an intensive grilling of the expert.
9. Return the favour. Share any information you have gained and show willing to help the source in future if the opportunity arises.
10. Say thank you. A short note as a follow-up is even better.

Getting the most out of a consultant

- Prepare a strategy in advance or if that is part of the consultancy, agree the strategy first. State in detailed terms the goals of the organization and how this particular application of information technology will achieve those goals.
- Agree a budget; this may exclude some experts right from the start but better to know that in advance than to waste time on

both sides. When evaluating cost estimates from consultants, do not confuse costs of a feasibility study or other type of study with a total project. That is, clients are often disappointed because they think they are buying a solution to a problem rather than a study which will produce several possible choices, and involve further investment to achieve a practical solution to the problem.
- Agree a timetable and request periodic status reports. Communication is essential and written reports, timetables and 'milestones' are ways of managing expert help.
- While it is important to have a precise brief for the consultancy, try to draw it in wide enough terms for the consultant to exercise his/her skills. Give the expert access to all types of people in the organization. An outsider can often break down barriers which exist within an organization and diagnose problems which are not apparent to the permanent staff members.
- Make certain the future maintenance of any system is spelled out. Systems are often time and capital intensive; it is not just the initial expense which is a concern but what the system will operate (and cost) two years from now.

The following section contains information sources for locating experts in information technology. Attention should be drawn to a major government initiative in the UK, the Alvey Programme for Advanced Information Technology. This joint venture between the Department of Trade and Industry, Ministry of Defence and the Department of Education and Science (acting through the Science and Engineering Research Council) was named after Mr John Alvey, chairman of the committee which recommended in 1982 that a programme be started as a response to increasing overseas competition in IT.

The five-year programme cost £350 million; its objective was to stimulate British IT research by funding government, academic and private industry research projects. In January 1988 the Alvey Programme was subsumed into the new Information Engineering Directorate of the Department of Trade and Industry which involves a joint effort with the SERC. The main publication of the programme, *Alvey News*, was filled with news of projects and experts in IT; it ceased publication in December 1988. The Information Engineering Directorate plans a new publication covering all the IED and SERC IT research activities. Details can be obtained from the Information Engineering Directorate.

Information sources

Associations (UK)

Aslib, The Association for
Information Management
20–24 Old Street
London EC1V 9AP
Tel. 071-253 4488
(Aslib has several specialist
groups with IT interests:
Computer Group, Electronics
Group and Informatics Group)

Association of Commonwealth
Universities
36 Gordon Square
London WC1H 0PF
Tel. 071-387 8572

British Computer Society
13 Mansfield Street
London W1M 9FH
Tel. 071-637 0471

The Confederation of
Information Communication
Industries
19 Bedford Square
London WC1B 3HJ
Tel. 071-580 6321

Information Engineering
Directorate
Kingsgate House
66–74 Victoria Street
London SW1E 6SW
Tel. 071-215 7877

Institute of Data Processing
Management
21 Russell Street
London WC2B 5UB
Tel. 071-240 3304

Institute of Information
Scientists
44/45 Museum Street
London WC1A 1LY
Tel. 071-831 8003

Institution of Electrical
Engineers
Savoy Place
London WC2R 0BL
Tel. 071-240 1871

Library Association
7 Ridgmount Street
London WC1E 7AE
Tel. 071-636 7543

Management Consultancies
Association
11 Halkin Street
London SW1X 8JL
Tel. 071-235 3897

Management Consultancy
Information Service
38 Blenheim Avenue
Gants Hill
Ilford
Essex IG2 6JQ
Contact: Anne Mallach
Tel. 081-554 4695

Associations (USA)

American Library Association
50 East Huron Street
Chicago, Illinois 60611

American Society for Information Science (ASIS)
1424 16 Street N.W. Suite 404
Washington, DC 20036

Association for Computing Machinery
11 West 42 Street
New York, NY 10036

Computer Society of the IEEE
1730 Massachusetts Avenue
Washington, DC 20036

Special Libraries Association
1700 Eighteenth Street N.W.
Washington, DC 20009

Directories and yearbooks

Directory of British Associations, Beckenham, CBD Research Ltd, 10th edn, 1990.
A comprehensive directory of thousands of British associations, societies, institutes and similar organizations which have a voluntary membership.

CICI Directory of Information Products and Services, Harlow, Longman.
The Confederation of Information Communication Industries listing of over 1600 organizations in the information industry.

Centres & Bureaux
A directory of concentrations of effort, information and expertise.

Computer Users' Year Book 1989 (in 4 volumes). London, VNU.
Volume 1: *Equipment (computer and comms manufacturers)*.

Volume 2: *Services (lists firms providing computer-related services; includes consultants, technical authors)*.

Volume 3: *Installations (mainframe and minicomputer departments in major organizations around the UK & Eire)*.

Volume 4: *Suppliers (lists firms computer-related supplies; peripherals)*.

Current British Directories, Lindsay Sellar (ed.), Beckenham, CBD Research Ltd, 1987.
A directory of nearly 1000 diverse specialist centres and bureaux. This directory is useful since it identifies small organizations which might otherwise be difficult to trace or small units within a larger organization where specialist interests are pursued.

Current Research in Britain, Boston Spa, British Library Science, Technology and Industry Division, published in four parts:

Physical sciences—annual (two parts)
Biological sciences—annual (two parts)
Social Science—annual
Humanities—biennial
The set contains details of 65 000 current research projects in universities, polytechnics, colleges and other institutions in the United Kingdom. Indexes include an alphabetical listing of researchers and subject area by keyword. The arrangement allows identification by parent organization or department within an organization.

Index of Conference Proceedings Received, Boston Spa, British Library Science, Technology and Industry Division.
Published monthly and then in annual cumulations. This is an excellent source for identifying the specialist conferences, workshops and seminars held throughout the world.

Consultants

Management Consultancies Association; Directory of Member Firms and their Services to Clients 1988. Management Consultancies Association.

Management Consultancy Information Service.
A central source of information on management consultants in the UK. Assists in the selection of management consultants with skills appropriate to the client's requirements.

Directory of Information Brokers and Consultants 1989/80, Marshall Crawford and Mary Moody (eds.), London, Information Marketmakers.
Lists over 160 individuals or firms providing information services. Contains an index of information expertise as well as one for subject expertise.

Inside Information 1989/90; a Directory of Organizations, Products and Services in the Information Sector, Catherine Smith (ed.), London, TFPL.
Over 800 organizations are listed with names of key personnel.

British Library Information Guide 8: Directory of Consultants and Researchers in Library and Information Science, Christine Smith (ed.), Boston Spa, British Library Science, Technology and Industry Division.
Lists 262 consultants/contacts in the field. A subject index identifies those with specialist skills.

Consultants and Consulting Organizations Directory, 1989 (in two volumes). Detroit, Gale Research.
More than 14 000 firms and individuals in the US and Canada are listed; well indexed.

Directory of Fee-based Information Services 1989, Helen Burwell (ed.), Houston, Burwell Enterprises.
Lists 473 commercial information services in the US plus a selection of others in the rest of the world.

Yearbook of International Organizations 1988/89, edited by the Union of International Associations, Brussels. Munich, K.G. Saur.
A directory of over 10 000 international organizations. There are multiple indexes but the subject index to keywords is particularly useful for locating organizations specializing in information technology.

Academic/research establishments

Commonwealth Universities Yearbook 1988 (four volume set). London, Association of Commonwealth Universities.
A detailed directory of universities in the Commonwealth with an index to more than 180 000 individuals in those universities.

World of Learning 1988, London, Europa Publications.
A directory which covers all countries in the world, identifying centres of knowledge such as national academics, learned societies, research institutes, libraries, museums, universities and colleges.

Scientific and Technical Organizations and Agencies Directory, Margaret L. Young (ed.), Detroit, Gale Research, 1985 (six-volume set).
A guide to 12 000 organizations concerned with the physical sciences, engineering and technology. Organizations include associations, computer information services, consulting firms, education institutions, government agencies, libraries and information centres, patents sources, research and development centres, standards organizations.

Government Research Directory, Kay Gill and Susan Tufts (eds.), Detroit, Gale Research, 4th edn, 1987.
A guide to 3000 U.S. government research and development centres, laboratories, data collection and analysis centres in the subject fields of agriculture, business, education, energy, engineering,

environment, humanities, medicine, military science, and basic and applied sciences.

Information USA, Matthew Lesko (ed.) New York, Viking Penguin.
A guide to the thousands of information sources within the U.S. government and its funded agencies. The emphasis is on free or low cost information and access via telephone or online databases. A massive reference work which is almost too comprehensive to describe.

Online/electronic information

BEST (British Expertise in Science and Technology). Longman Cartermill Ltd, Technology Centre, St Andrews, Fife KY16 9EA. Tel. 0334 77660
Database of British specialists in all fields of science and technology working in UK establishments (universities, polytechnics, government establishments).

BRIT-LINE 1989, Directory of British Databases, Shaun Ince (ed.)
EDI Guide to over 350 Databases covering all kinds of information.

Directory of Online Databases. Cuadra/Elsevier, 1990. (Published quarterly).

Encyclopedia of Information Systems and Services 1989, Amy Lucas (ed.).
Volume 1: *United States listings*

Encyclopedia of Information Systems and Services, 1989, Amy Lucas (ed.) Gale Research.
Volume 1: *Descriptive listings*
Volume 2: *Indexes*
Guide to over 4400 organizations involved in the production and distribution of information in electronic form (includes online, CD-ROM, videotex, teletext).

Periodicals/journals

Alvey News
Aslib Information
Aslib Proceedings
Business Computing and Communications
Business Information Review

CADCAM International
Communicate
Communications
Communications Management
Computer Bulletin (official journal of the British

Computer Society)
Computer Journal (official journal of the British Computer Society)
Computer System Europe
Computer Weekly
Computing
Datalink
Desktop Publishing
Desktop Publishing Today
DTP
Industrial Computing
Inform (IIS)
Infomatics
Information and Library Manager
Information Management Journal
Information Media and Technology
Information Technology for Development
Information Technology Intelligence
Information Technology for Local Government
Information World Review
IT Focus
Journal of Information Technology
Library Association Record
Library and Information Technology Abstracts
Micro Decision
Netlink (Aslib)
Online
Online Review
PC Magazine
PC User
PC Week
Personal Computer Magazine
Personal Computer World
Practical Computing
Program (Aslib)
Systems International

CHAPTER NINETEEN

Standards

L. JACKSON

Introduction

Standards are an important part of information technology and they enable us to use products and services from a variety of manufacturers. They are especially important in the procurement of equipment. From the users' point of view, products which conform to specified standards effectively have a seal of approval.

Many new technologies have emerged from the research and development departments of the large manufacturers. For example, optical fibres and Unix were created at the AT&T Bell Laboratories; the most common desktop publishing features were developed at Palo Alto by Rank Xerox, and Philips in the Netherlands has a special interest in interactive video developments. In Japan a lot of research effort has been spent on developing high definition television. All of these ideas are protected by patents. Once the concept has reached the production line, it is volume of sales which determines which products will become the norm and which will fold through lack of support. IBM has created a *de facto* standard through marketing by capturing the lead position for sales of personal computers, for example. In the early 1980s this had a knock-on effect for software producers. The operating system for the IBM PC, MS-DOS (produced by Microsoft) became a standard for operating systems and the majority of PC software products operate under MS-DOS. Since then IBM have developed a new operating system OS/2, with the apparent intention of making this a replacement standard for MS-DOS. Other manufacturers are looking at alternatives to OS/2 including Unix.

Dealers and distributors also play a part in the development of standards because they tend to stock items from companies which can offer good discounts or have substantial marketing budgets. Other manufacturers can benefit from products with large markets by reverse engineering existing products to get back to the same base and then adding other features to enhance them. For example, Hayes modems have become a widely–emulated standard; for mainframe to micro transmission and other PC peripherals one needs a SCSI interface; for CAD/CAM workstations one thinks of Sun and for windows and mice, the name Apple Macintosh springs to mind. Good ideas are often taken up and developed to produce new or different standards. An example of this is Unix, where several manufacturers have made their own versions to suit their own products. One company which specializes in assessing computer products and networks on an international scale is Datapro in Lausanne, Switzerland. Datapro publishes reports and loose-leaf subscription services (available through McGraw-Hill) which cover the emerging standards.

The costs associated with bringing new technologies to a wide purchasing public are now so great that the hardware manufacturers are forming alliances with one another and with those companies which can make their products sell. It is here that standards come into their own on an international as well as a regional or national scale.

As certain elements of information technology become familiar they acquire popular names which no longer need an explanation. Examples are ASCII, Ethernet and Token Ring which all started life as standards. ASCII is an American National Standards Institute standard for 7-bit character interchange agreed in 1986 and has an ISO equivalent. Ethernet and Token Ring started life as IEEE 802 local area networking standards before moving into the international arena. A group of manufacturers developed a standard format for CD-ROM discs called the 'High Sierra' format to ensure interchangeability of discs regardless of the drive manufacturer in advance of ISO 9660 adopted in June 1987. Just occasionally the service name is adopted as the name of the standard. An example is Prestel which is the UK videotex standard and the name of the British Telecom viewdata service.

International standards

The majority of international standards are glossaries or methods of test. They provide the necessary precursors to the development of product specifications. Methods of test can be viewed as a means of communication or a technical language. To gain the maximum benefit everyone should use the same language and test equipment since this cuts the costs associated with tooling a test bed and avoids confusion over what is being tested.

Like the regional and national bodies, the international organizations are divided into technical and sub-committees by subject interest. Representatives are sent from the national organizations which in turn have drawn their representatives from within the membership of industrial, professional and trade associations. Some of the larger companies may send representatives direct and for special projects an expert may be co-opted. At the top level, in the field of information technology, there is the International Electrotechnical Commission (IEC) working in conjunction with the International Organization for Standardization (IOS) in Geneva. The Joint Technical Committee for information technology meets every two years. However the many sub-committees meet every year and details appear in the *IEC Yearbook*.

Draft proposals, draft international standards and amendments of these sub-committees are listed in the *IEC Yearbook* as work items together with the date the item was registered, what stage it has reached and the expected target date. All the entries are in English and French but the *Yearbook* cannot be used for current information of the various committee meetings since the publication is often late. The IEC issues books which define the concepts and symbols used to describe the work in progress and the diagrams used. These are published via the book-trade but they are also available from the Geneva office.

The IEC also publishes a catalogue which lists and describes the 2000 international electrotechnical standards. News of meetings, reports of these and what standards have been issued will be found in the *IEC Bulletin* issued six times a year. It is free to members.

The ISO/IEC have issued a *KWIC Index of International Standards* covering their own standards and those of twenty-seven other international organizations. This is intended to meet the need for a single comprehensive reference source that helps to identify all existing international standards for a given subject. New editions appear every two years but only the introduction is in both French and English at the moment. The product is a spin–off from the ISONET database to which 60 national members contribute. Each national member acts as a reference point for other members to exchange information as and when required. The addresses, telephone, telex and fax numbers of the participating members and whether they are ISO agents are listed at the front of the book together with IEC national committees and the twenty-seven international publishing bodies. Standards issued by the

International Telegraph and Telephone Consultative Committee (CCITT) are included. As the entries are title based no abbreviations or acronyms will appear. It is advisable to look under several headings since this can widen the scope of the search considerably.

Since standards are necessary for international trade, there is a flurry of activity within the regional groupings especially within Europe in the lead up to the European Single Market in 1992. The main body is the European Committee for Electrotechnical Standardization (CENELEC). Its Electronics Components Committee (CECC) is taking over other national standards such as the BS9000 series although dual numbering is permitted. Individual countries may choose whether or not to adopt a complete CEC standard. However, once a standard has joined the official European Community official EN series, all local references and deviations must be withdrawn. Information regarding the progress of these unified standards may be obtained via seminars and news items in the individual countries, notice of which is passed to the membership and published in the various newsletters.

New independent standards bodies are springing up to undertake the technical work for CEN/CENELEC. The European Workshop for Open Systems (EWOS) handles OSI profiles, working loosely with the NIST in the USA and the Asian and Oceanic Workshop (AWOS) in Japan. The European Telecommunications Standards Institute was set up mainly by the national telecommunications bodies. It issues its own European Telecommunication Standards (ETS) but its association with CENELEC is still evolving.

There are other regional groupings such as EFTA which have very close links with the European Community and an English-speaking group based round the Pacific basin. Details of the latter may be found in C.D. Sullivan's *Standards & Standardization: Basic Principles and Applications* (Marcel Dekker Inc., 1983). This book covers the history of standards as well as the committee structure of international and US standards bodies. The appendices cover information sources and addresses, GATT, a list of abbreviations and the book itself is well indexed. Another title worth reading is *Information Technology Standardisation: Theory, Process and Organisations* (Digital Press, 1989) by C.F. Cargill.

National organizations

Most of the industrialized countries have a single standards body which coordinates the development of standards for all areas.

Below is a list of some of the national standards organizations around the world:

- American National Standards Institute (ANSI)
- Association Française de Normalisation (AFNOR)
- British Standards Institution (BSI)
- Deutsches Institut für Normung (DIN)
- National Institute for Standards of Technology (NIST)
- USSR State Committee for Standards (GOST)

Governments now take a great interest in information technology since they perceive it playing an important role in the overall economy of a country. An overview of standards in various countries is to be found in *Information Technology Standardization* (London, BSI/DTI, 1989) by J. Bogod.

USA

The USA has several hundred independent standards developing bodies. Major professional institutions such as the IEEE are responsible for standards in specific areas such as telecommunications.

The National Institute for Standards of Technology (NIST) (formerly the National Bureau of Standards (NBS)) is one of the most important standards bodies in the USA. NIST issues a monograph series which includes literature reviews. These form a useful source of information during the early stages of development in a new technology. In the field of IT the particular department responsible for developing standards is the National Computer and Telecommunications Laboratories (formerly ICST).

UK—British Standards Institution

The British Standards Institution Information Technology Service (BITS) was developed to keep abreast of developments in IT standards. A subscription to the *BITS Newsletter* costs £160 per annum for twelve issues and covers:

- Open Systems Interconnection (OSI)
- Local Area Networks (LANs)
- Computer graphics
- Database languages
- CAD/CAM product data exchange (STEP/IGES/EDIF)
- Document structure and interchange (ODA/ODIF/SGML)
- Messaging (MHS/MMS)
- MAP and TOP
- PROWAY C, Field Bus, MAP/EPA

Details are available from the Marketing Department, BSI, Milton Keynes. BITS also publishes other documents including the current work from international and regional standards bodies. Names or contacts and country representatives to specialist committees overseas are published in the *BSI Catalogue*. The same holds true for other national standards bodies: names, committees and general information are to be found in the relevant catalogues.

Current awareness services for members are available from the national standards bodies' libraries. The BSI library offers the Worldwide Standards Information Service (WSI) which is a monthly listing of all standards and technical regulations received in the BSI Library. It is available by subject and country of reference. Alternatively, there is the Overseas Standards Updating Service (OSUS) which monitors changes to the users' list of overseas standards. Monitoring and customized searches from its own database are available on a daily basis from ILI in Ascot.

One service which appears to be unique is the Technical Help for Exporters section of the BSI. Its function is to help exporting companies to comply with the necessary electrical safety, radio interference and certification requirements of the importing country, either by writing test reports or by visiting firms on a consultancy basis. No IT equipment can be exported without a test certificate. The certification bodies such as the Underwriters Laboratories in the USA and Canada hold the key to whether goods are acceptable for import.

Professional associations also issue research papers where they perceive a new technology impacting upon their area of expertise. One such example is the British Library's interest in CD-ROM covered by several R & D reports outlining the various developments prior to any one particular standard emerging.

Databases

One of the most comprehensive databases is the INTERNATIONAL STANDARDS AND SPECIFICATIONS FILE on Dialog. It covers standards from the major industrialized countries including Japan, the USA, UK, France, Canada, Australia and Germany. Standards from the international organizations such as ISO and IEC are also covered, as are national organizations such as the IEEE, ANSI and EIA. It is produced by Information Handling Services in the USA.

The purpose of national standards bodies is to define, write and issue standards for use within their territories. Information about the standards is made available through annual catalogues by the issuing bodies. In addition, there are three well known databases for standards in Europe—STANDARDLINE from the BSI, NORIANE from the Association Française de Normalisation (AFNOR) and DITR from the Deutsches Institut für Normung (DIN). These three organizations have joined together to produce a CD-ROM—PERINORM—containing all the current, full and draft standards and specifications, plus European and international standards produced by ISO, IEC and CEN/CENELEC. Technical rules for France and Germany are included so that this source of roughly 100 000 records is the most up-to-date and detailed one available. It is updated monthly and is available on subscription from the standards bodies.

Japanese and US standards as well as European and international standards are also available on CD-ROM. STANDARDS INFODISK contains 125 000 standards and specifications from over 60 organizations. It is updated monthly at a subscription rate of £750 a year. The producers are: ILI (Infonorme London Information), Index House, Ascot, Berks SL5 7EU. This company specializes in providing information from the various standards issuing bodies such as ANSI, CCITT, the Reliability Analysis Centre (RAC) and the IEEE. Individual catalogues are available on request.

Specialist areas

Electronic data interchange (EDI)

Further down the scale there are specialist areas such as Electronic Data Interchange (EDI). This technology pervades many industry sectors and each has its own requirements especially when describing items. The Article Numbering Association is the key organization in this field with its standards on bar codes.

National standards emerge because trading links and alliances are formed through the use of the same equipment and services; especially when a country initiates the technology, as with the Tradacoms formats for EDI in the UK. The United Nations is developing its own EDI standard—EDIFACT—which will eventually be adopted by many countries. Information on these standards can be found in *Library & Information Briefings: the Book* (London, LITC, 1989) based on the periodical *Library & Information Briefings* which is published ten times a year.

Standards 333

Open Systems Interconnection (OSI)

The UK government has issued its own OSI guidelines (GOSIP), to ensure that companies are not locked into or out of specific trading activities because of the particular hardware used. OSI is the enabling technology to allow EDI. The first glimmerings of future standards are to be found in the conference proceedings and papers whether formal or informal and at exhibitions when the products first appear.

Documentation standards

Much confusion and frustration in the development of information technology perhaps could have been avoided if companies were to insist on standard documentation. An excellent book by M. Gray and K. London called *Documentation Standards* (Business Books, 1969) covers the purpose, type, structure and usage of the various documents from the initial user request through to evaluation and maintenance.

Quality assurance

Quality assurance which includes documentation, is an integral part of IT standards. The national standards body such as the BSI runs a quality assurance scheme specifically for electronic components and is responsible in the UK for the operation of its Western European and international counterparts, the CECC and IECQ schemes. The *Buyers Guide* is issued annually and is arranged by Standard Industry Classification numbers. All firms registered as manufacturers, maintenance specialists or stockists are listed. There is a Canadian, Australian and New Zealand tie-up to this service and a Swiss section also. The *Guide* replaces the HMSO publication *Register of Quality Assessed United Kingdom Companies*.

To encourage more companies to join the scheme the BSI has made available the guides from the International Federation of the Application of Standards. These guides cover methods for determining the advantages of common standards projects as well as the when, how and international aspects of Quality Assurance. They are available in the PD series.

Conclusion

It is clear that no technology can exist within national boundaries and international standards provide the key to future developments. Some European standards will become international standards without further alteration. One such is the IECQ standard for printed circuit boards. Bodies such as the Standards Promotion Application Group in Europe, the Asian Forum for Standardization in Japan and the Corporation for Open Systems in America all have an important role to play in the development of international standards.

INDEX

3RD BASE SOFTWARE REGISTRY, 60
4GLs (Fourth-generation languages), 55
Abstracts and indexes, 173
　robotics, 26
Academic institutions, 204
　consultancies, 206
　data collections, 205
　documents, 205
　libraries, 207
　personnel, 206
　research groups, 206
　staff, 207
Academic journals, 273
ACCIS (UN Advisory Committee for the Co-ordination of Information Systems), 139, 263
ACM (Association for Computing Machinery), 201
ACM Guide to Computing Literature, 175
ACM Guide to Computing Machinery, 18, 27
Addresses
　database hosts, 47
　database producers, 164
　directory publishers (output technologies), 49
　foreign-language material, 313
　journal publishers (output technologies), 39
　market information providers, 226
　organizations (output technologies), 47

AFRI (Association Française de Robotique Industrielle), 30
Alvey Programme, 233
American Society of Mechanical Engineers (ASME), 29, 35
Analysis (systems), 52
Applications, 122
　databases, 157
Applications generators, 55
Applications software (see Software), 57, 144
Applications-specific journals, 276
Applied Science Research Institute, 182
Article Numbering Association, 117, 118
Artificial intelligence, 122
ARTIFICIAL INTELLIGENCE, 157
Aslib, 127, 193
Aslib Directory of Information Sources in the UK, 191
Aslib Shorter Guide to Institutions, 191
ASME (American Society of Mechanical Engineers), 29, 35
Association for Computational Linguistics, 39
Association for Computing Machinery (ACM), 23, 201
Association Française de Robotique Industrielle (AFRI), 30
Association of Commonwealth Universities, 180
Association of Control Manufacturers, 36

Index

Associations and professional bodies, 190, 200
Australian Robot Association, 30
Automated manufacturing directories, 171
Automated Manufacturing Directory, 34

BAAS (British Society for the Advancement of Science), 201
Bar codes, 10
BCS (British Computer Society), 202
BEAMA, 36
BETA (Business Equipment Trade Association), 194
Bibliographies
 optical media, 80
Bibliothèque National, 188
BITS (BSI Information Technology Service), 86
BIVA (British Interactive Video Association), 87
BMMG (British Microcomputer Manufacturers Group), 194
Books (see Text books)
BOOKS IN PRINT PLUS, 163
BOSTON SPA PERIODICALS, 270
Bowker Complete Source Book of Personal Computing, 169
Britain (see United Kingdom), 183
Britain's Computer Industry, 172
Britain's Data Communications Equipment Suppliers, 170
British Computer Society (BCS), 35, 77, 202
British Interactive Video Association (BIVA), 87
British Library, 188
 Document Supply Centre, 188
 Science Reference and Information Service (SRIS), 25, 189
British Microcomputer Manufacturers Group (BMMG), 194
British Office Technology Manufacturers Alliance, 20, 23
British Radio and Electronic Equipment Manufacturers Association, 194
British Robot Association, 30
British Society for the Advancement of Science (BAAS), 201
British Society of Audiology, 39
British Sources of Information, 167
British Standards Institution, 330

British Universities Film and Video Council (BUFVC), 86
Broadsheets
 foreign-language material, 289
Brokers, 211
BROKERSGUIDE, 161
Brookhaven National Laboratory, 182
BUFVC (British Universities Film and Video Council), 86
Business Equipment Trade Association (BETA), 194
BUSINESS SOFTWARE DATABASE, 59, 127, 156

C-MOS, 93
Cable TV, 129
CAD International Directory, 171
CAD/CAM (database), 32
CADCAM, 26
CADCAM Association Yearbook, 208
CAM-I (Computer Aided Manufacturing International), 231
CAR (microfilm), 88
CBI (Confederation of British Industry), 193
CCIA (Computing and Communications Industry Association), 195
CCITT (International Telegraph and Telephone Consultative Committee), 39, 101, 113, 329
CCTA (Central Computer and Telecommunications Agency), 113, 140
CD-I (Compact Disk Interactive), 77
CD-ROM, 77
 standards, 80, 85
CD-ROM databases, 162
CECUA (Confederation of European Computer Users Associations), 195
CELEX, 255
CENELEC, 329
Centre National d'Études des Télécommunications (CNET), 183
Centre National de la Recherche Scientifique (CNRS), 183
CHEMICAL ABSTRACTS, 247
CHEMICAL PATENTS INDEX, 252
China patent searching, 249
Chinese foreign-language material, 293
Chinese Society of Automation, 25

CICI (Confederation of Information and Communication Industries), 139, 195
CICI Directory of Information Products and Services, 167
Cimtech, 77
Claims
  patents, 244
Classification, 176
  patents, 246
CNET (Centre National d'Études des Télécommunications), 183
CNRS (Centre National de la Recherche Scientifique), 183
Coarse-grained parallel processors, 73
COM (Computer output microfilm), 88
COMECON system
  patents, 242
Communication Yearbook, 170, 208
Communications, 170
Communications Management Yearbook, 170
Communications Source Book, 167
Communications technology (see Transmission of information)
Compact disk interactive (CD-I), 77
Compact disk read-only memory (see CD-ROM), 77
Companies, 210
Company journals
  input technologies, 5
  output technologies, 19
COMPENDEX, 27, 32, 156, 162
Components (see also Hardware), 62, 69
Computer Abstracts, 90, 174
Computer Aided Manufacturing International (CAM-I), 231
Computer and Control Abstracts, 4, 18, 32, 174
Computer and Peripherals Equipment Training Association, 24
Computer Books Review, 91
Computer Contents, 175
COMPUTER DATABASE, 19, 154, 247
COMPUTER EXPRESS, 127
Computer graphics
  directories, 171
Computer Graphics Directory, 171
Computer languages (see Programming languages), 55
Computer output microfilm (COM), 88

Computer Periodicals Currently Received by the Library of Congress, 209
Computer Peripherals Review, 19
Computer Retailers Association (CRA), 194
Computer Science Source Book, 167
Computer security, 144
Computer Terminals Review, 19
Computer Users' Yearbook, 169, 208
COMPUTER-SPECS, 162
Computers and Computing Information Resources Directory, 168, 211
Computing and Communications Industry Association (CCIA), 195
Computing Information Directory, 167
Computing Services Association (CSA), 127, 195
Computing Services Association Official Reference Book and Buyers' Guide, 168
Concise Encyclopedia of Information Technology, 62
Confederation of British Industry (CBI), 193
Confederation of European Computer Users Associations (CECUA), 195
Confederation of Information and Communication Industries (CICI), 195
Conference Papers Index, 282
CONFERENCE PAPERS INDEX, 283
CONFERENCE PROCEEDINGS INDEX, 283
Conferences, 281
  facsimile transmission, 110
  foreign-language material, 288
  hardware, 65
  information network systems, 118
  ISDN, 116
  listings, 282
  magnetic media, 92
  micrographics, 89
  networks, 105
  open systems interconnection, 113
  optical fibres, 107
  optical media, 83
  organizers, 283
  output technologies, 23
  proceedings
    databases, 283
  foreign-language material, 289
  process control, 34

338 Index

programming languages, 56
robotics, 29
satellite television, 108
semiconductor storage, 95
speech synthesis, 38
storage devices, 77
video technology, 87
Construction Industry Computing
    Association, 196
Consultancies
    academic institutions, 206
Consultants, 318, 322
Control engineering, 31
Copyright legislation, 140
COSMIC, 60
Council of Europe, 143
CRA (Computer Retailers
    Association), 194
CRI Directory of Expert Systems, 171
CRIB, 235
CRIP, 237
CSA (Computing Services
    Association), 195
CSIRO RESEARCH IN PROGRESS, 235
*Cuadra (Directory of Online
    Databases)*, 159
Current British Directories, 166, 223
*Current Contents. Engineering
    Technology & Applied Science*,
    175
Current European Directories, 166,
    223
*Current Papers in Electrical and
    Electronics Engineering*, 174
*Current Papers on Computers and
    Control*, 174
Current Research in Britian, 191

DARPA (Defense Advanced Research
    Project Agency), 231
DAT (Digital audio tape), 89
Data broadcasting, 117
Data collections
    academic institutions, 205
*Data Communications Product
    Directory*, 170
Data privacy, 142
Data processing (see also Software,
    Operating systems, Programming
    languages), 51
Data Processing Digest, 175
Data protection, 142
Data security, 142, 144

Data sources, 91
Data storage (see Storage devices), 74
Database directories, 159
Database Directory, 159
Database hosts
    addresses, 47
Database producers
    addresses, 164
Database systems, 126
Databases, 151
    applications, 157
    conference proceedings, 283
    experts, 324
    European Community, 264
    hardware, 63
    law, 267
    legislation, 267
    operating systems, 57
    research, 234
    software, 59
    standards, 331
    United Nations, 263
Databases on CD-ROM, 162
DATA CHANNELS, 128
DataComms Book, 170
Datapro Directory of Online Services,
    169
*Datapro Directory of Small
    Computers*, 169
Dataquest, 217
Datareviews, 70
DBMSs (Database management
    systems), 126
Defense Advanced Research Project
    Agency (DARPA), 231
Deferred examination (patents), 241
Department of Education and Science
    (DES), 186
Department of Trade and Industry
    (DTI), 184
Derwent Publications Ltd, 251
DES (Department of Education and
    Science), 186
Design (systems), 52
Desktop publishing, 136
Deutsche Bibliothek, 187
*DIAL Industry: Electrical, Electronics,
    Computers, Instrumentation*, 168
DIANE Guide, 159
Dictionaries, 172
    foreign-language, 300
    robotics, 26
Digital audio tape (DAT), 89
Digitization, 11

Index 339

Direct broadcasting by satellite (see Satellite television), 107
DIRECT-NET, 60, 127
Directories, 167
  automated manufacturing, 171
  communications, 170
  computer graphics, 171
  electronics, 168
  expert systems, 171
  facsimile transmission, 109
  information network systems, 118
  ISDN, 116
  magnetic media, 91
  market information, 171
  microcomputers, 169
  micrographics, 88
  networks, 104
  open systems interconnection, 112
  optical fibres, 107
  optical media, 80
  output technologies
  publishers' addresses, 49
  packet switching, 114
  regional, 168
  satellite television, 108
  semiconductor storage, 94
  software, 58, 169
  storage devices, 76
  telecommunications, 170
  transmission of information, 100
  video technology, 87
Directory of British Associations, 191
Directory of Computer Graphics Suppliers, 171
Directory of Directories, 166
Directory of European Industrial and Trade Associations, 192
Directory of Online Databases, 159
Directory of Published Proceedings, 282
Disks, 89
Dissertation Abstracts International, 239
Dissertations, 238
Document supply
  translations, 307
Document Supply Centre (see British Library Document Supply Centre), 188
Documentation standards, 333
Documents
  academic institutions, 205
DTI (Department of Trade and Industry), 184

DTP (Desktop publishing), 136
DUNDIS, 263
DVI (Digital video interactive), 77

E-mail (see Electronic mail), 128
E-PUBS (ELECTRONIC PUBLISHING ABSTRACTS), 4, 76, 133, 157, 283
EABS, 291
EC (see European Community), 143, 180
ECHO, 161
ECMA (European Computer Manufacturers Association), 196
ECTEL, 197
EDI (Electronic Data Interchange), 117, 332
EDI Association, 118
EDICON, 118
Education and Science, Department of, 186
EEPROMs (Electrically erasable programmable ROMs), 93
EIIA (European Information Industry Association), 196
Electrical and Electronics Trades Directory, 168
ELECTRICAL PATENTS INDEX, 252
Électro Annuaire Électricité— Électronic, 168
Electro Electronics Buyers' Guide, 168
Electronic components (see Components), 62, 69
Electronic data interchange (see EDI), 117, 332
Electronic Engineering Association, 196
Electronic Engineering Index, 168
Electronic mail, 128
Electronic Market Data Book, 216
Electronic Materials Information Service (EMIS), 69
Electronic office, 134
Electronic Publishing Abstracts, 4, 76, 167
Electronics
  directories, 168
Electronics and Communications Abstracts, 94, 175
Electronics and Instruments Directory, 169, 208
Electrotechnical Laboratory, Japan, 182
EMIS (Electronic Materials Information Service), 69

Encyclopedia of Computer Science and Technology, 68
Encyclopedia of Information Systems and Services, 169
Encyclopedia of Microcomputers, 68
ENGINEERING & INDUSTRIAL SOFTWARE DIRECTORY, 60, 127
EPIE ON-LINE, 60
EPROMs (Erasable programmable ROMs), 93
ERA Technology Ltd, 199
ESPRIT, 231
Ethernet, 101
EUREKA, 232
Euroabstracts, 180, 290
EUROBASES, 291
EURODICAUTOM, 302
Europa World Yearbook, 178
European Association for the Transfer of Technologies, 181
European Association of Information Services (EUSIDIC), 196
European Community, 143, 180
 foreign-language material, 289
 intellectual property, 254
 online databases, 264
 publications, 263
 research programmes, 231
European Computer Manufacturers Association (ECMA), 196
European Computing Services Association, 196
European Electronic Component Distributor Directory, 169
European Information Industry Association (EIIA), 196
European Patent Convention, 294
European Patent Office, 180, 248
European Single Market, 144
EUSIDIC (European Association of Information Services), 196
Exhibitions
 foreign-language material, 288
Expert systems, 124
 directories, 171
Experts, 315
 databases, 324
 finding, 316
 information sources, 320
 journals, 324
 using, 315

Facsimile transmission, 108
 conferences, 110
 directories, 109
 journals, 109
 newsletters, 109
 state-of-the-art reviews, 109
 text books, 109
 trade literature, 110
FANATEL, 133
FAST (Federation Against Software Theft), 144
FAST (Forecasting and Assessment in Science and Technology), 232
Fax (see Facsimile transmission), 108
FEDERAL RESEARCH IN PROGRESS, 235
Federation of Microsystems Centres, 197
Fibre optics (see Optical fibres), 106
Fifth-generation Computer Project, 230
Fine-grained parallel processors, 73
Forecasting and Assessment in Science and Technology (FAST), 232
Foreign-language material, 285
 addresses, 313
 broadsheets, 289
 Chinese, 293
 conferences, 288
 conference proceedings, 289
 dictionaries, 300
 European Community, 289
 exhibitions, 288
 Japanese, 292
 journals, 288
 organizations, 289
 patents, 294
 production of, 312
 scanning, 298
 weekly popular periodicals, 287
FORKAT, 235
Fourth generation languages (4GLs), 55
France
 organizations, 183
 patent searching, 249
Frauenhofer Society for the Advancement of Applied Research, 183

Gallium arsenide, 71
GAMBICA, 36, 194
General sources
 hardware, 62
 input technologies, 3
Germany
 organizations, 183

Index 341

Government publications (UK), 257
Government statistics, 214
Graphics (see Computer graphics)
Green papers (UK legislation), 265
Guide to Official Industrial Property Publications, 296
Guide to Reference Books, 166

Hacking, 144
Hardware (see also Components), 62
  books, 65
  conferences, 65
  databases, 63
  general sources, 62
  journals, 62
  market information, 63
  research programmes, 64
  suppliers, 209
HATRICS, 190
Health and Safety Executive (HSE), 186
HERTIS, 190
High Sierra Group, 85
HMSO
  publications, 257
  publicity catalogues, 258
HSE (Health and Safety Executive), 186

ICC INTERNATIONAL BUSINESS RESEARCH DATABASE, 225
ICP Software Directory, 58
IDC, 217
Identifying journals, 270
IEC (International Electrotechnical Commission), 180, 236
IEE (Institution of Electrical Engineers), 35, 101, 107, 203
IEEE (Institute of Electrical and Electronic Engineers), 35, 101, 113, 202
IEEIE (Institute of Electrical and Electronics Incorporated Engineers), 203
IEPRC (International Electronic Publishing Research Centre), 199
IFAC (International Federation of Automated Control), 35
IFIP (International Federation for Information Processing), 204
IIS (Institute of Information Scientists), 101, 127, 203
Index to Conference Proceedings Received, 282
Index to Information Technology, 283
Index to Theses, 238
Indexes
  legislation, 267
Indexing journals, 173
Industrial Research Institute, Japan, 182
INFOMAT, 220
Information brokers, 211
Information Engineering Directorate, DTI, 185
Information network systems, 117
  conferences, 118
  directories, 118
  journals, 118
  newsletters, 117
  organizations, 118
  state of-the-art reviews, 117
  text books, 118
Information policy (see Policy), 138
Information Processing Society of Japan (IPSJ), 202
Information retrieval systems, 126
Information technology applications (see Applications), 122
Information Technology Yearbook, 167
Information transmission (see Transmission of information), 96
Infra-red keyboard links, 8
Inmos, 73
INPADOC, 250
Input technologies, 3
  company journals, 5
  general sources, 3
  journals, 4
  libraries, 3
  secondary sources, 3
  organizations, 5
Inside Information, 191
INSIDE R&D, 237
Inspec, 204
INSPEC (database), 4, 18, 27, 32, 63, 153, 271, 283, 297
Institute de l'Information Scientifique et Technique, 183
Institute for Computer Sciences and Technology, 182
Institute for Future Technology, 182
Institute of Acoustics, 39
Institute of Data Processing Management, 202
Institute of Electrical and Electronics Engineers (see IEEE), 35, 101, 113, 202

Institute of Information Scientists (IIS), 101, 127, 203
Institute of Measurement and Control, 35
Institution of British Telecommunications Engineers, 203
Institution of Electrical Engineers (IEE), 35, 101, 107, 203
Institution of Mechanical Engineers, 30, 35
Institution of Production Engineers, 35, 204
Instrument Society of America, 35
Integrated services digital network (see ISDN), 115
Intellectual property (see also Patents, Copyright legislation), 254
European Community, 254
INTELSAT (International Telecommunications Satellite Organization), 108
Interactive video, 86
Intergovernmental Bureau for Informatics, 180
International agencies, 178
information policy, 141
International Computer Graphics Directory, 208
International Directory of Telecommunications, 288
International Economic and Trade Information Centre, 183
International Electronic Publishing Research Centre (IEPRC), 199
International Electrotechnical Commission (IEC), 180
International Federation for Information Processing (IFIP), 181, 204
International Federation of Automated Control (IFAC), 35
International official publications, 261
International Organization for Standardization (ISO), 85, 113, 328
International Patent Classification (IPC), 246
International standards, 327
INTERNATIONAL STANDARDS AND SPECIFICATIONS FILE, 331
International Telecommunication Union (ITU), 101, 179
International Telecommunications Satellite Organization (INTELSAT), 108
International Telegraph and Telephone Consultative Committee (CCITT), 101
International trade, 144
Inventions (IT-related), 245
INVESTEXT, 225
IPC (International Patent Classification), 246
IPSJ (Information Processing Society of Japan), 202
IR-SOFT, 127
ISDN (Integrated services digital network), 115
conferences, 116
directories, 116
journals, 116
newsletters, 116
organizations, 116
state-of-the-art reviews, 116
text books, 116
ISIS SOFTWARE DATENBANK, 60
ISMEC, 32
ISO (International Organization for Standardization), 85, 113, 328
ISONET, 85
IT Focus, 174
IT PROJECTS, 237
ITU (International Telecommunication Union), 101, 179

JANET (Joint Academic Network), 114
Japan
organizations, 182
patents, 296
searching, 249
research programmes, 230
Japan Electronics Almanac, 216
Japan External Trade Organization, 182
Japan Industrial Robot Association (JIRA), 30
Japanese
foreign-language material, 292
language learning, 299
JAPIO, 296
JEDI (United Nations Joint EDI Task Force), 118
JICST, 236
JIRA (Japan Industrial Robot Association), 30

Joint Academic Network (JANET), 114
Journals, 275
  applications-specific, 276
  experts, 324
  facsimile transmission, 109
  foreign-language material, 288
  hardware, 62
  identifying journals, 270
  information network systems, 118
  input technologies, 4
  ISDN, 116
  magnetic media, 90
  micrographics, 88
  networks, 104
  open systems interconnection, 112
  operating systems, 56
  optical fibres, 106
  optical media, 77
  output technologies, 17
    addresses of publishers, 39
  packet switching, 114
  process control, 31
  robotics, 24
  satellite television, 108
  semiconductor storage, 93
  software engineering, 53
  speech synthesis, 37
  storage devices, 75
  transmission of information, 99
  video technology, 86
Joysticks, 9

Key Abstracts, 174
Key Abstracts: Business Automation, 18
Key Abstracts: Computer Communications and Storage, 76
Key Abstracts: Electronic Instrumentation, 32
Key Abstracts: Robotics and Control, 32
Key Abstracts: Software Engineering, 51
Key pads, 8
Keyboards, 6
Kompass, 7, 92

Language learning, 298
  Japanese, 299
Language recognition, 300

Languages (computer—see Programming languages), 55
LANs (Local area networks), 101
Law, 138
  databases, 267
  UK, 264
Learned and professional societies, 272
Learned journals, 272
Learned societies, 200
Learning languages, 298
Legislation, 138
  indexes, 267
  online databases, 267
  UK, 264
Lenin State Library, 188
Libraries, 177
  academic institutions, 207
  input technologies, 3
  national, 187
Library and Information Technology Centre, 127
Library of Congress, 187
Linguistic Aid Service, 308
Listings (Research), 234
Local Area Networking Sourcebook, 170
Local area networks (LANs), 101
LOGIBASE, 60
Logica, 217

Machine code, 55
Machine translation, 311
Machine-readable sources, 149
MAGB (Microfilm Association of Great Britain), 89
Magnetic disks, 89
Magnetic media, 89
  conferences, 92
  directories, 91
  journals, 90
  secondary sources, 90
  text books, 91
  trade literature, 91
Magnetic tape, 89
Mainframe computers, 66
Manufacturers, 207
Manufacturing and Information Technology Division, DTI, 185
Market information (see also Trade literature), 213
  directories, 171
  hardware, 63

output technologies, 20
robotics, 27
Market information providers
 addresses, 226
Market research, 217
Mass storage (see Storage devices), 74
Max-Planck Society for the
 Advancement of Science, 183
MENU—THE INTERNATIONAL SOFTWARE
 DATABASE, 59, 127, 155
Micro Abstracts, 52
MICRO CITY, 60
MICROCOMPUTER INDEX, 59, 155
Microcomputer Index, 52
MICROCOMPUTER SOFTWARE AND
 HARDWARE GUIDE, 155
MICROCOMPUTER SOFTWARE GUIDE, 59
Microcomputers, 68
 directories, 169
Microelectronics and Computer
 Technology Cooperative, 230
Microfiche, 88
Microfilm, 88
Microfilm Association of Great Britain
 (MAGB), 89
Micrographics, 88
 conferences, 89
 directories, 88
 journals, 88
 newsletters, 88
 organizations, 89
 text books, 88
*Micrographics and Optical Equipment
 Review*, 76
Microinfo, 211
MICROREVIEWS FOR BUSINESS, 60
MICROSEARCH, 60
MINERVA, 235
Minicomputers, 67
Ministry of International Trade and
 Industry (MITI), 182
MITI (Ministry of International Trade
 and Industry), 182
Monitors, 16
Monographs (see Text books)
MOS memory (Metal oxide
 semiconductor memory), 93
Mouse, 9

NASA, 182
National Bureau of Standards, 182
NATIONAL BUREAU OF STANDARDS
 BULLETIN, 236
National Computer and
 Telecommunications
 Laboratories, 330
National Computing Centre (NCC),
 113, 127, 197
NATIONAL E-MAIL WHITE PAGES, 128
National Economic Development
 Office (NEDO), 183
National Electronic Council, 186
National Electronics Centre, 198
National Engineering Laboratory, 182
National Engineering Research
 Laboratory, 36
National information centres, 182
National Information Standards
 Organization (NISO), 85
National Institute for Standards of
 Technology (NIST), 330
National Interactive Video Centre
 (NIVC), 87
National libraries, 187
National Library of Scotland, 189
National Library of Wales, 189
National Materials Handling Centre,
 36
National organizations, 181
National standards, 329
National Technical Information
 Service, 182
National Translations Center, 306
NCC (National Computing Centre),
 113, 127, 197
Netherlands Organization for Applied
 Scientific Research (TNO), 199
Networks, 101
 conferences, 105
 directories, 104
 journals, 104
 newsletters, 103
 organizations, 106
 text books, 104
 trade literature, 105
Newsletters, 260
 facsimile transmission, 109
 information network systems, 117
 ISDN, 116
 micrographics, 88
 networks, 103
 open systems interconnection, 112
 optical media, 77
 output technologies, 19
 packet switching, 114
 satellite television, 108
 semiconductor storage, 93
 storage devices, 74

transmission of information, 99
video technology, 86
NEWSNET, 19, 27
Newspapers, 220
NISO (National Information Standards Organization), 85
NIST (National Institute for Standards of Technology), 330
NIVC (National Interactive Video Centre), 87
Non-Roman Alphabets, 8
NORIANE, 332
North America
 research programmes, 230
NTIS, 297
Numerical Engineering Society, 204

Object-oriented languages, 55
Occam, 73
OCR (Optical character recognition), 9
OECD (Organization for Economic Cooperation and Development), 143, 180
Office automation, 134
Office of the Data Protection Registrar, 127
Official publications, 257
 international, 261
Official Publications Library, 188
Online costs, 151
Online databases (see Databases), 151
ONLINE MICROCOMPUTER SOFTWARE GUIDE AND DIRECTORY, 59, 127
Online search services, 161
Online training, 161
Open systems interconnection (OSI), 110
 conferences, 113
 directories, 112
 journals, 112
 newsletters, 112
 organizations, 113
 state-of-the-art reviews, 112
 text books, 112
Operating systems, 57
 databases, 57
 journals, 56
OPERATING SYSTEMS & NETWORKS, 57
Optical character recognition (OCR), 9
Optical circuits, 71
Optical components, 71
Optical computers, 71

Optical Disk Forum, 85
Optical disks, 77
Optical fibres, 106
 conferences, 107
 directories, 107
 journals, 106
 organizations, 107
 text books, 107
Optical media, 77
 bibliographies, 80
 conferences, 83
 directories, 80
 journals, 77
 newsletters, 77
 organizations, 85
 secondary sources, 77
 textbooks, 80
 trade literature, 83
Optical read-only memory (OROM), 77
Optical Society of America, 107
Optical Systems Information Service (OSIS), 85
Organizations, 177
 foreign-language material, 289
 France, 183
 Germany, 183
 information network systems, 118
 input technologies, 5
 international, 178
 ISDN, 116
 Japan, 182
 location of 178
 micrographics, 89
 national, 181
 networks, 106
 open systems interconnection, 113
 optical fibres, 107
 optical media, 85
 output technologies, 23
  addresses, 47
 packet switching, 115
 process control, 35
 robotics, 30
 satellite television, 108
 Soviet Union, 182
 speech synthesis, 39
 storage devices, 77
 transmission of information, 101
 United Kingdom, 183
 USA, 182
 video technology, 87
OROM (Optical read-only memory), 77

346 *Index*

OSI (see Open systems interconnection), 110
  standards, 333
OSIS (Optical Systems Information Service), 85
Output technologies, 14
  books, 20
  company journals, 19
  conferences and exhibitions, 23
  directories
    publishers addresses, 49
  journals, 17
  publishers addresses, 39
  market information, 20
  newsletters, 19
  organizations, 23
    addresses, 47
  secondary sources, 18
  standards, 22
  trade literature, 22
Overseas Technical Information Unit (OTIU), 185

Packet switching, 113
  directories, 114
  journals, 114
  newsletters, 114
  organizations, 115
  state-of-the-art reviews, 114
  text books, 114
  trade literature, 115
Parallel processing, 72
Parliamentary bills (UK legislation), 265
Patents, 240
  applications, 241
  claims, 244
  classification, 246
    UK patents, 246
    US patents, 246
    IPC, 246
  COMECON system, 242
  deferred examination, 241
  foreign-language material, 294
  Japan, 296
  legislation, 140
  literature, 247
  references, 255
  searching, 248
    China, 249
    France, 249
    Japan, 249
    USA, 249
  specifications, 242
  technical information, 253
  techno-commercial information, 254
  traditional, 242
PATOLIS, 296
PATSTAT-PLUS, 253
PC Yearbook, 58, 208
PCT, 294
PEOPLE IN ELECTRONIC MAIL SYSTEMS, 128
PERA (Production Engineering Research Association), 36, 199, 204
PERA Abstracts, 32
PERINORM, 85, 332
Periodicals (see Journals, see also Newsletters), 269
Personnel (academic institutions), 206
PIRA, 11
Piracy, 144
Plotters, 16
Pointers, 9
Policy, 138
  international, 141
  UK, 142
  US, 141
POLIS (Parliamentary On-line Information System), 268
Polytechnics, 204
PR HI-TECH ALERT, 128, 133
Press (see also Journals, Newsletters), 220
Printers, 15
Privacy, 142
Private companies, 210
Private sector
  organizations, 207
  research, 233
Proceedings in Print, 282
Process control, 31
  conferences, 34
  journals, 31
  marketing information, 33
  organizations, 35
  secondary sources, 32
  standards, 34
  text books, 33
  trade literature, 33
Process Engineering Directory, 171
Product data, 223
PRODUCT DATA STORE, 222
Product news, 277
Production Engineering Research Association (PERA), 36, 199, 204

Professional bodies and associations, 190, 200
Professional journals, 274
PROFILE, 220
Programming languages, 55
  conferences, 56
PTS, 220
PTS NEWSLETTER DATABASE, 57
PTS PROMT, 156
Public libraries, 190
Publications
  European Community, 263
  United Nations, 262

QMC Industrial Research, 199
Quality assurance, 333
RACE (R&D in Advanced Communications for Europe), 232
RAM (Random access memory), 90, 93
Random access memory (RAM), 90, 93
Read-only memory (ROM), 90
Reference works, 166
References
  patents, 255
  transmission of information, 118
Referral services, 177
Regional directories, 168
Research, 229
  academic institutions, 206
  establishments, 323
  databases, 234
  hardware, 64
  journals, 274
  listings, 234
  private sector, 233
  programmes, 229
    Europe, 231
    Japan, 230
    North America, 230
  robotics, 30
Research associations, 198
Research in progress, 234
ROBOMATIX, 27
Robotics, 24
  abstracts and indexes, 26
  conferences, 29
  dictionaries, 26
  journals, 24
  market information, 27
  monographs, 27
  organizations, 30
  research, 30
  secondary sources, 26
  trade literature, 27
ROM (Read-only memory), 90
Romtec, 217
Royal Institute of International Affairs, 139
Russia (see Soviet Union), 182

Satellite broadcasting (see Satellite television), 107
Satellite television, 107
  conferences, 108
  directories, 108
  journals, 108
  newsletters, 108
  organizations, 108
  state-of-the-art reviews, 108
  text books, 108
SB-1, 135
Science and Engineering Research Council (SERC), 186
Science Citation Index, 271
Science Reference and Information Service (British Library), 25, 189
Scientific Documentation Centre (SDC), 200
SCISEARCH, 272
SCITECH REPORT, 236
Scotland
  National Library of Scotland, 189
Scottish Science Library, 189
SDC (Scientific Documentation Centre), 200
SDF (System Development Foundation), 231
Search services, 161
Searching patents, 248
Secondary sources, 166
  input technologies, 3
  magnetic media, 90
  optical media, 77
  output technologies, 18
  process control, 32
  robotics, 26
  semiconductor storage, 94
  speech synthesis, 38
  storage devices, 76
  translations, 305
  transmission of information, 100
  video technology, 86
Security, 144
Select committees
  UK legislation, 267

Semiconductor Research Corporation (SRC), 231
Semiconductor storage, 93
  conferences, 95
  directories, 94
  journals, 93
  newsletters, 93
  secondary sources, 94
  text books, 94
  trade literature, 95
Semiconductors, 69
SERC (Science and Engineering Research Council), 186
Service providers, 210
SIGPLAN (ACM Special Interest Group on Programming Languages), 56
SIGSOFT (ACM Special Interest Group on Software Engineering), 54
SIRI (Società Italiana Robotica Industriale), 30
SITRAFO, 236
Società Italiana Robotica Industriale (SIRI), 30
Society of Fiber Science and Technology, 107
Society of Photo-optical Instrumentation Engineers (SPIE), 72
Software, 57, 144
  databases, 59
  directories, 58, 169
  engineering, 52
  journals, 53
  monographs, 52
  houses, 207
  piracy, 144
  producers, 208
SOFTWARE, 60
Software Catalog, 59
SOFTWARE COMPETITIVE INTELLIGENCE, 60
Software Encyclopedia, 59, 208
SOFTWARE LOCATOR, 60
Software packages (see Software), 57, 144
Software Publishers' Association, 144
SOFTWARE SPECIAL INTERVIEW PROGRAM, 61
Software Systems and Techniques Abstracts, 52
Software Users' Year Book, 58, 169, 208

SOFTWARE-CD, 162
Soviet Academy of Sciences, 182
Soviet Union
  organizations, 182
SPAG (Standards Promotions and Applications Group), 113
Specifications (Patents), 242
Speech recognition, 11
Speech synthesis, 36
  books, 38
  conferences, 38
  journals, 37
  organizations, 39
  secondary sources, 38
SPIE (Society of Photo-Optical Instrumentation Engineers), 72
Spreadsheets, 126
SRC (Semiconductor Research Corporation), 231
SRIS (Science Reference and Information Service), 189
SSIE CURRENT RESEARCH, 236
Staff
  academic institutions, 207
STANDARDLINE, 332
Standards, 326
  CD-ROM, 80, 85
  databases, 331
  international, 327
  national, 329
  output technologies, 22
  process control, 34
STANDARDS INFODISK, 332
Standards Promotions and Applications Group (SPAG), 113
State-of-the-art reviews
  facsimile transmission, 109
  information network systems, 117
  ISDN, 116
  open systems interconnection, 112
  packet switching, 114
  satellite television, 108
Statistics, 213
  government, 214
Statutory instruments (UK legislation), 266
Stockbroker research, 225
Storage devices, 74
  conferences, 77
  directories, 76
  journals, 75
  newsletters, 74
  organizations, 77
  secondary sources, 76

Index 349

text books, 76
Supercomputers, 66
Superconductors, 72
Suppliers, 207
Swedish Industrial Robot Association (SWIRA), 30
SWIRA (Swedish Industrial Robot Association), 30
Symbolic languages, 55
Synthesis by analysis (Speech synthesis), 36
System Development Foundation (SDF), 231
Systems analysis, 52
Systems analysis and design, 52

Tape (see Magnetic tape), 89
TEAM, 302
Technical information
  patents, 253
Techno-commercial information
  patents, 254
Technology-specific journals, 275
Telecomms Abstracts, 175
Telecommunications (see Transmission of information), 96
Telecommunications Alert, 167
Telecommunications Engineering and Manufacturing Association (TEMA), 198
Telecommunications Managers Association (TMA), 101
Teletex, 117
TEMA (Telecommunications Engineering and Manufacturing Association), 198
Terminals, 69
Terminology, 300
  databanks, 302
TERMIUM, 302
Text books
  facsimile transmission, 109
  hardware, 65
  information network systems, 118
  ISDN, 116
  magnetic media, 91
  micrographics, 88
  networks, 104
  open systems interconnection, 112
  optical fibres, 107
  optical media, 80
  output technologies, 20
  packet switching, 114
  process control, 33
  robotics, 27
  satellite television, 108
  semiconductor storage, 94
  software engineering, 52
  speech synthesis, 38
  storage devices, 76
  transmission of information, 100
  video technology 87
Text retrieval systems, 126
Text-to-speech (Speech synthesis), 37
TEXTLINE, 19, 27, 32, 220
Theses, 238
Thomas, 7
TMA (Telecommunications Managers Association), 101
TNO (Netherlands Organization for Applied Scientific Research), 199
Token Ring, 101
Touch screens, 9
Touch-tablets, 8
Tradacoms, 117
Tradanet User Group, 118
Trade, 144
Trade associations (see also Research associations), 192
Trade literature (see also Market information)
  facsimile transmission, 110
  magnetic media, 91
  networks, 105
  optical media, 83
  output technologies, 22
  packet switching, 115
  process control, 33
  robotics, 27
  semiconductor storage, 95
  transmission of information, 101
Trade press (see also Trade literature), 277
Trade statistics, 213
Traditional patents, 242
Training (online), 161
Trans-border data flow, 143
Translations, 285, 303
  document supply, 307
  indexes, 306
  journals, 304
  registers, 304
  secondary sources, 305
  services, 308
Translators, 309
Transmission of information, 96
  directories, 100, 170
  journals, 99

350 Index

newsletters, 99
organizations, 101
references, 118
secondary sources, 100
text books, 100
trade literature, 101
Transputers, 73
Turing Institute, 200

UK
  information policy, 142
  law, 264
  organizations, 183
  legislation, 264
    green papers, 265
    parliamentary bills, 265
    select committees, 267
    statutory instruments, 266
    white papers, 265
  patent classification, 246
UKOP (Catalogue of United Kingdom Official Publications), 261
Ulrich's International Periodical Directory, 270
UNCTAD, 179
UNISIST, 263
United Kingdom (see UK)
United Nations, 179
  online databases, 263
  publications, 262
United States (see USA),
Universities, 204
USA
  information policy, 141
  organizations, 182
  patent classification, 246
  patent searching, 249
Use of patent information, 253
Using experts, 315
Using online databases, 157
USSR (see Soviet Union), 182

VADS (Value-added and data services), 117
Value-added and data services (see VADS), 117
Vanguard project, 118

VESA (Video Electronics Standards Association), 22
Video Electronics Standards Association (VESA), 22
Video technology, 86
  conferences, 87
  directories, 87
  journals, 86
  newsletters, 86
  organizations, 87
  secondary sources, 86
  textbooks 87
Videodisc, 86
Videotape, 86
Videotex, 131
Viewdata, 131
VINITI (All-Union Institute for Scientific and Technical Information), 182

Wales
  National Library of Wales, 189
WANs (Wide area networks), 101
Weekly journals
  foreign-language, 287
WHITAKERS, 163
White papers (UK legislation), 265
Wide area networks (WANs), 101
WIPO (World Intellectual Property Organization), 139
Wissenschaftsrat, 183
WOODs (Write-once optical disks), 77
Word processing, 136
Workstations, 69
World Guide to Special Libraries, 210
World Patent Abstracts, 296
WORLD PATENT INDEX, 252
WORMS, 77

X.25, 114

YANKEENET, 128, 133
Yearbook of International Organizations, 192
Yearbook of World Electronics Data, 213
Yearbooks, 215